You teach the world to read

McGraw-Hill

Reading

D1230914

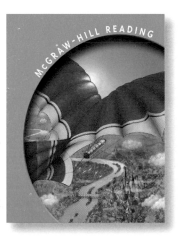

We give you the support you need for success

McGraw-Hill

Reading

Where all students are motivated to read.

Meet Angela Shelf Medearis

As a child, Angela Shelf Medearis loved to read. At the age of thirty, she began to write her own books. "I want to write the kind of books I always longed to find in the library when I was a child," she says. Now her talent and humor have made Medearis one of Texas's most popular children's book authors.

Meet Karen Chandler

Karen Chandler uses computers to do her artwork. For *The Roundup at Rio Ranch*, she mixed photos with illustrations in a computer program called PhotoShop. Ms. Chandler is also the illustrator of *The Keeper of the Swamp*.

The Roundup at Rio Ranch

By Angela Shelf Medearis
Illustrated by Karen Chandler

RICH VARIETY OF LITERATURE

◀ **FICTION**

- From fantasy to realistic fiction, students enjoy the best of literature

▶ **NONFICTION**

- Content-rich nonfiction and expository text—in contrast to narrative style as used in most fiction—develops critical reading and prepares students for test-taking

TIME FOR KIDS
SPECIAL REPORT

Ships

Look at the big ship.

Spiders at Work

by Diane Hoyt-Goldsmith

▲ DECODABLE LITERATURE

- Promotes early reading success
- Award-winning authors and illustrators throughout the grades
- From decodable to authentic literature, selections progress from easier to more complex stories

▲ LEVELED BOOKS

guarantee independent reading for every child

McGraw-Hill Reading
provides a rich variety of literature.

Where phonics and decoding are the keys to early reading success.

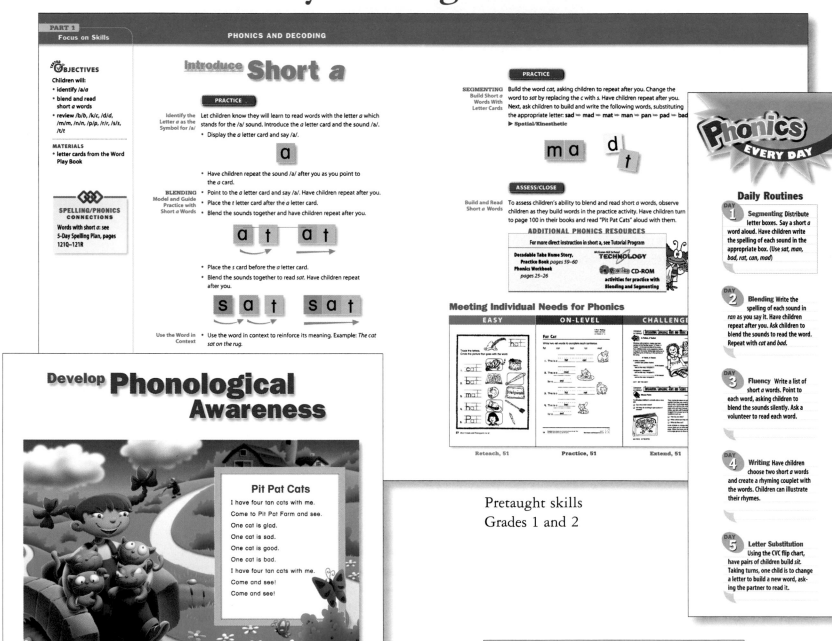

▲ DIRECT, EXPLICIT INSTRUCTION IN PHONICS

- Begins with phonological awareness
- Includes blending and substitution
- Provides daily routines

SPELLING/PHONICS CONNECTIONS

▲ Every day—Every grade

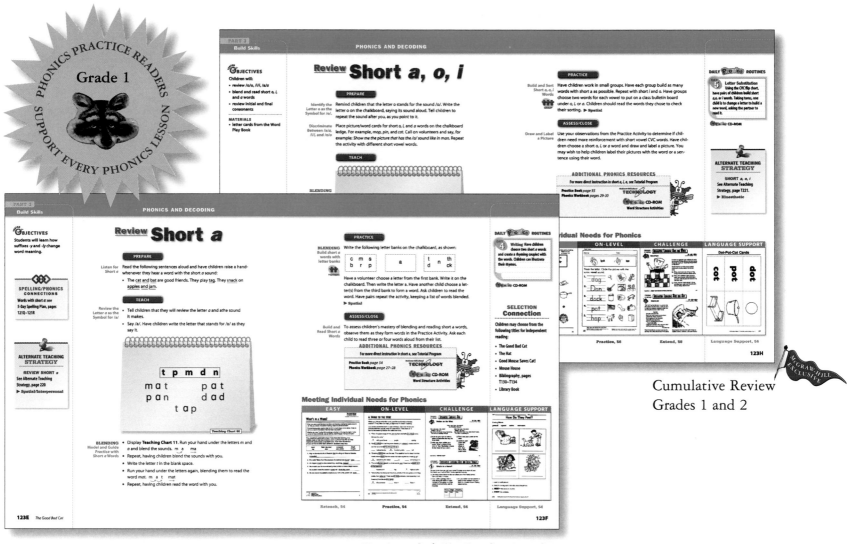

Cumulative Review
Grades 1 and 2

Reviewed skills Grades 1 and 2

▲ SYSTEMATIC, SEQUENTIAL PHONICS APPROACH

- Pretaught before the selection
- Reinforced and applied throughout the decodable stories
- Reviewed immediately in the same plan—Multiple repetitions
- Cumulative Review for skills retention and application

Phonics CD-ROM

▲ Technology parallels the program skills

McGraw-Hill Reading
combines explicit instruction with a sequential,
systematic approach to build early reading success.

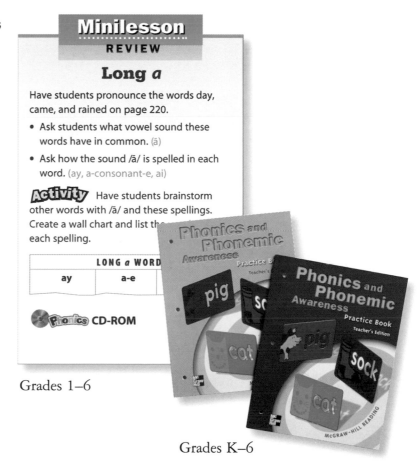

Minilesson
REVIEW

Long *a*

Have students pronounce the words day,
came, and rained on page 220.

- Ask students what vowel sound these
  words have in common. (ā)
- Ask how the sound /ā/ is spelled in each
  word. (ay, a-consonant-e, ai)

Activity Have students brainstorm
other words with /ā/ and these spellings.
Create a wall chart and list the
each spelling.

LONG *a* WORD	
ay	a-e

Phonics CD-ROM

Grades 1–6

Grades K–6

Where direct instruction leads to reading success.

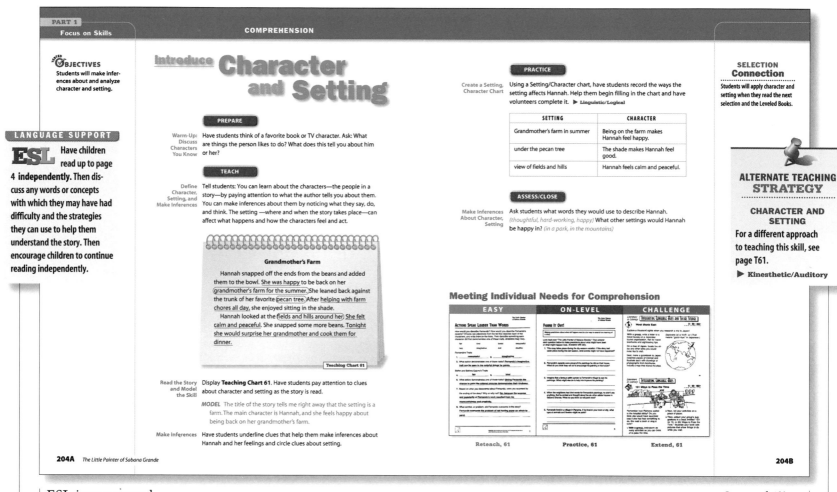

OBJECTIVES
Students will make inferences about and analyze character and setting.

LANGUAGE SUPPORT

ESL Have children read up to page 4 independently. Then discuss any words or concepts with which they may have had difficulty and the strategies they can use to help them understand the story. Then encourage children to continue reading independently.

Introduce Character and Setting

PREPARE

Warm-Up: Discuss Characters You Know
Have students think of a favorite book or TV character. Ask: What are things the person likes to do? What does this tell you about him or her?

TEACH

Define Character, Setting, and Make Inferences
Tell students: You can learn about the characters—the people in a story—by paying attention to what the author tells you about them. You can make inferences about them by noticing what they say, do, and think. The setting —where and when the story takes place—can affect what happens and how the characters feel and act.

Grandmother's Farm

Hannah snapped off the ends from the beans and added them to the bowl. She was happy to be back on her grandmother's farm for the summer. She leaned back against the trunk of her favorite pecan tree. After helping with farm chores all day, she enjoyed sitting in the shade.

Hannah looked at the fields and hills around her. She felt calm and peaceful. She snapped some more beans. Tonight she would surprise her grandmother and cook them for dinner.

Teaching Chart 61

Read the Story and Model the Skill
Display **Teaching Chart 61**. Have students pay attention to clues about character and setting as the story is read.

MODEL The title of the story tells me right away that the setting is a farm. The main character is Hannah, and she feels happy about being back on her grandmother's farm.

Make Inferences
Have students underline clues that help them make inferences about Hannah and her feelings and circle clues about setting.

PRACTICE

Create a Setting, Character Chart
Using a Setting/Character chart, have students record the ways the setting affects Hannah. Help them begin filling in the chart and have volunteers complete it. ▶ Linguistic/Logical

SETTING	CHARACTER
Grandmother's farm in summer	Being on the farm makes Hannah feel happy.
under the pecan tree	The shade makes Hannah feel good.
view of fields and hills	Hannah feels calm and peaceful.

ASSESS/CLOSE

Make Inferences About Character, Setting
Ask students what words they would use to describe Hannah. (thoughtful, hard-working, happy) What other settings would Hannah be happy in? (in a park, in the mountains)

Meeting Individual Needs for Comprehension

EASY	ON-LEVEL	CHALLENGE
Reteach, 61	Practice, 61	Extend, 61

SELECTION Connection
Students will apply character and setting when they read the next selection and the Leveled Books.

ALTERNATE TEACHING STRATEGY

CHARACTER AND SETTING
For a different approach to teaching this skill, see page T61.
▶ Kinesthetic/Auditory

ESL incorporated throughout

Same skill—
Different approach

▲ DIRECT INSTRUCTION
- Prepare, Teach, Practice, Assess/Close
- Leveled practice
- Alternate Teaching Strategy

EVERY LESSON INCLUDES:

Phonics
Comprehension
Vocabulary
Study Skills

McGRAW-HILL•LECTURA
- Spanish-language program parallels skills, themes, instruction, and components

▼ GUIDED INSTRUCTION IN ALL STORIES

- Key skill is the focus of instruction
- Pretaught skill applied throughout the selection

Creates independent readers

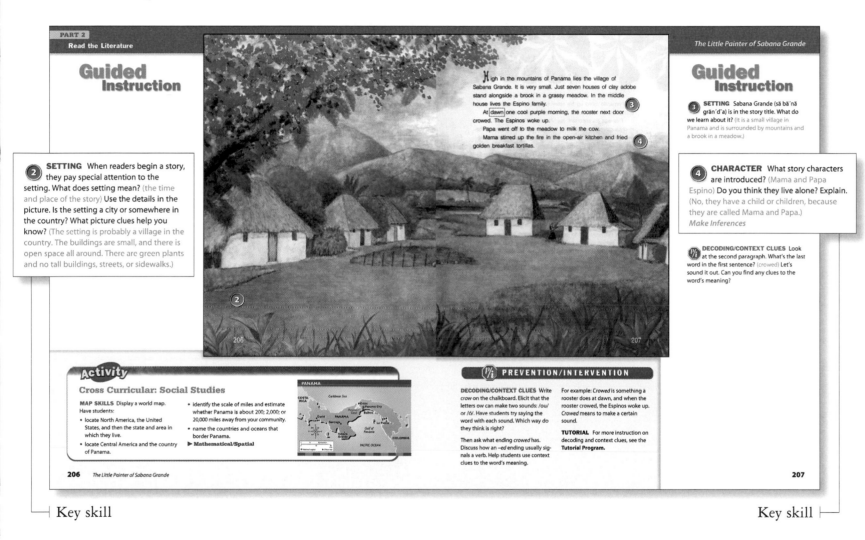

Guided Instruction

2 **SETTING** When readers begin a story, they pay special attention to the setting. What does setting mean? (the time and place of the story) Use the details in the picture. Is the setting a city or somewhere in the country? What picture clues help you know? (The setting is probably a village in the country. The buildings are small, and there is open space all around. There are green plants and no tall buildings, streets, or sidewalks.)

High in the mountains of Panama lies the village of Sabana Grande. It is very small. Just seven houses of clay adobe stand alongside a brook in a grassy meadow. In the middle house lives the Espino family.

At dawn one cool purple morning, the rooster next door crowed. The Espinos woke up.

Papa went off to the meadow to milk the cow.

Mama stirred up the fire in the open-air kitchen and fried golden breakfast tortillas.

Guided Instruction

3 **SETTING** Sabana Grande (sä bä´nä grän´d´a) is in the story title. What do we learn about it? (It is a small village in Panama and is surrounded by mountains and a brook in a meadow.)

4 **CHARACTER** What story characters are introduced? (Mama and Papa Espino) Do you think they live alone? Explain. (No, they have a child or children, because they are called Mama and Papa.)
Make Inferences

DECODING/CONTEXT CLUES Look at the second paragraph. What's the last word in the first sentence? (crowed) Let's sound it out. Can you find any clues to the word's meaning?

206 / 207

Activity

Cross Curricular: Social Studies

MAP SKILLS Display a world map. Have students:
- locate North America, the United States, and then the state and area in which they live.
- locate Central America and the country of Panama.
- identify the scale of miles and estimate whether Panama is about 200; 2,000; or 20,000 miles away from your community.
- name the countries and oceans that border Panama.
▶ **Mathematical/Spatial**

(P/I) PREVENTION/INTERVENTION

DECODING/CONTEXT CLUES Write *crow* on the chalkboard. Elicit that the letters *ow* can make two sounds: /ou/ or /ō/. Have students try saying the word with each sound. Which way do they think is right?

Then ask what ending *crowed* has. Discuss how an *–ed* ending usually signals a verb. Help students use context clues to the word's meaning.

For example: *Crowed* is something a rooster does at dawn, and when the rooster crowed, the Espinos woke up. *Crowed* means to make a certain sound.

TUTORIAL For more instruction on decoding and context clues, see the **Tutorial Program.**

206 *The Little Painter of Sabana Grande*

Key skill

Key skill

▲ MEETING INDIVIDUAL NEEDS

- **Prevention/Intervention**
- **Alternate Teaching Strategy**
- **ESL**
- **Leveled Books**
- **Leveled Practice**
- **Language Support**
- **Fluency**

FEATURED THROUGHOUT
GRADES K–6

McGraw-Hill Reading
teaches all students to become skillful readers.

Where learning-to-read opportunities reach every child.

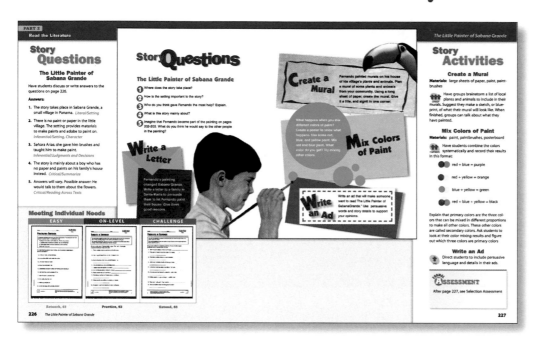

◄ STORY QUESTIONS
- Comprehension, thinking, and writing

STORY ACTIVITIES
- Cross-Curricular

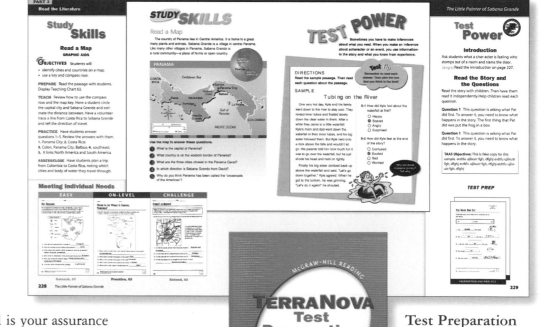

► STUDY SKILLS
- Maps, charts, graphs, and other reading resources

TEST POWER
- Test-taking skills and practice

STANDARDIZED TEST PREPARATION MATERIALS
Aligned & Validated

THE PRINCETON REVIEW
THE NATION'S LEADER IN TEST PREPARATION
McGRAW-HILL EXCLUSIVE

This seal is your assurance that all test preparation materials are aligned and validated by The Princeton Review.

TERRANOVA Test Preparation and Practice Book

Test Preparation

TerraNova

SAT-9

ITBS

Kindergarten Readiness

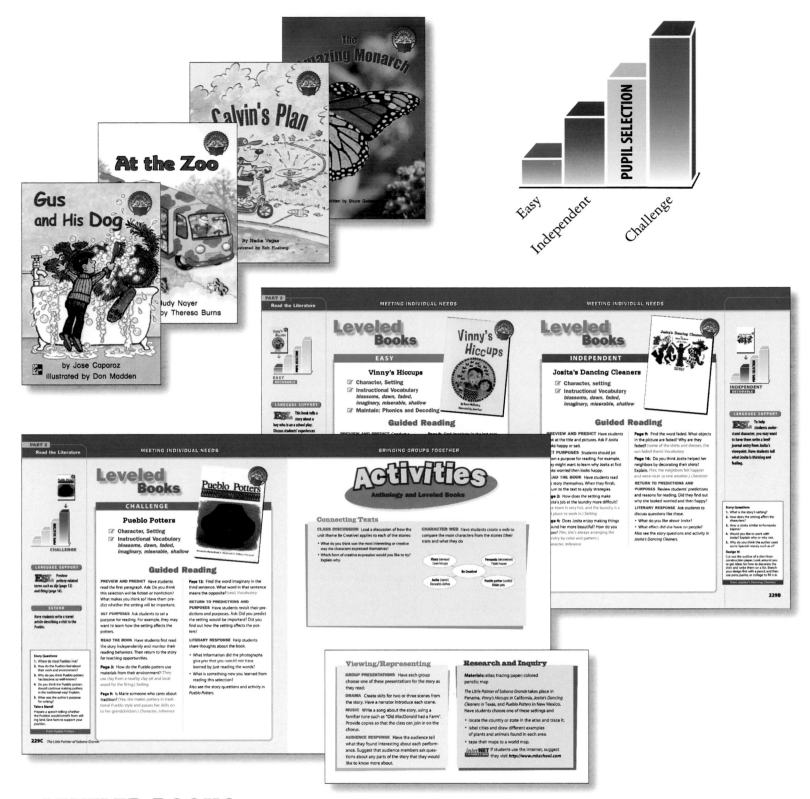

▲ LEVELED BOOKS

- Successful reading opportunities for all levels—regardless of ability
- Encourage reading growth from Easy to Independent to Challenge levels
- Includes Viewing/Representing and Research and Inquiry

McGRAW-HILL READING AND ACCELERATED READER: EASY AS 1-2-3

1. Support for every selection and leveled book; computer quizzes test student knowledge
2. Immediate and constructive feedback for teachers and students
3. Exciting, student-friendly design inspires and motivates learning

McGraw-Hill Reading
places opportunities to learn at the fingertips of every child.

Where the direction you need is all in one plan.

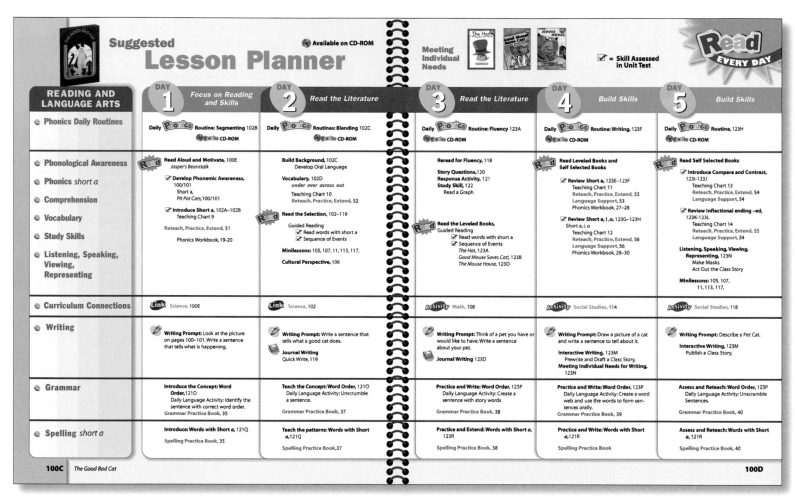

READING AND LANGUAGE ARTS	DAY 1 — Focus on Reading and Skills	DAY 2 — Read the Literature	DAY 3 — Read the Literature	DAY 4 — Build Skills	DAY 5 — Build Skills
• Phonics Daily Routines	Daily **Phonics** Routine: Segmenting 102B — CD-ROM	Daily **Phonics** Routines: Blending 102C — CD-ROM	Daily **Phonics** Routine: Fluency 123A — CD-ROM	Daily **Phonics** Routine: Writing, 123F — CD-ROM	Daily **Phonics** Routine, 123H — CD-ROM
• Phonological Awareness • Phonics *short a* • Comprehension • Vocabulary • Study Skills • Listening, Speaking, Viewing, Representing	**Read** Read Aloud and Motivate, 100E *Jasper's Beanstalk* ☑ Develop Phonemic Awareness, 100/101 Short a, *Pit Pat Cats*, 100/101 ☑ Introduce Short a, 102A–102B Teaching Chart 9 Reteach, Practice, Extend, 51 Phonics Workbook, 19-20	Build Background, 102C Develop Oral Language Vocabulary, 102D *under over across out* Teaching Chart 10 Reteach, Practice, Extend, 52 **Read** Read the Selection, 102–119 Guided Reading ☑ Read words with short a ☑ Sequence of Events Minilessons: 105, 107, 11, 113, 117, Cultural Perspective, 106	Reread for Fluency, 118 Story Questions, 120 Response Activity, 121 Study Skill, 122 Read a Graph **Read** Read the Leveled Books, Guided Reading ☑ Read words with short a ☑ Sequence of Events *The Hat*, 123A *Good Mouse Saves Cat!,* 123B *The Mouse House,* 123D	**Read** Read Leveled Books and Self Selected Books ☑ Review Short a, 123E–123F Teaching Chart 11 Reteach, Practice, Extend, 53 Language Support, 53 Phonics Workbook, 27–28 ☑ Review Short a, i ,o, 123G–123H Short a, i, o Teaching Chart 12 Reteach, Practice, Extend, 56 Language Support, 56 Phonics Workbook, 29–30	**Read** Read Self Selected Books ☑ Introduce Compare and Contrast, 123I-123J Teaching Chart 13 Reteach, Practice, Extend, 54 Language Support, 54 ☑ Review Inflectional ending –ed, 123K-123L Teaching Chart 14 Reteach, Practice, Extend, 55 Language Support, 54 Listening, Speaking, Viewing, Representing, 123N Make Masks Act Out the Class Story Minilessons: 105, 107, 11, 113, 117,
• Curriculum Connections	**Link** Science, 100E	**Link** Science, 102	**Activity** Math, 108	**Activity** Social Studies, 114	**Activity** Social Studies, 118
• Writing	Writing Prompt: Look at the picture on pages 100–101. Write a sentence that tells what is happening.	Writing Prompt: Write a sentence that tells what a good cat does. Journal Writing Quick Write, 119	Writing Prompt: Think of a pet you have or would like to have. Write a sentence about your pet. Journal Writing 123D	Writing Prompt: Draw a picture of a cat and write a sentence to tell about it. Interactive Writing, 123M Prewrite and Draft a Class Story, Meeting Individual Needs for Writing, 123N	Writing Prompt: Describe a Pet Cat. Interactive Writing, 123M Publish a Class Story,
• Grammar	Introduce the Concept: Word Order,121O Daily Language Activity: Identify the sentence with correct word order. Grammar Practice Book, 35	Teach the Concept: Word Order, 121O Daily Language Activity: Unscramble a sentence. Grammar Practice Book, 37	Practice and Write: Word Order, 123P Daily Language Activity: Create a sentence with story words Grammar Practice Book, 38	Practice and Write: Word Order, 123P Daily Language Activity: Create a word web and use the words to form sentences orally. Grammar Practice Book, 39	Assess and Reteach: Word Order, 123P Daily Language Activity: Unscramble Sentences. Grammar Practice Book, 40
• Spelling *short a*	Introduce: Words with Short a, 121Q Spelling Practice Book, 35	Teach the patterns: Words with Short a, 121Q Spelling Practice Book, 37	Practice and Extend: Words with Short a, 123R Spelling Practice Book, 38	Practice and Write: Words with Short a, 121R Spelling Practice Book	Assess and Reteach: Words with Short a, 121R Spelling Practice Book, 40

▲ 5-DAY LESSON PLANNER

• Easy-to-use lessons
• Interactive Lesson Planner available on CD-ROM allows teachers to create and customize lesson plans

DAILY
INTEGRATED LANGUAGE ARTS

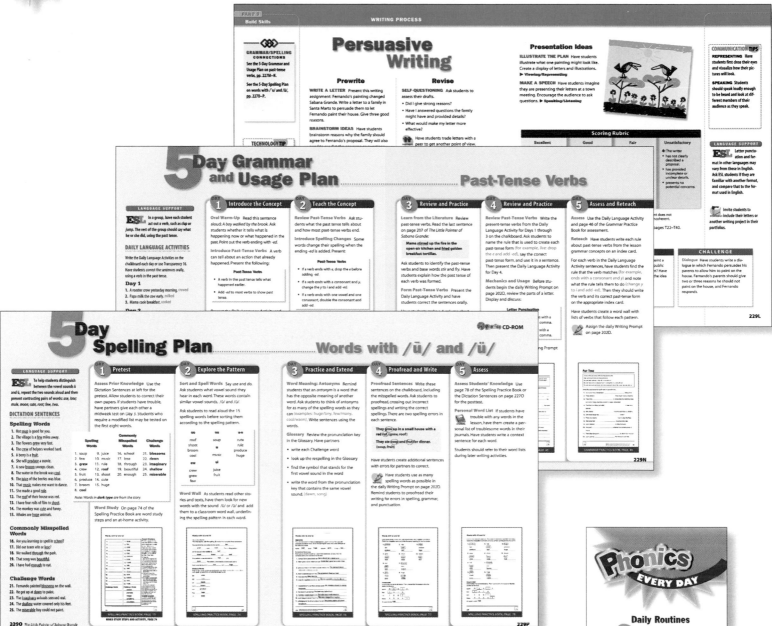

DAILY
ACTIVITIES

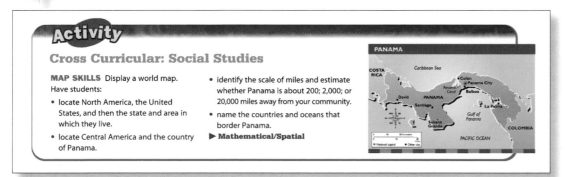

Activity

Cross Curricular: Social Studies

MAP SKILLS Display a world map. Have students:

- locate North America, the United States, and then the state and area in which they live.
- locate Central America and the country of Panama.

- identify the scale of miles and estimate whether Panama is about 200; 2,000; or 20,000 miles away from your community.
- name the countries and oceans that border Panama.

▶ **Mathematical/Spatial**

McGraw-Hill Reading

One company, one program, one lesson plan gives teachers the tools for reading success.

McGraw-Hill Reading

COMPONENT CHART

LITERATURE	K	1	2	3	4	5	6
Pupil Edition	•	•	•	•	•	•	•
Leveled Books: Patterned	•						
Literature Anthology Pupil Edition—Volumes 1 and 2		•					
Leveled Books: Easy		•	•	•	•	•	•
Leveled Books: Independent		•	•	•	•	•	•
Leveled Books: Challenge		•	•	•	•	•	•
ABC Big Books	•						
Big Book of Phonics Rhymes and Poems	•						
Big Book of Real Life Reading	•						
Big Book of Decodable Stories	•						
Literature Big Books	•	•	•	•			
Take-Home Books and Daily Activities Blackline Masters	•	•	•	•			

K/1 READINESS	K	1	2	3	4	5	6
McGraw-Hill Readiness Pupil Edition	•	•					
McGraw-Hill Readiness Teacher's Edition	•	•					

SKILLS AND PRACTICE	K	1	2	3	4	5	6
Practice Book	•	•	•	•	•	•	•
Practice Book Teacher's Annotated Edition	•	•	•	•	•	•	•
Reteach Blackline Masters		•	•	•	•	•	•
Extend Blackline Masters		•	•	•	•	•	•
Phonics/Phonemic Awareness Practice Book Pupil Edition	•	•	•	•	•	•	•
Phonics/Phonemic Awareness Practice Book Teacher's Annotated Edition	•	•	•	•	•	•	•
Language Support: Lessons and Practice Blackline Masters	•	•	•	•	•	•	•
Grammar Practice Book		•	•	•	•	•	•
Spelling Practice Book		•	•	•	•	•	•
Word Building Manipulative Cards: Letters, Sounds, and Words	•	•	•				
Word Building Manipulative Cards: Words and Word Parts				•	•	•	•
Letter Cards	•	•					
Phonics Picture Cards	•	•					
Phonics Picture Posters	•	•					

TEACHER'S MATERIALS	K	1	2	3	4	5	6
Teacher's Edition	•	•	•	•	•	•	•
Literature Anthology Teacher's Edition		•					
Daily Language Activities Transparencies		•	•	•	•	•	•
Daily Language Activities Blackline Masters		•	•	•	•	•	•
Writing Process Transparencies		•	•	•	•	•	•
Teaching Charts		•	•	•	•	•	•
Teaching Charts Transparencies		•	•	•	•	•	•
Graphic Organizers Transparencies		•	•	•	•	•	•
Phonics Kit	•	•	•				

ASSESSMENT	K	1	2	3	4	5	6
Diagnostic/Placement Evaluation Blackline Masters Teacher's Edition	•	•	•	•	•	•	•
Unit Test Booklets	•	•	•	•	•	•	•
Mid-Year Test Booklets	•	•	•	•	•	•	•
End-Year Test Booklets	•	•	•	•	•	•	•
Comprehensive Assessment Blackline Masters and Teacher's Manual (includes Unit, Mid-, and End-Year Assessment)	•	•	•	•	•	•	•
Selection Assessments Pupil Edition		•	•	•	•	•	•
Selection Assessments Teacher's Annotated Edition		•	•	•	•	•	•
Standardized Test Preparation and Practice Book	•						
Standardized Test Preparation and Practice Book Teacher's Edition	•						
TerraNova Test Preparation and Practice Book Pupil Edition		•	•	•	•	•	•
TerraNova Test Preparation and Practice Book Teacher's Annotated Edition		•	•	•	•	•	•
SAT-9 Test Preparation and Practice Book Pupil Edition		•	•	•	•	•	•
SAT-9 Test Preparation and Practice Book Teacher's Annotated Edition		•	•	•	•	•	•
ITBS Test Preparation and Practice Book Pupil Edition		•	•	•	•	•	•
ITBS Test Preparation and Practice Book Teacher's Annotated Edition		•	•	•	•	•	•
Student Profile Booklet	•	•	•	•	•	•	•

TECHNOLOGY	K	1	2	3	4	5	6
Adventures with Buggles: Phonics CD-ROM	•	•	•	•			
Accelerated Reader Quizzes		•	•	•	•	•	
Internet Research and Inquiry Activities	•	•	•	•	•	•	•
Interactive Lesson Planner	•	•	•	•	•	•	•
Listening Library Audiocassettes	•	•	•	•	•	•	•
Internet Assessment	•	•	•	•	•	•	•

Macmillan/McGraw-Hill Edition

McGRAW-HILL READING

 **McGraw-Hill School Division**

New York   Farmington

Contributors

The Princeton Review, Time Magazine, Accelerated Reader

The Princeton Review is not
affiliated with Princeton
University or ETS.

McGraw-Hill School Division ⚛

A Division of The McGraw·Hill Companies

McGraw-Hill School Division
Two Penn Plaza
New York, New York 10121

Printed in the United States of America

ISBN 0-02-184759-2/3, Bk.1, U.1
        6 7 8 9 043/073 04 03 02 01

McGRAW-HILL READING

McGraw-Hill
School Division

New York   Farmington

Selected Quizzes Prepared by  **Accelerated Reader**

McGraw-Hill Reading
Authors
Make the Difference...

Dr. James Flood

Ms. Angela Shelf Medearis

Dr. Jan E. Hasbrouck

Dr. Scott Paris

Dr. James V. Hoffman

Dr. Steven Stahl

Dr. Diane Lapp

Dr. Josefina Villamil Tinajero

Dr. Karen D. Wood

Contributing
Authors

Dr. Barbara Coulter

Ms. Frankie Dungan

Dr. Joseph B. Rubin

Dr. Carl B. Smith

Dr. Shirley Wright

iv

Part 1
START TOGETHER

Focus on Reading and Skills

All students start with the SAME:

- Read Aloud
- Pretaught Skills
  Phonics
  Comprehension
- Build Background
- Selection Vocabulary

...Never hold a child back. Never leave a child behind.

Part 2
MEET INDIVIDUAL NEEDS

Read the Literature

Core Selection **Leveled Books** **Leveled Practice**

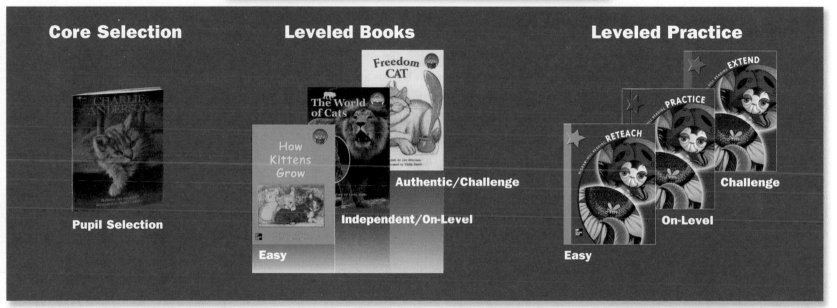

Pupil Selection

Easy

Independent/On-Level

Authentic/Challenge

Easy

On-Level

Challenge

Examples Taken From Grade 2

Part 3
FINISH TOGETHER

Build Skills

All students finish with the SAME:

- Phonics
- Comprehension
- Vocabulary
- Study Skills
- Assessment

McGraw-Hill Reading
Applying the Research

Phonological Awareness

Phonological awareness is the ability to hear the sounds in spoken language. It includes the ability to separate spoken words into discrete sounds as well as the ability to blend sounds together to make words. A child with good phonological awareness can identify rhyming words, hear the separate syllables in a word, separate the first sound in a word (onset) from the rest of the word (rime), and blend sounds together to make words.

Recent research findings have strongly concluded that children with good phonological awareness skills are more likely to learn to read well. These skills can be improved through systematic, explicit instruction involving auditory practice. McGraw-Hill Reading develops these key skills by providing an explicit Phonological Awareness lesson in every selection at grades K-2. Motivating activities such as blending, segmenting, and rhyming help to develop children's awareness of the sounds in our language.

Guided Instruction/ Guided Reading

Research on reading shows that guided instruction enables students to develop as independent, strategic readers. The *reciprocal-teaching model* of Anne-Marie Palincsar encourages teachers to model strategic-thinking, questioning, clarifying, and problem-solving strategies for students as students read together with the teacher. In McGraw-Hill Reading, guided instruction for all Pupil Edition selections incorporates the Palincsar model by providing interactive questioning prompts. The *guided-reading model* of Gay Su Pinnell is also incorporated into the McGraw-Hill Reading program. Through the guided-reading lessons provided for the leveled books offered with the program, teachers can work with small groups of students of different ability levels, closely observing them as they read and providing support specific to their needs.

By adapting instruction to include successful models of teaching and the appropriate materials to deliver instruction, McGraw-Hill Reading enables teachers to offer the appropriate type of instruction for all students in the classroom.

Phonics

Our language system uses an alphabetic code to communicate meaning from writing. Phonics involves learning the phonemes or sounds that letters make and the symbols or letters that represent those sounds. Children learn to blend the sounds of letters to decode unknown or unfamiliar words. The goal of good phonics instruction is to enable students to read words accurately and automatically.

Research has clearly identified the critical role of phonics in the ability of readers to read fluently and with good understanding, as well as to write and spell. Effective phonics instruction requires carefully sequenced lessons that teach the sounds of letters and how to use these sounds to read words. The McGraw-Hill program provides daily explicit and systematic phonics instruction to teach the letter sounds and blending. There are three explicit Phonics and Decoding lessons for every selection. Daily Phonics Routines are provided for quick reinforcement, in addition to activities in the Phonics/Phonemic Awareness Practice Book and technology components. This combination of direct skills instruction and applied practice leads to reading success.

Curriculum Connections

As in the child's real-world environment, boundaries between disciplines must be dissolved. Recent research emphasizes the need to make connections between and across subject areas. McGraw-Hill Reading is committed to this approach. Each reading selection offers activities that tie in with social studies, language arts, geography, science, mathematics, art, music, health, and physical education. The program threads numerous research and inquiry activities that encourage the child to use the library and the Internet to seek out information. Reading and language skills are applied to a variety of genres, balancing fiction and nonfiction.

Integrated Language Arts

Success in developing communication skills is greatly enhanced by integrating the language arts in connected and purposeful ways. This allows students to understand the need for proper writing, grammar, and spelling. McGraw-Hill Reading sets the stage for meaningful learning. Each week a full writing-process lesson is provided. This lesson is supported by a 5-day spelling plan, emphasizing spelling patterns and spelling rules, and a 5-day grammar plan, focusing on proper grammar, mechanics, and usage.

Meeting Individual Needs

Every classroom is a microcosm of a world composed of diverse individuals with unique needs and abilities. Research points out that such needs must be addressed with frequent intensive opportunities to learn with engaging materials. McGraw-Hill Reading makes reading a successful experience for every child by providing a rich collection of leveled books for easy, independent, and challenging reading. Leveled practice is provided in Reteach, Practice, and Extend skills books. To address various learning styles and language needs, the program offers alternative teaching strategies, prevention/intervention techniques, language support activities, and ESL teaching suggestions.

Assessment

Frequent assessment in the classroom makes it easier for teachers to identify problems and to find remedies for them. McGraw-Hill Reading makes assessment an important component of instruction. Formal and informal opportunities are a part of each lesson. Minilessons, prevention/intervention strategies, and informal checklists, as well as student self-assessments, provide many informal assessment opportunities. Formal assessments, such as weekly selection tests and criterion-referenced unit tests, help to monitor students' knowledge of important skills and concepts. McGraw-Hill Reading also addresses how to adapt instruction based on student performance with resources such as the Alternate Teaching Strategies. Weekly lessons on test preparation, including test preparation practice books, help students to transfer skills to new contexts and to become better test takers.

McGraw-Hill School
TECHNOLOGY

*inter*NET For information
CONNECTION on research that
supports this program, visit
www.mhschool.com/reading

McGraw-Hill Reading

Theme Chart

MULTI-AGE Classroom

Using the same global themes at each grade level facilitates the use of materials in multi-age classrooms.

GRADE LEVEL	Experience Experiences can tell us about ourselves and our world.	Connections Making connections develops new understandings.
Kindergarten	**My World** We learn a lot from all the things we see and do at home and in school.	**All Kinds of Friends** When we work and play together, we learn more about ourselves.
Subtheme 1	At Home	Working Together
Subtheme 2	School Days	Playing Together
1	**Day by Day** Each day brings new experiences.	**Together Is Better** We like to share ideas and experiences with others.
2	**What's New?** With each day, we learn something new.	**Just Between Us** Family and friends help us see the world in new ways.
3	**Great Adventures** Life is made up of big and small experiences.	**Nature Links** Nature can give us new ideas.
4	**Reflections** Stories let us share the experiences of others.	**Something in Common** Sharing ideas can lead to meaningful cooperation.
5	**Time of My Life** We sometimes find memorable experiences in unexpected places.	**Building Bridges** Knowing what we have in common helps us appreciate our differences.
6	**Pathways** Reflecting on life's experiences can lead to new understandings.	**A Common Thread** A look beneath the surface may uncover hidden connections.

Themes: Kindergarten – Grade 6

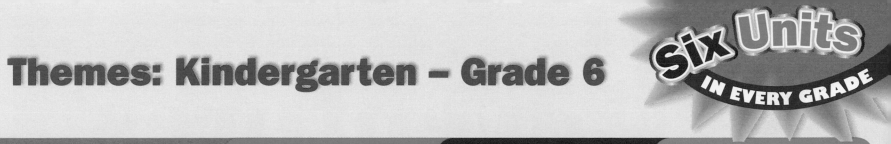

Six Units IN EVERY GRADE

Expression	Inquiry	Problem Solving	Making Decisions
There are many styles and forms for expressing ourselves.	By exploring and asking questions, we make discoveries.	Analyzing information can help us solve problems.	Using what we know helps us evaluate situations.
Time to Shine We can use our ideas and our imagination to do many wonderful things.	**I Wonder** We can make discoveries about the wonders of nature in our own backyard.	**Let's Work It Out** Working as part of a team can help me find a way to solve problems.	**Choices** We can make many good choices and decisions every day.
Great Ideas	In My Backyard	Try and Try Again	Good Choices
Let's Pretend	Wonders of Nature	Teamwork	Let's Decide
Stories to Tell Each one of us has a different story to tell.	**Let's Find Out!** Looking for answers is an adventure.	**Think About It!** It takes time to solve problems.	**Many Paths** Each decision opens the door to a new path.
Express Yourself We share our ideas in many ways.	**Look Around** There are surprises all around us.	**Figure It Out** We can solve problems by working together.	**Starting Now** Unexpected events can lead to new decisions.
Be Creative! We can all express ourselves in creative, wonderful ways.	**Tell Me More** Looking and listening closely will help us find out the facts.	**Think It Through** Solutions come in many shapes and sizes.	**Turning Points** We make new judgments based on our experiences.
Our Voices We can each use our talents to communicate ideas.	**Just Curious** We can find answers in surprising places.	**Make a Plan** Often we have to think carefully about a problem in order to solve it.	**Sorting It Out** We make decisions that can lead to new ideas and discoveries.
Imagine That The way we express our thoughts and feelings can take different forms.	**Investigate!** We never know where the search for answers might lead us.	**Bright Ideas** Some problems require unusual approaches.	**Crossroads** Decisions cause changes that can enrich our lives.
With Flying Colors Creative people help us see the world from different perspectives.	**Seek and Discover** To make new discoveries, we must observe and explore.	**Brainstorms** We can meet any challenge with determination and ingenuity.	**All Things Considered** Encountering new places and people can help us make decisions.

Great Adventures

Life is made up of big and small experiences.

"Closed, I am a mystery" a poem by *Myra Cohn Livingston*

GRANDFATHER'S JOURNEY **12A**

written and illustrated by **Allen Say**

SKILLS			
Study Skill	**Comprehension**	**Vocabulary**	**Phonics**
• Using Parts of a Book: Book Parts	• **Introduce** Story Elements • **Review** Story Elements • **Introduce** Make Predictions	• **Introduce** Compound Words	• Short Vowels

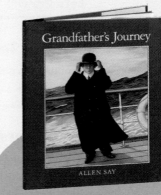

BIOGRAPHICAL STORY

PHOEBE AND THE SPELLING BEE **48A**

written and illustrated by **Barney Saltzberg**

SKILLS			
Study Skill	**Comprehension**	**Vocabulary**	**Phonics**
• Using Parts of a Book: Glossary	• **Introduce** Prob-lem and Solution • **Review** Problem and Solution • **Review** Make Predictions	• **Introduce** Prefixes	• Long *a* and Long *e*

HUMOROUS FICTION

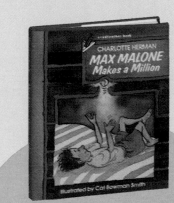

Unit Planner

	WEEK 1 Grandfather's Journey	WEEK 2 Phoebe and the Spelling Bee
Leveled Books	**Easy:** *Journey to America* **Independent:** *Ruthie Rides the Trolley* **Challenge:** *Jason and the Argonauts*	**Easy:** *The Family Game* **Independent:** *The Secret of the Super Sinker* **Challenge:** *The Thousand-Year-Old Game*
✓ **Tested Skills**	☑ **Comprehension** Story Elements, 14A–14B, 47E–47F Make Predictions, 47G–47H ☑ **Vocabulary** Compound Words, 47I–47J ☑ **Study Skills** Parts of a Book, 46	☑ **Comprehension** Problem and Solution, 50A–50B, 77E–77F Make Predictions, 77G–77H ☑ **Vocabulary** Prefixes, 77I–77J ☑ **Study Skills** Parts of a Book, 76
Minilessons	**Phonics and Decoding:** Short Vowels, 39 **Suffixes,** 21 **Summarize,** 25 **Make Inferences,** 41	**Phonics and Decoding:** Long *a* and Long *e*, 67 **Summarize,** 63 **Inflectional Endings,** 65 **Make Inferences,** 71
Language Arts	**Writing:** Personal Narrative, 47K **Grammar:** Statements and Questions, 47M–47N **Spelling:** Words with Short Vowels, 47O–47P	**Writing:** Personal Narrative, 77K **Grammar:** Commands and Exclamations, 77M–77N **Spelling:** Words with Long *a* and Long *e*, 77O–77P

Activities

Curriculum Connections	**Read Aloud:** "From the Bellybutton of the Moon," 12E	**Read Aloud:** "The Wind and the Sun," 48E
	Stories in Art: *The Emigrants*, 12/13	**Stories in Art:** *Heroes on Wheels*, 48/49
	Math: Measure Distances, 18	**Science:** Dinosaurs, 54
	Art: College, 26	**Social Studies:** Careers, 58
	Social Studies: Immigration, 28	**Health:** Stress and Health, 64
	Science: Birds, 36	**Math:** Multiplication, 68
CULTURAL PERSPECTIVES	Dress, 34	Amazing Alphabets, 52

WEEK **3** Opt: An Illusionary Tale	WEEK **4** Max Malone	WEEK **5** Champions of the World	WEEK **6** Review, Writing Process, Assessment
Easy: *Journey Across the Desert* **Independent:** *Magical Illusions: Simple Tricks You Can Do!* **Challenge:** *Houdini: Master of Escape*	**Easy:** *Special Delivery* **Independent:** *The Wonder Ball* **Challenge:** *The Saltaire Voice*	Self-Selected Reading of Leveled Books	Self-Selected Reading
☑ **Comprehension** Steps in a Process, 80A–80B, 105E–105F Story Elements, 105G–105H ☑ **Vocabulary** Prefixes, 105I–105J ☑ **Study Skills** Parts of a Book, 104	☑ **Comprehension** Problem and Solution, 108A–108B, 127E–127F Story Elements, 127G–127H ☑ **Vocabulary** Compound Words, 127I-127J ☑ **Study Skills** Parts of a Book, 126	☑ **Comprehension** Make Predictions, 130A–130B Steps in a Process, 137E–137F ☑ **Vocabulary** Compound Words, 137G–137H Prefixes, 137I–137J ☑ **Study Skills** Technology, 136	☑ **Assess Skills** Story Elements Make Predictions Problem and Solution Steps in a Process Compound Words Prefixes Parts of a Book ☑ **Assess Grammar and Spelling** Review Sentences, 139G Review Spelling Patterns, 139H ☑ **Unit Progress Assessment** ☑ **Standardized Test Preparation**
Phonics and Decoding: Long *i* and Long *o*, 91 **Context Clues,** 83 **Summarize,** 93 **Make Inferences,** 99	**Phonics and Decoding:** /ū/ and /ü/, 119 **Analyze Character,** 113 **Suffixes,** 115 **Main Idea,** 117		
✎ **Writing:** Personal Narrative, 105K **Grammar:** Subjects, 105M–105N **Spelling:** Words with Long *i* and Long *o*, 105O–105P	✎ **Writing:** Personal Narrative, 127K **Grammar:** Predicates, 127M–127N **Spelling:** Words with /ū/ and /ü/, 127O–127P	✎ **Writing:** Personal Narrative, 137K **Grammar:** Sentence Combining, 137M–137N **Spelling:** Words From Physical Education, 137O–137P	✎ **Unit Writing Process:** Personal Narrative, 139A–139F
Read Aloud: "The Wolf and His Shadow," 78E	**Read Aloud:** "If I Find a Penny," 106E	**Read Aloud:** "Take Me Out to the Ball Game," 128E	**Cooperative Theme Project Research and Inquiry:** People on the Move, 10
Stories in Art: *The Art of Conversation,* 78/79	**Stories in Art:** *Lemonade Stand,* 106/107	**Stories in Art:** *Hockey at Malvern Girls College,* 128/129	
Science: Color, 82	**Math:** Division, 112		
Math: Geometric Shapes, 92	**Social Studies:** Foreign Currency, 114		
Social Studies: Monarchies, 94	**Music:** Singing, 116		
Art: Background Colors, 96	**Science:** The Appendix, 120		
Art and Perspectives, 86	Baseball Hall of Fame, 110		

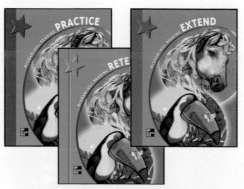

LITERATURE

LEVELED BOOKS

Easy
- *Journey to America*
- *The Family Game*
- *Journey Across the Desert*
- *Special Delivery*

Independent
- *Ruthie Rides the Trolley*
- *The Secret of the Super Sinker*
- *Magical Illusions: Simple Tricks You Can Do!*
- *The Wonder Ball*

Challenge
- *Jason and the Argonauts*
- *The Thousand-Year-Old Game*
- *Houdini: Master of Escape*
- *The Saltaire Voice*

THEME BIG BOOK Share *Two Foolish Cats* to set the unit theme and make content-area connections.

LISTENING LIBRARY AUDIOCASSETTE Recordings of the student book selections and poetry

SKILLS

LEVELED PRACTICE

Practice Book: Student practice for phonics, comprehension, vocabulary, and study skills; plus practice for instructional vocabulary and story comprehension. Take-Home Story included for each lesson.

Reteach: Reteaching opportunities for students who need more help with each assessed skill.

Extend: Extension activities for vocabulary, comprehension, story, and study skills.

TEACHING CHARTS Instructional charts for modeling vocabulary and tested skills. Also available as transparencies.

WORD BUILDING MANIPULATIVE CARDS Cards with words and structural elements for word building and practicing vocabulary.

LANGUAGE SUPPORT BOOK
ESL Parallel teaching lessons and appropriate practice activities for students needing language support.

PHONICS/PHONEMIC AWARENESS PRACTICE BOOK Additional practice focusing on vowel sounds, phonograms, blends, digraphs, and key phonetic elements.

LANGUAGE ARTS

GRAMMAR PRACTICE BOOK Provides practice for grammar and mechanics lessons.

SPELLING PRACTICE BOOK Provides practice with the word list and spelling patterns. Includes home involvement activities.

DAILY LANGUAGE ACTIVITIES Sentence activities that provide brief, regular practice and reinforcement of grammar, mechanics, and usage skills. Available as blackline masters and transparencies.

McGraw-Hill School
TECHNOLOGY

Phonics CD-ROM provides extra phonics support.

*inter*NET **CONNECTION** extends lesson activities through Research and Inquiry ideas.

Visit
www.mhschool.com/reading

Resources for Meeting Individual Needs

	EASY	ON-LEVEL	CHALLENGE	LANGUAGE SUPPORT

UNIT 1

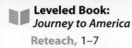

Grandfather's Journey

EASY
Leveled Book: *Journey to America*
Reteach, 1–7
Alternate Teaching Strategies, T60-T66
✏ **Writing:** Title and Caption, 47L
💿 **Phonics CD-ROM**

ON-LEVEL
Leveled Book: *Ruthie Rides the Trolley*
Practice, 1–7
Alternate Teaching Strategies, T60-T66
✏ **Writing:** Oral History, 47L
💿 **Phonics CD-ROM**

CHALLENGE
Leveled Book: *Jason and the Argonauts*
Extend, 1–7
✏ **Writing:** Journal Entry, 47L

LANGUAGE SUPPORT
Teaching Strategies, 14C, 15, 17, 31, 33, 47A, 47B, 47C, 47L
Language Support, 1–8
Alternate Teaching Strategies, T60-T66
✏ **Writing:** Write a Letter, 47K-47L
 💿 **Phonics CD-ROM**

Phoebe and the Spelling Bee

EASY
Leveled Book: *The Family Game*
Reteach, 8-14
Alternate Teaching Strategies, T60-T66
✏ **Writing:** Peculiar Pizzas, 77L
💿 **Phonics CD-ROM**

ON-LEVEL
Leveled Book: *The Secret of the Super Sinker*
Practice, 8-14
Alternate Teaching Strategies, T60-T66
✏ **Writing:** Diary Entry, 77L
💿 **Phonics CD-ROM**

CHALLENGE
Leveled Book: *The Thousand-Year-Old Game*
Extend, 8-14
✏ **Writing:** Dialogue, 77L

LANGUAGE SUPPORT
Teaching Strategies, 50C, 51, 67, 69, 77A, 77B, 77C, 77L
Language Support, 9-16
Alternate Teaching Strategies, T60-T66
✏ **Writing:** Write a Personal Narrative, 77K-77L
 💿 **Phonics CD-ROM**

Opt: An Illusionary Tale

EASY
Leveled Book: *Journey Across the Desert*
Reteach, 15-21
Alternate Teaching Strategies, T60-T66
✏ **Writing:** Caption, 105L
💿 **Phonics CD-ROM**

ON-LEVEL
Leveled Book: *Magical Illusions: Simple Tricks You Can Do!*
Practice, 15-21
Alternate Teaching Strategies, T60-T66
✏ **Writing:** Directions, 105L
 💿 **Phonics CD-ROM**

CHALLENGE
Leveled Book: *Houdini: Master of Escape*
Extend, 15-21
✏ **Writing:** Thank-You Letter, 105L

LANGUAGE SUPPORT
Teaching Strategies, 80C, 81, 83, 85, 91, 95, 105A, 105B, 105C, 105L
Language Support, 17-24
Alternate Teaching Strategies, T60-T66
✏ **Writing:** Write a Story, 105K-105L
 💿 **Phonics CD-ROM**

Max Malone

EASY
Leveled Book: *Special Delivery*
Reteach, 22-28
Alternate Teaching Strategies, T60-T66
✏ **Writing:** Thank-You Card, 127L
 💿 **Phonics CD-ROM**

ON-LEVEL
Leveled Book: *The Wonder Ball*
Practice, 22-28
Alternate Teaching Strategies, T60-T66
✏ **Writing:** Biographical Article, 127L
 💿 **Phonics CD-ROM**

CHALLENGE
Leveled Book: *The Saltaire Voice*
Extend, 22-28
✏ **Writing:** Citizen-of-the-Month Award, 127L

LANGUAGE SUPPORT
Teaching Strategies, 108C, 109, 113, 115, 127A, 127B, 127C, 127L
Language Support, 25-32
Alternate Teaching Strategies, T60-T66
✏ **Writing:** Write an Article, 127K-127L
  💿 **Phonics CD-ROM**

Champions of the World

EASY
Review
Reteach, 29-35
Alternate Teaching Strategies, T60-T66
✏ **Writing:** Make a Cartoon, 137L

ON-LEVEL
Review
Practice, 29-35
Alternate Teaching Strategies, T60-T66
✏ **Writing:** Goals and Needs, 137L

CHALLENGE
Review
Extend, 29-35
✏ **Writing:** Sammy's Story, 137L

LANGUAGE SUPPORT
Teaching Strategies, 130C, 131, 137L
Language Support, 33-40
Alternate Teaching Strategies, T60-T66
✏ **Writing:** Write an Essay, 137K-137L

INFORMAL

Informal Assessment

- Comprehension, 14B, 42, 43, 47F, 47H; 50B, 72, 73, 77F, 77H; 80B, 100, 101, 105F, 105H; 108B, 122, 123, 127F, 127H; 130B, 133, 137F
- Vocabulary, 47J, 77J, 105J, 127J, 137H, 137J

Performance Assessment

- Scoring Rubrics, 47L, 77L, 105L, 127L, 137L
- Research and Inquiry, 11, 139
- Writing Process, 47K, 77K, 105K, 127K, 137K, 139A–F
- Listening, Speaking, Viewing Activities, 12E, 12/13, 14C, 14–45, 47D, 47K–L; 48E, 48/49, 50C, 50–75, 77D, 77K–L; 78E, 78/79, 80C, 80–103, 105D, 105K–L; 106E, 106/107, 108C, 108–125, 127D, 127K–L; 128E, 128/129, 130C, 130–135, 137D, 137K–L
- Portfolio, 47L, 77L, 105L, 127L, 137L
- Writing, 47K–L, 77K–L, 105K–L, 127K–L, 137K–L
- Cross-Curricular Activities, 14C, 18, 26, 28, 36, 50C, 54, 58, 64, 68; 80C, 108C, 82, 92, 94, 96, 108C, 112, 114, 116, 120, 130C

Leveled Practice

Practice, Reteach, Extend

- **Comprehension**
  Story Elements, 1, 5, 20, 27
  Make Predictions, 6, 13, 29
  Problem and Solution, 8, 12, 22, 26
  Steps in a Process, 15, 19, 33
- **Vocabulary Strategies**
  Compound Words, 7, 28, 34
  Prefixes, 14, 21, 35
- **Study Skills**
  Parts of a Book, 4, 11, 18, 25, 32

FORMAL

Selection Assessments

- **Skills and Vocabulary Words**
  Grandfather's Journey, 1–2
  Phoebe and the Spelling Bee, 3–4
  Opt: An Illusionary Tale, 5–6
  Max Malone, 7–8
  Champions of the World, 9–10

Unit 1 Test

- **Comprehension**
  Story Elements
  Make Predictions
  Problem and Solution
  Steps in a Process
- **Vocabulary Strategies**
  Compound Words
  Prefixes
- **Study Skills**
  Parts of a Book

Grammar and Spelling Assessment

- **Grammar**
  Sentences, 5, 11, 17, 23, 29, 31–32
- **Spelling**
  Words with Short Vowels, 6
  Words with Long *a* and Long *e,* 12
  Words with Long *i* and Long *o,* 18
  Words with /ū/ and /ü/, 24
  Words from Physical Education, 30
  Unit 1 Assessment, 31–32

Diagnostic/Placement Evaluation

- Individual Reading Inventory, 31–32
- Running Record, 33–34
- Grade K Diagnostic/Placement
- Grade 1 Diagnostic/Placement
- Grade 2 Diagnostic/Placement
- Grade 3 Diagnostic/Placement

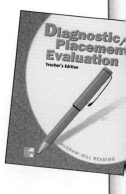

Test Preparation

- TAAS Preparation and Practice Booklet, 20–29
- See also Test Power in Teacher's Edition, 47, 77, 105, 127, 137

Assessment Checklist

Student ....Grade........

Teacher ....

	Grandfather's Journey	Phoebe and the Spelling Bee	Opt: An Illusionary Tale	Max Malone	Champions of the World	Assessment Summary
LISTENING/SPEAKING						
Participates in oral language experiences						
Listens and speaks to gain knowledge of culture						
Speaks appropriately to audiences for different purposes						
Communicates clearly						
READING						
Uses a variety of word identification strategies:						
• Short Vowels						
• Long *a* and Long *e*						
• Long *i* and Long *o*						
• /ū/ and /ü/ spelled *u-e, oo, ew, ui, ou, u*						
• Compound Words						
• Prefixes						
Reads with fluency and understanding						
Reads widely for different purposes in varied sources						
Develops an extensive vocabulary						
Uses a variety of strategies to comprehend selections:						
• Make Predictions						
• Problem and Solution						
• Steps in a Process						
Responds to various texts						
Analyzes the characteristics of various types of texts:						
• Story Elements (Character, Setting, Plot)						
Conducts research using various sources:						
• Parts of a Book						
Reads to increase knowledge						
WRITING						
Writes for a variety of audiences and purposes						
Composes original texts using the conventions of written language such as capitalization and penmanship						
Spells proficiently						
Composes texts applying knowledge of grammar and usage						
Uses writing processes						
Evaluates own writing and writing of others						

+ Observed   − Not Observed

Introducing the Theme

Great Adventures

Life is made up of big and small experiences.

PRESENT THE THEME Read the theme statement to students. Encourage them to think of experiences they've had that they'll always remember. Call on volunteers to share their memories. Then ask if quiet moments can be as memorable as big events. Help students think of different kinds of adventures, from sailing to a new land to finding a secret hideout in one's own house.

READ THE POEM Point out that every day holds fresh discoveries for people. Read aloud "Closed, I am a mystery" by Myra Cohn Livingston. Ask students to try to discover the subject of the poem as you read. Why do they think the poet compares a book to a friend? What experiences do friends share? Lead them to see that books, too, can be partners in great adventures.

LISTENING LIBRARY AUDIOCASSETTE

MAKE CONNECTIONS Have students preview the unit by reading the selection titles and looking at the illustrations. Then have them work in small groups to brainstorm a list of ways that the stories, poems, and the *Time for Kids* magazine article relate to the theme Great Adventures.

Groups can then compare their lists as they share them with the class.

THEME SUMMARY

Each of the five selections relates to the unit theme Great Adventures as well as the global theme Experience. These thematic links will help students to make connections across texts.

Grandfather's Journey A man's life's journey takes him back and forth between two lands.

Phoebe and the Spelling Bee Phoebe uses her imagination to overcome her fear.

Opt: An Illusionary Tale In a kingdom of optical illusion things aren't always what they seem.

Max Malone Two boys earn lots of money, then learn its true worth.

Champions of the World The Toms River team wins the Little League World Series.

Great Adventures

Closed, I am a Mystery

Closed, I am a mystery.
Open, I will always be
a friend with whom you think and see.

Closed, there's nothing I can say.
Open, we can dream and stray
to other worlds, far and away.

by Myra Cohn Livingston

11

LEARNING ABOUT POETRY

Literary Devices: Figurative Language As you read the poem aloud, have students use hand gestures to express "open" and "closed." Point out the comparison (metaphor) between a book and a person (friend). Ask in what ways people can be either open or closed to new experiences and adventures. Reread the poem aloud with the class to reinforce the ideas.

Poetry Activity Have students write a poem about a Great Adventure that they have had. Students might want to use this poem as a model to follow when they write, or choose another one.

Research and Inquiry

Theme Project: People on the Move Invite teams of students to brainstorm historical events, journeys, or explorations they want to know more about, for example: Orbiting the Earth, Discovering the Wreck of the *Titanic*. Students will choose one adventure for a project that will capture the experiences of the people who participated.

List What They Know Once students have chosen an "adventure," have them list what they already know about it.

Ask Questions and Identify Resources Ask students to brainstorm questions they would to answer to prepare their presentations. Have them list possible resources.

QUESTIONS	POSSIBLE RESOURCES
• How did the people travel? • What dangers did they face? • What did they take with them? • How long was the journey?	• Encyclopedias • Search on the Internet • First-person account (diaries, interviews) • Visit to a museum

interNET **CONNECTION** Have students visit **www. mhschool.com/reading.**

Create a Presentation When their research is complete, students will reenact the experience. Ask them to develop a cast of characters who can give different points of view. Students should portray both dramatic and quiet moments. Encourage them to use costumes and props to add authenticity. See Wrap Up the Theme, page 139.

Grandfather's Journey

Selection Summary A man grows to love the two different lands that he calls home as his life journey takes him back and forth between them.

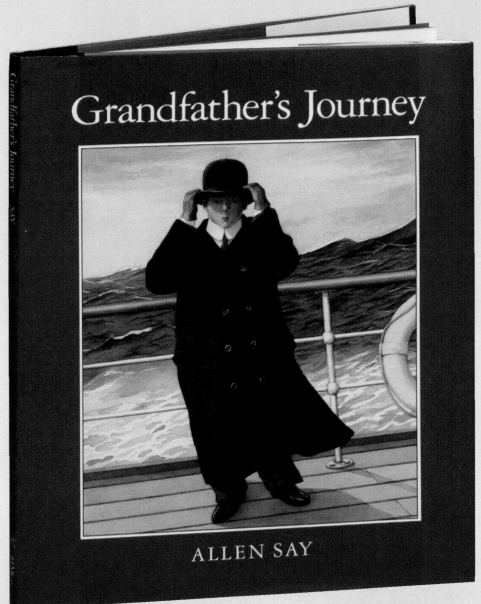

**Listening
Library
Audiocassette**

INSTRUCTIONAL
Pages 14–47

About the Author/Illustrator Allen Say writes and illustrates many of his own stories. The idea for *Grandfather's Journey* came to Say when he started thinking about Japan and the United States, the two countries where he had lived. "In a sense, I used my grandfather's experience to tell my own life story," he says. When Say was twelve, a Japanese cartoonist taught him how to draw. Years later, Say drew pictures for many children's books. He was awarded the Caldecott Medal for *Grandfather's Journey*.

Resources for Meeting Individual Needs

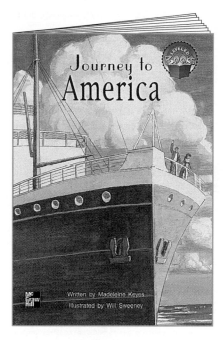

EASY
Pages 47A, 47D

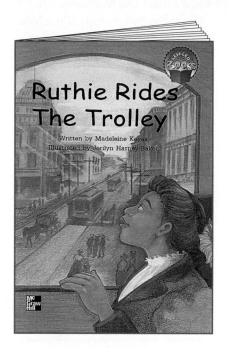

INDEPENDENT
Pages 47B, 47D

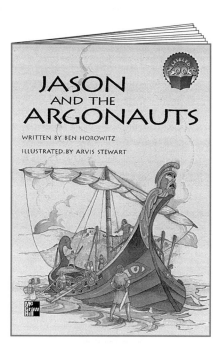

CHALLENGE
Pages 47C, 47D

🏠 *Take-Home version available*

LEVELED PRACTICE

Reteach, 1–7
blackline masters with reteaching opportunities for each assessed skill

Practice, 1–7
workbook with Take-Home stories and practice opportunities for each assessed skill and story comprehension

Extend, 1–7
blackline masters that offer challenge activities for each assessed skill

ADDITIONAL RESOURCES

- **Language Support Book,** pp. 1–8
- **Take-Home Story, Practice** p. 2a
- **Alternate Teaching Strategies,** pp. T60–T66
- **Selected Quizzes Prepared by** Accelerated Reader

McGraw-Hill School
TECHNOLOGY

Phonics CD-ROM provides extra phonics support.

interNET CONNECTION Research & Inquiry ideas. Visit **www.mhschool.com/reading.**

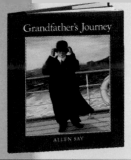

Suggested Lesson Planner

 Available on CD-ROM

READING AND LANGUAGE ARTS

	DAY 1 *Focus on Reading and Skills*	**DAY 2** *Read the Literature*
Comprehension	**Read Aloud and Motivate,** 12E "From the Bellybutton of the Moon"	**Build Background,** 14C Develop Oral Language
Vocabulary	**Develop Visual Literacy,** 12/13	**Vocabulary,** 14D
Phonics/Decoding	☑ **Introduce Story Elements,** 14A–14B **Teaching Chart 1** Reteach, Practice, Extend, 1	*astonished journey surrounded* *enormous scattered towering*
Study Skills		**Teaching Chart 2** **Word Building Manipulative Cards** Reteach, Practice, Extend, 2
Listening, Speaking, Viewing, Representing		**Read the Selection,** 14–43 Guided Instruction ☑ Story Elements
		Minilessons, 21, 25, 39, 41
		Cultural Perspectives, 34

Curriculum Connections	Fine Arts, 12/13	Social Studies, 14C

Writing	**Writing Prompt:** Think about a trip you took. Where did you go? What did you do? Write about it.	**Writing Prompt:** Describe your town or city in a short paragraph to be included in a guidebook. **Journal Writing,** 43 Quick-Write

Grammar	**Introduce the Concept: Statements and Questions,** 47M Daily Language Activity 1. She explored North America . 2. he missed California. He 3. I was born in Japan . **Grammar Practice Book,** 1	**Teach the Concept: Statements and Questions,** 47M Daily Language Activity 1. Did he miss his friends ? 2. are their tall buildings in the city? Are there 3. He went to Calforina . **Grammar Practice Book,** 2

Spelling	**Pretest: Words with Short Vowels,** 47O Spelling Practice Book, 1–2	**Explore the Pattern: Words with Short Vowels,** 47O Spelling Practice Book, 3

DAY 3 — Read the Literature

Reread for Fluency, 42

Story Questions, 44
Reteach, Practice, Extend, 3
Story Activities, 45

Study Skill, 46
☑ Parts of a Book
Teaching Chart 3
Reteach, Practice, Extend, 4

Test Power, 47

 Read the Leveled Books,
Guided Reading
Short Vowels
☑ Story Elements
☑ Instructional Vocabulary
 CD-ROM

 Activity Math, 18

Writing Prompt: Write a paragraph comparing different ways to travel.

Writing Process: Personal Narrative, 47K
Prewrite, Draft

Review and Practice: Statements and Questions, 47N
Daily Language Activity
1. they returned to the village. They
2. He remembered the songbirds
3. What did he see ?
Grammar Practice Book, 3

Practice and Extend: Words with Short Vowels, 47P
Spelling Practice Book, 4

DAY 4 — Build Skills

 Read the Leveled Books and Self-Selected Books

☑ **Review Story Elements,** 47E–47F
Teaching Chart 4
Reteach, Practice, Extend, 5
Language Support, 6

☑ **Introduce Make Predictions,** 47G–47H
Teaching Chart 5
Reteach, Practice, Extend, 6
Language Support, 7

 Activity Art, 26

Writing Prompt: Imagine your friend just took a trip. Write three questions you want to ask about the trip.

Writing Process: Personal Narrative, 47K
Revise

Meeting Individual Needs for Writing, 47L

Review and Practice: Statements and Questions, 47N
Daily Language Activity
1. he did not see land. He
2. What did he want ?
3. It was called the New World .
Grammar Practice Book, 4

Proofread and Write: Words with Short Vowels, 47P
Spelling Practice Book, 5

DAY 5 — Build Skills

 Read Self-Selected Books

☑ **Introduce Compound Words,** 47I-47J
Teaching Chart 6
Reteach, Practice, Extend, 7
Language Support, 8

Listening, Speaking, Viewing, Representing, 47L
Illustrate Letters
Read Aloud

Minilessons, 21, 25, 41

Phonics Review,
Short Vowels, 39
Phonics/Phonemic Awareness Practice Book, 7–12
 CD-ROM

Activity Science, 36

Writing Prompt: Choose a place you would like to visit. Write a letter convincing your teacher to plan a class trip to your chosen location.

Writing Process: Personal Narrative, 47K
Edit/Proofread, Publish

Assess and Reteach: Statements and Questions, 47N
Daily Language Activity
1. what did he explore? What
2. He returned to his home .
3. he is homesick for Japan. He
Grammar Practice Book, 5–6

Assess and Reteach: Words with Short Vowels, 47P
Spelling Practice Book, 6

Link
Social Studies

Read Aloud
and Motivate

**From the Bellybutton
of the Moon
Del ombligo de la luna**
by Francisco X. Alarcón

cuando
digo
"México"

whenever
I say
"Mexico"

siento
en la cara
el mismo viento

I feel
the same wind
on my face

que sentía
al abrir
la ventanilla

I felt when
I would open
the window

Continued on pages T2-T5

Oral Comprehension

LISTENING AND SPEAKING Motivate students to think about character and setting by reading aloud this bilingual poem about Mexico. Encourage them to picture the setting of the poem as you read it. When you have finished, ask them, "How would you describe the character of the person in the poem?" Then ask, "Which words in the poem describe the setting?" Reread the poem with the students and ask them to discuss what they like about the poem. How does it make them feel?

Activity Discuss with students places they would like to visit. Encourage them to think of and write down everything they know about the place that they choose. Then ask them to draw a picture or a map of their eventual destination, labeling the details.

▶ **Visual/Spatial**

Develop Visual Literacy

Link

Works of Art

Anthology pages 12–13

Stories in Art

Some paintings seem to tell a story. There are many details which add to the story. Each tells us something about what is happening.

Look at this setting. What can you tell about it? Did the people live a long time ago? How can you tell? Where do you think the people are going? How do they feel?

Close your eyes. Think about the painting. What do you remember? Why?

The Emigrants by Thomas Falcon

12   13

Objective: Analyze Character and Setting

VIEWING *The Emigrants,* a realistic painting, captures the feelings of people leaving their homeland to start new lives elsewhere. Have students describe what they see in the painting. Encourage them to notice how both the boats and the clothing provide clues to the time period that is portrayed. Then discuss with students what the people are doing. Why are many of the men and women looking back instead of ahead?

Read the page with students, encouraging individual interpretations of the painting. Ask students to support interpretations they make about the characters and

setting. For example:

- The clothing and the boats are old-fashioned. The painting depicts a time long ago.
- Some of the characters are waving or crying. They are probably feeling sad about leaving.

REPRESENTING Have students imagine why the people are leaving home. (For example, some of them might be leaving to find new jobs.) Invite students to prepare dramatizations of the boat scene. Through the characters' dialogue, students can reveal the nature of the journey.

12/13

^{TESTED}**OBJECTIVES**

Students will:

• make inferences about character.

• analyze setting.

TEACHING TIP

MANAGEMENT To make the Teaching Charts more interactive, use the acetate overlay provided. Have students underline or circle answers or clues on the overlay using a nonpermanent marker.

PREPARE

Discuss Characters You Know Have students think of a favorite book or TV character. Ask: What does that person really like to do? What does that tell you about him or her?

TEACH

Explain Inferences, Character, and Setting Tell students that you can make inferences—guesses based on clues in the text—about the characters in a story based on what they say, do, and think. The setting—where and when the story takes place—can affect how the characters think, feel, and act.

A First Trip to New York City

Kiku (excitedly) held her mother's hand as they took a taxi away from the bustling airport toward the city. It looked so much bigger than her little town in Japan. But when the driver let her out onto the crowded sidewalk Kiku (was nervous.) She (suddenly missed) her quiet, tree-lined roads from home. Horns blared and people were everywhere. Kiku wondered why she had come to this noisy city.

"Look," her mother said, pointing up. Kiku lifted her head. She (gasped.) "It's the Empire State Building!" Kiku smiled. Now she remembered why she had come.

Teaching Chart 1

Read the Story and Model the Skill Display **Teaching Chart 1**. Have students pay attention to clues about character and setting as the story is read.

> **MODEL** The title of the story tells me that the setting is New York City. In the first sentence, I see that Kiku is the main character. She seems to feel excited and scared about being in such a big city.

Find Clues in the Text Have students circle the clues that help them make inferences about Kiku, and underline clues about setting.

PRACTICE

Create a
Setting/Character
Chart

GROUP

Using a Setting/Character chart, have students record the ways the setting affects Kiku in the story. Help them begin filling in the chart and have volunteers complete it. ▶ **Visual/Linguistic**

SETTING	CHARACTER
bustling airport	Kiku is excited to be so close to New York City.
crowded sidewalks	Kiku is nervous because of the crowds.
near the Empire State Building	Kiku is amazed by the sight of the Empire State Building and is glad she came to New York City.

ASSESS/CLOSE

Make Inferences
About Character
and Analyze
Setting

Ask students how they would describe Kiku. (not used to noise and crowds; likes to explore, even if she is sometimes fearful) How would Kiku be likely to act if she were visiting a town as small as her own? Would a small-town setting show the same things about Kiku?

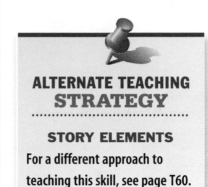

ALTERNATE TEACHING STRATEGY

STORY ELEMENTS
For a different approach to teaching this skill, see page T60.

Meeting Individual Needs for Comprehension

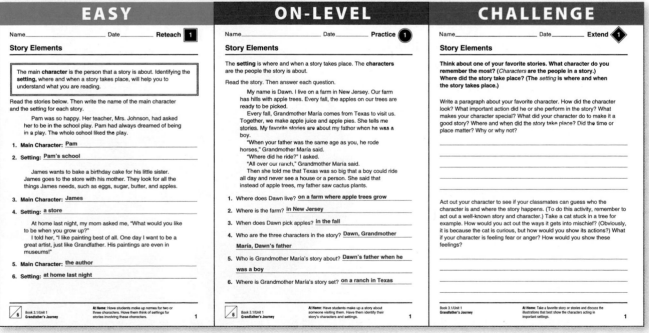

EASY — Reteach, 1

ON-LEVEL — Practice, 1

CHALLENGE — Extend, 1

Build Background

Social Studies

Anthology and Leveled Books

Evaluate Prior Knowledge

CONCEPT: JOURNEYS The characters in these stories are affected by the journeys they take. Have students share experiences of journeys they have taken.

COMPARE METHODS OF TRAVEL Have students brainstorm methods of travel from long ago and methods of travel today. Ask them to make a Venn diagram showing these methods of travel. ▶ **Spatial/Interpersonal**

METHODS OF TRAVEL

Then	Then and Now	Now
horse horse-pulled vehicle	boat/ship train walking	airplane car bus

Graphic Organizer 14

PLAN A TRIP Have students work in small groups to plan imaginary day trips. Ask them to make an itinerary for their trip. Students should include the time and place of departure, method of travel, arrival time, day's scheduled events (including free time and lunch), and return time.

GROUP   WRITING

Develop Oral Language

DISCUSS METHODS OF TRAVEL Ask

ESL students to brainstorm a list of ways they have traveled and ways they could travel. If possible, bring in photos of cars, trains, boats, buses, and airplanes.

Write words such as *car*, *train*, *plane*, *boat*, and *taxicab* on the chalkboard. Discuss the meaning of each word and have students use the word in a sentence.

Have students work in pairs. Invite one student to role-play being the driver or pilot of a car, taxicab, plane, train, or boat. The partner can role-play being a passenger in the vehicle. Encourage partners to talk to each other about the people and places they see.

Vocabulary

Key Words

An Amazing Trip

1. Grandfather made his first (journey) from Japan to America on a steamship. **2.** For three weeks he was (surrounded) by water; the Pacific Ocean was all he could see <u>on every side</u> of the ship. **3.** Grandfather <u>traveled many years</u> to explore this (enormous) country. **4.** There were times when <u>he could not believe his eyes</u>, the beauty of the country so (astonished) him. **5.** Of all the places he saw, Grandfather most loved California with its (towering) mountains that <u>seemed to scrape the sky</u>. **6.** Deserts, with hundreds of wild flowers (scattered) across them, amazed him.

> **Teaching Chart 2**

Vocabulary in Context

IDENTIFY VOCABULARY WORDS
Display **Teaching Chart 2** and read the passage with students. Have volunteers circle each vocabulary word and underline other words that are clues to its meaning.

DISCUSS MEANINGS
Ask questions like these to help clarify word meanings:

- When you make a journey, do you remain in one place or take a trip?

- If you are surrounded by water, what is all around you?

- How much time would you need to explore an enormous country—a lot or a little?

- If you were astonished by something, would you be expecting it or surprised by it?

- Are you towering over someone if you are shorter than he or she is?

- If you scattered seeds, did you plant them in neat rows or spread them in all directions?

Practice

PLAY 20 QUESTIONS Have partners take turns choosing vocabulary cards and asking "Yes/No" questions, such as, "Is it an adjective?" or "Does it begin with *e*?" Continue until all words have been correctly determined.
▶ **Linguistic/Oral**

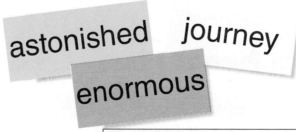

> **Word Building Manipulative Cards**

WRITE CONTEXT SENTENCES Have partners write context sentences, leaving a blank for each vocabulary word. Have them exchange papers to fill in the blanks. Students can refer to the Glossary as needed. ▶ **Linguistic/Interpersonal**

Definitions

journey (p. 17) a long trip

surrounded (p. 30) to have something on all sides of

enormous (p. 20) extremely large

astonished (p. 17) surprised very much; amazed

towering (p. 23) rising high up in the air

scattered (p. 38) thrown or spread in different directions

SPELLING/VOCABULARY CONNECTIONS
See Spelling Challenge Words, pages 470–47P.

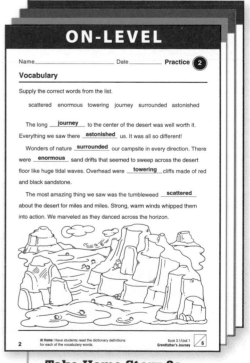

Take-Home Story 2a
Reteach 2
Practice 2 • Extend 2

Guided Instruction

Preview and Predict

Have students read the title and preview the story, looking for pictures that give clues about the setting and characters.

- What clues about the main character do the title and the pictures give?
- When might this story take place?
- What will the story most likely be about?
- This story is a biography. How can you tell? (The title and pictures make it seem as if it will be about a real person.) *Genre*

Have students record their predictions.

PREDICTIONS	WHAT HAPPENED
The story is about a grandfather who travels.	
The story takes place in a different time.	

Set Purposes

What do students want to find out by reading the story? For example:

- Why does the grandfather make the journey?
- How does his life change?

MEET ALLEN SAY

Allen Say has been an artist almost all of his life. At the age of thirteen, he already had a job drawing backgrounds for a famous cartoonist in Japan. When Say came to the United States, his interest in art kept growing. In time he began to write and illustrate his own stories.

Say begins creating a story by drawing the pictures first. Then he thinks of a story idea and the words to go with his drawings. Say tries to produce a book a year, which he admits is hard work. But he says, "I love what I'm doing so much that although it's difficult, it makes me happy."

Other books that you might enjoy by this writer and illustrator are *The Lost Lake*, *El Chino*, and *Tree of Cranes*.

14

Meeting Individual Needs • Grouping Suggestions for Strategic Reading

EASY	ON-LEVEL	CHALLENGE
Read Together Read the story with students or have them use the **Listening Library Audiocassette**. Have students use the Setting/Character chart to record information about setting and characters. Guided Instruction and Intervention prompts offer additional help with decoding, vocabulary, and comprehension.	**Guided Reading** Preview the story words on page 15. Then choose from the Guided Instruction questions as you read or review the story with students. They can play the **Listening Library Audiocassette** to hear a dramatic performance of the story.	**Read Independently** Have students read independently. Remind them that making inferences about character and setting will help them understand the story. Have students set up a Setting/Character chart as on page 15. After reading, have them use their charts to help summarize the story.

Grandfather's Journey

WRITTEN AND ILLUSTRATED BY
ALLEN SAY

15

LANGUAGE SUPPORT

This chart is available as a black-line master in the **Language Support Book.**

Name _____ Date _____

Setting	Character

LANGUAGE SUPPORT, 5

Guided Instruction

☑ **Story Elements**

Strategic Reading Paying attention to how the setting affects the character will help you understand the character and the story as a whole.

Before we begin reading, let's prepare Setting/Character charts so we can write down story notes.

SETTING	CHARACTER

1 SETTING What does the picture tell you about the time and place of this story? (The young man in the picture is wearing old-fashioned clothes, so the story takes place long ago. Since the young man is on a boat, the story is probably about more than one place.)

Story Words

The words below may be unfamiliar. Have students check their meanings and pronunciations in the Glossary on page 388:

• steamship, p. 17

• New World, p. 18

• marveled, p. 23

15

Guided Instruction

 CHARACTER What story character is introduced on this page? What can you say about what kind of person he might be? (adventurous) What makes you think that? (He leaves his home even though he is a young man, just so he can see the world.)

 Who is telling this story? (a grandchild) How do you know? (The title tells me that the story is about a grandfather, and only a grandchild would refer to someone as a grandfather.) *Make Inferences*

TEACHING **TIP**

INSTRUCTIONAL As students read, have them look for clues that this story took place some time ago. Tell them they will find these clues in the author's words and pictures.

My grandfather was a young man when he left his home in Japan and went to see the world.

16

He wore European clothes for the first time and began his journey on a steamship. The Pacific Ocean astonished him.

17

Guided Instruction

4 What can you tell about the grandfather's past experience with traveling? (He has not traveled much before.) **How do you know?** (He is wearing European clothes for the first time. The ocean probably astonishes him because he never knew it was so large.) *Make Inferences*

5 **SETTING** What can you tell about when this story takes place, since the grandfather is crossing the Pacific Ocean by steamship instead of some faster method of travel?

MODEL If he had the choice, the grandfather would probably travel by airplane so he could get across the ocean faster. Since he is not on an airplane, I think he doesn't have that choice, so the story must take place before airplanes were used for traveling.

LANGUAGE SUPPORT

ESL Point out the word *European* on page 17. Tell students this word comes from the word *Europe* and write both words on the board. Then point out Europe and some of its countries on a world map. Ask students to guess what the word *European* means. If necessary, explain that it describes something or some- one from Europe.

Next point to the picture on page 16. Ask: What kind of clothes is he wearing? (Japanese clothes, Asian clothes) Then point to the picture on page 17 and ask: What kind of clothes is he wearing? (European clothes)

Guided Instruction

6 What was travel like when the grandfather made his journey? How was it different from travel today? (It must have been difficult—it took him three weeks to get from Japan to the New World.) *Make Inferences*

TEACHING TIP

MANAGEMENT You may wish to wait and use the cross-curricular activities and minilessons during a second reading of the story.

6 For three weeks he did not see land. When land finally appeared it was the New World.

18

Activity

Cross Curricular: Math

MEASURE DISTANCES Have students think of a faraway place where they have visited. (Some students may have visited other countries while others may have only visited other states or cities.) Then, using a world map, have students use a piece of string to measure the distance from that place to where they live now. Each student can use the scale of miles to determine how far he or she journeyed to get there.

▶ **Spatial/Mathematical**

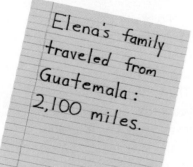

Elena's family traveled from Guatemala: 2,100 miles.

He explored North America by train and riverboat, and often walked for days on end.

19

Guided Instruction

7 Now that the main character has arrived in North America, what do you think will happen next? *(His journey will continue.)* Will we get to see what he saw on his journey? Explain your answer. *(Yes, because the title makes it sound like the whole book will be about his journey.) **Make Predictions***

8 What are some possible reasons the grandfather would walk for days on end? *(no trains or riverboats where he wanted to go; limited travel money) **Make Inferences***

COMPOUND WORDS Reread pages 17 and 19. What words do you see that look like they are made up of two smaller words? *(steamship and riverboat)* Do you know what these words mean?

PREVENTION/INTERVENTION

COMPOUND WORDS Remind students that a compound word is a word made up of two smaller words.

- Write the words *steamship* and *riverboat* on the chalkboard.

- Have volunteers circle the separate words in each compound word.

- Ask students the definition of each base word, and write their responses beneath each one.

- Have students put the base word meanings together to arrive at a definition for each compound word.

19

Guided Instruction

(9) CHARACTER, SETTING How does the setting affect the grandfather? Why do you think he is affected this way? Do you think the setting in his home of Japan is similar to the setting in North America? Explain.

MODEL I see how small he is compared to the huge rocks of the desert. I understand why he is amazed by them. I don't think the place where the grandfather is from is the same as this. He probably wouldn't be so amazed by this place if he had seen similar sights at home.

TEACHING TIP

INSTRUCTIONAL You might want to refer to a map of the United States as you read. Students can look at it to try to guess where the grandfather might be at different points during his travels around the country. For example, on page 20, you might ask students to find deserts that the grandfather might be visiting.

9 Deserts with rocks like ⎟enormous⎟ sculptures amazed him.

10

20

The endless farm fields reminded him of the ocean he had crossed.

21

Guided Instruction

10 **CHARACTER, SETTING** Let's write down what we know about the settings in the story so far and how they have affected the main character, the grandfather.

SETTING	CHARACTER
Pacific Ocean	He is astonished by the ocean.
desert	He is amazed by the rock sculptures.

11 **How are the farm fields and the ocean the same?** (They are both endless.) **How are they different?** (The ocean is deep and wet. The farm fields are not even as tall as the grandfather and they are dry.) *Compare and Contrast*

Minilesson
REVIEW/MAINTAIN
Suffixes

Review that understanding suffixes can help students determine the meaning of unfamiliar words.

- Have students point out the suffix in the word *endless* on page 21. (*-less*)
- Tell students that *-less* is a suffix meaning "having no; without."
- Based on this definition, ask students what *endless* means. (having no end; without end)

Activity Have students add *-less* to the following words and then define them: *use, price, hope.*

Guided Instruction

 **CHARACTER, SETTING** What can you tell about the grandfather's character based on his reaction to the places he has visited so far? (He is an explorer; he is excited and moved by it all.)

Huge cities of factories and tall buildings bewildered and yet excited him.

22

He marveled at the towering mountains and rivers as clear as the sky.

23

13 Did everyone correctly predict that we would see more of the grandfather's journey? Do you think there will be even more to see? *Make Predictions*

 FIGURATIVE LANGUAGE/SIMILE
Read the sentence on page 23. What does the author say are *as clear as the sky?* (the rivers)

PREVENTION/INTERVENTION

FIGURATIVE LANGUAGE/SIMILE
Explain to students that a simile compares two things that are different. Similes use the word *like* or *as.*

- Ask students to point out the simile on this page. (*rivers as clear as the sky*)

- Have them brainstorm descriptive words for rivers, based on this comparison. Write their ideas on the chalkboard.

- Ask students how this simile helps them in their reading. (It paints a picture of the rivers with words.)

Guided Instruction

(14) **SETTING** What does this illustration tell you about what life must have been like at this time in history?

MODEL First, I notice that the men are wearing old-fashioned clothes. The clothes look more formal than most of the clothes we wear today. I also notice that the street in front of the shops is unpaved; it looks like dirt. Traveling over dirt roads was probably pretty rough.

(15) What can you tell about the population of North America at the time that the grandfather was traveling and shaking people's hands? (It was a land made up of many different kinds of people.) *Draw Conclusions*

He met many people along the way. He shook hands with black men and white men, with yellow men and red men.

24

The more he traveled, the more he longed to see new places, and never thought of returning home.

25

Guided Instruction

16 **CHARACTER, SETTING** Do you think the grandfather has been changed by his journey? How has he changed? (His journey has made him want to keep traveling.)

17 **CHARACTER** How likely do you think it is that the grandfather will return to Japan? (It is likely. Usually when people go on a journey they eventually return to where they started from.) *Make Predictions*

Minilesson
REVIEW/MAINTAIN
Summarize

Remind students that summarizing is telling the main events of a story. It is a way to help keep the story's action clear.

Activity Ask students to write three sentences to summarize the story so far. Then have them make a tri-fold summary:

• Fold a piece of paper into thirds.

• Write one of the sentences at the bottom of each section.

• Draw a simple picture in each section.

• Share the summaries with the class.

Guided Instruction

18 **CHARACTER, SETTING** Where do you think the grandfather would most like to live out of all the places he has visited on his journey? (California) Why would he want to live there? (He loves the sunlight, mountains, and coast.)

Let's add to our charts.

SETTING	CHARACTER
Pacific Ocean	He is astonished by the ocean.
desert	He is amazed by the rock sculptures.
California	He loves the sunlight, mountains, and coast.

19 How can a seacoast be *lonely*? What do you think the author means by this? Does the illustration help you figure it out? (There are no people in the illustration, so maybe a lonely seacoast is one without people.) *Make Inferences*

18 Of all the places he visited, he liked California best. He loved the strong sunlight there, the Sierra **19** Mountains, the lonely seacoast.

26

Activity

Cross Curricular: Art

COLLAGE The grandfather has been to many different sorts of places, but he likes California best. Ask students:

- What place do you like best?
- What about the place makes it special?

Activity Have students cut out pictures and images from magazines to paste on construction paper to make collages of their favorite places.
▶ **Spatial/Interpersonal**

After a time, he returned to his village in Japan to marry his childhood sweetheart. Then he brought his bride to the new country.

27

Guided Instruction

20 **CHARACTER** Based on what you have learned about the grandfather's character so far, why do you think he is bringing his bride to the new country? (He loves it there and wants to share it with her.)

P/i **PHONICS/DECODING** Read the second sentence on page 27. Say the third word in this sentence out loud. (*brought*) Do you hear all the letters in this word? (No, the *gh* in this word is silent.)

P/i PREVENTION/INTERVENTION

PHONICS/DECODING Remind students that often a word will contain silent letters. Write the word *brought* on the chalkboard.

- Ask students which letters they don't hear in *brought*. (*gh*)
- Write the following words on the chalkboard: *thought, eight, sight*.
- Have students name the silent letters in each one. (*gh*)

- Ask students to name other silent letters they know. (Possible answers: *k* as in *know*, *w* as in *write*, *b* as in *comb*)
- Write these words on the board: *know, walk, write, comb*. Have volunteers circle the silent letter in each word. (*k* in *know*, *l* in *walk*, *w* in *write*, *b* in *comb*)

Guided Instruction

21 Do you know who the baby girl is in relation to the grandchild narrator? (She is probably the narrator's mother.) **How do you know?** (I know she is the daughter of the narrator's grandfather, so, unless he and his wife have more children, she must be the narrator's mother.) *Draw Conclusions*

21 They made their home by the San Francisco Bay and had a baby girl.

28

Activity

Cross Curricular: Social Studies

IMMIGRATION Tell students that many people came to live in the United States in the early part of the twentieth century.

RESEARCH AND INQUIRY Have students pick a country and research how many people immigrated from that country to the United States in any year between 1900 and 1910. They should post their findings on a bulletin board.

▶ **Intrapersonal/Interpersonal**

inter NET CONNECTION Go to **www.mhschool.com** **/reading** for more information about immigration.

In 1907, 258,943 people immigrated to the United States from Russia.

As his daughter grew, my grandfather began to think about his own childhood. He thought about his old friends.

29

22 **CHARACTER** How do you think the grandfather is feeling? (homesick for Japan) **What makes you think that?** (He is thinking of his childhood, which he spent in Japan, and his old friends from Japan.)

23 What is the event that has caused the grandfather to feel homesick? (Watching his own daughter grow up reminded him of growing up himself, and he started to miss his childhood home.) *Make Inferences*

Guided Instruction

24 **CHARACTER, SETTING** How does the memory of the mountains and rivers of his home affect the grandfather? (It makes him homesick and sad.) Let's add to our charts.

SETTING	CHARACTER
Pacific Ocean	He is astonished by the ocean.
desert	He is amazed by the rock sculptures.
California	He loves the sunlight, mountains, and coast.
memory of mountains and rivers in Japan	He is homesick and sad.

25 What do you think the grandfather will do now that he has started to change his thoughts about Japan? *Make Predictions*

SELF-MONITORING

STRATEGY

REREAD Rereading a part of the story can help a reader to understand why the characters behave as they do.

MODEL I'm not sure why the grandfather has surrounded himself with songbirds. Maybe if I reread a bit I can find out. His daughter growing up has reminded him of his own childhood in Japan, so now he is homesick. It is because he is homesick that he has surrounded himself with songbirds to remind him of home.

24 He remembered the mountains and rivers of his home. He surrounded himself with songbirds, but he could not forget.

25

30

Guided Instruction

Finally, when his daughter was nearly grown, he could wait no more. He took his family and returned to his homeland.

31

26 Which happens first: The grandfather takes his family to Japan or his daughter is grown? (His daughter grows up.) What is the word on this page that tells you that returning to Japan happens last? *(finally)* *Sequence of Events*

LANGUAGE SUPPORT

ESL To help students understand how the grandfather is feeling, have them look at the illustration on page 30. Ask some either/or questions using familiar words. For example: Is he feeling happy or sad? Is he remembering or forgetting? Is he thinking about the United States or Japan? Is he homesick or content? After students have answered these questions, ask one student to sum up how the grandfather is feeling.

Guided Instruction

27 How many of us correctly predicted that the grandfather would move back to Japan? *Confirm Predictions*

27 Once again he saw the mountains and rivers of his childhood. They were just as he had remembered them.

32

Once again he exchanged stories and laughed with his old friends.

33

Guided Instruction

28 **CHARACTER, SETTING** What is the setting now? (the mountains and rivers of Japan; lots of friends around) **How is it affecting the grandfather?** (He is happy and laughing.) **Let's add to our charts.**

SETTING	CHARACTER
Pacific Ocean	He is astonished by the ocean.
desert	He is amazed by the rock sculptures.
California	He loves the sunlight, mountains, and coast.
memory of mountains and rivers in Japan	He is homesick and sad.
mountains and rivers in Japan; friends	He is happy and laughing.

LANGUAGE SUPPORT

ESL Help students understand the meaning of the word *exchanged* on page 33. Ask a student to give you his or her pencil and then immediately give that student your pencil. As you do this, say: We are exchanging pencils. When you have finished, say: We exchanged pencils.

Then explain that *exchange* means giving and taking. Tell students that we usually exchange physical objects like presents, but in the story the grandfather and his friends exchanged stories. Point out the sentence on page 33 and read it aloud to the students.

33

Guided Instruction

29 Why do you think the village was not right for a daughter from San Francisco? (Villages are pretty small. Life there was probably too simple compared to the city life she was used to.) *Make Inferences*

30 The grandfather knew the village was not the right place for his daughter to live, yet he wanted to be near where he grew up. How did he solve this problem? (He bought a house in a large city nearby.) *Problem and Solution*

But the village was not a place for a daughter from San Francisco. So my grandfather bought a house in a large city nearby.

29

30

34

CULTURAL PERSPECTIVES

DRESS In the illustration on page 34, the daughter wears western clothes. In her wedding photo on page 35, she wears a traditional garment called a kimono.

RESEARCH AND INQUIRY Have students select a culture whose dress they would like to research.

Have them display an illustration of that culture's traditional dress and present their findings orally.

▶ **Spatial/Interpersonal**

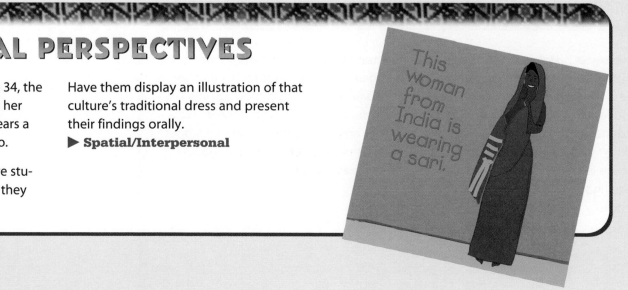

This woman from India is wearing a sari.

There, the young woman fell in love, married, and sometime later I was born.

35

Guided Instruction

31 Who is the new character introduced on this page? (the author) How do you know? (The story is a biography, or a real story about a real person, so the *I* who is telling the story must be the author.)

WORD STRUCTURE Look at the word *married* on this page. What is the present-tense form of this word? *(marry)*

PREVENTION/INTERVENTION

WORD STRUCTURE Write the words *married* and *marry* on the chalkboard. Use the words to review past tense and present tense. Have a volunteer come to the board and change *marry* to *married.* Then ask the class what needed to be done. (Change the *y* to *i* and add *ed.*)

Brainstorm with students other words that form the past tense by dropping a *y* and adding *ied.*

Guided Instruction

32 **CHARACTER** Do you think his experiences in California are still affecting the grandfather now that he is in Japan? Explain.

MODEL He doesn't seem sad right now, but I think he is still affected by his experiences in California, because he likes to tell his grandson stories about them.

32 When I was a small boy, my favorite weekend was a visit to my grandfather's house. He told me many stories about California.

36

Activity

Cross Curricular: Science

BIRDS Discuss how the grandfather raised songbirds in Japan as well as in the United States.

RESEARCH AND INQUIRY Ask pairs of students to choose a bird. Have them research their bird's habitats and needs. Ask students to make a poster showing what they learned.

▶ **Spatial/Interpersonal**

Toucans

He raised warblers and silvereyes, but he could not forget the mountains and rivers of California. So he planned a trip.

Guided Instruction

33 How is this page different from page 30? (The grandfather is wearing traditional Japanese clothing instead of western clothes; he is thinking about California instead of Japan; the windows are covered with bamboo shades instead of uncovered.) *Compare and Contrast*

34 What inference can you make about warblers and silvereyes? Where do you think they come from? What makes you think this? (They are probably birds from California. Since he raised songbirds to remind him of Japan when he was living in California, it makes sense that he would raise birds that might be from the United States to remind him of California while he is living in Japan.) *Make Inferences*

35 **CHARACTER, SETTING** How does the grandfather feel about Japan? (He loves Japan.) How does he feel about California? (He loves California.) How do you know? (When he is in one place he longs for the other.)

Guided Instruction

36 **CHARACTER, SETTING** How has the setting of the story changed? (It has gone from peaceful to violent.) How might this affect the grandfather and his family? (They may have to leave the city.) *Make Predictions*

37 What happens to leaves during a storm? (They get torn from branches and blown in many different directions.) So, what does *scattered our lives like leaves in a storm* mean? (It probably means that they all had to move from one place to another or that they could no longer live near each other.) Why do you think the author wrote it this way? (The image of leaves being scattered in a storm helps us to understand how the war affected their lives.) *Figurative Language*

TEACHING TIP

INSTRUCTIONAL You might want to ask students if they have any idea what war this was. (World War II) You can then discuss that the United States and Japan were at war with each other, which would have made travel between the two countries difficult, if not impossible.

36 But a war began. Bombs fell from the sky and scattered our lives like leaves in a storm.

37

38

When the war ended, there was nothing left of the city and of the house where my grandparents had lived.

 38

 39

39

Guided Instruction

38 What is one effect war had on the grandfather and the other people who lived in his city? (It destroyed their homes.) *Cause and Effect*

39 Who do you think the children in the illustration on page 39 are? (They are children whose homes have been destroyed during the war.) Why do you think the author shows them to us? (To show us the effect of the war on people's lives.) *Make Inferences*

PHONICS KIT
HANDS-ON ACTIVITIES AND PRACTICE

Minilesson
REVIEW/MAINTAIN
Short Vowels

Have students pronounce the words *began, fell, city,* and *bombs* from pages 38 and 39.

- Ask students to identify the short vowel in each word. (*a,* in *began; e,* in *fell; i,* in *city; o,* in *bombs*)

Activity Have students brainstorm other words with short vowels. Create a word wall of words with short vowel sounds.

Phonics CD-ROM Have students use the interactive phonics activities on the CD-ROM for more reinforcement.

Guided Instruction

40 **CHARACTER, SETTING** What is the setting now? (the grandparents' village) Is this enough to make the grandfather feel happy again after the war? (no) How do you know? (He isn't keeping birds to remind him of the places he loves.) Let's add to our charts.

SETTING	CHARACTER
Pacific Ocean	He is astonished by the ocean.
desert	He is amazed by the rock sculptures.
California	He loves the sunlight, mountains, and coast.
memory of mountains and rivers in Japan	He is homesick and sad.
mountains and rivers in Japan; lots of friends	He is happy and laughing.
village in Japan, after the war	He refuses to keep songbirds; he is sad.

40 So they returned to the village where they had been children. But my grandfather never kept another songbird.

40

The last time I saw him, my grandfather said that he longed to see California one more time. He never did.

41

41

Guided Instruction

41 Do you think the grandson will ever visit California? Why or why not?
Make Predictions

42 What was the grandfather's final wish? (He wanted to go back to California.)
What stopped him? (the war; his age; his death)
Cause and Effect

Minilesson

REVIEW/MAINTAIN

Make Inferences

Remind students that good readers pay attention to a character's words and actions to understand that character's feelings and emotions.

• Ask students to find places in the story that tell how the grandfather felt about California.

• Ask them how they think he felt about not getting to see it one more time.

Activity Have students write a sentence telling what effect they think the grandfather's feelings about California have on his grandson.

41

Guided Instruction

43 CHARACTER, SETTING How did the setting affect the grandfather throughout this story? Let's review.

SETTING	CHARACTER
Pacific Ocean	He is astonished by the ocean.
desert	He is amazed by the rock sculptures.
California	He loves the sunlight, mountains, and coast.
memory of mountains and rivers in Japan	He is homesick and sad.
mountains and rivers in Japan; lots of friends	He is happy and laughing.
village in Japan, after the war	He refuses to keep songbirds; he is sad.

RETELL THE STORY Ask volunteers to tell the major events of this story. Students may refer to their charts. Then have partners write two sentences that summarize the story.
Summarize

STUDENT SELF-ASSESSMENT

- How did using the strategy of analyzing character and setting help me to understand the story?
- How did the Setting/Character chart help?

TRANSFERRING THE STRATEGY

- When might I try using this strategy again?
- In what other reading could the chart help?

And when I was nearly grown, I left home and went to see California for myself.

42

REREADING FOR *Fluency*

PARTNERS Have students choose a favorite section from the story to read to a partner. Encourage students to read with feeling and expression.

READING RATE You may want to evaluate a student's reading rate. Have the student read aloud from *Grandfather's Journey* for one minute. Ask the student to place a self-stick note after the last word read. Then count the number of words he or she has read.

Alternatively, you could assess small groups or the whole class together by having students count words and record their own scores.

A Running Record form provided in **Diagnostic/Placement Evaluation** will help you evaluate reading rate(s).

After a time, I came to love the land my grandfather had loved, and I stayed on and on until I had a daughter of my own.

But I also miss the mountains and rivers of my childhood. I miss my old friends. So I return now and then, when I can not still the longing in my heart.

The funny thing is, the moment I am in one country, I am homesick for the other.

I think I know my grandfather now.
I miss him very much.

43

Guided Instruction

Return to Predictions and Purposes

Review with students their story predictions and reasons for reading the story. Were their predictions correct? Did they find out what they wanted to know?

PREDICTIONS	WHAT HAPPENED
The story is about a grandfather who travels.	As a young man, the grandfather travels from Japan to North America to see the world. He ends up staying there for a while but eventually returns to Japan. He is always torn between the two places.
The story takes place in a different time.	The story begins long ago, before air travel. Time moves on, in the story, until well after World War II.

INFORMAL ASSESSMENT

ANALYZE CHARACTER, SETTING

HOW TO ASSESS

- Ask how the settings affect the grandfather.
- Ask students to draw conclusions about him from his actions.

Students should recognize the effect of settings on the grandfather's feelings.

FOLLOW UP

If students have trouble analyzing character, help them brainstorm words to describe the grandfather. Ask for supporting details.

If students have trouble seeing the importance of setting, ask them why the grandfather misses one place when he is in the other.

LITERARY RESPONSE

QUICK-WRITE Invite students to record their thoughts about the story. These questions may help get them started:

- How would you describe the grandfather?
- How is the grandson like his grandfather?

- Can you understand the idea of wanting to live in two places at once?

ORAL RESPONSE Have students share their journal writings and discuss in what ways, if any, the story reminds them of their own lives.

Story Questions

Have students discuss or write answers to the questions on page 44.

Answers:

1. deserts, farm fields, and huge cities
Literal/Setting

2. At first, he was very excited and interested in seeing as much as possible.
Inferential/Character, Setting

3. He missed the mountains and rivers of Japan. *Inferential/Make Inferences*

4. The main idea is that you may be torn between two places. *Critical/Main Idea*

5. Possible answer: They love their homeland, but they will love their new home as well.
Critical/Reading Across Texts

Write a Letter For a full writing-process lesson related to this writing suggestion, see pages 47K–47L.

Story Questions & Activities

1 What were three things that the grandfather saw when he came to North America?

2 At first, how did the grandfather feel about his travels?

3 What do you think he missed most when he was living in the United States?

4 What is the main idea of this selection?

5 If the grandfather could talk to the people in the picture on pages 12–13, what might he tell them?

Write a Letter

Think about a trip you have taken. Write a letter to your best friend telling about the place you visited and how you got there. Include lots of details about the place.

Meeting Individual Needs

EASY

Name_____ Date_____ Reteach **2**

Vocabulary

Read each clue. Then find the vocabulary word in the row of letters and circle it.

astonished enormous journey scattered surrounded towering

1. surprised   p a s t o n i s h e d m z
2. spread out   s c a t t e r e d y w o s
3. trip   b s y j o u r n e y y j i
4. large   v i c p s e n o r m o u s
5. tall   i t o w e r i n g o a t s
6. circled   b e s u r r o u n d e d z

Story Comprehension   Reteach **3**

Write a ✔ next to every sentence that tells about "Grandfather's Journey."

✔ 1. Grandfather leaves Japan to see the world.

___ 2. Grandfather wants to live near farms and factories in North America.

✔ 3. Grandfather brings his wife and daughter to live in Japan.

✔ 4. The grandson learns about California from Grandfather.

✔ 5. A war prevents Grandfather from visiting California again.

✔ 6. California and Japan both feel like home to the grandson.

At Home: Have students make up two more sentences that describe "Grandfather's Journey."

2–3   Book 3.1/Unit 1
                       Grandfather's Journey 6

Reteach, 3

ON-LEVEL

Name_____ Date_____ Practice **3**

Story Comprehension

Read each statement. Write **T** if the statement describes "Grandfather's Journey." Write **F** if the statement does not correctly describe "Grandfather's Journey."

1. __F__ The grandfather first left Japan when he was an old man.

2. __T__ Grandfather traveled to North America on his journey.

3. __T__ Grandfather saw the desert on his trip to the New World.

4. __F__ The grandfather explored North America by covered wagon.

5. __T__ For part of his journey, Grandfather traveled by steamship.

6. __F__ The grandfather liked Florida best.

7. __T__ Grandfather returned to Japan to get married and because he was homesick.

8. __T__ The grandson went to California because his grandfather had told him stories about the place.

9. __T__ The grandfather, his new wife, and baby daughter lived in San Francisco.

10. __F__ The grandson now lives in China.

At Home: Have students imagine a faraway place that they would like to visit. Have them write down reasons why they would like to go and things they would expect to find there.

3   Book 3.1/Unit 1
                      Grandfather's Journey 10

Practice, 3

CHALLENGE

Name_____ Date_____ Extend **2**

Vocabulary

| astonished | enormous | journey |
| scattered | surrounded | towering |

Imagine you're far from home in a place of your choice. Write a letter home using some of the words in the box. Remember to include details about the places you are seeing.

Extend **3**

Story Comprehension

Grandfather's Journey

[illustration box]   Work with a partner. Choose a setting from "Grandfather's Journey." Draw one detail about the setting. Then choose a title for your illustration.

At Home: Draw a timeline together tracing some of the main events in Grandfather's life.

2–3   Book 3.1/Unit 1
                      Grandfather's Journey

Extend, 3

Draw a Picture

Think about the times you have spent with a grandparent or an older adult. Choose one special time that you shared together. Draw a picture that shows your experience.

Save a Memory

Choose a special moment from your life and think of a way to help you remember it. Create a "remembering" device, such as a box of objects, a photo collection, a poem, or a story. Display your "remembering" device in the classroom.

Find Out More

If you could move to a faraway place, where would it be? Find that place on a map and trace a route there. Then find out three things you did not know about this place. Use an encyclopedia or a travel guide.

45

Story Activities

Draw a Picture

Materials: paper, felt-tipped markers

ONE Ask students to picture some special times in their mind and then to choose one to draw. When they have finished illustrating, have them write a caption for their drawings.

Save a Memory

ONE Have students think of special moments in their lives. If necessary, help them think of an appropriate "remembering" device. Then have them share their memories and their "remembering" devices with the class.

Find Out More

RESEARCH AND INQUIRY Display a world map for partners to use in their **PARTNERS** searches, and provide easy access to sources of information about other countries. Have them report their findings to the class.

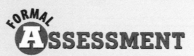 *inter***NET** **CONNECTION** Go to *www.mhschool.com/reading* for more information or activities on the topic.

FORMAL ASSESSMENT

After page 45, see Selection Assessment.

Study Skills

PARTS OF A BOOK

OBJECTIVES

Students will:

- identify the title, author, and illustrator of a book.
- use a table of contents.

PREPARE Look at the cover and table of contents with the students. Display **Teaching Chart 3**.

TEACH Discuss the information on a book's cover and how to use a table of contents.

PRACTICE Have students answer questions 1–5. Review the answers with them.
1. Living in Japan **2.** Author: Carol Johnson; illustrator: Harvey Kramer **3.** eight **4.** on pages 21–24 **5.** Yes, because the book tells about New Year's Day and other celebrations.

ASSESS/CLOSE Have students use a book's table of contents and answer the first three questions on page 46.

Study Skills

Use Book Parts

Has life in Japan changed much since the grandfather's time? You can find out by looking at a book about Japan. The **cover** and **table of contents** of one book about Japan are shown below.

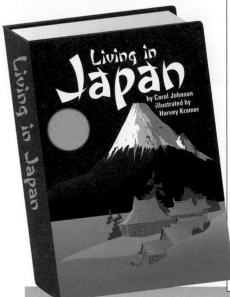

∼ LIVING IN JAPAN ∼

Use the cover and table of contents to answer these questions.

1 What is the title of the book?

2 Who are the author and the illustrator?

3 How many chapters does the book have?

4 On what pages could you find information about family traditions?

5 If you wanted to learn about holidays in Japan, would this be a good book to check? Why or why not?

Meeting Individual Needs

EASY	ON-LEVEL	CHALLENGE

EASY

Name_____ Date_____ Reteach **4**

Use Book Parts

A **table of contents** is a guide to what is inside a book. Most books are broken down into chapters. The table of contents also shows you the page numbers of the chapters.

In a book about a trip, the table of contents could show you where the author has traveled.

Through the West by Train

by Tom Harris

Illustrated by Lynn Jacobson

Table of Contents

Leaving St. Louis 3
Nebraska's Flatlands 10
Here Come the Mountains 18
Denver: Frontier Town 25
Yosemite National Park 33
Death Valley and the Desert 56
Sequoias—Tallest Trees on Earth 77
The Waves of the Pacific 101

Use the cover and table of contents to answer these questions.

1. Who wrote *Through the West by Train?* **Tom Harris**
2. What is the book about? **a train trip**
3. In what city does the journey start? **St. Louis**
4. On page 25, what city would you learn about? **Denver**
5. Which does the book describe first, a desert or the mountains? **mountains**

Book 3.1/Unit 1
Grandfather's Journey

At Home: Have students choose a book and write two questions that can be answered by reading the table of contents. **4**

ON-LEVEL

Name_____ Date_____ Practice **4**

Use Book Parts

The **author** and the **title** of a book appear on both the front cover and the side of the book, or **spine**.

Old Friends	Joe Parker		Cooking with Woks	Li Woo
Victorian Porches	Selma Davidson		*Kindergarten Art*	Harry Waters
Painting Easter Eggs	Paula Brunst		JUMP ROPE	Rhonda Newcomb
COMPUTER REPAIR	Kathy Verang		Bonsai Trees	Larry Larsen
Wigs and Hats	Rhonda Newcomb		Scary Stories	Paula Arnot

Use the stacks of books to answer these questions.

1. Who wrote a book about art in kindergarten? **Harry Waters**
2. What is the title of the book written by Joe Parker? **Old Friends**
3. If your computer was broken, which book would you need? **Computer Repair**
4. Who wrote more than one book in these piles? **Rhonda Newcomb**
5. What is the title of the book about cooking? **Cooking with Woks**
6. Who wrote Scary Stories? **Paula Arnot**
7. What is the name of the book that Larry Larsen wrote? **Bonsai Trees**
8. Which book did Paula Brunst write? **Painting Easter Eggs**

Book 3.1/Unit 1
Grandfather's Journey

At Home: Ask students which book they would look in to find information about miniature trees. **4**

CHALLENGE

Name_____ Date_____ Extend **4**

Use Book Parts

Suppose you wanted to write a book about holidays in the United States. There are several ways you could organize your book into chapters. One way would be to have a chapter for each holiday. Think of other ways your book could be organized, and write them below.

Answers will vary. Some possibilities are by season, by month, by national holidays and state holidays.

Now use your method of organization to make a sample table of contents for your book. Use another sheet of paper if you need more room.

Holidays in the United States
Table of Contents

_____
_____
_____
_____
_____
_____
_____
_____
_____
_____
_____
_____

Book 3.1/Unit 1
Grandfather's Journey

At Home: Read through the table of contents of a book. Then quiz each other on the information that can be found in the book, and how that information is organized. **4**

Reteach, 4   Practice, 4   Extend, 4

TEST POWER

THE PRINCETON REVIEW

Test Tip

Read the story slowly and carefully.

DIRECTIONS:

Read the story. Then read each question about the story.

SAMPLE

The Discovery

Tony and Jennie played in a field by Jennie's house one day. They were digging in the dirt to build a fort. Jennie's fingers hit a flat, sharp rock.

"What is this?" Jennie asked. She picked up a rock shaped like a triangle.

"Wow! That's an arrow-head!" Tony said. He looked at the rock. "I read that Native Americans made arrows from straight sticks," he said. "They used stone for the tips of the arrows and tied them to the end of the sticks."

Jennie put the arrowhead into her pocket. "Let's give this arrowhead to the museum. Then everyone can learn more about arrowheads," she said.

1 When Jennie picked up the arrowhead, Tony was—

   ○ angry

   ○ sad

   ● surprised

   ○ tired

2 Where was Jennie digging?

   ○ At the museum

   ○ In the yard outside the school

   ● In a field near Jennie's house

   ○ In Tony's backyard

47

Test Power

Read the Page

Have students read the story, questions, and answer choices to themselves. Instruct students to choose the best answer choice and be able to discuss why it is the best choice.

Discuss the Questions

QUESTION 1: This question requires students to understand Tony's feelings. Discuss what information in the story is a clue to how Tony feels. One clue: Tony said "Wow!" after he saw the arrowhead. Ask students: Does Tony appear happy or sad? Work through the choices.

QUESTION 2: This question asks students to recall the setting of the story. Teach students to work through the answer choices using process of elimination.

ITBS/TEST PREPARATION

TERRANOVA/TEST PREPARATION

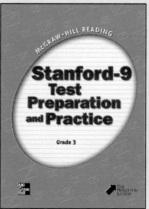

SAT 9/TEST PREPARATION

EASY

Answers to Story Questions

1. They went on a steamship.
2. Marco and Lena were concerned about their friends and went to help them.
3. They are kind people who help their friends.
4. The story is about an Italian couple who journeys across the ocean to America.
5. Answers will vary.

Story Questions and Writing Activity

1. How did Marco and Lena get to America?
2. What did Marco and Lena do after the storm was over?
3. How would you describe Marco and Lena?
4. What is this story mostly about?
5. If Marco and Lena met the grandfather from *Grandfather's Journey* what might they talk about?

Save Your Money!

A boat trip to America in the 1880s cost about $35 for each adult and $17.50 for each child. It cost $25 per person to enter the country. People also had to save money for food and a place to stay. Write a list of what you would need to make this trip with your family and add up how much it would cost.

from *Journey to America*

Leveled Books

EASY

Journey to America

Short Vowels

☑ **Story Elements**

☑ **Instructional Vocabulary:**
astonished, enormous, journey, scattered, surrounded, towering

Guided Reading

PREVIEW AND PREDICT Conduct a **picture walk** through page 10, having students pay attention to character and setting. Then have them predict what the story may be about.

SET PURPOSES Have students write what they want to find out as they read the story.

READ THE BOOK Use the following prompts while students are reading, or after they have read the story independently.

Pages 2–3: How are Marco and Lena feeling about boarding the ship? (excited) *Character*

Page 5: How does the setting of the hold affect the passengers that stay there? (Because the hold is crowded, smelly, and at the bottom of the ship, people get sick.) *Setting*

Page 7: Why does Lena start to cry? (She misses her family.) How does Marco make her feel better? (He tells her they'll make new friends.) *Character*

Page 8: Read the first paragraph. Find the

word *surrounded* in the third sentence. What nearby phrases help you understand the meaning of *surrounded?* (far out at sea, no land in sight) *Vocabulary*

Page 15: Why do you think Marco and Lena hugged when they saw the Statue of Liberty? (They knew their new life was about to begin.) *Character*

Page 16: Read the first sentence. Which word has the /i/ sound? (ship) Make a list of other short *i* words you find. (begin, his, think, it) *Phonics and Decoding*

RETURN TO PREDICTIONS AND PURPOSES Review students' predictions and reasons for reading.

LITERARY RESPONSE Discuss these questions:

- Why do you think Marco and Lena were traveling to America?
- What might life in America be like for Marco and Lena?

Also see the story questions and activity in *Journey to America.*

See the  **CD-ROM** for practice using words with short vowels.

Leveled Books

INDEPENDENT

Ruthie Rides the Trolley

☑ **Story Elements**

☑ **Instructional Vocabulary:**
astonished, enormous, journey, scattered, surrounded, towering

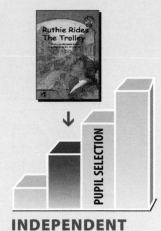

INDEPENDENT

Guided Reading

PREVIEW AND PREDICT Conduct a **picture walk**, discussing each illustration up to page 8. Have students predict whether the setting will be important.

SET PURPOSES Have students write down questions they would like to have answered as they read. For example, they may want to know how a trolley works.

READ THE BOOK Use questions like the following to guide students' reading, or after they have read the story independently

Page 3: How do you think Ruthie feels about the journey she is about to take? (excited) How can you tell? (She says she can't wait; she looks excited in the picture.) *Character*

Page 8: Describe what Ruthie sees from the trolley. (the countryside, wagons bumping along dirt roads.) *Setting*

Page 9: How does Elkhart differ from Chestnut Ridge? (much bigger, with smokestacks, apartment buildings, and streetlights) *Setting/Compare and Contrast*

Page 12: Why does the steam train salute the trolley? (The trolley won the race.) *Make Inferences*

Page 13: Find the word *enormous* in the first paragraph. What looks enormous? (Indianapolis) Do you think the city seems large or small to Ruthie? (large) What do you think *enormous* means? (extremely large) *Vocabulary*

RETURN TO PREDICTIONS AND PURPOSES Review students' predictions and reasons for reading. Ask: Did you predict the setting would be important?

LITERARY RESPONSE Discuss these questions:

• What might Ruthie's journey to Chicago have been like aboard a steam train?

• How might Ruthie travel from Chestnut Ridge to Chicago today? Do you think the journey would be as exciting?

Also see the story questions and activity in *Ruthie Rides the Trolley.*

Answers to Story Questions

1. Ruthie and her mother are going to Chicago.
2. Cars and buses probably took their place.
3. Ruthie probably enjoyed the smooth ride even more after watching the bumpy road.
4. This story is about what it was like to travel on the trolley system many years ago.
5. Answers will vary.

Story Questions and Writing Activity

1. Where were Ruthie and her mother going?
2. Why do you think we no longer have the kind of trolley network found in the story?
3. Why might watching the road have made Ruthie feel good about being on the trolley?
4. What is this story mostly about?
5. If the trolley Ruthie rode on went as far as the Mississippi River and the grandfather from *Grandfather's Journey* used it to travel farther east, what might he have seen?

How Far?

Make a map of Ruthie's route from Chestnut Ridge to Chicago. Use this information to label your map.

Chestnut Ridge to Elkhart	135 miles
Elkhart to Indianapolis	135 miles
Indianapolis to Chicago	100 miles

How far did Ruthie travel on her whole trip? Write two or three sentences explaining your answer.

from *Ruthie Rides the Trolley*

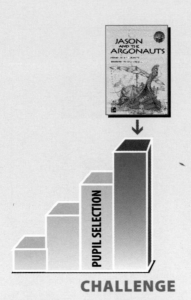

PUPIL SELECTION

CHALLENGE

EXTEND

Discuss difficult journeys students might have made and how they felt about them.

Answers to Story Questions

1. The Argo is a large, fast ship that Jason and the Argonauts used on their journey.
2. King Aeson wanted his son to be safe, and to grow up to be a fine young man.
3. Jason was proud of his father and wanted King Aeson to take his rightful place on the throne.
4. The story is about a brave young man who goes on a difficult journey to secure the magical Golden Fleece in order to free his father from prison and restore him to the throne.
5. Answers will vary.

Story Questions and Writing Activity

1. What is the Argo?
2. Why do you think Jason's father wanted his son to stay with the centaur?
3. Why was it important to Jason to restore the crown to his father?
4. What is the story mostly about?
5. How was Jason's journey different from the grandfather's in *Grandfather's Journey*?

Write a Problem

Make up some addition word problems using the characters in the story. For example, you might write, "Jason and the Argonauts fought off six soldiers. Then seven more soldiers came to fight. How many soldiers did they fight altogether?" Exchange word problems with a classmate and try to solve them.

---

from *Jason and the Argonauts*

Leveled Books

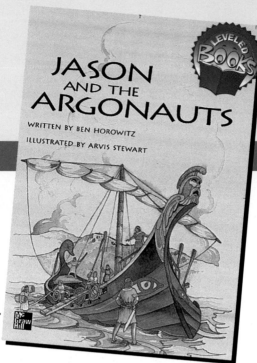

JASON AND THE ARGONAUTS
WRITTEN BY BEN HOROWITZ
ILLUSTRATED BY ARVIS STEWART

CHALLENGE

Jason and the Argonauts

☑ **Story Elements**

☑ **Instructional Vocabulary:** *astonished, enormous, journey, scattered, surrounded, towering*

Guided Reading

PREVIEW AND PREDICT Read the story title and chapter titles. Then conduct a **picture walk**. Ask students to predict what the story may be about.

SET PURPOSES Have students write down questions they would like to have answered as they read the story. For example: *Will Jason encounter the dragon on his journey*?

READ THE BOOK Have students read the story independently. Then return to the story for teaching opportunities.

Page 3: Why did Chiron train Jason so hard? (to make him strong and brave) *Character*

Pages 4–5: What does Pelias tell Jason to do? (bring him the Golden Fleece) What kind of person do you think Pelias is? Explain. (He put his brother in prison and sends Jason off to his death, so he must be very greedy and cruel.) *Character*

Page 10: The Clashing Cliffs were made up of two towering mountains. Do you think *towering* means "rising high in the air" or "staying near to the ground"? *Vocabulary*

Page 14: Is the Golden Fleece located in a safe or dangerous place? How can you tell? (Dangerous, because it hangs in a garden that's guarded by a dragon.) *Setting*

Page 16: How does King Aeson feel about his son, Jason? Why? (Proud, because Jason found the Golden Fleece and restored the throne.) *Character*

RETURN TO PREDICTIONS AND PURPOSES Review students' predictions and reasons for reading.

LITERARY RESPONSE Discuss these questions:

- What does Jason mean when he says, "It was you who made me who I am, father"?
- What is a hero? What qualities make a person heroic? Do you have any heroes?

Also see the story questions and activity in *Jason and the Argonauts*.

Activities

Anthology and Leveled Books

Connecting Texts

GRAPHIC ORGANIZER
Write the word *Journeys* in the center of the graphic organizer. Write the story titles in each of the other four boxes. Discuss with students the journey taken in each story using questions like the following:

- What is the purpose of the journey?

- What different settings do the characters experience?

- What do the characters discover about themselves and their surroundings on their travels?

Call on volunteers from each reading level and write their suggestions in the appropriate box.

Grandfather's Journey
- The grandfather journeyed by ship from Japan to America to start a new life.
- The ocean he crossed astonished him.
- He sometimes missed Japan and other times missed California.

Journey to America
- Marco and Lena traveled by ship from Italy to America to start a new life.
- They experienced a storm at sea.
- They helped their friends who are less fortunate.

JOURNEYS

Ruthie Rides the Trolley
- Ruthie and her mother journeyed by trolley from a small town to Chicago.
- On her journey, Ruthie was amazed by the smokestacks and streetlights of the cities.

Jason and the Argonauts
- Jason had to make a long journey to capture the Golden Fleece and restore his father's throne.
- Jason was clever and strong and won many battles during his difficult journey.

Viewing/Representing

GROUP PRESENTATIONS Divide the class into groups, one for each of the four books read in the lesson. (For *Grandfather's Journey*, combine students of different reading levels.) Have each group write and/or draw pictures for a travel journal for the main character in the assigned story. Journal entries and/or drawings should portray what the traveler feels and sees during the journey. Have each group present its journal to the class.

AUDIENCE RESPONSE Ask students to tell what they found interesting about each group's presentation. Allow time for questions after each presentation.

Research and Inquiry

MORE ABOUT JOURNEYS Have students ask themselves: What are some reasons people go on journeys? Then invite them to do the following:

- Ask a parent or grandparent to share the story of an important journey he or she took.

- Research methods of travel in use in the late 1800s and early 1900s.

- Look up the story of Ellis Island in an encyclopedia.

interNET CONNECTION For more information about this topic, have students log on to **www.mhschool.com/reading** for links to Web pages.

OBJECTIVES

Students will analyze and make inferences about character and setting.

TEACHING TIP

INSTRUCTIONAL Tell students they can understand how a character feels by thinking of experiences in their own lives that might be similar to those in the character's life. For example, students who have moved should be able to relate to the grandfather's feeling of being torn between two homes.

Review Story Elements

PREPARE

Discuss Character and Setting

Review: To make inferences about the characters in a story, pay attention to their actions, thoughts, and words. The setting (when and where the story takes place) can affect how the characters feel and act. Ask students: How did the setting affect the main character in the selection we just read?

TEACH

Read "Home and Homesick" and Model the Skill

Ask students to pay close attention to character and setting as you read the passage on **Teaching Chart 4** with them.

Home and Homesick

My grandfather looked at the mountains and rivers of his childhood and smiled with delight. He exchanged warm greetings with his old friends. He was very glad to be in Japan, to be home.

Later, he felt confused. He got up and looked out the window. He took a deep breath and could not smell the bay or hear the surf. He was not in San Francisco anymore.

He had waited for years to come home. Now he was homesick for California. He started thinking about when he might see California again.

Teaching Chart 4

Discuss clues in the passage that help readers to make inferences about the setting and character.

MODEL I can tell the grandfather is happy to be home because of his response to his surroundings and his friends. I can also tell that he misses San Francisco because he thinks about when he might see California again.

Make Inferences About Character, Setting

GROUP

Have students underline clues in "Home and Homesick" that help them to make inferences about the grandfather's character. Have them circle clues about the setting.

Then ask students how the setting affected the character's feelings and actions. (His old home made the grandfather happy and homesick at the same time. It made him think about when he might visit California again.) ▶ **Logical/Interpersonal**

ASSESS/CLOSE

Rewrite a Familiar Tale with a New Setting

Ask students to think of a favorite tale or fable, such as "The Fox and the Grapes" or "The Three Billy Goats Gruff." Ask them to think of a new setting for the tale—a new time, a new place, or both. Ask students how the new setting will affect the characters. Have them write their new version of the story and share it with the class.

ALTERNATE TEACHING STRATEGY

STORY ELEMENTS

For a different approach to teaching this skill, see page T60.

SELF-SELECTED Reading

Students may choose from the following titles:

ANTHOLOGY

- *Grandfather's Journey*

LEVELED BOOKS

- *Journey to America*
- *Ruthie Rides the Trolley*
- *Jason and the Argonauts*

Bibliography, pages 76-T77

Meeting Individual Needs for Comprehension

EASY	ON-LEVEL	CHALLENGE	LANGUAGE SUPPORT

Reteach, 05   **Practice, 05**   **Extend, 05**   **Language Support, 06**

OBJECTIVES

Students will make predictions about outcomes.

TEACHING TIP

INSTRUCTIONAL Tell students the word *predict* means to tell beforehand. The *pre/* part of the word comes from Latin and means "before," or "in front of." The *-dict* part of the word also comes from Latin, and means "to tell."

Introduce Make Predictions

PREPARE

Discuss Make Predictions

Tell students that trying to predict what will happen in a story reinforces what they know about the characters and what has already happened in a story. Predictions—correct or incorrect—can lead to students' improved understanding of a story.

TEACH

Read "In His Grandfather's Footsteps" and Model the Skill

Read "In His Grandfather's Footsteps" with the students. Have them focus on clues that will help them predict the outcome of the story.

In His Grandfather's Footsteps

My son said he has something important to tell me. I've been awaiting this day since I first found him crawling down the street. My son is just like his grandfather, the wanderer.

Father left his home in Japan when he was a young man. My father loved California, but he often had a faraway look in his eyes. Finally we moved back to Japan. In Japan, Father missed California.

Now that my son is a young man, I see that same faraway look in his eyes. I know what he has to tell us. I will miss him.

Teaching Chart 5

Ask students to predict the outcome of this story. What do they think the son is going to tell his mother? How did they reach that conclusion?

MODEL I think that the son is going to tell his mother that he is going away. First the title tells us that the grandson is going to follow in his grandfather's footsteps. Then we learn that the grandson is just like his grandfather, who is a wanderer.

PRACTICE

Find Clues in the Passage

Ask students what question arose with the very first sentence of the passage. (What does the son have to discuss with his mother?) Then ask students to underline clues in the passage that helped them to answer this question and to predict what will happen next.

▶ **Logical/Interpersonal**

ASSESS/CLOSE

Rewrite the Passage to Have a Different Outcome

Have students look back at the clues they underlined to make their predictions. Ask students to think of a different outcome (the son wants to stay home, join the circus, become a doctor, and so on) and change the clues to reflect that outcome. Then have them share the revised stories with the class to see if the other students can predict the new outcomes.

ALTERNATE TEACHING STRATEGY

MAKE PREDICTIONS

For a different approach to teaching this skill, see page T62.

LOOKING AHEAD

Students will apply this skill as they read the next selection, *Phoebe and the Spelling Bee.*

Meeting Individual Needs for Comprehension

EASY	ON-LEVEL	CHALLENGE	LANGUAGE SUPPORT

EASY

Name_____ Date_____ Reteach **6**

Make Predictions

You can use what you know about story characters to **predict** what the characters would do in other situations.

Read the story below. Then make predictions about what will happen next. Write your answers on the lines. Answers will vary.

Cassie liked helping her mother take care of the yard. Her mother knew that Cassie shared her love of yard work. Today, though, Cassie had to help her brother James finish his geography project. Cassie looked out the window and could see her mother weeding. She wanted to be outside. James was becoming impatient. Cassie wasn't paying attention.

Just then, their father came home from work. "Hi, kids!" he said. "What's that you're doing? Do you need any help?"

1. How do you think Cassie will answer her father's question?
   She will probably ask her father if he would help James.

2. How do you think James will answer his father's question?
   He will probably ask his father to help him.

3. Do you think that Cassie will stay inside and continue to help James? Explain why or why not. Since she likes to work in the yard, she will probably let her father help James while she goes outside.

4. How do you think the yard will look after Cassie's mother is finished working? Explain your answer. It will look neat and pretty because Cassie's mother takes pride in her yard.

5. Do you think James and his father will help with the yard work? Why or why not? No; James needs help on his project.

5 Book 3.1/Unit 1 Grandfather's Journey | At Home: Have students make another prediction about the story. | 6

ON-LEVEL

Name_____ Date_____ Practice **6**

Make Predictions

You can use what you have learned about a character in a story to **predict** what this character might do. Read each story. Then answer the questions.

Tanisha is good at solving problems. She also likes taking care of her little brother. Last summer, Tanisha and her family went on a camping trip. One afternoon, Tanisha and her little brother got lost on the way from their tent to the car. Tanisha's brother became scared and started to cry.

1. Will the children find their way back to the tent? How do you know?
   Yes; Tanisha is good at solving problems.

Tonight, Jerry has to finish a science project for school. Tomorrow is the science fair. They are giving prizes for the best project. Jerry would really like to win a prize. Tonight, Jerry's favorite TV show is on from eight o'clock to eight-thirty. Jerry has to go to bed at eight-thirty.

2. Will Jerry finish his science project? Why? Yes; he wants to win a prize.

3. When will Jerry work on his science project? before his TV show

Wendy lives in the country. The ocean is far away. Her favorite books are about boats. She dreams of sailing far and fast across the ocean.

Last summer, Wendy's father asked her to choose what they would do on their next summer trip.

4. What will Wendy and her father do on their next summer trip?
   They will go sailing.

4 Book 3.1/Unit 1 Grandfather's Journey | At Home: Have students pick a character from a movie. Ask students to describe what the character is like and predict something that the character might do. | 6

CHALLENGE

Name_____ Date_____ Extend **6**

Make Predictions

Some things that happen can change everyone's life. In "Grandfather's Journey," the war started. "Bombs fell from the sky and scattered our lives like leaves in a storm." Write what you think might have happened to the author and his grandfather if the war had not started.

_____

Answers will vary. Some students may predict that Allen Say and his grandfather journeyed to California again.

Would you guess that the author of the story would feel the same way about journeys that his grandfather did? Why or why not?

_____

Some may indicate that because they both took a trip away from their homeland, they would feel the same way.

Book 3.1/Unit 1 Grandfather's Journey | At Home: Have students make predictions about what they might do next Saturday. | 6

LANGUAGE SUPPORT

Name_____ Date_____

What Will Happen Next?

what you think the boy did next. What actually happened in the story?

_____

I miss the mountains and rivers of my childhood. I miss my old friends.

Took a Vacation To See Old Friends | **Bought Songbirds**

Grade 3 | Language Support/Blackline Master 3 • Grandfather's Journey 7

Reteach, 06   **Practice, 06**   **Extend, 06**   **Language Support, 07**

OBJECTIVES

Students will learn to identify and define compound words.

....

MATERIALS

• **Teaching Chart 6**

TEACHING TIP

INSTRUCTIONAL Explain that there are two kinds of compound words—closed and open. Closed compound words, as their name indicates, do not have a space between their base words. *Grandfather* and *homesick* are closed compound words. Open compound words have a space or a hyphen between the base words. *High school* and *mother-in-law* are open compound words.

Introduce Compound Words

PREPARE

Discuss Compound Words

Explain: A compound word is a word made up of two smaller words. You can figure out the meaning of a compound word from the meaning of its parts.

TEACH

Read the Passage and Model the Skill

Have the students look for compound words as they read the passage on **Teaching Chart 6.**

Knowing <u>Grandfather</u>

Although my <u>grandfather</u> died when I was still a boy, it was only after I became a man that I truly came to know him. That is when I left my <u>homeland</u>, traveled to California, and felt his love for that land. California's strong <u>sunlight</u> and lonely <u>seacoast</u> won my heart the way they did my <u>grandfather's</u>. I even chose to settle there, as he once did.

Making a new home for <u>myself</u> taught me more about my <u>grandfather</u>. I learned why his heart was always in two places. For, like him, I have found that as much as you love your new home you can still be <u>homesick</u> for your old one.

Teaching Chart 6

Help students determine what *sunlight* means.

MODEL The word *sunlight* in the third sentence is a compound word. It is made up of two words, *sun* and *light*. I can figure out the meaning of this compound word by looking at these two words. *Sunlight* means "the light of the sun."

Have students define *seacoast* in the third sentence by looking at its shorter words.

Identify Compound Words

GROUP

Have students underline each compound word in "Knowing Grandfather." Then have students discuss the meanings of the shorter words and the words in compound form. ▶ **Logical/Linguistic**

ASSESS/CLOSE

Form Compound Words and Use Them in a Paragraph

Have students form three or more compound words by combining a word from the first column below with a word from the second column. Then ask them to write a paragraph using the compound words. They may want to draw a picture to go with their paragraph.

grand	birds
river	boat
sea	coast
song	father
steam	light
sun	ship

ALTERNATE TEACHING STRATEGY

COMPOUND WORDS

For a different approach to teaching this skill, see page T63.

Meeting Individual Needs for Vocabulary

EASY	ON-LEVEL	CHALLENGE	LANGUAGE SUPPORT

EASY

Name_____ Date_____ Reteach **7**

Compound Words

When two words are put together to make one word, the bigger word is called a **compound word**. Use the meaning of each of the smaller words to help you figure out the meaning of the compound word.

Look at the compound words below. Write the two smaller words that make up each compound word. Then write the meaning of the compound word.

backyard
1. back   2. yard
3. the yard in the back

sunlight
4. sun   5. light
6. light from the sun

grandfather
7. grand   8. father
9. the father of one's father or mother

riverboat
10. river   11. boat
12. a boat that travels on a river

homesick
13. home   14. sick
15. missing home

16. Now write a compound word that you know. Answers will vary.

At Home: Ask students to name the words in the compound words *baseball, blueberry,* and *homemade.*

7   Book 3.1/Unit 1 Grandfather's Journey   /16

ON-LEVEL

Name_____ Date_____ Practice **7**

Compound Words

A **compound word** is a word that is made up of two smaller words. Each word in a compound word can stand alone.

brake + man = brakeman

Use the picture clues to write the compound word. The first part of the compound word appears below.

	First Word	Compound Word
1.	basket	basketball
2.	rail	railroad
3.	home	homework
4.	camp	campground or campfire
5.	jelly	jellyfish

At Home: Ask students to tell you three more examples of compound words.

7   Book 3.1/Unit 1 Grandfather's Journey   /5

CHALLENGE

Name_____ Date_____ Extend **7**

Compound Words

Compound words are made by putting two words together. The words *basket* and *ball* make the word basketball.

Use the words below to write as many new compound words as you can.

grand	steam	sick	river	sea	father	ship
boat	coast	land	end	parent	home	week

Suggested responses:	
grandfather	homeland
steamship	weekend
riverboat	grandparent
seacoast	homesick
	steamboat

Choose some of these compound words and write a story about someone you know who has gone on a journey.

_____
_____
_____
_____
_____
_____

Create a class compound word chart. Display it in the classroom. Add words to the chart during the year.

At Home: Ask students to think of compound words that will have something to do with what they will do that day.

7   Book 3.1/Unit 1 Grandfather's Journey

LANGUAGE SUPPORT

Name_____ Date_____

What is the Meaning?

Look at the example. ▭▭▷ what each new word means.

grand + father
grand - special importance + father - a man who has a child

1. grandfather = a father of special importance

steam + ship
steam - mist from hot water + ship - large boat which moves by power

2. steamship – hot water powered boat

river + boat
river - stream of water + boat - something that travels on water

3. riverboat = a boat that travels on a stream of water

sun + light
sun - star that heats Earth + light - to brighten

4. sunlight = starlight that brightens Earth

sea + coast
sea - great body of salty water + coast - land

5. seacoast = land that meets salty water

8 Grandfather's Journey • Language Support/Blackline Master 4   Grade 3

Reteach, 7	Practice, 7	Extend, 7	Language Support, 8

GRAMMAR/SPELLING
CONNECTIONS

See the 5-Day Grammar and Usage Plan on pages 47M–47N.

See the 5-Day Spelling Plan on pages 47O–47P.

TEACHING TIP

A spell-checker won't tell you if you have spelled the names of persons and places correctly. You should always read over your letters yourself to check for correct spelling.

Personal Narrative

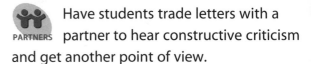

Prewrite

WRITE A LETTER Present this writing assignment: In *Grandfather's Journey,* the grandfather took a long and exciting journey as a young man. Think about a trip you have taken. Write a letter to your best friend telling about the place you visited and how you got there. Be sure to describe the setting with lots of details.

FREE WRITE Have students free write ideas for their letters. They should try to write as many ideas as they can without lifting their pens or pencils from the paper. Tell them not to worry about spelling, grammar, or punctuation as they free write. Ask them to choose one idea from this exercise and then free write on that.

Strategy: Make an Outline Have students organize their ideas chronologically in an outline. Tell them the more exciting or interesting parts of their trip might call for more details.

Draft

USE THE OUTLINE Ask students to write their letters by using their outlines as a guide. Remind them to add lots of details and to express their feelings in order to bring their experience to life for their readers. Tell students that letters should include a heading with the writer's address and date, a greeting, and a closing signature. There should also be an introductory sentence or paragraph.

Revise

SELF-QUESTIONING Ask students to assess their drafts.

- Did I tell about my trip in an order my reader can follow?
- Did I express my feelings about the event?
- Did I give enough details?

PARTNERS Have students trade letters with a partner to hear constructive criticism and get another point of view.

Edit/Proofread

CHECK FOR ERRORS Students should reread their letters to check clarity, spelling, grammar, and punctuation.

Publish

SEND THE LETTERS Students can address their letters and deliver them to the recipient's desk.

---

214 Puffin Place
Springfield, Massachusetts
August 23, 20__

Dear Lisa,
   I hope you are having fun at your grandparents' in Boston. I miss you.
   We just got back from Cape Cod. It was a great trip! Well, the ride was not so great. My baby brother screamed in my ear for four hours.
   Everyone stopped screaming when we got to our cottage. It was right on the beach! The water was as cold as a snowmelt, but the sun was as hot as an oven, so we still swam every day. We built huge sand castles. We buried each other in the sand. (I wanted to leave my brother buried there when we went home, but Mom didn't like that idea.) I ate sticky, sweet ice cream every day.
   Now I am home. I hope you are home soon, too.
Your friend,
Lucinda

Presentation Ideas

ILLUSTRATE LETTERS Have each student choose a scene from his or her letter to illustrate. Create a display of the letters and illustrations. ▶ **Viewing/Representing**

READ ALOUD Have students read their letters to the class. Ask listeners to close their eyes and try to visualize what the readers are describing in their letters. After each letter is read, discuss which scenes were easiest to visualize and why. ▶ **Speaking/Listening**

COMMUNICATION TIPS

REPRESENTING Have students close their eyes and think of the scene from their trip they want to illustrate. Ask them to try to remember as many details as possible.

LISTENING Tell students that as they listen to the letters being read, they should listen for something that interests them that they can ask the reader about after the reading.

Consider students' creative efforts, possibly adding a plus (+) for originality, wit, and imagination.

Scoring Rubric

Excellent	Good	Fair	Unsatisfactory
4: The writer • introduces the topic and presents the information in a particular sequence. • expresses his or her feelings about a personal experience. • provides many details to make the letter interesting.	**3:** The writer • introduces the topic and presents most of the information in sequence. • Includes an account of a personal experience and feelings. • provides some supporting details and descriptions.	**2:** The writer • introduces the topic, but does not present the information in any particular sequence. • only mentions a personal experience. • presents few supporting details.	**1:** The writer • does not introduce the topic, and does not present the information in any particular order. • does not include any personal experience. • presents no details.

0: The writer leaves the page blank or fails to respond to the writing task. The student does not address the topic or simply paraphrases the prompt. The response is illegible or incoherent.

LANGUAGE SUPPORT

To help students include more personal feelings in their letters, have them complete the sentence "I feel _____, when I think of _____ (a place or person from their trip)."

PORTFOLIO Invite students to include their letters or another writing project in their portfolios.

Meeting Individual Needs for Writing

EASY

Title and Caption Have students draw a picture of something from a trip they took. Then ask them to give the picture a title and write a brief caption describing what is going on in the picture.

ON-LEVEL

Oral History Have students make a list of questions to ask a grandparent or older adult about life when she or he was young. Have students do the interview and share what they learned with the class. Ask them to bring in a photo or draw a picture of the person.

CHALLENGE

Journal Entry Ask students to imagine they are the grandson as a young man writing about his first trip from Japan to the U.S. Encourage students to write about how the grandson feels as he looks at the same things his grandfather saw on his journey many years before.

5 Day Grammar and Usage Plan

 ESL Say the following fragments: *Born in Japan. Had many friends. My grandfather and I.* Explain to students that these are not sentences because they don't express a complete thought. Then repeat the fragments and ask different students to turn them into complete sentences.

DAILY LANGUAGE ACTIVITIES

Write the Daily Language Activities on the chalkboard each day or use **Transparency 1.** Ask students to correct the sentences orally.

Day 1

1. She explored North America .
2. he missed California. He
3. I was born in Japan .

Day 2

1. Did he miss his friends ?
2. are there tall buildings in the city? Are
3. He went to California .

Day 3

1. they returned to the village. They
2. He remembered the songbirds .
3. What did he see ?

Day 4

1. he did not see land. He
2. What did he want ?
3. It was called the New World .

Day 5

1. what did he explore? What
2. He returned to his home .
3. he is homesick for Japan. He

Daily Language Transparency 1

DAY 1 Introduce the Concept

Oral Warm-Up Write this phrase on the chalkboard: *My favorite bird.* Then write: *My favorite bird is a robin.* Ask students which one tells a complete thought.

Introduce Statements Present the following:

Statements

- A **sentence** is a group of words that expresses a complete thought.
- A **sentence fragment** is a group of words that does not tell a complete thought.
- A **sentence** begins with a capital letter and ends with a period.
- A **statement** is a **sentence** that tells about something.

Present the Daily Language Activity and have students correct orally. Then have students write three statements about someone they know.

 WRITING Assign the daily Writing Prompt on page 12C.

Grammar Practice Book, Page 1

Name_____ Date_____ Grammar ①

What Is a Sentence?

- A **sentence** is a group of words that tells a complete thought.
- Every sentence begins with a capital letter.
  Sentence: *My grandfather walked for days.*
  Not a sentence: *Walked for days.*

Write **yes** if the words make a sentence. Write **no** if they do not.

1. My grandfather was born in Japan. ___yes___
2. He came to America on a ship. ___yes___
3. He married and lived in California. ___yes___
4. Land of sunlight and sea. ___no___
5. Homesick for Japan. ___no___
6. He moved his family to Japan. ___yes___
7. Mountains and rivers of his childhood. ___no___
8. Laughed with old friends. ___no___
9. He raised songbirds. ___yes___
10. Missed California. ___no___

Book 3.1/Unit 1 Grandfather's Journey   Extension: Have students write three sentences about their family.   1

GRAMMAR PRACTICE BOOK, PAGE 1

DAY 2 Teach the Concept

Review Statements Ask students what kind of sentence a statement is and how to recognize a statement.

Introduce Question Ask a student to give an example of a question. Write it on the board. Have another student answer the question. Display and discuss:

Questions

- A **question** is a sentence that asks something.
- A question ends with a question mark.

Present the Daily Language Activity and have students write three questions about places they have visited.

 WRITING Assign the daily Writing Prompt on page 12C.

Grammar Practice Book, Page 2

Name_____ Date_____ Grammar ②

Statements and Questions

- A **statement** is a sentence that tells something. It ends with a period.
- A **question** is a sentence that asks something. It ends with a question mark.
  Statement: *My grandfather liked to travel.*
  Question: *Do you like to travel?*

Write **statement** if the sentence tells something. Write **question** if the sentence asks something. Put the correct end mark at the end of the sentence.

1. My grandfather's ship crossed an ocean. ___statement___
2. Have you seen an ocean? ___question___
3. Is an ocean deep? ___question___
4. My grandfather explored America. ___statement___
5. He saw huge cities. ___statement___
6. Do you know how many people live in cities? ___question___
7. Where is San Francisco Bay? ___question___
8. My grandfather missed Japan. ___statement___
9. There are rivers in Japan. ___statement___
10. Are there mountains in Japan? ___question___

Extension: Have students work in pairs. Ask each student to write a question about the story. Then have them write a statement to answer each other's question.   Book 3.1/Unit 1 Grandfather's Journey

GRAMMAR PRACTICE BOOK, PAGE 2

Statements and Questions

Learn from the Literature Review statements and questions. Read the first sentence on page 24 of *Grandfather's Journey*:

> **He met many people along the way.**

Ask students if this sentence is a statement or question. Ask students to explain their answers. Then have students change that sentence into a question.

Write Statements and Questions
Present the Daily Language Activity and have students correct orally.

Have partners work together to write statements and questions. Ask students to write questions about *Grandfather's Journey*. Then have students exchange papers and answer their partner's questions by writing statements.

 Assign the daily Writing Prompt on page 12D.

Review Statements and Questions
Write these three sentences on the board: *He traveled for weeks. When did she visit Japan? He loves songbirds.* Ask students to identify whether each sentence on the board is a statement or a question. Then have them explain the rules to support their answer. Present the Daily Language Activity for Day 4.

Mechanics and Usage Review capitalization and punctuation for statements and questions. Display and discuss:

Sentence Punctuation

- Every sentence begins with a capital letter.
- A statement ends with a period.
- A question ends with a question mark.

 Assign the daily Writing Prompt on page 12D.

Assess Use the Daily Language Activity and page 5 of the **Grammar Practice Book** for assessment.

Reteach Have students work in small groups to play Twenty Questions. Two students can think of a famous person, book, or movie while other students try to guess who or what it is by asking questions. Students should respond with statements rather than *yes* or *no*.

Have students write sentences and questions from the game and add them to the classroom word wall.

 Assign the daily Writing Prompt on page 12D.

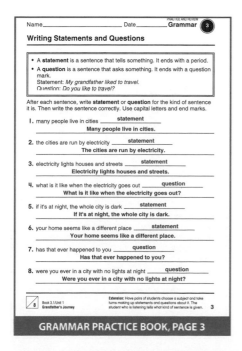

GRAMMAR PRACTICE BOOK, PAGE 3

GRAMMAR PRACTICE BOOK, PAGE 4

GRAMMAR PRACTICE BOOK, PAGE 5

GRAMMAR PRACTICE BOOK, PAGE 6

47N

5 Day Spelling Plan

LANGUAGE SUPPORT

ESL To give students extra practice with the vowel sounds, display a picture for each one and label it with the letter. Examples: short *a*: bat; short *o*: dot; short *u*: bug. Then ask students to give other examples of words with each of these vowel sounds.

DICTATION SENTENCES

1. My pet broke her <u>leg</u>.
2. The book cover is <u>black</u>.
3. He ate too <u>much</u>.
4. The <u>bag</u> was heavy.
5. He jumped over the <u>rocks</u>.
6. She <u>kept</u> the children home.
7. The boy <u>hid</u> the toy.
8. The girl walked by the <u>window</u>.
9. I went for a ride in the <u>van</u>.
10. <u>Mix</u> the eggs in a dish.
11. I can <u>rub</u> the spot out of the new dress.
12. Do you <u>ever</u> fall down?
13. That noise is the <u>buzz</u> of a bee.
14. The <u>body</u> of the child was thin.
15. Put that <u>thing</u> down!

Challenge Words

16. The bad weather <u>astonished</u> her.
17. The new house is <u>enormous</u>.
18. I went on a <u>journey</u> by car.
19. She <u>scattered</u> the flowers.
20. The children <u>surrounded</u> the toy.

DAY 1 Pretest

Assess Prior Knowledge Use the Dictation Sentences at left and **Spelling Practice Book** page 1 for the pretest. Allow students to correct their own papers. If students have trouble, have partners give each other a midweek test on Day 3. Students who require a modified list may be tested on the first eight words.

Spelling Words		Challenge Words
1. leg	9. van	16. **astonished**
2. **black**	10. mix	17. **enormous**
3. **much**	11. rub	18. **journey**
4. bag	12. ever	19. **scattered**
5. **rocks**	13. buzz	20. **surrounded**
6. **kept**	14. body	
7. hid	15. thing	
8. window		

*Note: Words in **dark type** are from the story.*

Word Study On page 2 of the **Spelling Practice Book** are word study steps and an at-home activity.

DAY 2 Explore the Pattern

Sort and Spell Words Say the words *cat, men, sit, top, up.* Ask students to identify the short-vowel sound in each word. Then have them say the Spelling Words and sort them by short-vowel sound.

Short *a*	Short *i*	Short *o*
black	hid	rocks
bag	window	body
van	mix	
	thing	**Short *u***
Short *e*		much
leg		rub
ever		buzz
kept		

Spelling Patterns A word or syllable with a short-vowel sound usually has the pattern CVC (consonant-vowel-consonant). Variations are CCVC, CVCC, and CCVCC. Have students make a diagram with one box for each sound and then fill in the letters that spell each sound.

SPELLING PRACTICE BOOK, PAGE 1

WORD STUDY STEPS AND ACTIVITY, PAGE 2

SPELLING PRACTICE BOOK, PAGE 3

Words with Short Vowels

DAY 3 — Practice and Extend

Word Meaning: Compound Words
Remind students that a compound word is two short words joined together to make one longer word. Ask students to list as many compound words as they can think of that contain at least one spelling word. Write their words on the the chalkboard and discuss their meanings. (Examples: *chalkboard, blacktop, whoever, whenever, wherever somebody, everything, something, everybody*)

Glossary Review the pronunciation key in the Glossary. Have partners:

- look up each Challenge Word.

- write its pronunciation respelling on an index card.

- mix up the cards and place them in a pile.

- take turns picking a card, writing the regular spelling of the word on the reverse side of the index, then checking the spelling by looking it up in the Glossary.

DAY 4 — Proofread and Write

Proofread Sentences Write these sentences on the chalkboard, including the misspelled words. Ask students to proofread, circling incorrect spellings and writing the correct spellings. There are two spelling errors in each sentence.

> The ⊙blac cat jumped out the ⊙wendow.
> (black, window)
>
> He tripped over some ⊙roks and hurt his ⊙legg. (rocks, leg)

Have students create additional sentences with errors for partners to correct.

Writing Cross-Reference Have students use as many Spelling Words as possible in the daily Writing Prompt on page 12D. Remind students to proofread their writing for errors in spelling, punctuation, and grammar.

DAY 5 — Assess and Reteach

Assess Students' Knowledge Use page 16 of the **Spelling Practice Book** or the Dictation Sentences on page 47 O for the posttest.

Personal Word List If students have trouble with any words in the lesson, have them create a personal list of troublesome words in their journals. Have students write a context sentence for each word.

Students should refer to their word lists during later writing activities.

Worksheet — Page 4

Name_____ Date_____ SPELLING **4**

Words with Short Vowels

leg	bag	hid	mix	buzz
black	rocks	window	rub	body
much	kept	van	ever	thing

What's the Word?
Complete each sentence with a spelling word.

1. The **black** spider crawled slowly along the wall.
2. Crickets **rub** their front wings together to chirp.
3. The humming sound of a bee is a **buzz**.
4. Dad hurt his **leg** and could not walk.
5. When our dog **hid** the bone, I found it under a pillow.
6. I opened a **bag** of chips for the party.
7. I can't do one more **thing** today.
8. The dress didn't fit the doll's **body**.
9. Mom **kept** our drawings in a box.
10. We washed the **window** with a glass cleaner.

Define It!
Write the spelling words that have the same meanings as the words or phrases below.

11. a kind of truck **van**
12. always **ever**
13. a great amount **much**
14. stir together **mix**
15. stones **rocks**

Challenge Extension: Ask students to write a "fill in the blank" sentence for each Challenge Word and then exchange papers with a partner to complete the sentences.

Book 3.1/Unit 1 **15**
4 Grandfather's Journey

SPELLING PRACTICE BOOK, PAGE 4

Worksheet — Page 5

Name_____ Date_____ SPELLING **5**

Words with Short Vowels

Proofreading
There are six spelling mistakes in this visitor's guide to the zoo. Circle the misspelled words. Write the words correctly on the lines below.

A zoo is a ⊙winndow to the animal kingdom. If you wonder how wild animals live, visit the zoo. Come by bus, car, ⊙vann or train. Remember this: these animals are not pets.

Follow these safety rules. Don't throw ⊙roks at the birds. Don't put your arm or ⊙legg through a bar of a cage. A dangerous animal might be ⊙kept there. Don't pet the animals.

There is a lot you can do at the zoo. Watch the seals play in the water. See a ⊙blak bear. Have fun!

1. **window**   2. **van**   3. **rocks**
4. **leg**   5. **kept**   6. **black**

Writing Activity
Write a postcard to a friend describing the zoo. Use at least four spelling words in your description.

_____
_____
_____
_____
_____

10 Book 3.1/Unit 1
Grandfather's Journey   5

SPELLING PRACTICE BOOK, PAGE 5

Worksheet — Page 6

Name_____ Date_____ SPELLING **6**

Words with Short Vowels

Look at the words in each set. One word in each set is spelled correctly. Use a pencil to color in the circle in front of that word. Before you begin, look at the sample sets of words. Sample A has been done for you. Do Sample B by yourself. When you are sure you know what to do, you may go on with the rest of the page.

Sample A
- Ⓐ dec
- ● deck
- Ⓒ dek
- Ⓓ deak

Sample B
- Ⓔ haz
- Ⓕ hass
- ● has
- Ⓗ hazs

1.
- Ⓐ mutch
- Ⓑ moch
- Ⓒ mouch
- ● much

6.
- Ⓔ windoe
- Ⓕ windo
- Ⓖ whindow
- ● window

11.
- Ⓐ hidd
- Ⓑ heid
- Ⓒ hiid
- ● hid

2.
- ● thing
- Ⓕ thinge
- Ⓖ thinq
- Ⓗ thinng

7.
- ● mix
- Ⓑ miks
- Ⓒ mikz
- Ⓓ mixe

12.
- Ⓔ evver
- Ⓕ everr
- ● ever
- Ⓗ evah

3.
- Ⓐ kepped
- ● kept
- Ⓒ kepet
- Ⓓ cept

8.
- Ⓔ lage
- Ⓕ legg
- ● leg
- Ⓗ lege

13.
- Ⓐ baag
- Ⓑ bage
- ● bag
- Ⓓ bagg

4.
- Ⓐ blak
- Ⓕ blac
- ● black
- Ⓗ blacke

9.
- Ⓐ rox
- ● rocks
- Ⓒ rocs
- Ⓓ rockse

14.
- ● buzz
- Ⓕ buz
- Ⓖ buze
- Ⓗ bous

5.
- Ⓐ roub
- ● rub
- Ⓒ rubb
- Ⓓ rubbe

10.
- Ⓔ boddy
- ● body
- Ⓖ boddie
- Ⓗ bodee

15.
- Ⓐ vaane
- ● van
- Ⓒ vann
- Ⓓ vean

6 Book 3.1/Unit 1
Grandfather's Journey **15**

SPELLING PRACTICE BOOK, PAGE 6

Phoebe and the Spelling Bee

Selection Summary A girl uses her imagination to make learning fun and to overcome her fears of spelling and competition.

Listening Library Audiocassette

INSTRUCTIONAL
Pages 50–77

About the Author/Illustrator Barney Salzberg lives in Los Angeles with his wife, two children, and many pets. He owns, among other animals, two dogs, a cat, a bunch of frogs, fish, and a hamster named Pinky. He has written and illustrated several books and pop-ups for children, including *Mrs. Morgan's Lawn*, *Show and Tell*, *This Is a Great Place for a Hot Dog Stand*, and *Backyard Cowboy*.

Resources for Meeting Individual Needs

EASY
Pages 77A, 77D

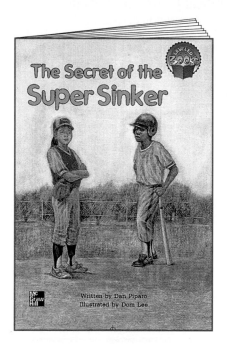

INDEPENDENT
Pages 77B, 77D

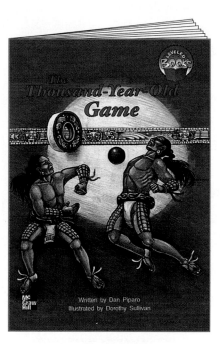

CHALLENGE
Pages 77C, 77D

🏠 *Take-Home version available*

LEVELED PRACTICE

Reteach, 8–14

blackline masters with reteaching opportunities for each assessed skill

Practice, 8–14

workbook with Take-Home stories and practice opportunities for each assessed skill and story comprehension

Extend, 8–14

blackline masters that offer challenge activities for each assessed skill

ADDITIONAL RESOURCES

- **Language Support Book,** pp. 9–16
- **Take-Home Story, Practice** p. 9a
- **Alternate Teaching Strategies,** pp. T60–T66
- **Selected Quizzes Prepared by** Accelerated Reader®

McGraw-Hill School
TECHNOLOGY

Phonics CD-ROM provides extra phonics support.

interNET CONNECTION Research & Inquiry ideas. Visit **www.mhschool.com/reading.**

READING AND LANGUAGE ARTS	**DAY 1** *Focus on Reading and Skills*	**DAY 2** *Read the Literature*
● **Comprehension** ● **Vocabulary** ● **Phonics/Decoding** ● **Study Skills** ● **Listening, Speaking, Viewing, Representing**	**Read Aloud and Motivate,** 48E "The Wind and the Sun" **Develop Visual Literacy,** 48/49 ☑ **Introduce Problem and Solution,** 50A–50B **Teaching Chart 7** Reteach, Practice, Extend, 8	**Build Background,** 50C Develop Oral Language **Vocabulary,** 50D *continue embarrass legend* *correct groaning unusual* **Teaching Chart 8** **Word Building Manipulative Cards** Reteach, Practice, Extend, 9 **Read the Selection,** 50–73 Guided Instruction ☑ Problem and Solution ☑ Make Predictions **Minilessons,** 63, 65, 67, 71 **Cultural Perspectives,** 52
● **Curriculum Connections**	**Link** Fine Arts, 48/49	**Link** Social Studies, 50C
● **Writing**	**Writing Prompt:** Your friend is organizing a spelling bee. Write three rules she expects everyone to follow.	**Writing Prompt:** You won a spelling bee! You are excited! Write to your aunt and tell her what happened. **Journal Writing,** 73 Quick-Write
● **Grammar**	**Introduce the Concept: Commands and Exclamations,** 77M Daily Language Activity 1. Study your spelling words . 2. Find a partner to help you . 3. Prepare for the spelling bee . **Grammar Practice Book** 7	**Teach the Concept: Commands and Exclamations,** 77M Daily Language Activity 1. How exciting this is ! 2. Gosh, that one is hard ! 3. Next time, study more . **Grammar Practice Book,** 8
● **Spelling**	**Pretest: Words with Long *a* and Long *e*,** 77O **Spelling Practice Book,** 7–8	**Explore the Pattern: Words with Long *a* and Long *e*,** 77O **Spelling Practice Book,** 9

Meeting Individual Needs

☑ = **Skill Assessed in Unit Test**

DAY 3 — Read the Literature

Reread for Fluency, 72

Story Questions, 74
  Reteach, Practice, Extend, 10
Story Activities, 75

Study Skills, 76
  ☑ Parts of a Book
  Teaching Chart 9
  Reteach, Practice, Extend, 11

Test Power, 77

 Read the Leveled Books,
  Guided Reading
  ☑ Long *a* and Long *e*
  ☑ Problem and Solution
  ☑ Instructional Vocabulary
   **CD-ROM**

 Science, 54, **Social Studies,** 58

 Writing Prompt: Choose a spelling word from the story. Write a short, exciting story using that word.

Writing Process: Personal Narrative, 77K
  Prewrite, Draft

Review and Practice: Commands and Exclamations, 77N
  Daily Language Activity
  1. Do not forget your spelling list .
  2. Wow, there are too many words !
  3. Just learn them one at a time .
Grammar Practice Book, 9

Practice and Extend: Words with Long *a* and Long *e*, 77P
Spelling Practice Book, 10

DAY 4 — Build Skills

 Read the Leveled Books and Self-Selected Books

☑ **Review Problem and Solution,** 77E–77F
  Teaching Chart 10
  Reteach, Practice, Extend, 12
  Language Support, 14

☑ **Review Make Predictions,** 77G–77H
  Teaching Chart 11
  Reteach, Practice, Extend, 13
  Language Support, 15

 Health, 64

 Writing Prompt: Explain how to prepare for a spelling bee. Include tips on how to remember hard words.

Writing Process: Personal Narrative, 77K
  Revise

Meeting Individual Needs for Writing, 77L

Review and Practice: Commands and Exclamations, 77N
  Daily Language Activity
  1. What a long word that is !
  2. How difficult it seems !
  3. Try a little harder .
Grammar Practice Book, 10

Proofread and Write: Words with Long *a* and Long *e*, 77P
Spelling Practice Book, 11

DAY 5 — Build Skills

 **Read Self-Selected Books**

☑ **Introduce Prefixes,** 77I–77J
  Teaching Chart 12
  Reteach, Practice, Extend, 14
  Language Support, 16

Listening, Speaking, Viewing, Representing, 77L
  Illustrate the Story
  Make a Tape

Minilessons, 63, 65, 71

Phonics Review,
  Long *a* and Long *e*, 67
  Phonics/Phonemic Awareness Practice Book, 31–38
  CD-ROM

Math, 68

Writing Prompt: Imagine a friend hurt your feelings. Explain what happened and how you felt. Include exclamations.

Writing Process: Personal Narrative, 77K
  Edit/Proofread, Publish

Assess and Reteach: Commands and Exclamations, 77N
  Daily Language Activity
  1. Get ready for the spelling bee .
  2. Spell the word *actor* .
  3. I am the best speller ever !
Grammar Practice Book, 11–12

Assess and Reteach: Words with Long *a* and Long *e*, 77P
Spelling Practice Book, 12

48D

Link
Language Arts

Read Aloud
and Motivate

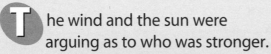

The Wind and the Sun

a fable by Aesop
told by Margaret Hughes

The wind and the sun were arguing as to who was stronger.

"I am," said the wind, blowing out his cheeks so hard that all the trees bent down before him and men turned up the collars of their overcoats.

"There," he said to the sun, "I can make the trees bend. You can't do that. You just shine and people lie down and bask in the warmth."

"Well, then," said the sun, "if you're so sure, why don't we arrange a contest, then everyone will know which of us is stronger."

"Good idea," said the wind. "See the traveler down below. Let's see which of us can make him take off his coat."

The sun agreed to the contest and told the wind to try first. The wind took a deep breath and blew and blew. A great storm came up and everything shook. But the traveler didn't take off his coat. Instead he drew it closer around him, gripping it tightly, trying to shut out the wind.

At last the wind was exhausted with blowing and he had to give up.

Continued on pages T2-T5

Oral Comprehension

LISTENING AND SPEAKING Encourage students to think about the author's purpose by reading aloud this fable about strength. After you have finished, ask students, "Do you think the author wrote this fable just to entertain, or did he have another purpose?" Then ask, "Do you think the author succeeded in his purpose? Why or why not?" Remind students to look for the author's purpose in other stories or poems as they read.

Activity Encourage students to make up dances based on the movements of wind. Have students perform their dance in small groups, with one student taking the stationary role of the sun in the center of the group. If possible, play appropriate music as students perform their dances.

▶ **Kinesthetic/Interpersonal**

Anthology pages 48–49

Stories in Art

Some paintings are filled with many details. You find yourself looking carefully at the picture to discover what is happening.

Look at this painting. What can you tell about it? How does the artist show you that it is a race? Pretend that you are one of the bicycle riders. What would you do to try to win the race?

Close your eyes. What do you remember about the painting? Why?

Heroes on Wheels
by Jane Wooster Scott

48

49

Objective: Identify Problem and Solution

VIEWING This colorful painting features a world cycling championship. Have children note the vivid details, such as the flags in the foreground and background, the uniforms of the racers, and the stadium filled with spectators. What do the different flags and uniforms show about the race? Have children read the title of the work. How does the artist feel about the cyclists' efforts?

Read the page with students, encouraging individual interpretations of the painting.

Have students describe what they might try to do to win the race. For example:

- go very slowly until the end and then surprise everyone with a burst of speed.
- cycle very hard from the start of the race to the finish.

REPRESENTING Have children choose a main character from the painting and imagine a problem that the person had to solve before the race. Have children tell the class what the problem was and its solution.

OBJECTIVES

Students will identify problems and analyze possible solutions to them.

TEACHING TIP

MANAGEMENT Pair ESL students with native English-speakers and have them collaborate on their responses to the Practice and Assess/Close activities.

Introduce Problem and Solution

PREPARE

Discuss Solutions to Problems

Have students think of a problem a well-known fairy-tale character experienced (or they can refer to a TV program). Ask: What was the problem? How was the problem solved? Was the solution a good one? Why?

TEACH

Define Problem and Solution

State that in many stories, the main character has a problem. The story tells how the main character tries to solve the problem.

Mayor for a Day

A buzz of excitement ran through the class when Ms. Rosado told them about the contest. The student who wrote the best essay about their city's history would be named "Mayor for a Day"!

Jackie knew that she wanted this more than anything. To be named Mayor for a Day, all she had to do was write the best essay. Still, she had to admit that she didn't know very much about the city's history.

The excitement began to drain out of her. But she refused to give up. The key, she knew, was to learn that history—and fast.

Teaching Chart 7

Read the Story and Model the Skill

Display **Teaching Chart 7**. Have students identify the main problem as the story is read.

MODEL I know what Jackie wants—to be mayor for a day. I see the main problem she faces. It's that she has to write an essay about the city's history and she doesn't know enough about its history.

Identify Problem and Solution

Have students underline clues that help them identify the problem faced by the main character. Have them circle clues that help them to predict how the main character will solve that problem.

PRACTICE

Write Solutions to Problem

Discuss the problem faced by Jackie and begin a Problem/Solution chart. In the chart, list the possible solutions suggested by students.

GROUP

▶ **Spatial/Interpersonal**

PROBLEM	POSSIBLE SOLUTIONS
Jackie doesn't know about the city's history.	Go to the library.
	Visit City Hall.
	Question older residents about their memories of the city.

ASSESS/CLOSE

Analyze Solutions to Problem

Ask students to imagine that Jackie has only one week to complete her essay. Which is the best solution to her problem? Which solutions would not solve the problem quickly? Why?

SELECTION
Connection

Students will apply problem and solution when they read *Phoebe and the Spelling Bee* and the Leveled Books.

ALTERNATE TEACHING
STRATEGY

PROBLEM AND SOLUTION

For a different approach to teaching this skill, see page T64.

Meeting Individual Needs for Comprehension

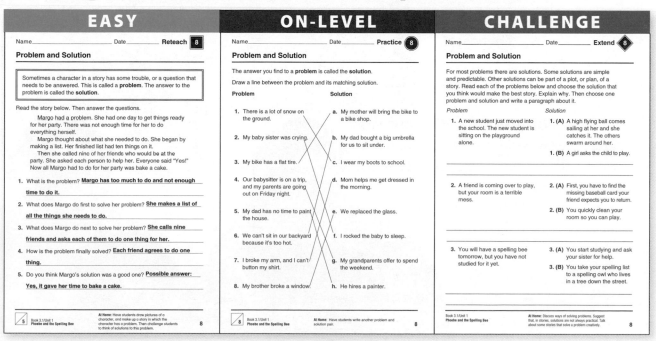

EASY	ON-LEVEL	CHALLENGE
Reteach, 8	Practice, 8	Extend, 8

50B

Build Background

Link Anthology and Leveled Books

Social Studies

Evaluate Prior Knowledge

CONCEPT: CONTESTS The characters participate in contests. Have students share experiences or knowledge they have of contests or competitions.

IDENTIFY CONTESTS Have students list different kinds of contests or competitions. Create a word web to organize their responses.

▶ **Spatial/Interpersonal**

- Baseball
- Spelling Bees
- Sports
- School
- Gymnastics
- Science Fairs
- Contests
- Political
- Elections

Graphic Organizer 29

WRITE A PARAGRAPH Have students write a paragraph about a contest they participated in or one they could imagine participating in. Encourage them to tell how they felt during the contest.

Develop Oral Language

DISCUSS CONTESTS **ESL** Bring in magazine pictures or photos of people involved in competitive activities. Ask students to describe the feelings the people in the competitions might be having.

List the feelings on the chalkboard. Discuss the meaning of each word and have students use the word in a sentence.

Ask students to imagine that they are participating in the competitions. Have students work in pairs and choose one magazine picture or photo. One student in each pair should play the part of a TV reporter interviewing the other, who plays a participant in that contest or competition. Encourage students to use words listed on the chalkboard.

TEACHING TIP

INSTRUCTIONAL Keep a box full of colorful magazines in the classroom, dealing with topics such as sports or travel. The illustrations and photographs can be used to motivate and interest students in the Develop Oral Language activity.

LANGUAGE SUPPORT

See the **Language Support Book, pages 9–12,** for teaching suggestions for Build Background and Vocabulary.

Vocabulary

Key Words

Katie's Legend

1. Katie said to Phoebe, "Let me tell you the (legend) of the purple shirt, which was passed down from my grandmother to my mother, then to me." **2.** It was an (unusual) story, full of strange events about how a boy in a purple shirt won the first spelling bee. **3.** In the story, anyone who wore a purple shirt would give (correct) spellings without any mistakes. **4.** When Katie stopped, Phoebe asked her to (continue). **5.** "I don't want to (embarrass) you or make you feel ashamed," said Katie, "but the story isn't true." **6.** Phoebe began (groaning), because she was sad that the purple shirt could not help her.

> **Teaching Chart 8**

Vocabulary in Context

IDENTIFY VOCABULARY WORDS
Display **Teaching Chart 8** and read the passage with students. Have volunteers circle each vocabulary word and underline other words that are clues to its meaning.

DISCUSS MEANINGS Ask questions like these to help clarify word meanings:

- Is a legend a story that is completely true?
- Is an unusual thing something you see every day?
- Is 5 the correct answer to this problem: $2 + 2 = ?$
- Can you think of a word that means the opposite of *continue*?
- How do you feel when you are embarrassed?
- When you are groaning, are you feeling happy or sad?

Practice

DEMONSTRATE WORD MEANING Have partners choose vocabulary cards and use them in a dialogue that shows the words' meanings. ▶ **Linguistic/Interpersonal**

> **Word Building Manipulative Cards**

CREATE A WORD PUZZLE Divide students into pairs. Have each pair create a word-search puzzle or a simple crossword puzzle using the six vocabulary words. Have pairs exchange papers and solve the puzzles.

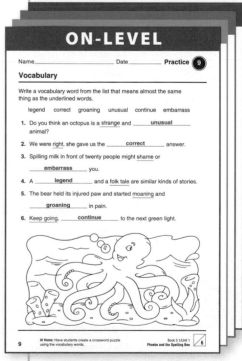

ON-LEVEL

Name_____ Date_____ Practice **9**

Vocabulary

Write a vocabulary word from the list that means almost the same thing as the underlined words.

legend   correct   groaning   unusual   continue   embarrass

1. Do you think an octopus is a strange and _____**unusual**_____ animal?

2. We were <u>right</u>, she gave us the ____**correct**____ answer.

3. Spilling milk in front of twenty people might <u>shame</u> or ____**embarrass**____ you.

4. A ____**legend**____ and a <u>folk tale</u> are similar kinds of stories.

5. The bear held its injured paw and started <u>moaning</u> and ____**groaning**____ in pain.

6. Keep going, ____**continue**____ to the next green light.

9

Take-Home Story 9a
Reteach 9
Practice 9 • Extend 9

50D

Guided Instruction

Preview and Predict

Have students read the title and preview the story, looking for pictures that give strong clues about problem and solution.

- Who is the story's main character?
- What clues about the main character's problem do the title and pictures give?
- What will the story most likely be about?
- Will the story be a realistic one or a fantasy? How can you tell? (Students may feel the illustrations suggest it will be a fantasy; others may see that it is set in school and will be realistic.) *Genre*

Have students record their predictions about the story and the main character.

PREDICTIONS	HOW IT TURNED OUT
The story is about a girl with a good imagination.	
She is unhappy about something in school.	
The story will be realistic.	

Set Purposes

What do students want to find out by reading the story? For example:

- Why is the girl unhappy in school?

Meet Barney Saltzberg

Things are always hopping at Barney Saltzberg's house. In addition to two dogs, a cat, a fish, and a hamster named Pinky, he also keeps a bunch of frogs.

Even with a house full of pets, Saltzberg has still managed to find time to write and illustrate several award-winning and correctly spelled picture books for children. You might also like to read *This Is a Great Place for a Hot Dog Stand*, *Mrs. Morgan's Lawn*, and *Backyard Cowboy*.

50

Meeting Individual Needs · Grouping Suggestions for Strategic Reading

EASY	ON-LEVEL	CHALLENGE
Read Together Read the story with students or have them use the **Listening Library Audiocassette**. Have students use the Problem/Solution chart to record important information about problems and solutions. Guided Instruction and Intervention prompts offer additional help with decoding, vocabulary, and comprehension.	**Guided Reading** Suggest that students read the selection together using the Guided Instruction. You may also want to have the students read the story first on their own. Have them use the Problem/Solution chart to record meaningful information during reading.	**Read Independently** Remind students that identifying problems and solutions will help them understand the story. Have students set up a Problem/Solution chart as on page 51. After reading, they can use their charts to summarize the story.

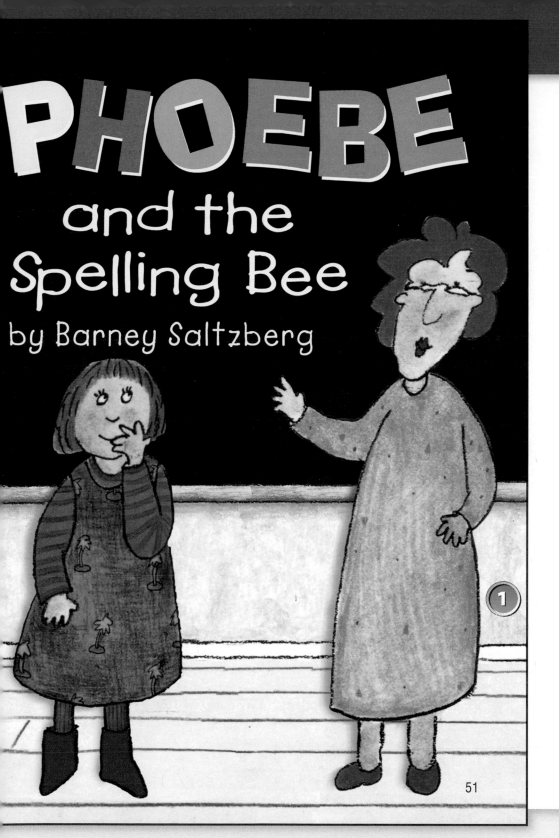

PHOEBE
and the Spelling Bee
by Barney Saltzberg

51

Guided Instruction

☑ **Problem and Solution**
☑ **Make Predictions**

Strategic Reading Paying attention to problem and solution will help you understand what is happening in the story. Before we begin reading, let's prepare a Problem/Solution chart for story notes.

PROBLEM	SOLUTION

(1) MAKE PREDICTIONS Can you predict anything about the story from this picture? Can you predict where it takes place? Can you predict if it will be mainly serious or mainly humorous? (The story mainly takes place in school. The picture is humorous, so the story will be, too.)

Story Words

The words below may be unfamiliar. Have students check their meanings and pronunciations in the Glossary beginning on page 388.

- mock, p. 61
- consonant, p. 65
- disaster, p. 68
- pedestrian, p. 71

LANGUAGE SUPPORT

A blackline master of the Problem/ Solution chart is available in the **Language Support Book**.

LANGUAGE SUPPORT, 13

Guided Instruction

2 **PROBLEM AND SOLUTION** When you begin a story, it's often a good idea to pay attention to how a main character tries to solve his or her problems. Who is the main character of this story? Can you see a problem that she has?

MODEL As I read, I see that Phoebe is the main character. I think that the problem she has is that she is not ready for the spelling bee.

3 Phoebe says two things on this page. What can you tell about her character based on what she says? (She doesn't like spelling. She has a sense of humor.)
Analyze Character

"Friday we will have our first spelling bee," announced Ms. Ravioli. "Here's a list of words you should know."

I slid down in my chair. "I'm going to be sick on Friday," I whispered to Katie.

2 "Don't be silly, Phoebe," said Katie. "Spelling is easy."

"I'm allergic to spelling," I told her.

3 "I'll help you," said Katie.

4 We ate lunch together. Katie looked over the spelling list. "This will be a breeze!" she said.

52

CULTURAL PERSPECTIVES

AMAZING ALPHABETS Point out that in most alphabets, each letter or symbol stands for a sound. The Russian, or Cyrillic alphabet, has 33 letters and is based on the Greek alphabet. Ask:

• Have any of you ever seen Russian letters? Where?

Have students think of two or three sounds in the English language, such as short *e* or long *a*. Ask children to design their own symbols or letters to stand for the sounds. Ask students to display their letters.

▶ **Visual/Linguistic**

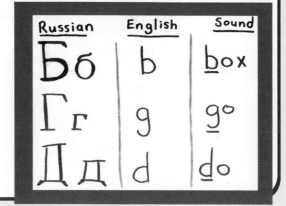

Russian	English	Sound
Бб	b	<u>b</u>ox
Гг	g	<u>g</u>o
Дд	d	<u>d</u>o

I drew dots all over my arm and started groaning, "Oooohhhh!"

"What's the matter?" asked Katie.

"I think I've got chicken pox!" I said.

"Spell **actor**," said Katie.

"**A-k-d-o-r**," I said.

"That's what it sounds like," said Katie, "but it's spelled differently."

She showed me the word on the spelling list. I saw that you could break the word into two parts—**act** and **or**.

53

Guided Instruction

4 **PROBLEM AND SOLUTION** Let's keep track of Phoebe's problems. As the story goes along, we can write down her solutions to these problems.

PROBLEM	SOLUTION
Phoebe is not ready for the spelling bee.	

5 Do you think that Phoebe really has chicken pox? Why or why not? (She is pretending to have chicken pox because she does not want to be in the spelling bee.) *Make Inferences*

6 **MAKE PREDICTIONS** Based on what you know about Phoebe so far, do you think that she will do well in the spelling bee? Why? (No, because she does not know how to spell *actor*.)

Guided Instruction

(7) MAKE PREDICTIONS Have you changed your prediction about how well Phoebe will do in the spelling bee? Has she learned anything about how to spell? What makes you think that?

MODEL I'll think about what I have learned about Phoebe and spelling so far. At first, she couldn't spell the word *actor*. But when Katie showed her the word, she saw that she could break it up into two smaller words. Then she knew how to spell it. I predict that she will do well in the spelling bee when she will be able to break up long words into smaller words.

"If I could **act or** spell, I'd **act**!" I said. "**A-c-t-o-r**!" (7)

"That's right!" said Katie.

"Try spelling **brontosaurus**," said Katie.

I dropped to the ground, holding my leg. "Oh, it's broken!" I cried. "A **brontosaurus** knocked me over, and I broke my leg!"

"I'm waiting!" said Katie.

"Race you to class backward," I shouted, and then I ran inside.

54

Cross Curricular: Science

DINOSAURS Display drawings of dinosaurs and ask students to identify each kind. Elicit students' knowledge about dinosaurs, such as when they lived.

RESEARCH AND INQUIRY Have students find pictures of dinosaurs. Small groups can make dioramas of dinosaurs in their environment and present them to the class.

▶ **Kinesthetic/Interpersonal**

*inter***NET** **CONNECTION** Students can learn more about dinosaurs by visiting *www.mhschool.com/reading.*

That night Katie called me to find out how I was doing with my spelling list. ⑧

"Great!" I said.

I was folding the spelling list into a paper airplane.

⑨

55

Guided Instruction

⑧ Who would like to role-play Phoebe and Katie for us? Phoebe and Katie, you are on the phone talking about the upcoming spelling bee. Can you tell us what you say to each other? Try to give us a good sense of your character and what she might say to the other person. *Role-Play*

⑨ **PROBLEM AND SOLUTION** Take a look at your Problem/Solution chart. What is Phoebe's problem? Do you think she has found a way yet to solve that problem? What makes you say this? (Phoebe is not ready for the spelling bee. She does not seem to be preparing herself for it.)

PROBLEM	SOLUTION
Phoebe is not ready for the spelling bee.	

Guided Instruction

10 Look at the words *actor* and *brontosaurus* on this page. Do you see something different about the way they look? Why do you think they are printed this way? (These words appear in darker letters, or boldface. Boldface is often used to emphasize words or show that they are different.) *Typographic Clues*

> ## TEACHING TIP
>
> **INSTRUCTIONAL** As students read, point out that one way to understand a character's problem is to compare that character's life with their own. Like Phoebe, have they been in a situation in which they were unprepared? How did they feel? What did they decide to do to solve the problem? Were they successful?

The next morning Ms. Ravioli asked how many students had been studying for the spelling bee.

Everyone raised their hand. Except me. I was under the table, studying my shoes.

"Phoebe," said Ms. Ravioli, "have you looked at your spelling list?"

 I sat up in my chair. "Once there was an **actor** who played a **brontosaurus**."

56

Everybody laughed. I sank in my chair.

"Settle down, class," said Ms. Ravioli. "It sounds like Phoebe has an unusual way of learning her words."

11

57

Guided Instruction

PHONICS AND DECODING Read the second word on page 57. *(laughed)* Now read the word in the third line spelled *P-h-o-e-b-e.* What sound do you hear in both words? *(the /f/ sound)*

11 **PROBLEM AND SOLUTION** How do you think Phoebe feels when the other students laugh? *(embarrassed)* Let's add this problem to our charts.

PROBLEM	SOLUTION
Phoebe is not ready for the spelling bee.	
The class laughs at Phoebe when she uses spelling words to tell a story.	

PREVENTION/INTERVENTION

PHONICS AND DECODING Remind students that sometimes different letters can combine to make the same sound. This is true of the sound /f/.

- Write *laughed* on the chalkboard. Underline the letters *gh.*
- Write *Phoebe* on chalkboard. Underline the letters *Ph.*

- Challenge students to come up with other words that use *gh* and *ph* to make the *f* sound. *(rough, tough, cough, phone, photograph)* Write the words on the chalkboard in a two-column chart as shown:

gh	ph

Guided Instruction

12 Do you think that Phoebe and Katie are good friends? What makes you think so? (Katie tries to help Phoebe. They call each other on the phone. They walk home from school together.) *Draw Conclusions*

I looked at Katie's spelling list on our way home.
"Try spelling **graceful**," she said.
"The **actor** who played a **brontosaurus** was **graceful**!" I said.

58

Activity

Cross Curricular: Social Studies

CAREERS Have students find examples in the text or illustrations for the following careers as they read the story: teacher, actor, ice-cream vendor, nurse, and pediatrician.

RESEARCH AND INQUIRY Have students brainstorm a list of professionals they know and create a bulletin-board display.
▶ **Spatial/Interpersonal**

"You're great at making up stories," said Katie.
"But the spelling bee is in three days!"

"I know," I said. Then I ran to get some ice cream.

I knew I had better study or I would really embarrass
myself at the spelling bee.

59

Guided Instruction

13 **PROBLEM AND SOLUTION** Let's think again about how a plot—the events that take place in a story—often concerns a problem that the main character has. Do you think that this is true so far about this story? Why do you say that? (So far, the events of this story have to do with Phoebe not wanting to be in the spelling bee. This is her problem.) *Analyze Plot*

14 **MAKE PREDICTIONS** What can you predict from the last sentence on this page? (Phoebe will find a way to prepare for the spelling bee.)

59

Guided Instruction

15
PROBLEM AND SOLUTION
Phoebe imagines she will win the contest if her paper airplane flies into the trash can. Do you think this is a good solution to her problem? *Make Judgments*

$\mathbb{S}$ELF-MONITORING

STRATEGY

SEARCH FOR CLUES Searching for clues on a page can help a reader figure out where or when part of a story is taking place.

MODEL When I got to this page I was confused. On the last page, Phoebe was getting ice cream. The pictures tell me that now she is in her pajamas. I can tell that it is nighttime now because her father says it is time for bed.

Fluency

READ WITH EXPRESSION

PARTNERS Have partners take turns reading aloud page 60. Point out the exclamation point at the end of the sixth paragraph.

Remind students to:

• think about how Phoebe is feeling and try to convey that feeling as they read.

• pause at the end of sentences.

• pause a little longer where there is extra space between paragraphs.

• vary the speed of the reading depending on the passage.

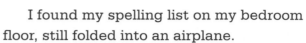

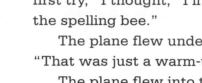

15 I found my spelling list on my bedroom floor, still folded into an airplane.

"If I can fly this into the trash can on the first try," I thought, "I'll be the winner of the spelling bee."

The plane flew under a chair.
"That was just a warm-up."

The plane flew into the wall.
"Didn't count."

I stood on a chair
and dropped the airplane
into the trash.
"Yes!"

I had a victory celebration
and danced around my room.
Then my father told me
it was time to go to bed.

60

The next morning Ms. Ravioli said we would have a mock spelling bee.

I decided it was time to get sick.

"Ooooh!" I moaned.

"What seems to be the problem?" asked Ms. Ravioli.

"I ate too many pieces of pizza with pineapple last night," I said. "I feel sick."

"I think a visit to the nurse's office would be a good idea," said Ms. Ravioli.

"You haven't studied at all, have you?" whispered Katie.

"Yes I have!" I said.

61

Guided Instruction

 MAKE PREDICTIONS Do you predict that Phoebe will do well in the mock spelling bee? Why do you think so? (Phoebe will not do well in the mock spelling bee because she has not studied for it.)

 DECODING/CONTEXT CLUES Look at the first sentence. Say the word spelled *m-o-c-k*. (mock) Do you know what the word means? Can you find any clues to the meaning?

 PREVENTION/INTERVENTION

DECODING/CONTEXT CLUES
Remind students to use the blending strategy to decode the word *mock*.

m o ck   mock

Help students also use context clues to find the word's meaning. Do they understand that it is not Friday yet and so this is not the real spelling bee, but a practice? Help students understand that *mock* means an imitation of something.

Guided Instruction

17 Who wants to role-play Phoebe for us? Phoebe, can you tell us what you are thinking as you walk down the hall to the nurse's office? *Character/Role-Play*

Visual Literacy

VIEWING AND REPRESENTING

Point out that you can tell a lot about the characters' feelings from their "body language," even if you cannot see their faces. Discuss the illustration on page 62: What does it show about how Phoebe is feeling? (Even though we can't see Phoebe's face, we can tell she is unhappy. Her shoulders are hunched, and her hands are thrust into her pockets.)

Ask students to draw several characters with bodies and heads, but no faces. Have students present their drawings to the class. Have other students try to guess the characters' feelings.

I dragged my feet to the nurse's office. Now my stomach really did feel awful.

I had never lied to Katie before. **18**

63

Guided Instruction

18 **PROBLEM AND SOLUTION** What new problem does Phoebe face now? Let's add to our chart.

PROBLEM	SOLUTION
Phoebe is not ready for the spelling bee.	
The class laughs at Phoebe when she uses spelling words to tell a story.	
Phoebe is upset because she lied to her friend Katie.	

Minilesson

REVIEW/MAINTAIN

Summarize

Review that good readers look for important details as they read. It is often useful to stop and summarize the most important details in order to understand the story.

• Ask students to review story events up to this point. What are the most important details of this story? How would you summarize what has happened so far?

Activity Have students write a short paragraph summarizing the most important details of the story to this point.

Guided Instruction

(19) **MAKE PREDICTIONS** How do you predict Phoebe will feel after she reads Katie's note? Does the picture help you make your prediction?

(20) Notice that the letters of Katie's note look different from the other letters on the page. Often, authors will use a different typeface to show an example of written text, like a note. Can you think of other examples that might be shown this way? (part of a newspaper article or book, telegram, student report, letter) *Author's Craft and Typographic Clues*

When I got back from the nurse's office, Katie handed me a note. It said:

YOU DIDN'T STUDY AND YOU **(19)** DIDN'T HAVE A STOMACHACHE AND REAL FRIENDS TELL EACH **(20)** OTHER THE TRUTH!

I didn't speak to Katie for the rest of the day.

64

Activity

Cross Curricular: Health

STRESS AND HEALTH Phoebe's stomach felt awful because she was upset about school and her friend. Point out that emotions such as stress or anxiety can affect how our bodies feel. Ask students:

• Are there things that give you stress?

• How does this make your body feel?

• What do you do to relieve the stress?

Ask students to talk to family, friends, and librarians about stress and how to relieve it. Have students present their findings to the class.

▶ **Logical/Interpersonal**

How to Relieve Stress
1. Make sure you get enough sleep.
2. Get exercise.
3. Take a hot bath.

That night I felt terrible. I hadn't been honest with my best friend, and I wasn't ready for the spelling bee. I looked at my spelling list.

The first word I learned was **method**. I thought of a caveman saying his name, "**Me**, **Thod**."

I learned **telephone** by thinking of a phone, which you *tell* your friends things on. The second **l** in **tell** becomes an **e**.

I even learned how to spell **consonant**. It was easy because I figured there were three parts, **con**, **son**, and **ant**.

65

Guided Instruction

21 **PROBLEM AND SOLUTION** In this paragraph, Phoebe is summarizing some of her problems. Can you state what they are? (She is not ready for the spelling bee. She has not been honest with her friend Katie.)

22 **PROBLEM AND SOLUTION** Has Phoebe found a solution to any of her problems? Let's see if we can add some information to our Problem/Solution chart.

PROBLEM	SOLUTION
Phoebe is not ready for the spelling bee.	She studies for the spelling bee.
The class laughs at Phoebe when she uses spelling words to tell a story.	
Phoebe is upset because she lied to her friend Katie.	

Minilesson
REVIEW/MAINTAIN
Inflectional Endings

Discuss how adding *-ed* to a verb changes its meaning. Write *learned* on the chalkboard. Ask a volunteer to name the base word and circle the ending. Review that *learn* tells about the present and *learned* tells about the past. Point out that if a verb already ends in *e*, the *e* is dropped before adding *-ed*. Have students find an example on page 65. *(figured)*

Activity Make a two-column chart. In the left column, write regular present-tense verbs such as *spell* and *lie*. In the right, have students add *-ed* to the word.

Guided Instruction

23 **MAKE PREDICTIONS** Do you predict that Phoebe will now do well in the spelling bee? Why or why not? (Phoebe is likely to do well because she has studied for the spelling bee.)

24 **PROBLEM AND SOLUTION** What problem is Phoebe trying to solve here? (Phoebe is trying to make up to Katie for having lied to her.)

TEACHING **TIP**

MANAGEMENT As students read aloud, make observations about fluency and decoding skills to determine where help may be needed. Classify problems by type, such as:

- reading rate

- fluency, accuracy, and expression

- decoding, using letter-sound correspondences

- recognizing common vowel spelling problems

23 The next day was Friday. Spelling bee day.
I brought Katie a tulip and said I was sorry for having lied.
24 Ms. Ravioli explained the rules. I could feel my heart beating fast. What if I looked stupid in front of the whole class?

66

I started to raise my hand to go to the nurse's office. I decided to have the flu.

Katie wished me good luck. I was happy she was still talking to me. I put down my hand.

I decided not to have the flu after all.

67

Guided Instruction

25 **PROBLEM AND SOLUTION** We know that Phoebe regrets having lied to her friend Katie. Do you think that Phoebe has solved this problem by apologizing and giving her a tulip? Explain. (Yes, because Katie wishes Phoebe good luck for the spelling bee. Phoebe realizes that Katie is still her friend.)

PHONICS KIT
HANDS-ON ACTIVITIES AND PRACTICE

Minilesson

REVIEW/MAINTAIN

Long *a* and Long *e*

Have students say the words *explained* and *raise* on pages 66 and 67. Ask:

• What vowel sound do these words have in common? (/ā/)

• How is the sound spelled in each word? (*ai*)

Have students say *bee* and *feel* on page 66.

• What vowel sound do these words have in common? (/ē/)

• How is the sound spelled in each word? (*ee*)

Activity Have students list other words with the /ē/ and /ā/ sounds and categorize the words according to the spelling of the sound.

Phonics CD-ROM Have students use the interactive phonics activities on the CD-ROM for more reinforcement.

LANGUAGE SUPPORT

ESL To help students understand the drama of a spelling bee, have a few volunteers demonstrate how a spelling bee works. Using simple words, have some students pretend to misspell a word and then have to sit down. The next person in line then spells the word correctly and remains standing.

Guided Instruction

26 Why do you think Jorge asked to go to the bathroom after not being able to spell the word *telephone*? (He may have been embarrassed, or he may not have felt well.)
Make Inferences

During the spelling bee, Sheldon couldn't spell **disaster**. So he had to sit down.

When Jorge couldn't spell **telephone** correctly, he asked to go to the bathroom. **26**

Marcia almost remembered how to spell **consonant**, but she forgot one of the **n**s.

I had to spell **Wednesday**. I knew the word had three parts, all with three letters.

I thought of a wedding day where chocolate chips were thrown instead of rice. **Wed** for wedding, **nes** for Nestlé chocolate, and **day**!

I spelled the word, "**W-e-d-n-e-s-d-a-y**."

"Nice job!" said Ms. Ravioli.

68

Activity

Cross Curricular: Math

MULTIPLICATION Point out to students that Phoebe says that she remembers how to spell *Wednesday* because it has three parts with three letters each. Challenge students to tell you how many letters are in *Wednesday*—without counting.

Ask how many letters would be in a word with four parts of four letters each and in a word with five parts of five letters each. Invite students to find the highest number they can multiply by itself. Ask if they think any word has so many letters.

▶ **Mathematical/Logical**

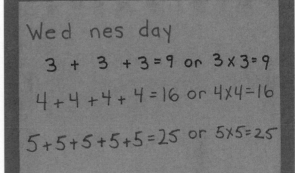

Wed nes day
$3 + 3 + 3 = 9$ or $3 \times 3 = 9$
$4 + 4 + 4 + 4 = 16$ or $4 \times 4 = 16$
$5 + 5 + 5 + 5 + 5 = 25$ or $5 \times 5 = 25$

Katie spelled her word perfectly.
"**N-a-t-u-r-a-l**," she said.

After a while there were only three of us still spelling, and then came **brontosaurus**. I tried sounding it out,
"**b-r-a-w-n-t-o-e-s-o-r-u-s**."

"That was a good try," said Ms. Ravioli, "but it's not the correct spelling."

"The **actor** was a **natural** and very **graceful**," I said. The whole class was staring at me.

69

Guided Instruction

27 **MAKE PREDICTIONS** Has Phoebe done well in the spelling bee? Was your prediction correct? (Phoebe has done well in the spelling bee. She is one of the last three remaining students.)

28 How would you describe Phoebe's character, based on the way she has tried to solve her problems? (She cares about her friends. She has a good imagination, and finds imaginative ways to solve her problems.) *Analyze Character*

LANGUAGE SUPPORT

ESL Ask Spanish-speaking students to help pronounce the name *Jorge* and explain the sounds made by the letters *j* and *g* in the Spanish language.

On a political map of North America, point out cities of San José in California, San Juan in Puerto Rico, and Tijuana in northwest Mexico.

Pronounce these names with students, and explain that these names are all taken from Spanish words. (Tijuana is from Spanish Tia Juana, meaning "Aunt Juana.")

Challenge students to share other Spanish words or names in which the letters *j* and *g* are pronounced differently than they are in English.

Guided Instruction

(29) **PROBLEM AND SOLUTION** Look at the pictures on these pages. What do you think the other students and Ms. Ravioli are feeling about Phoebe's spelling story? Do you think this will help her solve one of her problems?

MODEL I think they are enjoying Phoebe's story because they are smiling. They are not laughing at her.

WORD STRUCTURE Phoebe uses the words *brontosaurus* and *dinosaur* a lot in this story. Does anyone notice a similar part in both words? *(saur)*

"The **a-c-t-o-r** played a **brontosaurus** and met a caveman who said, '**Me**, **Thod**,' which is how you break down the spelling of **method**. Thod asked the dinosaur if he had heard about the volcano **disaster**. The dinosaur said no, but he wondered if Thod knew what a **c-o-n-s-o-n-a-n-t** was."

I looked at Ms. Ravioli.

"Please continue," she said.

So I did. "Thod and the dinosaur heard a **t-e-l-e-p-h-o-n-e** ringing in a tree!"

Katie smiled.

(29)

70

 PREVENTION/INTERVENTION

WORD STRUCTURE Write the words *brontosaurus* and *dinosaur* on the chalkboard. Explain that *brontosaurus* is a particular kind of *dinosaur*. Invite a volunteer to circle the part of each word that is the same.

After the student has circled *saur* in both words, explain that *saur* means *lizard*. Help students conclude that the people who named these creatures thought they must have been like lizards. Ask students to think of other dinosaur names that have *saur* or *saurus* in them.

"The call was for a **p-e-d-e-s-t-r-i-a-n** who was jogging by, eating a piece of **c-h-o-c-o-l-a-t-e**." I told my class that a great way to remember how to spell chocolate is to think of someone named *Choco*, who's *late*. **30**

"When Choco saw the **brontosaurus**, he screamed and ran the other way! The caveman and the dinosaur fell on the ground and laughed!" **31**

71

Guided Instruction

30 **PROBLEM AND SOLUTION** Phoebe found a new way to learn the spelling list. Do you think this was a good way to solve her problem of not being ready for the spelling bee? Why do you think this? (Students might suggest that it is a good method for someone with an active imagination.) *Make Judgments*

31 Can you think of some other words that can be spelled using Phoebe's method? Can you think of some words that cannot be spelled in this way? (Students might suggest that single-syllable words wouldn't work with Phoebe's method.) *Comparison and Contrast*

Minilesson
REVIEW/MAINTAIN
Make Inferences

Review that good readers use story clues and their own knowledge to understand the feelings and emotions of characters.

• Ask students to look at what Ms. Ravioli says on page 70. What do they infer Ms. Ravioli is feeling at that moment? Why does she ask Phoebe to continue?

Activity Have students write a sentence in which they state how they think Katie felt on page 70 and why.

Guided Instruction

32 **PROBLEM AND SOLUTION** How did Phoebe try to solve her problem of the class laughing at her? Did she succeed? Why do you think so? (Phoebe showed them a new way to learn spelling words. They clapped for her.)

33 **PROBLEM AND SOLUTION** Let's see if we can complete our Problem/Solution chart now.

PROBLEM	SOLUTION
Phoebe is not ready for the spelling bee.	She studies for the spelling bee.
The class laughs at Phoebe when she uses spelling words to tell a story.	She shows them a new way to learn spelling words.
Phoebe is upset because she lied to her friend Katie.	Phoebe apologizes to Katie and gives her a tulip.

RETELL THE STORY Ask volunteers to retell the major events of the story, referring to their charts if they need to. Then have partners write a few sentences that summarize the story. Have them focus on Phoebe's main problem and how it is solved. *Summarize*

STUDENT SELF-ASSESSMENT

- How did the Problem/Solution chart help me understand the story?
- How did using the strategy of Make Predictions help me?
  TRANSFERRING THE STRATEGY
- When might I use the Problem/Solution chart again? In what other reading might predicting outcomes help me?

"That's the **l-e-g-e-n-d** of Thod and the brontosaurus. You can remember how to spell legend by thinking of your **leg** and **end**!"

Everybody clapped when I finished. Even though I **32** couldn't spell **brontosaurus**, I had used up all the words on my list to tell a story. Charlie couldn't spell **33** **brontosaurus** either—but Katie could, so she won the spelling bee. She was great!

72

REREADING FOR *Fluency*

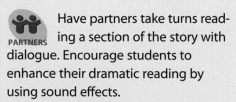 Have partners take turns reading a section of the story with dialogue. Encourage students to enhance their dramatic reading by using sound effects.

READING RATE You may want to evaluate a student's reading rate. Have the student read aloud from *Phoebe and the Spelling Bee* for one minute. Ask the student to place a self-stick note

after the last word read. Then count the number of words he or she has read.

Alternatively, you could assess small groups or the whole class together by having students count words and record their own scores.

A Running Record form provided in **Diagnostic/Placement Evaluation** will help you evaluate reading rate(s).

Ms. Ravioli gave Katie a certificate that said CHAMPION SPELLER.

I got a certificate, too, only mine said WONDERFUL IMAGINATION*!*

73

Guided Instruction

Return to Predictions and Purposes

Review with students their story predictions and reasons for reading the story.

PREDICTIONS	HOW IT TURNED OUT
The story is about a girl with a good imagination.	Phoebe uses her imagination to help her learn how to spell.
She is unhappy about something in school.	Phoebe is unhappy about being in the spelling bee.
The story will be realistic.	The story was realistic.

PROBLEM AND SOLUTION

HOW TO ASSESS

• Have students describe how Phoebe's personality helped her to solve her problems.

• Ask how the events of the plot arose because of Phoebe's original problem.

Students should recognize that Phoebe was able to use her imagination to come up with solutions to her problems.

FOLLOW UP

If students have trouble analyzing how Phoebe's character influenced her problem solving, ask them how other people might have solved the same problems.

If students have trouble connecting plot events to Phoebe's problem, ask them if the various events would have happened if Phoebe had been ready for the spelling bee.

LITERARY RESPONSE

QUICK-WRITE Invite students to record their thoughts about the story. These questions may help them get started:

• How would you describe Phoebe?

• What did you think of the way Phoebe solved her problems?

• What will you remember about this story?

ORAL RESPONSE Have students share their journal writings and discuss what part of the story they enjoyed most.

Story Questions

Have students answer the questions on page 74.

Answers:

1. Phoebe wanted to avoid the mock spelling bee. *Literal/Problem and Solution*

2. She broke words down and created stories. *Inferential/Character*

3. Answers will vary. Possible answer: Phoebe would win because she had found such a useful way to remember her spelling list. *Inferential/Make Predictions*

4. A girl who doesn't want to be in a spelling bee, but then finds a creative way to learn how to spell. *Critical/Summarize*

5. They rode their bikes every day and ate well. *Critical/Reading Across Texts*

Write a Personal Narrative For a full writing process lesson on Personal Narrative see pages 77K–77L.

Story Questions & Activities

1. Why did Phoebe pretend to feel sick?

2. What was unusual about the way that Phoebe learned to spell words?

3. Did you think that Phoebe might win the spelling bee? Explain.

4. What is this story mostly about?

5. Phoebe got ready for the spelling bee by thinking of a clever way to learn the words. How do you think the bike racers in the painting on pages 48–49 got ready for their race?

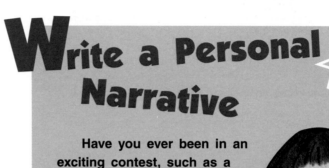

Write a Personal Narrative

Have you ever been in an exciting contest, such as a race or a game? Write about what happened. Tell how you felt before, during, and after the contest.

Meeting Individual Needs

EASY	ON-LEVEL	CHALLENGE
Name_____ Date_____ **Reteach 9**	Name_____ Date_____ **Practice 10**	Name_____ Date_____ **Extend 9**
Vocabulary	**Story Comprehension**	**Vocabulary**

EASY

Vocabulary

Use the correct word from the list.

continue correct embarrass groaning legend unusual

1. The story was very ___unusual___. But it wasn't a tall tale or a ___legend___. It was a true story!

2. I don't know the ___correct___ way to spell your name. Let me ___continue___ thinking about it.

3. My little cousin kept making these ___groaning___ sounds. Everyone was laughing! I told him that he didn't ___embarrass___ me at all!

Story Comprehension   Reteach 10

1. How does Phoebe avoid studying for the spelling bee? __Possible answers: by pretending to be sick, hiding, playing__

2. How does Phoebe remember the spelling of difficult words? __She breaks up the words and makes up stories about them.__

3. How does Phoebe remember how to spell *legend*? __She thinks of a leg and end.__

4. How does Phoebe probably feel after the spelling bee? __Possible answers: She is proud of herself; she is happy.__

9–10   At Home: Have students write a paragraph about the way they remember how to spell a word.   Book 3.1/Unit 1 **Phoebe and the Spelling Bee**

Reteach, 10

ON-LEVEL

Story Comprehension

Answer the questions about "Phoebe and the Spelling Bee."

1. Why is Phoebe afraid of Friday? __Phoebe is afraid because Mrs. Ravioli has planned a spelling bee.__

2. Why does Phoebe pretend to be sick at school? __She hasn't studied her spelling words.__

3. How is Katie different from her friend Phoebe? __Katie likes spelling, and she is not afraid of the spelling bee.__

4. How does Phoebe upset Katie? __Phoebe lied to her and the class.__

5. How does Phoebe make up for what she does to Katie? __She gives Katie a tulip and studies hard for the spelling bee.__

6. Why do Phoebe and Katie get certificates? __Katie gets her certificate for good spelling. Phoebe gets hers for good imagination.__

10   At Home: Have students choose a word they find difficult to spell. Then have them make a sign that gives a spelling tip for that word. Post the signs in a place where everyone can see them.   Book 3.1/Unit 1 **Phoebe and the Spelling Bee**

Practice, 10

CHALLENGE

Vocabulary

The correct spelling of some words is difficult to remember. Make up a short and funny story using these words and illustrate it.

continue correct legend unusual embarrass groaning

Do you find these words difficult to spell? Tell how you can remember them.

__Answers will vary. For example, some students might say that they remember there are 3 u's in *unusual*.__

Extend 10

Story Comprehension

Phoebe had a special way of studying her spelling words. Turn Phoebe's solution into a play. Have each person in your group take a character. First, find lines from the story for your character. Then predict what your character might say, and write some lines on your own. Act out the play you have written. Give the play a new ending.

9–10   At Home: Ask students to cut challenging spelling words out of magazines. Discuss how you can remember these words.   Book 3.1/Unit 1 **Phoebe and the Spelling Bee**

Extend, 10

Create a Poster

Gather information about the brontosaurus or another dinosaur. Use what you learn to make a poster. Include a drawing and some fun facts.

Make Your Own Spelling Book

Choose three words that you find difficult to spell. Write each word on one side of a piece of paper. On the other side, draw a picture that will remind you of how to spell the word. Punch a hole in the pages and tie them together with yarn to make a book.

Find Out More

Many words, like *consonant*, can be broken into smaller words. Flip through a dictionary and find a few such words. Then, with a partner, play a game of charades and try to guess each other's words.

75

Story Activities

Create a Poster

Materials: encyclopedia, poster board, pencils, colored markers

GROUP Have each group choose a dinosaur and find interesting facts in the encyclopedia to use in a poster. After groups have finished their posters, allow time to discuss them with the class.

Make Your Own Spelling Book

Materials: paper, pencil, colored markers, hole punch, yarn

ONE If students choose spelling words of two syllables or more for their Spelling Books, they can divide each word into syllables and add illustrations that will remind them of the individual syllables.

Find Out More

RESEARCH AND INQUIRY Guide students in using the dictionary to **PARTNERS** find longer words that are made up of smaller words. Let students act out each of these smaller words so that their partners can guess the whole.

 Have students visit **www.mhschool.com/reading**.

After page 75, see the Selection Assessment.

Study Skills

PARTS OF A BOOK

OBJECTIVES Students will:

- identify elements of a glossary.
- use a glossary to learn spelling, definitions, and parts of speech.

PREPARE Preview the glossary sample with students. Display **Teaching Chart 9**.

TEACH Review the elements of a glossary, including guide words, parts of speech, and definitions. Choose a word and have students identify its part of speech and its definition.

PRACTICE Have students answer questions 1–5. Review the answers with them. **1.** *Bound* **2.** Noun **3.** Before; the first letter *a* comes before the first letter *b* **4.** *bamboo/buffalo* **5.** Some leaves; The brontosaurus ate plants.

ASSESS/CLOSE Have students create a glossary page using the six vocabulary words from the selection.

Use a Glossary

A **glossary** can help you to spell a word correctly or to learn the meaning of a word. The words in a glossary appear in alphabetical order. Guide words at the top tell you the first and last words on the page.

B

bamboo/buffalo

bamboo A tall plant that is related to grass. The bamboo has woody stems that are often hollow and are used to make fishing poles, canes, and furniture. *Noun.*
—Made of *bamboo. Adjective.*
bam•boo (bam bü′) *noun, plural*
bamboos; *adjective.*

Word History
The word **bamboo** comes from the Malay word *bambu* for the same plant.

bamboo

Bapa Raja (bä′pə rä′jə).

beneath 1. Lower than; below; under. We stood *beneath* the stars. 2. Unworthy of. Telling a lie is *beneath* you.
be•neath (bi nēth′) *preposition.*

bound 1. To leap; spring; jump. The rabbit *bounded* away into the woods. 2. To spring back after hitting something. The ball *bounded* off the wall and hit my bicycle.
bound (bound) *verb,* **bounded, bounding.**

brontosaurus A huge, plant-eating dinosaur with a long neck and tail and a small head. This dinosaur is also called *brontosaur.*
bron•to•saurus (bron′tə sôrəs′) *noun.*

buffalo A large North American animal that has a big hump on its back; bison. Many years ago *buffalo* roamed free on the plains.
buf•fa•lo (buf′ ə lō) *noun, plural*
buffaloes or **buffalos** or **buffalo.**

Use the glossary to answer these questions.

1 What word comes before *brontosaurus* in the **glossary**?

2 Is *brontosaurus* a noun, a verb, or an adjective?

3 To find out what the word *actor* means, would you look before or after this page in the glossary? Explain.

4 What are the guide words for the page on which *brontosaurus* appears?

5 Which do you think a brontosaurus would rather eat, meat or leaves?

Meeting Individual Needs

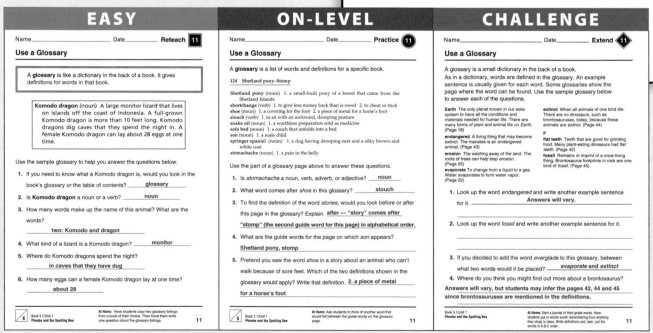

EASY

Name _____ Date _____ **Reteach** 11

Use a Glossary

A **glossary** is like a dictionary in the back of a book. It gives definitions for words in that book.

Komodo dragon (noun) A large monitor lizard that lives on islands off the coast of Indonesia. A full-grown Komodo dragon is more than 10 feet long. Komodo dragons dig caves that they spend the night in. A female Komodo dragon can lay about 28 eggs at one time.

Use the sample glossary to help you answer the questions below.

1. If you need to know what a Komodo dragon is, would you look in the book's glossary or the table of contents? __glossary__

2. Is **Komodo dragon** a noun or a verb? __noun__

3. How many words make up the name of this animal? What are the words?
__two: Komodo and dragon__

4. What kind of a lizard is a Komodo dragon? __monitor__

5. Where do Komodo dragons spend the night?
__in caves that they have dug__

6. How many eggs can a female Komodo dragon lay at one time?
__about 28__

Book 3.1/Unit 1
Phoebe and the Spelling Bee
At Home: Have students copy two glossary listings from a book of their choice. Then have them write one question about the glossary listings. 11

ON-LEVEL

Name _____ Date _____ **Practice** 11

Use a Glossary

A **glossary** is a list of words and definitions for a specific book.

124 Shetland pony–Stomp

Shetland pony (noun) 1. a small-built pony of a breed that came from the Shetland Islands
shortchange (verb) 1. to give less money back than is owed 2. to cheat or trick
shoe (noun) 1. a covering for the foot 2. a piece of metal for a horse's foot
slouch (verb) 1. to sit with an awkward, drooping posture
snake oil (noun) 1. a worthless preparation sold as medicine
sofa bed (noun) 1. a couch that unfolds into a bed
son (noun) 1. a male child
springer spaniel (noun) 1. a dog having drooping ears and a silky brown and white coat
stomachache (noun) 1. a pain in the belly

Use the part of a glossary page above to answer these questions.

1. Is *stomachache* a noun, verb, adverb, or adjective? __noun__

2. What word comes after *shoe* in this glossary? __slouch__

3. To find the definition of the word *stories*, would you look before or after this page in the glossary? Explain. __after — "story" comes after "stomp" (the second guide word for this page) in alphabetical order.__

4. What are the guide words for the page on which *son* appears?
__Shetland pony, stomp__

5. Pretend you saw the word *shoe* in a story about an animal who can't walk because of sore feet. Which of the two definitions shown in the glossary would apply? Write that definition. __2. a piece of metal for a horse's foot__

Book 3.1/Unit 1
Phoebe and the Spelling Bee
At Home: Ask students to think of another word that would fall between the guide words on this glossary page. 11

CHALLENGE

Name _____ Date _____ **Extend** 11

Use a Glossary

A glossary is a small dictionary in the back of a book. As in a dictionary, words are defined in the glossary. An example sentence is usually given for each word. Some glossaries show the page where the word can be found. Use the sample glossary below to answer each of the questions.

Earth The only planet known in our solar system to have all the conditions and materials needed for human life. There are many forms of plant and animal life on *Earth.* (Page 18)
endangered A living thing that may become extinct. The manatee is an *endangered* animal. (Page 43)
erosion The washing away of the land. The roots of trees can help stop *erosion.* (Page 25)
evaporate To change from a liquid to a gas. Water *evaporates* to form water vapor. (Page 22)

extinct When all animals of one kind die. There are no dinosaurs, such as brontosauruses, today, because these animals are extinct. (Page 44)
F
flat teeth Teeth that are good for grinding food. Many plant-eating dinosaurs had *flat teeth.* (Page 42)
fossil Remains or imprint of a once-living thing. Brontosaurus footprints in rock are one kind of *fossil.* (Page 45)

1. Look up the word *endangered* and write another example sentence for it. _____ **Answers will vary.**

2. Look up the word *fossil* and write another example sentence for it. _____

3. If you decided to add the word *everglade* to this glossary, between what two words would it be placed? __evaporate and extinct__

4. Where do you think you might find out more about a brontosaurus? __Answers will vary, but students may infer the pages 42, 44 and 45 since brontosauruses are mentioned in the definitions.__

Book 3.1/Unit 1
Phoebe and the Spelling Bee
At Home: Start a journal of third grade words. Have students put in words worth remembering from anything they study in class. Write definitions and, later, put the words in A-B-C order. 11

Reteach, 11   **Practice, 11**   **Extend, 11**

TEST POWER

DIRECTIONS:
Read the story. Then read each question about the story.

SAMPLE

A Pet for Bobby

Bobby's new dog Lucky did not listen. Every time Bobby said, "Sit," Lucky wagged his tail. Bobby was worried.

One day, Bobby had an idea. He went to the kitchen and got some dog biscuits. Then he went out to the backyard. Lucky came up to him, his tail wagging.

"Sit, Lucky! Sit!" Bobby said. But Lucky just wagged his tail.

Bobby took out a dog biscuit and held it above Lucky's head. Lucky just looked at the biscuit.

"Sit, Lucky!" Bobby said. Lucky did not understand. Bobby moved the biscuit a little until Lucky had to sit back to keep it in sight. "Sit, Lucky!"

Bobby said as Lucky sat. Bobby petted his dog and gave him the biscuit as a reward.

1 The next time he wants Lucky to listen, Bobby will probably—

○ not be able to find Lucky

● get a dog biscuit for Lucky

○ get Lucky's leash

○ bring a friend's dog over

2 How did Bobby feel when he first tried to get Lucky to sit?

○ Happy

○ Sad

○ Quiet

● Worried

77

Test Power

THE PRINCETON REVIEW

Read the Page

Have students read the story, questions, and answer choices. Tell students to choose the best answer choice.

Discuss the Questions

QUESTION 1: This question requires students to predict what Bobby will do the next time he wants Lucky to listen to him. Direct students to recall from the story what Bobby did to achieve his desired goal.

QUESTION 2: This question requires students to understand Bobby's feelings. Teach students to get in the habit of thinking about how characters feel. As students work through the answer choices, have them use process of elimination. For example, the first answer choice is "happy." Ask students if it is likely, given the information in the story, that Bobby was happy when Lucky would not sit?

ITBS/TEST PREPARATION

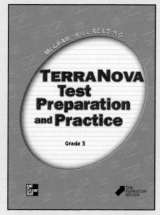

TERRANOVA/TEST PREPARATION

SAT 9/TEST PREPARATION

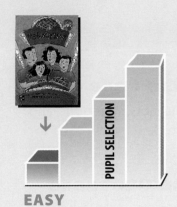

EASY

Answers to Story Questions

1. The Garzas were going to Orlando, Florida, to be on a TV game show called *The Family Game*.
2. Mrs. Garza rolled her eyes because she had spent so much time deciding what to wear on the show and she had to wear the standard *Family Game* T-shirt.
3. Paco would be pretending he didn't know the answer.
4. The Garza family goes on a TV game show.
5. Answers will vary.

Story Questions and Writing Activity

1. Where were the Garzas going?
2. Why did Mrs. Garza roll her eyes when they brought out the T-shirts?
3. What would it have meant if Paco had taken the pie?
4. What is the story mostly about?
5. If Phoebe from *Phoebe and the Spelling Bee* had been on the other team, how do you think her family would have done?

Be a TV Game Show Writer

Write five to ten more questions that Jason Jarman could have asked the families on *The Family Game*.

from *The Family Game*

Leveled Books

EASY

The Family Game

Long *a* and Long *e*
☑ **Problem and Solution**
☑ **Instructional Vocabulary:** *continue, correct, embarrass, groaning, legend, unusual*

Guided Reading

PREVIEW AND PREDICT Conduct a **picture walk**. Have students discuss the illustrations and predict what they think the story will be about. What do they think the TV show will be like? Review the words *groaning* and *embarrass* (page 2).

SET PURPOSES Students should decide what they want to find out as they read the story. For example, they might want to know the rules of the quiz show.

READ THE BOOK Have students read the story independently as you observe their reading behaviors. Then return to the text for opportunities to teach.

Pages 2–3: How does Mr. Garza feel about the family appearing on the show? (worried) What does Carla say to reassure him? (that it will be fun) *Problem and Solution*

Page 4: What does the word *unusual* mean? Is Mr. Garza telling the truth when he says it? Why or why not? (No. He is teasing.) *Vocabulary/Make Inferences*

Page 5: What words in the first sentence have the long *a* sound? (*amazed, they*) What other words can you think of that

have the long *a* spelled in each of these ways? *Phonics and Decoding*

Page 9: What do you get for a correct answer? (one point) What happens if you give a wrong answer? (You lose a point or get a pie in the face.) *Problem and Solution*

Pages 12–13: How does Carla come up with the right answer? (She thinks and thinks.) *Problem and Solution*

Page 16: Why does Carla's face turn red? (She's embarrassed.) *Character*

RETURN TO PREDICTIONS AND PURPOSES Review students' predictions and reasons for reading.

LITERARY RESPONSE Discuss these questions:

• What questions would you ask if you were the producer or host of the show?

• What was your favorite part of the story?

Also see the story questions and activity in *The Family Game*.

See the **Phonics** **CD-ROM** for practice using long *a* and long *e* words.

Leveled Books

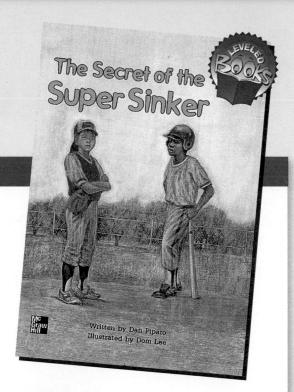

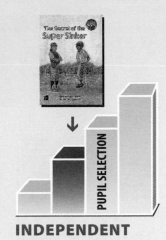

INDEPENDENT

The Secret of the Super Sinker

☑ **Problem and Solution**

☑ **Instructional Vocabulary:**
continue, correct, embarrass, groaning, legend, unusual

Guided Reading

PREVIEW AND PREDICT Conduct a **picture walk.** As they discuss the illustrations, ask students to predict what the story will be about. Chart their ideas.

SET PURPOSES Students should decide what they want to find out as they read the story. For example, they might want to know what the secret of a super sinker might be.

READ THE BOOK Have students first read the story independently. When they finish, return to the text to apply strategies.

Page 3: What does the pitcher do before she throws the ball? (wipes her forehead, tugs her cap) What does Jake say to himself? ("How did I mess up?") *Character and Setting*

Page 6: What does Jake mean when he says that he's not going down in Little League *legend* for this game? (Legendary figures are usually winners.) *Vocabulary*

Pages 8–9: What does Jenny think about Sally? (that Sally is cheating) Do you think Jenny is right or wrong? Why? (Answers will vary.) *Make Predictions*

Page 14: How does Jake prove that Jenny was right? (He finds grease on Sally's cap.) *Problem and Solution*

Page 15: Why do Jake, Manny, and Jenny feel so bad when they are right? (because they feel sorry for Sally) *Character*

RETURN TO PREDICTIONS AND PURPOSES Review students' predictions and reasons for reading. Did they find out what they wanted to know?

LITERARY RESPONSE Ask students to discuss questions like these:

- What would you do if you were on Sally's team and you knew her secret?

- What do you think should happen to Sally?

Also see the story questions and activity in *The Secret of the Super Sinker.*

INDEPENDENT

Answers to Story Questions

1. The main characters are Jenny, Jake, and Sally.
2. Jenny. She spoke to Jake, who tested the idea.
3. Sally always touched her cap before she threw the sinkerball that Jake couldn't hit.
4. The story is about a group of friends on a baseball team, who discover the pitcher on the other team is cheating. They resolve it quietly and effectively by speaking with the pitcher face to face.
5. Answers will vary.

Story Questions and Writing Activity

1. Who are the main characters?
2. Who had an idea that the pitcher might be cheating?
3. What did Jake observe that helped him figure out the secret?
4. What is the story mostly about?
5. If Phoebe from *Phoebe and the Spelling Bee* played on Jake's team, how might the story have been different?

Super Sports Sleuth

Write a mystery using your favorite sport as the setting. Remember to include details that the reader can use for clues. Let your readers figure out the solution to the mystery. Write the solution on the back of your paper.

from The Secret of the Super Sinker

Leveled Books

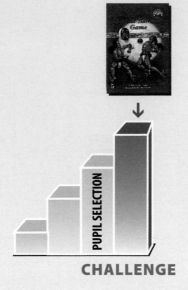

PUPIL SELECTION

CHALLENGE

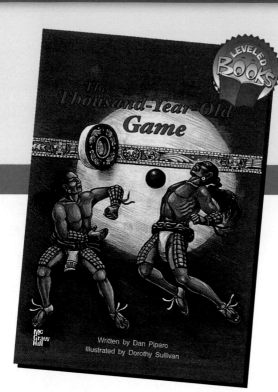

CHALLENGE

The Thousand-Year-Old Game

☑ **Problem and Solution**

☑ **Instructional Vocabulary:** *continue, correct, embarrass, groaning, legend, unusual*

Written by Dan Piparo
Illustrated by Dorothy Sullivan

Guided Reading

PREVIEW AND PREDICT Have students read the first two paragraphs. Ask: When do you think the story takes place? Why? What do you think will happen at the game? Ask students to chart their predictions in their journals.

SET PURPOSES Students should decide what they want to find out as they read the story. For example, they might want to know more about how the thousand-year-old game is played, or who wins the match.

READ THE BOOK Have students first read the stories independently as you monitor their reading behaviors. Then return to the text for opportunities to teach.

Page 3: How are the two brothers different? How are they alike? (One wants to be a player; the other wants to be a warrior. Both think they know what they want to be.) *Character*

Page 4: How was the boys' great-grandfather able to create a garden? (He built a reed mat, placed soil on top, and anchored it by planting trees.) *Problem and Solution*

Page 5: What is the legend of the Two Brothers that led to the sacred sport?

(There had been a battle between gods.) What is the difference between a legend and a true story? (A legend is not necessarily true.) *Vocabulary*

Page 10: What does each team try to do? (get the ball in the end zone) How else can teams score? (by hitting the ball through the ring) *Problem and Solution*

Page 13: Do you think Smoke Monkey will change his mind about becoming a player? Why or why not? (Possible answer: Yes, because a player can be a hero.) *Make Predictions*

RETURN TO PREDICTIONS AND PURPOSES Review students' predictions and purposes for reading. Did students find out what they wanted to know?

LITERARY RESPONSES Discuss these questions:

• Why might someone look up to an adult who was a great competitor?

• Why was Jaguar proud of his sons?

• Why might a great player become a hero?

Also see the story questions and activity in *The Thousand-Year-Old Game.*

Answers to Story Questions

1. It is called Tlachtli.
2. You would take the ball down to the other team's end zone by hitting it with your hips or knees. When the ball bounced off the wall of the end zone you would score a point. Getting the ball through the ring would end the game.
3. Possible answers: It is played on a court, it uses a ball, it has end zones, players wear pads to protect themselves, players hit the ball with their knees and hips.
4. It is about a ball game called Tlachtli played by the ancient Aztecs. The story tells how the game was played, and the type of court it was played on.
5. Answers will vary.

Story Questions and Writing Activity

1. What is the name of the Aztec ball game?
2. How would you score a point if you were playing Tlachtli?
3. How is the Aztec ball game like other sports you know?
4. What is the story mostly about?
5. If Two Deer and Smoke Monkey ever met Phoebe from *Phoebe and the Spelling Bee*, what would they talk about?

Court Sports

Make a drawing of what the Tlachtli court looked like. Label the different parts of the court. Write a brief description telling how the court is similar to a football field.

from The Thousand-Year-Old Game

Activities

Anthology and Leveled Books

Connecting Texts

CONTEST CHARTS
Write the story titles on a chart. Discuss with students the connections between the contests in the books. Call on volunteers from each reading level to explain the rules of the contest in each book.

Phoebe and the Spelling Bee	The Family Game	The Secret of the Super Sinker	The Thousand-Year-Old Game
• A spelling bee is held. • Phoebe does better than she thought she would.	• A family is accepted on a quiz show. • The game is more fun than they imagined.	• A Little League player doubts his abilities as a hitter. • He discovers that the pitcher is cheating.	• A father takes his sons to watch a sport he used to play. • They hope someday to play the sport, too.

Viewing/Representing

GROUP PRESENTATIONS Divide the class into groups, one for each of the four books. Have each group draw up rules for a class contest and read them to the class.

AUDIENCE RESPONSE Ask students to participate in each group's contest. Allow time for questions after each contest ends. Have students list rules for the contest such as these:

CONTEST RULES

1. Describe something.

2. Do not name it.

3. The person who guesses what it is wins.

Research and Inquiry

MORE ABOUT CONTESTS Have students ask themselves: What else would I like to know about contests and competitions? Then invite them to do the following:

- Look in encyclopedias to learn more about the rules of their own favorite games.

- Read about the rules of an ancient sport.

- Interview an adult about an important contest he or she once participated in.

interNET CONNECTION Students can find out more about this topic by visiting **www.mhschool.com/reading**.

Children can write and draw what they learned in their journals.

OBJECTIVES

Students will define problems and analyze possible solutions to them.

Review Problem and Solution

PREPARE

Discuss Problem and Solution

Review: In many stories, the plot centers on a problem of the main character. The story tells how the main character tries to solve the problem. Ask students how the main character in *Phoebe and the Spelling Bee* tried to solve her problem.

TEACH

Read "Posters by Phoebe" and Model the Skill

Ask students to pay close attention to problem and solution as you read the **Teaching Chart 10** passage with them.

Posters by Phoebe

Phoebe wanted to make posters for the bake sale. Ms. Ravioli said she could, if her drawings were good enough. So Phoebe drew a chocolate cake. "What a lovely picture of a table," Ms. Ravioli gushed. Phoebe wanted to hide.

Phoebe tried again with the drawing of a giant chocolate chip cookie. "Oh, that pizza looks delicious," Ms. Ravioli said, "but we are not selling pizza." Phoebe decided never to draw again.

Then Phoebe had an idea. She put real icing on her drawing of the cake and glued real chocolate chips to her drawing of the cookie. "What wonderful posters," Ms. Ravioli said. "They look good enough to eat."

Teaching Chart 10

Ask a volunteer to find and underline a sentence that tells what Phoebe wanted to do. Help students think about Phoebe's problems and how she solved them.

MODEL Phoebe wanted to make the posters for the bake sale. She tried twice, but both times Ms. Ravioli did not recognize what Phoebe had drawn. Her problem was that none of her drawings looked like what they were supposed to be.

Create a Problem/ Solution Chart

GROUP

Have students create a Problem/Solution chart for "Posters by Phoebe." ▶ **Interpersonal/Visual**

PROBLEM	SOLUTION
Phoebe wants to make posters for the bake sale but cannot draw well enough.	She uses real icing and chocolate chips in her drawings.

ASSESS/CLOSE

Write a Paragraph with a New Solution

In groups, have students imagine another solution for Phoebe's problem with the posters. Have each group write a paragraph describing its solution and present it to the class. Ask the class to discuss whether each was a good solution to Phoebe's problem.

ALTERNATE TEACHING STRATEGY

PROBLEM AND SOLUTION

For a different approach to teaching this skill, see page T64.

SELF-SELECTED Reading

Students may choose from the following titles.

ANTHOLOGY

- *Phoebe and the Spelling Bee*

LEVELED READERS

- *The Family Game*
- *The Secret of the Super Sinker*
- *The Thousand-Year-Old Game*

Bibliography, pages T76–T77

Meeting Individual Needs for Comprehension

EASY	ON-LEVEL	CHALLENGE	LANGUAGE SUPPORT

EASY

Name_____ Date_____ Reteach **12**

Problem and Solution

A **problem** is the difficulty or challenge that a character in a story faces. The **solution** is the way in which a character solves his or her problem.

Read the stories below. Then write the problem and the solution for each of the stories.

Three friends are at a picnic. Josie has only one piece of cake. Kim and Rosa didn't bring dessert to the picnic. Josie has an idea. She breaks her cake into three pieces. Now everyone can have dessert!

PROBLEM: There is only one piece of cake.

SOLUTION: Josie breaks the cake into three pieces, so everyone can have dessert.

There are twelve students. All of them want to be on the tennis team. Mr. Danforth needs only six players on the team. He would like everyone to get the chance to play. Finally, he decides to create two teams.

PROBLEM: Mr. Danforth needs only six players on the tennis team. Twelve students want to be on the team.

SOLUTION: Mr. Danforth decides to create two tennis teams.

At Home: Invite students to name an important problem a character faces in a movie they know. Have them explain how the problem is solved.

12   Book 3.1/Unit 1   *Phoebe and the Spelling Bee*   4

Reteach, 12

ON-LEVEL

Name_____ Date_____ Practice **12**

Problem and Solution

One subject in school presents **problems** for the main character in "Phoebe and the Spelling Bee." Read each problem in the chart below. Then write the solution Phoebe finds for the problem.

Problem	Solution
1. Phoebe needs to learn how to spell **actor** correctly.	1. She thinks of the word act and or in a sentence.
2. On Tuesday, Mrs. Ravioli asks Phoebe if she's looked at the spelling list yet. Phoebe has not spent a lot of time on spelling.	2. Phoebe shares a sentence with the class that shows that she has at least read the words.
3. Mrs. Ravioli gives a practice spelling bee, and Phoebe is not ready for it.	3. Phoebe pretends she is sick and goes to the nurse's office.
4. Katie is mad at Phoebe for lying to her.	4. Phoebe brings Katie a tulip and says she is sorry.
5. Phoebe wants to learn how to spell the word **method**.	5. She makes up a story about a caveman whose name is Me, Thod.
6. Phoebe misspells the word **brontosaurus**.	6. She shares her spelling stories with the class, and everyone enjoys them.

At Home: Have students use Phoebe's spelling techniques. Have them write stories to help them remember this week's spelling words.

12   Book 3.1/Unit 1   *Phoebe and the Spelling Bee*   5

Practice, 12

CHALLENGE

Name_____ Date_____ Extend **12**

Problem and Solution

Most problems have solutions. Some solutions are good. Other solutions are not so good. For each problem Phoebe had, write her solution. Then tell whether the solution was good or not so good. Answers may vary.

1. Katie tried to help Phoebe spell brontosaurus.

Solution: Phoebe fell to the ground, blamed the brontosaurus, and raced Katie back to class. This was not a good solution.

2. Katie called Phoebe to find out how she was doing with her spelling list.

Solution: Phoebe said "great," but she was really folding the spelling list into paper airplanes. This was not a good solution.

3. Ms. Ravioli announced a mock spelling bee. Phoebe was nervous.

Phoebe pretended she was sick, went to the nurse's office, and lied to Katie. This was not a good solution.

4. Phoebe felt very bad about lying to Katie.

Solution: Phoebe studied her spelling list, brought Katie a tulip, and told Katie that she was sorry for lying. This was a good solution.

5. Ms. Ravioli started the spelling bee.

Solution: Phoebe started to raise her hand to go to the nurse's office, but she decided not to have the flu. This was a good solution.

At Home: Debate Phoebe's and Katie's ways of learning spelling. Which works better?

12   Book 3.1/Unit 1   *Phoebe and the Spelling Bee*

Extend, 12

LANGUAGE SUPPORT

Name_____ Date_____

Match the Solution to the Problem

She made up stories to remember the word parts. ③	She could break words into small parts. ①	She pretended to be sick. ②

Problem	Solution
1. Phoebe did not know how to sound out spelling words.	①
2. Phoebe had not studied the spelling words.	②
3. Phoebe had to find a way to learn the words.	③

14 Phoebe and the Spelling Bee • Language Support/Blackline Master 6   Grade 3

Language Support, 14

TESTED
OBJECTIVES

Students will analyze how to predict outcomes.

LANGUAGE SUPPORT

ESL Review with students that understanding the roots of a word may help clarify its meaning. Explain that the prefix *pre-* means "before" and the root *dict* means to "say or write". To predict means to guess beforehand. Have students make predictions about the week's weather, the outcome of an upcoming sporting event, or other events pertinent to their lives.

1. Read
2. Underline Phoebe's problem
3. Predict how to solve
4. Circle any clues

Review **Make Predictions**

PREPARE

Discuss Making Predictions Explain: Many stories are about the main character's attempt to solve a problem. As you read, you can add to your understanding and enjoyment of a story by using what you have learned so far to make predictions about how the character will solve the problem.

TEACH

Read "The Science Fair" and Model the Skill Read the passage "The Science Fair." Focus students' attention on Phoebe's problem and predict what the outcome of the story might be.

The Science Fair

Phoebe's class was taking part in a school science fair. Each student in the class had to make a project on a different science topic. The science teacher told Phoebe that the topic for her project was: How does sunlight make plants grow?

Phoebe groaned when she heard her topic. She didn't know *anything* about how sunlight made plants grow! She wondered if she could find a way to not be in the fair. But then she remembered the spelling bee. No, she thought, maybe there was a better way to solve the problem.

Teaching Chart 11

Ask a volunteer to underline a sentence that tells what Phoebe's problem is. Help students think about Phoebe's problem and predict how she might solve it. Have them circle any clues they use to help make their prediction.

MODEL Phoebe knows nothing about her topic. She learned from the spelling bee that she can do well when she uses her imagination to help her prepare. I predict that she will use her imagination to help her prepare for her science project.

PRACTICE

Create a Predictions Chart

Have students create a Making Predictions chart. Help them get started.

PROBLEM	PREDICTION	REASON
Phoebe doesn't know much about her project topic.	She will use her imagination to help her prepare her project.	She learned in the spelling bee that she does well when she uses her imagination.

ASSESS/CLOSE

Write a New Ministory

On one sheet of paper, have pairs of students write a ministory from the beginning up to the final event. Remind students that they should include enough information for others to predict how the main character will behave. Have pairs turn the paper over and write the final event on the other side. Then have pairs trade stories with another pair. Have each pair predict on the bottom of the first side what the outcome of the mini-story will be, then turn over the paper to see if they were correct.

ALTERNATE TEACHING STRATEGY

MAKE PREDICTIONS

For a different approach to teaching this skill, see page T62.

LOOKING AHEAD

Students will apply this skill as they read the next selection, *Opt: An Illusionary Tale.*

Meeting Individual Needs for Comprehension

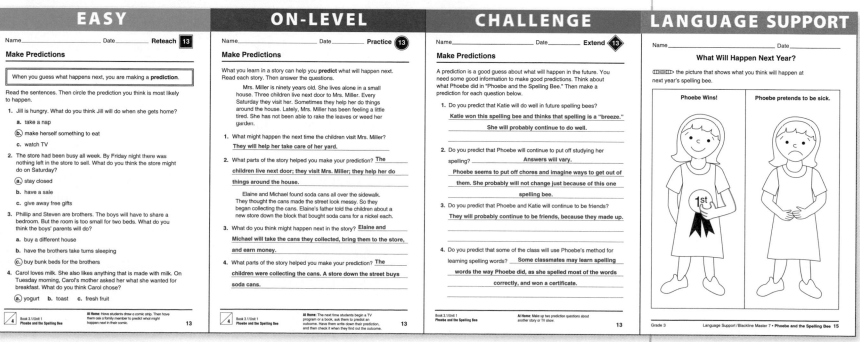

EASY	ON-LEVEL	CHALLENGE	LANGUAGE SUPPORT
Reteach, 13	Practice, 13	Extend, 13	Language Support, 15

 **OBJECTIVES**

Students will learn how the prefix *un-* changes word meaning.

....

MATERIALS

- **Teaching Chart 12**
- prefix **Word Building Manipulative Cards**

TEACHING TIP

INSTRUCTIONAL

- The letters *un-* at the beginning of a word are not always a prefix. (*under*)

- There is never a hyphen after the prefix *un-*. (*unhappy*)

- Letters are never dropped after the prefix *un-*, even when the next letter is an *-n*. (*unnecessary*)

- The prefix *un-* can also mean, "do the opposite of." (*unfold*)

Introduce

PREPARE

Discuss Meaning of the Prefix *un-* Explain: A prefix is a word part added to the beginning of a base word. Prefixes have their own meanings. The prefix *un-* usually means either "not" or "do the opposite." When a prefix is added to a word, the meaning of the word changes.

TEACH

Read the Passage and Model the Skill Have students read the passage on **Teaching Chart 12.**

An (Un)pleasant Day

Phoebe was feeling very (un)comfortable about what she had told Katie. She said she had studied for the test, but that was (un)true. Now she really did feel (un)well.

The door to the nurse's office was (un)locked, but Phoebe didn't go in. Why did she have to be in this spelling bee? It was so (un)fair!

Leaving the door (un)opened, Phoebe went back to the class. Katie gave her a note telling her it was (un)kind to tell a lie to a friend. Phoebe felt more (un)happy than ever. She decided never to be (un)prepared for a test again.

Teaching Chart 12

MODEL The word *untrue* in the second sentence begins with *un-*. The base word is *true*. If *un-* means "not," then *untrue* means "not true." Let me read that sentence again and see if that meaning makes sense.

Have students use the meaning of the prefix *un-* to define the word *unpleasant* in the title (not pleasant). Ask them whether that meaning makes sense for the rest of the passage.

PRACTICE

Identify Words with Prefixes

GROUP

Have volunteers underline each word in "An Unpleasant Day" that begins with the prefix *un-*, and then circle the prefix. Have students discuss the meaning of the words. ▶ **Logical**

ASSESS/CLOSE

Form Words with Prefixes and Use Them in a Paragraph

Have students write each of the words below on index cards. Then have them add the prefix *un-* (available from the Word Building Manipulative Cards) to each word. Ask partners to write a paragraph using all the words. They may want to draw a picture to go with their paragraphs.

safe   wise   grateful   lucky

ALTERNATE TEACHING STRATEGY

PREFIXES

For a different approach to teaching this skill, see page T65.

Meeting Individual Needs for Vocabulary

EASY	ON-LEVEL	CHALLENGE	LANGUAGE SUPPORT
Name_____ Date_____ **Reteach** 14	Name_____ Date_____ **Practice** 14	Name_____ Date_____ **Extend** 14	Name_____ Date_____
Prefixes	**Prefixes**	**Prefixes**	**un- Means "Not"**

EASY — Reteach 14

Prefixes

A **prefix** is a word part that can be added to the beginning of a word. It makes a new word with its own meaning. The prefix **un-** means "not," or "opposite of." For example, the word **unhappy** means "not happy."

prefix + base word = new word

un + happy = unhappy

Fill in the list below by writing the prefix and base word or the new word. Then write the meaning of the new word. The first one is done for you.

	Prefix	+	Base Word	= New Word	Meaning
1.	un		usual	unusual	not usual
2.	un		clear	unclear	not clear
3.	un		fair	unfair	not fair
4.	un		true	untrue	not true
5.	un		folded	unfolded	not folded
6.	un		known	unknown	not known
7.	un		kind	unkind	not kind
8.	un		wrap	unwrap	opposite of wrap
9.	un		wanted	unwanted	not wanted
10.	un		tie	untie	opposite of tie

At Home: Ask students to think of some other words that begin with the prefix un-.

14   Book 3.1/Unit 1 **Phoebe and the Spelling Bee**   10

ON-LEVEL — Practice 14

Prefixes

A **prefix** is a word part that can be added to the beginning of a word. It creates a new word with its own meaning. The prefix **un-** means "not," or "opposite of." For example, the word **unfair** means "not fair" or "the opposite of fair."

Below each sentence, write the word that includes the prefix **un-**. Then write the meaning of the word.

1. It was unlucky that Mona was sick on the first day of vacation.

   unlucky—not lucky

2. The story has an unusual character named Simon.

   unusual—not usual, different

3. The movie was very interesting, even though it was untrue.

   untrue—not true, false

4. It took the child a long time to unwrap her birthday present.

   unwrap—take off wrapping

5. The number of stars in the sky is unknown.

   unknown—not known

6. Jack was unhappy that he did not get a better score in the game.

   unhappy—not happy

At Home: Ask students to name three other words that begin with the prefix un-.

14   Book 3.1/Unit 1 **Phoebe and the Spelling Bee**   6

CHALLENGE — Extend 14

Prefixes

Word parts, such as *un* and *re* are called prefixes. The prefixes *un* and *re* can change the meaning of words. For example, *un* means "not," or "opposite" as in uncover. The word part *re* means "again," as in refill, or "back" as in replay.

Use *un* or *re* to change the meaning of the words below. Then write sentences using the words you created.

1. un lucky
2. un usual
3. un happy
4. re check
5. re fill
6. re play
7. un fair
8. re paint

At Home: Put up a list on the refrigerator with two columns—one for words with the prefix un and the other for words with the prefix re. Everyone should add words as they think of them. Keep the list up for several days.

14   Book 3.1/Unit 1 **Phoebe and the Spelling Bee**

LANGUAGE SUPPORT

un- Means "Not"

1. Read the sentences. Look at the words. 2. ✂ out the words.
3. ✏ each word in a blank to finish the sentences.

ready	usual	heard	tied	announced

1. Phoebe felt un ready for the spelling bee.

2. Phoebe had an un usual way of learning her words.

3. Phoebe spoke so softly that she was un heard .

4. Ms. Ravioli surprised the students with an un announced pop test.

5. Katie almost tripped because her shoes were un tied .

16 **Phoebe and the Spelling Bee** • Language Support/Blackline Master 8   Grade 3

Reteach, 14   **Practice, 14**   **Extend, 14**   **Language Support, 16**

GRAMMAR/SPELLING
CONNECTIONS

See the 5-Day Grammar and Usage Plan on pages 77M–77N.

See the 5-Day Spelling Plan on pages 77O–77P.

TECHNOLOGY TIP

A spell-checker won't catch a word that has been used incorrectly, such as a homophone. Use the spell-checker and read over the news story yourself.

Personal Narrative

Prewrite

WRITE A PERSONAL NARRATIVE
Present this writing assignment: Have you ever been in an exciting contest, such as a race or a game? Write about what happened. Tell how you felt before, during, and after the contest.

LIST DETAILS Have students list important details about the contest they have chosen, such as when and where it took place, how they felt, and what happened at different stages of the contest.

Strategy: Make a Sequence-of-Events Chart Have students arrange details from their list in the order in which they happened. Have them make a chart showing what happened during the beginning, middle, and end. Suggest the following:

• Check your chart to see if any important part has been left out.

• Mark a check next to the most exciting parts of the story.

Draft

USE THE CHART In their personal narratives students should include the important steps from their flowcharts. Presenting steps in the order in which they appear in the flowchart will keep the sequence clear. Remind students to include an opening that explains what the contest is and a closing that gives the results (or expected results) of participation.

Revise

SELF-QUESTIONING Ask students to assess their drafts, answering the following checklist:

• Have I made clear what the contest is?

• Did I explain clearly what it takes to participate in the contest?

• Does the order of steps make sense?

PARTNERS Have students trade news stories with a peer to get another point of view.

Edit/Proofread

CHECK FOR ERRORS Students should reread their personal narratives for spelling, grammar, format, and punctuation.

Publish

SHARE THE STORIES Students can write their stories out on construction paper and place them all together in a "Contest Binder" available for the whole class to read.

The Great Race

Last summer at camp, I ran in a special relay race. Each team had four runners. Each runner had to carry an egg on a spoon partway across a field. If the egg fell, your team was out.

Before the race I wasn't nervous. My friends and I just wanted to have fun. After the race began, I started to worry. What if I dropped the egg? I knew I would feel bad.

When it was my turn to run, I forgot about everything but the egg. After I handed it off to the next runner, I felt relieved.

My team came in third. In a way, we won, though. We had a great time!

Presentation Ideas

ILLUSTRATE THE STORY Have students draw pictures of photographs that might accompany their personal narrative and write photo captions below.

▶ **Viewing/Representing**

MAKE A TAPE Have students record a tape of their personal narrative. Encourage students listening to the tape to suggest sound effects or music where appropriate.

▶ **Speaking/Listening**

Consider students' creative efforts, possibly adding a plus (+) for originality, wit, and imagination.

Scoring Rubric

Excellent	Good	Fair	Unsatisfactory
4: The writer	**3:** The writer	**2:** The writer	**1:** The writer
• clearly and in detail describes his or her participation in the contest.	• describes his or her participation in the contest without detail.	• describes his or her participation with little clarity or detail.	• does not describe how he or she participated in the contest.
• explains each step in a logical sequence.	• explains steps in a mostly logical sequence.	• explains steps but does not arrange them in a logical sequence.	• leaves out steps of participation.
• tells what the results of the contest were (or will be).	• includes little information about the contest's results.	• leaves out information about the contest's outcome.	• gives no information about the contest's outcome.

0: The writer leaves the page blank or fails to respond to the writing task. The writer does not address the topic or simply paraphrases the prompt. The response is illegible or incoherent.

Meeting Individual Needs for Writing

EASY

Peculiar Pizzas Have students provide examples of edible but unusual pizza combinations, like Phoebe's pizza with pineapple. They can draw each pizza and describe it below. Have them write a sentence explaining which pizza is their favorite, and why.

ON-LEVEL

Diary Entry Have students imagine that they are Phoebe the night of her spelling bee. Have them write a diary entry describing what happened and how they felt. If they wish, students can add a drawing she might include in her diary.

CHALLENGE

Dialogue Have students write a dialogue between Phoebe and Katie walking home after the spelling bee. Encourage students to think about the characters and how they might actually talk to each other.

5 Day Grammar and Usage Plan

Invite students to play a game of "Simon Says." Point out that the game leader issues commands. Encourage them to note each command as they play.

DAILY LANGUAGE ACTIVITIES

Write the Daily Language Activities on the chalkboard each day or use **Transparency 2**. Have students correct the sentences orally, adding correct end punctuation.

Day 1
1. Study your spelling words .
2. Find a partner to help you .
3. Prepare for the spelling bee .

Day 2
1. How exciting this is !
2. Gosh, that one is hard !
3. Next time, study more .

Day 3
1. Do not forget your spelling list .
2. Wow, there are too many words !
3. Just learn them one at a time .

Day 4
1. What a long word that is !
2. How difficult it seems !
3. Try a little harder .

Day 5
1. Get ready for the spelling bee .
2. Spell the word *actor* .
3. I am the best speller ever !

Daily Language Transparency 2

DAY 1 — Introduce the Concept

Oral Warm-Up Invite students to re-state the definition of *sentence* that they learned last week. Then read this sentence aloud: *Hold your pencil above your head.* Point out that in this sentence you are telling them to do something. Invite students to make up other sentences that tell people to do things.

Introduce Commands Explain that the sentences that tell others to do something are called *commands*. Present:

Commands

- A **command** tells or asks someone to do something. It ends with a period.

Present the Daily Language Activity. Then have students write two commands and punctuate them correctly.

 WRITING Assign the daily Writing Prompt on page 48C.

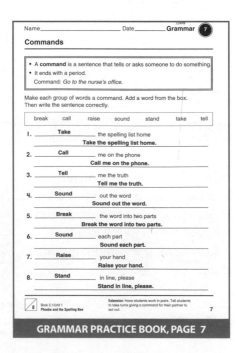

GRAMMAR PRACTICE BOOK, PAGE 7

DAY 2 — Teach the Concept

Review Commands Ask students to explain what a command is and what punctuation follows a command.

Introduce Exclamations Ask students what sort of things they would say while playing a sport. Identify those utterances that would qualify as exclamations. Present:

Exclamations

- An **exclamation** shows strong feeling. It ends with an exclamation mark.

Present the Daily Language Activity. Then have students write two exclamations and punctuate them correctly.

 WRITING Assign the daily Writing Prompt on page 48C.

GRAMMAR PRACTICE BOOK, PAGE 8

DAY 3 — Review and Practice

Learn from the Literature Review commands and exclamations. Read the following sentences from pages 52 and 53 of *Phoebe and the Spelling Bee*.

> **"This will be a breeze!"**
> **"Spell *actor*,"** said Katie.

Ask students to identify the kinds of sentences Katie said. Ask what end punctuation they would use if the command stood alone. (period)

Write Commands and Exclamations Present the Daily Language Activity and have students orally supply the end punctuation.

Ask each student to write three commands and three exclamations that might be heard during a spelling bee. Invite students to share aloud their sentences, and have the rest of the class identify them as commands or exclamations.

 Assign the daily Writing Prompt on page 48D.

DAY 4 — Review and Practice

Review Commands and Exclamations Write the sentences from the Daily Language Activities for Days 1 through 3 on the chalkboard. Ask students to identify each as a command or an exclamation. Then present the Daily Language Activity for Day 4.

Mechanics and Usage Review punctuation for commands and exclamations. Display and discuss:

Commands and Exclamations

- A command ends with a period.
- An exclamation ends with an exclamation point.

 Assign the daily Writing Prompt on page 48D.

DAY 5 — Assess and Reteach

Assess Use the Daily Language Activity and page 11 of the **Grammar Practice Book** for assessment.

Reteach Have students write each rule about commands and exclamations on an index card. Ask students to write on strips of paper two commands or exclamations that might be heard at mealtime, and invite several volunteers to read aloud a sentence. Have class members hold up the card that gives the rule for that kind of sentence. Do the same for each sentence in the Daily Language Activities. Have students place their sentences on a bulletin board under the headings COMMANDS and EXCLAMATIONS.

Use page 12 of the **Grammar Practice Book** for additional reteaching.

 Assign the daily Writing Prompt on page 48D.

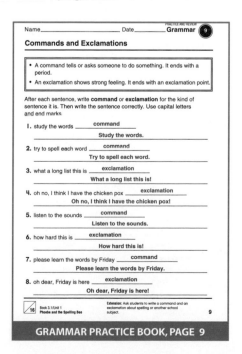

GRAMMAR PRACTICE BOOK, PAGE 9

GRAMMAR PRACTICE BOOK, PAGE 10

GRAMMAR PRACTICE BOOK, PAGE 11

GRAMMAR PRACTICE BOOK, 12

5 Day Spelling Plan

ESL Spanish speakers may spell long *a* as *e* and long *e* as *i*. Write the Spelling Words and then erase the letters that spell the vowel sounds. Have students say and complete the words.

DICTATION SENTENCES

1. He has a toy plane.
2. The boys play on a team.
3. Raise your hand when you are ready.
4. The breeze came through the window.
5. The class has to write a paper.
6. Would she marry him?
7. I weigh more than a child.
8. The bank thief was caught.
9. The cream is sweet.
10. That boy is wide awake.
11. Can you tell me my test grade?
12. The water in the creek is cold.
13. The mule can carry the pack.
14. The boat has a large sail.
15. Her neighbor lived by the corner.

Challenge Words

16. Continue with the test.
17. The answer is correct.
18. The joke could embarrass you.
19. The legend started years before.
20. Her coins are unusual.

DAY 1 — Pretest

Assess Prior Knowledge Use the Dictation Sentences at left and **Spelling Practice Book** page 7 for the pretest. Allow students to correct their own papers. If students have trouble, have partners give each other a midweek test on Day 3. Students who require a modified list may be tested on the first eight words.

Spelling Words		Challenge Words
1. plane	9. **cream**	16. **continue**
2. team	10. awake	17. **correct**
3. **raise**	11. grade	18. **embarrass**
4. **breeze**	12. creek	19. **legend**
5. **paper**	13. carry	20. **unusual**
6. marry	14. sail	
7. weigh	15. neighbor	
8. thief		

*Note: Words in **dark type** are from the story.*

Word Study On page 8 of the **Spelling Practice Book** are word study steps and an at-home activity.

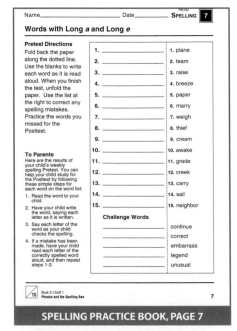

SPELLING PRACTICE BOOK, PAGE 7

WORD STUDY STEPS AND ACTIVITY, PAGE 8

DAY 2 — Explore the Pattern

Sort and Spell Words Say the words *plane* and *team*. Ask students what long-vowel sounds they hear. These are long *a* and long *e*. Have students read the spelling words aloud and sort them according to the spelling of each word.

Words with long *a* spelled

a	a-e	eigh
paper	plane	weigh
ai	awake	neighbor
raise	grade	
sail		

Words with long *e* spelled

ea	ee	y
team	breeze	marry
cream	creek	carry
	ie	
	thief	

Spelling Patterns In the spelling pattern CVC*e* (consonant-vowel-consonant-*e*), the silent *e* helps make the vowel sound long. Compare the vowel sounds in *plane* and *plan*. Have students write more words with this pattern.

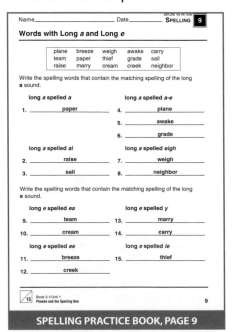

SPELLING PRACTICE BOOK, PAGE 9

..... Words with Long *a* and Long *e*

DAY 3 — Practice and Extend

Word Meaning: Endings Explain to students that they can change the verbs (action words) on the list to show the past tense by adding *ed* to the final letter. Point out that if the word ends in *e*, they drop the *e* and add *ed*. Then discuss how to change words that end in *y* to the past by changing the *y* to *i* and adding *ed*. Have students write the past-tense form of the following spelling words: *raise, marry, weigh, carry, sail.*

Glossary Have students look up the Challenge Words in the Glossary and find the part of speech of each word. (One word has two parts of speech.) Have them write the words followed by their parts of speech.

DAY 4 — Proofread and Write

Proofread Sentences Write these sentences on the chalkboard, including the misspelled words. Ask students to proofread, circling incorrect spellings and writing the correct spellings. There are two spelling errors in each sentence.

> He will (merry) his (nieghbor). (marry, neighbor)
>
> The (breaze) blew across the (creke). (breeze, creek)
>
> The (theif) broke in when she was (awaik). (thief, awake)

Have students create additional sentences with errors for partners to correct.

WRITING Have students use as many Spelling Words as possible in the daily Writing Prompt on page 48D. Remind students to proofread for errors in spelling, punctuation, and grammar.

DAY 5 — Assess and Reteach

Assess Students' Knowledge Use page 12 of the **Spelling Practice Book** or the Dictation Sentences on page 77O for the posttest.

Personal Word List If students have trouble with any words in the lesson, have them create a personal list of troublesome words in their journals. Have students write a context sentence for each word.

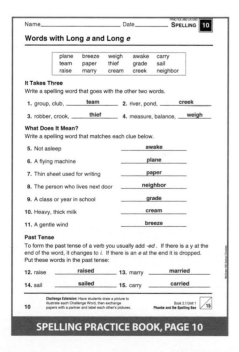

SPELLING PRACTICE BOOK, PAGE 10

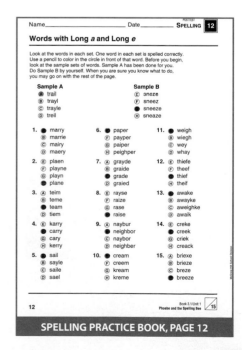

SPELLING PRACTICE BOOK, PAGE 11

SPELLING PRACTICE BOOK, PAGE 12

Opt:
An Illusionary Tale

Selection Summary With a jester as their guide, students will explore the royal world of optical illusion and discover that things aren't always what they seem.

AN ILLUSIONARY TALE
OPT
BY ARLINE AND JOSEPH BAUM

INSTRUCTIONAL
Pages 80–105

About the Authors Arlene Baum, once an assistant to a magician, and Joseph Baum, a former art director, make up the talented team who bring us this fascinating story of Opt, the land of illusion. The authors used their special backgrounds to create this children's book. *Opt: An Illusionary Tale* , which won an Outstanding Science Trade Book award, takes young readers to an exciting place where looks are almost always deceptive. Joseph and Arlene Baum like to entertain children as they teach them about the art of illusion.

Resources for
Meeting Individual Needs

LEVELED BOOKS

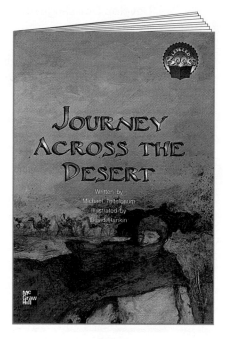

EASY
Pages 105A, 105D

INDEPENDENT
Pages 105B, 105D

CHALLENGE
Pages 105C, 105D

🏠 *Take-Home version available*

LEVELED PRACTICE

Reteach, 15–21
blackline masters with reteaching opportunities for each assessed skill

Practice, 15–21
workbook with Take-Home stories and practice opportunities for each assessed skill and story comprehension

Extend, 15–21
blackline masters that offer challenge activities for each assessed skill

ADDITIONAL RESOURCES

- **Language Support Book,** pp. 17–24
- **Take-Home Story, Practice** p. 16a
- **Alternate Teaching Strategies,** pp. T60–T66
- **Selected Quizzes Prepared by** 📘 Accelerated Reader®

McGraw-Hill School
TECHNOLOGY

💿 **Phonics CD-ROM** provides extra phonics support.

interNET CONNECTION Research & Inquiry ideas. Visit **www.mhschool.com/reading.**

READING AND LANGUAGE ARTS	DAY **1** *Focus on Reading and Skills*	DAY **2** *Read the Literature*

READING AND LANGUAGE ARTS

- **Comprehension**
- **Vocabulary**
- **Phonics/Decoding**
- **Study Skills**
- **Listening, Speaking, Viewing, Representing**

DAY 1 — Focus on Reading and Skills

 Read Read Aloud and Motivate, 78E
"The Wolf and His Shadow"

Develop Visual Literacy, 78/79

 ☑ **Introduce Steps in a Process,** 80A–80B
Teaching Chart 13
Reteach, Practice, Extend, 15

DAY 2 — Read the Literature

Build Background, 80C
Develop Oral Language

Vocabulary, 80D

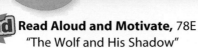

| gift | length | straighten |
| guard | royal | within |

Teaching Chart 14
Word Building Manipulative Cards
Reteach, Practice, Extend, 16

 Read Read the Selection, 80–101
Guided Instruction
☑ Steps in a Process
☑ Make Predictions

Minilessons, 83, 91, 93, 99

Cultural Perspectives, 86

Curriculum Connections

Link Fine Arts, 78/79

Link Science, 80C

Writing

 Writing Prompt: You are taking a picture of your uncle. He is standing next to an elephant. Your uncle is tall but he looks quite short. Did he suddenly shrink? Write what happened.

Writing Prompt: You are riding a bike down a road. It looks as if the road is going to end and you will fall off. Will you? Tell why or why not.

Journal Writing, 101
Quick-Write

Grammar

Introduce the Concept: Subjects, 105M
Daily Language Activity
1. The balloon is green. The balloon
2. Some dots disappeared. Some dots
3. The king reads. The king
Grammar Practice Book, 13

Teach the Concept: Subjects, 105M
Daily Language Activity
1. The queen laughed. The queen
2. ___ came to the party. A lady
3. ___ goes fishing. The prince
Grammar Practice Book, 14

Spelling

Pretest: Words with Long *i* and Long *o*, 105O
Spelling Practice Book, 13–14

Explore the Pattern: Words with Long *i* and Long *o*, 105O
Spelling Practice Book, 15

DAY 3 — Read the Literature

Rereading for Fluency, 100

Story Questions, 102
Reteach, Practice, Extend, 17
Story Activities, 103

Study Skill, 104
Teaching Chart 15
☑ Parts of a Book
Reteach, Practice, Extend, 18

Test Power, 105
TAAS Preparation and Practice Book, 24–25

 Read the Leveled Books,
Guided Reading
Long *i* and Long *o*
☑ Steps in a Process
☑ Instructional Vocabulary
Phonics CD-ROM

 Activity Science: Color, 82

 Writing Prompt: Write a paragraph describing the dragon from Opt. How is it different from other dragons you have read about?

Writing Process: Personal Narrative, 105K
Prewrite, Draft

Review and Practice: Subjects, 105N
Daily Language Activity
1. ___ are huge. Castles
2. ___ came to the castle. A messenger
3. Flowers grow in the sun. Flowers
Grammar Practice Book, 15

Practice and Extend: Words with Long *i* and Long *o*, 105P
Spelling Practice Book, 16

DAY 4 — Build Skills

 Read the Leveled Books and Self-Selected Books

☑ **Review Steps in a Process,** 105E–105F
Teaching Chart 16
Reteach, Practice, Extend, 19
Language Support, 22

☑ **Review Story Elements** 105G–105H
Teaching Chart 17
Reteach, Practice, Extend, 20
Language Support, 23

 Activity Math: Geometric Shapes, 92

Writing Prompt: Think about an unusual place you have visited. Write a letter to a friend describing the place and what you did while you were there.

Writing Process: Personal Narrative, 105K
Revise

Meeting Individual Needs for Writing, 105L

Review and Practice: Subjects, 105N
Daily Language Activity
1. ___ is ready. The hall
2. A throne is a place to sit. A throne
3. The zookeeper heard the news. The zookeeper

Grammar Practice Book, 16

Proofread and Write: Words with Long *i* and Long *o*, 105P
Spelling Practice Book, 17

DAY 5 — Build Skills

 Read Self-Selected Books

☑ **Review Prefixes,** 105I–105J
Teaching Chart 18
Reteach, Practice, Extend, 21
Language Support, 24

Listening, Speaking, Viewing, Representing, 105L
Make a Cover
Read Aloud

Minilessons, 83, 93, 99

Phonics Review,
Long *i* and Long *o*, 91
Phonics/Phonemic Awareness Practice Book, 39–42, 53–56
Phonics CD-ROM

 **Activity** Art: Background Colors, 96

Writing Prompt: Write about a birthday party or other celebration you have been to. What made it special?

Writing Process: Personal Narrative, 105K
Edit/Proofread, Publish

Assess and Reteach: Subjects, 105N
Daily Language Activity
1. The blue star shines brightly. The blue star
2. ___ are many colors. The banners
3. A sign points the way. A sign
Grammar Practice Book, 17–18

Assess and Reteach: Words with Long *i* and Long *o*, 105P
Spelling Practice Book, 18

Read Aloud and Motivate

Language Arts

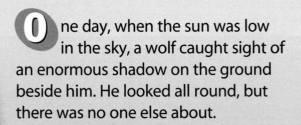

The Wolf and His Shadow

a fable by Aesop
retold by Margaret Clark and
Charlotte Voake

One day, when the sun was low in the sky, a wolf caught sight of an enormous shadow on the ground beside him. He looked all round, but there was no one else about.

"Why, that's my shadow," said the wolf. "What a wonderful animal I must be! I've never even seen another animal as big as that. The lion calls himself king, but he's not nearly as big as I am. I'm going to be king from now on."

So the wolf strutted about, thinking of all the things he would do now he was king. He was so busy thinking about himself, he didn't even notice the lion, who suddenly sprang on him and swallowed him whole.

As the lion licked his lips, he said, "What a silly wolf! Everyone knows that sometimes your shadow is big, sometimes it's small, and sometimes you have no shadow at all."

Oral Comprehension

LISTENING AND SPEAKING Motivate students to think about forming generalizations by reading aloud this fable about a foolish wolf. Ask students to think about what the author is saying in the fable. When you have finished reading, ask, "What was the author saying about the wolf?" Then ask, "Is this true of only this particular character, or could it apply to many people? Why or why not?" Encourage students to think about forming generalizations as they read other stories.

Activity Have students retell this story by role-playing the characters in the fable. Remind them that the characters are animals. Encourage students to base their characters on the movements and sounds of the different animals.

▶ **Kinesthetic/Interpersonal**

Develop **Visual Literacy**

Works of Art

Look at the painting quickly. What did you see? Look at it again. What is happening to the leaves? What other details can you see?

Sometimes a painting seems to change before your eyes. You may need to look at it carefully to see everything that is going on.

Close your eyes. What do you remember about the painting? Why?

The Art of Conversation
by René Magritte

78

79

Objective: Identify Steps in a Process

VIEWING In this work by Belgian painter René Magritte, objects are full of surprises. Ask students what they notice first about the painting. What do they notice next? Have them focus on differences between the foreground and the background. Would they call the painting realistic? Ask students to describe some of the elements that make the painting seem dreamlike. Invite them to close their eyes and tell what details they remember about the painting.

Read the page with students, encouraging individual interpretations of the painting.

Ask students to describe step by step what seems to be happening in the painting. For example:

- The green leaves grow straight up.
- They turn into birds.
- Small birds seem to grow into bigger birds.

REPRESENTING Have students pretend the painting represents a dream. Invite them to make up a story to go with the dream.

78/79

TESTED OBJECTIVES

Students will:

- identify steps in a process.
- follow directions.

LANGUAGE SUPPORT

 Write and define *optical* on the chalkboard. Explain that *optical* comes from the Greek word *ops*, meaning "eye." Have ESL students share how they say *to see* and *eye* in their native language.

Introduce Steps in a Process

PREPARE

Introduce Steps in a Process

Ask: Which distance is greater—from here to the cafeteria or from the cafeteria to the end of the playground? If you wanted to find out how much greater the distance was, what would you need to do? Discuss a step-by-step plan.

TEACH

Explain Steps in a Process

Explain to students that there are steps that must be taken to complete most tasks. Explain that sometimes the steps in a process consist of directions. All other times, students will need to figure out the steps on their own.

Pasqual's Picture

Pasqual had a picture of Buckingham Palace from his trip to England. He decided to frame the picture. He needed to get the right size and style for the frame. First, Pasqual used a ruler to measure the length and height of the picture. Next, he went to a picture frame shop. He looked carefully to choose the right color and style frame. After finding the size, color, and style he wanted, Pasqual bought the frame.

At home he put the picture in the frame and hung it in his room. Now he would always be reminded of what a great trip he had.

Teaching Chart 13

Read the Story and Model the Skill

Display **Teaching Chart 13**. Have students pay attention to clues about steps in a process as the story is read.

MODEL I see the clue words *first* and *next*, which tell me the first two steps Pasqual took. The next sentence does not have a word that signals a step in the series. I think that choosing a color and style is important to help complete the process, so this must be one of the steps.

Identify Steps in a Process

Have students underline the series of steps that Pasqual took to choose the right frame. Then have students list the steps.

1. Pasqual measured the picture with a ruler.

2. He went to a picture frame shop.

3. He chose a frame carefully.

4. He bought the frame.

5. At home, he put the picture in the frame and hung it up.

▶**Logical**

ASSESS/CLOSE

Follow Directions Using a List of Steps

Have students bring in a picture or postcard. Help them follow these directions to make their own frames out of construction paper. Be sure the students use their rulers.

1. Measure the length and width of the picture.

2. Choose a piece of colored paper. Draw a rectangle one inch longer and wider than your picture.

3. Cut out the rectangle you have drawn. It is your frame.

4. Tape your picture to the center of your frame.

5. Decorate the edges of your frame.

Meeting Individual Needs for Comprehension

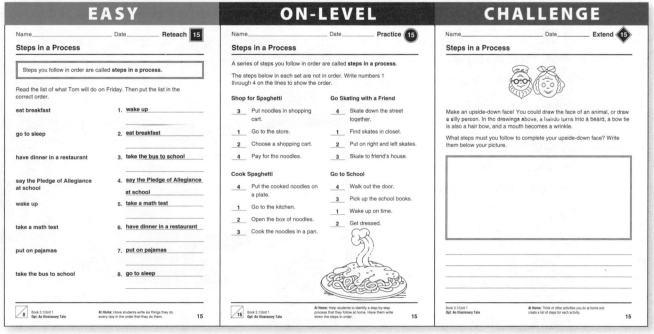

Reteach, 15   Practice, 15   Extend, 15

LANGUAGE SUPPORT

See the **Language Support Book**, pages 17–20, for teaching suggestions for Build Background and Vocabulary.

Build Background

 **Anthology and Leveled Books**

Science

Evaluate Prior Knowledge

CONCEPT: ILLUSIONS Explain that optical illusions are pictures or forms that give the viewer a false impression. Not everything is what it appears to be. For example, sometimes the illusions used in magic tricks are so convincing that you cannot believe your eyes.

COMPARE ILLUSIONS AND REALITY
Have students brainstorm to create a word web of different magic illusions they know about. Discuss the difference between magical illusions and reality. ▶ **Logical/Visual**

Graphic Organizer 29

EXPLAIN A TRICK Have
  students pretend
ONE   WRITING   they are magicians.
Ask each student to write a short explanation for how he or she created an illusion. They should use their imaginations to explain the trick.

Develop Oral Language

DISCUSS AN OPTICAL ILLUSION

ESL Before students arrive, fill a tall glass with water. Pour the water into a wide bowl. Refill the glass. Display both and an empty glass that is the same size.

Ask: Is there more water in the glass or the bowl? Survey the class. Have students, in turn, raise their hands if they think the glass has more water, the bowl has more water, or both contain the same amount.

Then pour the water from the bowl into the empty glass. Discuss why people often are fooled by this illusion.

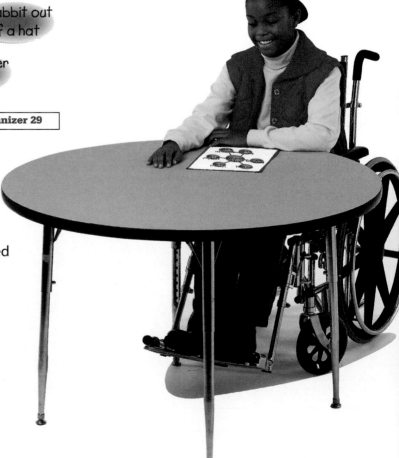

Vocabulary

Key Words

A Message for a Dragon

1. The King gave his royal messenger a letter to bring to the dragon. **2.** The messenger knew the length of the road to the dragon's cave, as he had made the walk from the castle to the cave before. **3.** There was no guard outside the cave, because the dragon could protect himself. **4.** The messenger stopped to straighten his crooked hat before he called the dragon. **5.** The dragon smiled at the letter, which was a thank-you note for the birthday gift he had given the Prince. **6.** There was even a drawing of the dragon folded within the envelope.

Teaching Chart 14

Definitions

royal (p. 85) involving or belonging to a king or queen or a member of his or her family

length (p. 89) the distance from one end of something to the other

guard (p. 84) a person who protects a person or place

straighten (p. 92) to make something straight

gift (p. 100) a present

within (p. 94) inside

SPELLING/VOCABULARY CONNECTIONS

See Spelling Challenge Words, pages 105O–105P.

Vocabulary in Context

IDENTIFY VOCABULARY WORDS
Display **Teaching Chart 14** and read the passage with students. Have volunteers circle each vocabulary word and underline other words that are clues to its meaning.

DISCUSS MEANINGS Ask questions like these to help clarify word meanings:

- Who besides the King is a member of the royal family?
- Can you measure the length of your foot? Show me.
- Would you feel safe with a guard dog?
- What shorter base word do you see in *straighten*? Does it mean the opposite or same as *bent*?
- When might you get gifts?
- If you are in the classroom, are you within the school?

Practice

DEMONSTRATE WORD MEANING
Have partners take turns choosing Vocabulary Cards from a pile, and demonstrating word meaning using pantomime.
▶ **Kinesthetic/Linguistic**

Word Building Manipulative Cards

MATCH DEFINITIONS AND PICTURES
On separate cards have partners define and illustrate each vocabulary word, using their Glossary as needed. Have partners take turns matching definitions and pictures. ▶ **Linguistic/Visual**

ON-LEVEL

Name_____ Date_____ Practice 16

Vocabulary

Supply the correct words from the list:

length guard royal within gift straighten

Once a prince and a princess lived happily in an underground castle. There was one problem, though. The ____royal____ kingdom always looked boring and dull. So the prince had an idea. As a birthday ____gift____ he bought the princess some paintings to decorate the castle walls.

The princess was thrilled! Her favorite painting showed a small face tucked ____within____ a larger face. She hung this one on the castle door, next to the ____guard____ who protected them. Another painting showed a group of bent and slanted lines. If you looked at the lines long enough, they seemed to ____straighten____ out. Looking at this will keep people busy, she thought.

After three days all of the paintings were hung, except one. This last painting is shown below. Do you think the lines are the same ____length____ ?

16 At Home: Use each of the vocabulary words in a sentence. Book 3.1/Unit 1 Opt: An Illusionary Tale 6

Take-Home Story 16a
Reteach 16
Practice 16 • Extend 16

80D

Guided Instruction

Preview and Predict

Have students read the title and preview the story. Have them do a **picture walk**, looking for pictures that give strong clues about the story.

- Do you notice anything unusual about the illustrations?
- What do you think this story will be about?
- Will this story be a realistic one or a fantasy? How can you tell? (A fantasy; the characters and surroundings look make-believe.) *Genre*

Have students record their predictions about the story.

PREDICTIONS	WHAT HAPPENED
The story is about a royal family.	
The illustrations are clues.	

Set Purposes

What do students want to find out by reading the story? For example:

- Why are there so many geometric shapes?
- Why are there two kinds of writing?

MEET
ARLINE AND JOSEPH BAUM

Arline and Joseph Baum are a husband-and-wife team who are fascinated by the art of illusion. Arline Baum once worked as an assistant to a magician. Joseph Baum was an art director for an advertising agency. His ability to create illusions with art won him many awards.

In *Opt: An Illusionary Tale,* the Baums have created a land of optical illusions. The book begins like this: "Seeing is believing, but sometimes our eyes deceive us. When this happens, it is called an optical illusion. Opt is a land of optical illusions." This book won an award for being an outstanding science trade book.

80

Meeting Individual Needs • Grouping Suggestions for Strategic Reading

EASY	ON-LEVEL	CHALLENGE
Read Together Read the story with students or have them read the story in small groups. Have students record what they learn about optical illusions. Guided Instruction and Prevention/Intervention prompts offer additional help with decoding, vocabulary, and comprehension.	**Guided Reading** Preview the story words on page 81. Choose from the Guided Instruction questions as you read the story with students or after they have read the story on their own. Have students record any important information.	**Read Independently** Thinking questions through and taking steps to find the right answers will help students understand the story. Have students make notes about the steps they took to figure out an illusion. After reading independently, they can use their notes to give an example of how to find an illusion in the story.

AN ILLUSIONARY TALE

OpT

BY ARLINE AND JOSEPH BAUM

81

☑ **Steps in a Process**

☑ **Make Predictions**

✤ **TEKS ELA 3.7: C; 3.9: B**

Strategic Reading Before we begin reading, let's find a prop that will help us figure out some of the optical illusions in the story. Let's use a ruler.

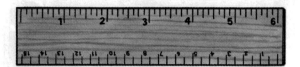

① **STEPS IN A PROCESS** How can you find out if the boy's legs are the same length? (Take the following steps: Measure both legs with your ruler. Compare the measurements.) *Story Prop*

Story Words

The words below may be unfamiliar. Have students check their meanings and pronunciations in the Glossary beginning on p. 388.

- banners, p. 82
- prongs, p. 84
- crooked, p. 85

LANGUAGE SUPPORT

A blackline master of a 6-inch ruler can be found in the **Language Support Book.**

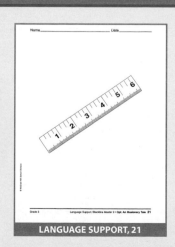

LANGUAGE SUPPORT, 21

Guided Instruction

2 A Sunny Day in Opt, a day of
3 banners, balloons, and surprises

2 **MAKE PREDICTIONS** Read the words at of the top of this page. Can you predict what this selection will be about? What do the words *banners* and *balloons* make you think of? What about *surprises*? (a party or a celebration)

Can you make my balloon change from white to green? For thirty seconds stare at the red. Now look at the white—is it green instead?

82

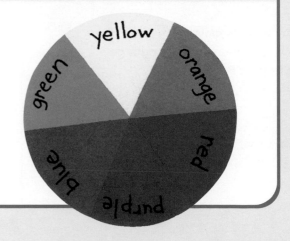

Activity

Cross Curricular: Science

COLOR Tell students that as they looked at red, one part of their eyes got tired. When they looked at the white, a different part of their eyes took over and they saw green. Green is the complementary color of red. Have students draw complementary-color wheels. Each student will:

- divide a circle into six equal slices with red, purple, and blue next to one another.
- color complementary colors opposite each other (purple/yellow, red/green, orange/blue).

▶ **Visual/Spatial**

The Wall surrounding the castle

Where white lines cross, gray dots are seen.
One disappears where one has been.

83

Guided Instruction

③ The setting of the story is where it takes place. What is the setting of this story? (a kingdom called Opt) *Setting*

Minilesson

REVIEW/MAINTAIN

Context Clues

Review that good readers look at the words surrounding an unfamiliar word to help them understand the word's meaning.

- Ask students to look at the second word in the last sentence on page 83. (*disappears*)
- Ask: What words give a clue to its meaning? (*where one has been*)

Activity Have students brainstorm a list of words or phrases that could be used as context clues for the word *disappears*.

LANGUAGE SUPPORT

ESL Explain that the text along the top of the pages is larger than the text along the bottom. Point out that the different-sized type is an invitation to read this story in two steps. It can be read as a simple story by reading only the top text. It also can be read as a story filled with tricks for the eyes by reading the bottom text.

Ask ESL students to read the bottom text with an English-fluent partner the first time through. Suggest that the two students read this text and try out the tricks together.

TEKS ELA 3.7: C; 3.9: B

83

Guided Instruction

4 **STEPS IN A PROCESS** How many prongs do you see? Are you sure? (Students may see either two or three.) Let's check this step-by-step. *Judgments and Decisions*

MODEL This is tricky. I can't tell whether the trident has two prongs or three. Let me cover up the top half and just look at the bottom. I see two prongs. Now I'll cover up the bottom half and just look at the top. I see three prongs. That doesn't make sense. This must be an illusion.

5 Some stories have a character, called a *narrator*, who tells the story from his or her point of view. Who is the narrator for this story? (the jester) How can you tell? (There is a picture of the jester in each bottom box. The jester asks questions about each page.) *Point of View*

The Castle Guard with his trident

How many prongs do you see?
I see two on the bottom—but on the top, three.

84

Visual Literacy

VIEWING AND REPRESENTING

Ask volunteers to define the words *trident* and *prongs*. How does the illustration on page 84 help demonstrate word meanings? (The illustrator shows the guard holding something with pointed tips like a fork. This must be the trident. The pointed tips must be the prongs.)

Have each student make up a nonsense word and its definition. Then ask a student to write a sentence for the word and draw a picture to go with it. Students can share their pictures with partners and guess word meanings.

The Royal Messenger arriving with a letter for the King

The vertical lines of the messenger's cloak are crooked.
The red tape on the letter is longer than the blue.
But is this really true?
Remember, now you are in OPT!

85

Guided Instruction

6 **MAKE PREDICTIONS** Do you think the vertical lines on the messenger's cloak are crooked? Is the red tape longer than the blue? What sentences make you think the answer to both questions is *no*? (*But is this really true? Remember, now you are in Opt!*)

7 **STEPS IN A PROCESS** How can we find out the truth about the lines on the messenger's cloak and the tape on the letter? Let's use our rulers. *Story Prop*

MODEL The lines on the messenger's cloak look crooked, but, since this is the land of Opt, I'd better check to be sure. I'll hold the ruler up to each line and see if it's straight. Just as I predicted, my eyes were deceiving me. The lines look crooked, but they are not.

Now I'll measure the red line. It's about 1½ inches. How about the blue? It's about 1½ inches, too. The lines are the same length. I'm surprised! The red line looks longer, for some reason.

Guided Instruction

8 **STEPS IN A PROCESS** What do your eyes tell you about which trumpeter is smaller? Based on what you have seen so far in this story, can you believe your eyes? Tell what steps you would take to figure out which trumpeter is smaller. Be sure to use your rulers. (Students should indicate they would first measure one trumpeter, then the other, and compare the results.) **Story Prop**

The Trumpeters announcing the arrival of the messenger

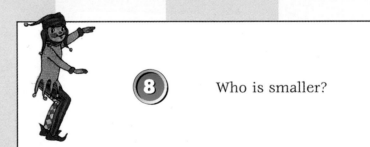

8 Who is smaller?

86

CULTURAL PERSPECTIVES

ART AND PERSPECTIVE Explain to students that Western artists make objects look farther away by making them smaller than objects in the foreground. Japanese artists make objects look farther away by placing them higher in their paintings.

Activity Provide each group with a long scroll of paper. Each group will:

- draw a landscape scene of their school or community.
- create perspective by drawing things that are far away at the top of the scroll.

▶ **Spatial/Logical**

✦ TEKS ELA 3.2: A,C; 3.3: A,B

The King and Queen waiting for the message

 Who is taller? **9**

87

Guided Instruction

9 **MAKE PREDICTIONS** Who is taller, the King or Queen? Try to predict the answer. Remember what you've read and seen so far in the story. How likely is it that things really are as they appear to be? (The King looks taller but I think that this may be an optical illusion like the other illustrations in the story.)

PHONICS AND DECODING
Read the word *waiting* in the first sentence on page 87. Sound out the word. What vowel sounds do you hear? (long *a*, short *i*)

PREVENTION/INTERVENTION

PHONICS AND DECODING
Students may need help decoding the /ā/ sound in *waiting*. Write the word *waiting* on the chalkboard. Use different-colored chalk to circle letters *ai*. Remind students that the letters *ai* make the long *a* sound. Model blending together w ai t i n g waiting.

List other words with long *a* spelled *ai* on the chalkboard. (Examples: *claim, stain, faint, paint*) Underline the letters that make the /ā/ sound in each word. *(ai)*

87

Guided Instruction

10 **STEPS IN A PROCESS** Sometimes we determine the steps we need to take to get information. At other times the steps are given to us in the form of directions. What are the directions on this page? (*First tilt the book, then take a look.*) What do we learn when we follow these directions? (*The message reads, "Coming to Tower."*)

The Message for the King to read

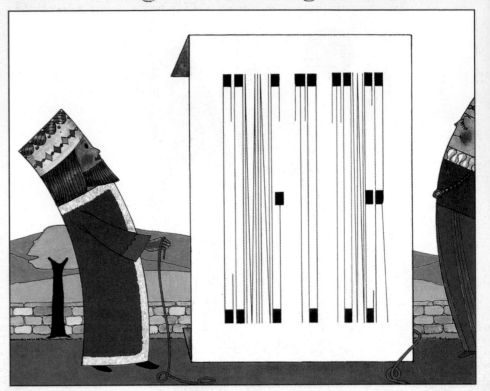

A clue to make the message clear.
10 First tilt the book, then take a look.
Who sent the message?

88

Fluency

ADJUST READING RATE

PARTNERS Have partners take turns reading sentences aloud from pages 88 and 89 (bottom sections only). Point out that this selection features many short sentences and many sentences with unusual phrasing and word order. It also includes rhymes. Encourage students to read slowly and carefully. Remind them to:

- use inflection when reading questions.
- vary the speed of their reading, depending on what is happening in the passage.
- emphasize rhyming words.

The Royal Art Gallery, dusted and tidied

Are the top of the lampshade and the top of the lamp base the same length?
Two ladies framed—or is it four?
Hidden elsewhere, you'll see two more.

11
12

89

Guided Instruction

11 **STEPS IN A PROCESS** How can we tell if the top of the lampshade and the top of the lamp base are the same length? Write the steps you will take to find out which is longer. (1. Use a ruler to measure the two lengths. 2. Compare the two lengths.) *Story Prop*

12 The authors hint that there are four ladies framed, not two, and tell us that there are two more faces hidden elsewhere. How can we see these faces? (Look at the pictures very closely. If you don't see the other faces, look away and then look at the picture again.)

COMPOUND WORDS Read the sentences that contain the words *lampshade* and *elsewhere* on page 89. How are these words alike? (They are both compound words—words that are made up of other smaller words.) How can you figure out the meanings of compound words?

PREVENTION/INTERVENTION

COMPOUND WORDS Write *lampshade* and *elsewhere* on the chalkboard. Ask volunteers to write the two words that make up each of these compound words on the chalkboard. (*lamp* and *shade, else* and *where*) Help students use the definitions of the two words to define each compound word.

Have students search for other compound words in the selection (page 94: *within* and *zookeeper;* page 97: *anywhere;* page 100: *birthday*). Have students figure out the definition of each compound word based on the meaning of its base words.

Guided Instruction

13 **STEPS IN A PROCESS** Can we figure out which line is the fishing rod and which is the branch? List the steps you would take to determine which is which. (1. Hold a ruler up to the rod. 2. See where the line continues on the other side of the tree. 3. Identify this as the fishing rod, not the tree branch.) *Story Prop*

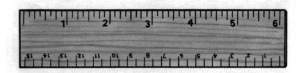

14 **MAKE PREDICTIONS** There's something special going on in Opt. Based on what you've read so far, how do you know? (There are balloons, banners, and surprises; a message for the King; the King and Queen clean the castle.) We learn the that the Prince has a new fishing rod. What could the special event be? (the Prince's birthday)

⑤ELF-MONITORING

STRATEGY

ASK FOR HELP Asking someone for help can often help a reader understand confusing words or sentences.

MODEL Some of these sentences are hard. I'm not sure what the authors are talking about. Perhaps if I ask classmates or the teacher, they will be able to help me understand what to look for in the illustration.

The Prince goes fishing with his new rod

13 Which is the rod and which the branch of the tree? Now look at the Prince's shirt. What do you see? **14** Is the space between the shirt's black dots larger than those same black spots?

90

The Princess picking a special bouquet

Flowers fair, flowers bright.
Which flower center is larger—
the black or the white?

15

91

Guided Instruction

15 **STEPS IN A PROCESS** What steps can we take to figure out which flower center is larger? Can you think of more than one way to answer the jester's question? (Use tracing paper to measure one center, then hold it over the other; or use a ruler to measure both flower centers.) *Story Prop*

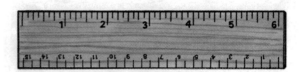

PHONICS KIT
HANDS-ON ACTIVITIES AND PRACTICE

Minilesson

REVIEW/MAINTAIN

Long *i* and Long *o*

Have students find the word *bright* on page 91 and the word *float* on page 99. Ask:

- What vowel sounds do you hear in these words? (long *i* and long *o*)
- How is the /ī/ sound spelled in the word *bright*? (*igh*)
- How is the /ō/ sound spelled in float? (*oa*)

Activity Ask students to brainstorm other words with the /ī/ and /ō/ sounds spelled *igh* and *oa*. Make a list of the words on the chalkboard.

Phonics CD-ROM Have students use the interactive phonics activities on the CD-ROM for more reinforcement.

91

Guided Instruction

16 **MAKE PREDICTIONS** We now know that there is going to be a party. What kind of party do you think it might be? For whom? What have you read so far that gives you a clue? (Maybe the fishing rod was a birthday gift for the Prince. A lot of children have birthday parties, so maybe this is a birthday party for the Prince.)

17 **STEPS IN A PROCESS** How can you tell if the mirror is crooked? (Use a ruler or a sheet of paper to trace the mirror to see if it is straight.)

18 Can anyone find the eight hidden faces in the illustration on page 92? Look back to page 89. Where were the faces hidden in that illustration? What steps will you take to figure out the illusion on this page? (Students should recall that they had to look closely to figure out the illusion on page 89. They should do the same for page 92.)
Use Illustrations

16 The Great Hall, ready for the party

17 Should the Queen straighten the mirror on the wall?
There are eight more faces.
Can you find them all?

18

92

Activity

Cross Curricular: Math

GEOMETRIC SHAPES Point out that there are many geometric shapes in the illustration on page 92.

RESEARCH AND INQUIRY Have students research other geometric shapes to compare with the ones used in the illustration. Have them make their own fantasy illustrations using some of these shapes.

▶ **Spatial/Mathematical**

*inter***NET** **CONNECTION** Students can learn more about geometric shapes by visiting **www.mhschool.com/reading**.

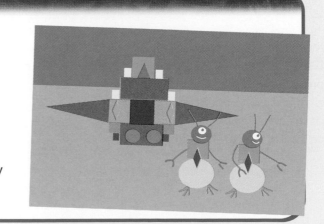

The Opt Sign pointing the way to the zoo ⑲

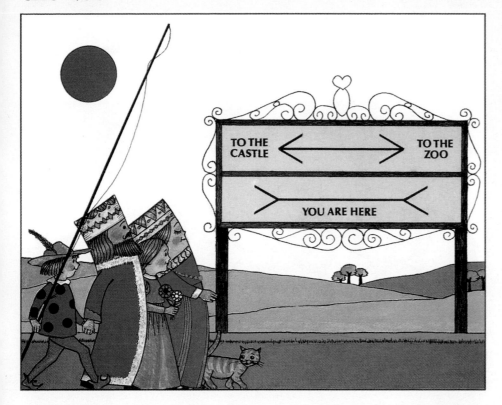

By the sign the royal family will stop.
Which line is longer, the bottom or top?
The King knows who the guest will be.
So do I—just follow me.

93

Guided Instruction

⑲ **MAKE PREDICTIONS** Can you predict where the royal family is going? (to the zoo) How can you tell? (The top sentence says that the sign is pointing the way to the zoo, and when I look at the illustration, I see that the royal family is walking in that direction.)

Minilesson

REVIEW/MAINTAIN

Summarize

Tell students that summarizing can help them better understand the story. Discuss how *Opt: An Illusionary Tale* is really two stories: one about the Prince's birthday, the other about optical illusions.

- Which of these stories do they think is the main story?

- How would they summarize the selection up to this point?

Activity Ask students to brainstorm a list of alternative titles for the part of the story that deals only with the optical illusions. Then ask them to brainstorm a list of titles for the selection if it were strictly a story about the Prince's birthday. Suggest they use their summaries to help them write their titles.

Guided Instruction

20 **STEPS IN A PROCESS** What directions are given on page 94? (*Turn the book around to find faces within faces.*) What happens when you follow the directions?

21 **MAKE PREDICTIONS** The body of the royal pet looks shorter than its neck, but is it? This is Opt! Should we trust what our eyes first tell us? Why or why not?

MODEL Since my eyes have been playing tricks on me throughout the book, I predict that its body is probably not shorter than its neck.

TEACHING TIP

MANAGEMENT As students read, encourage them to discuss how they feel about the illustrations. Do they enjoy trying to figure out how each illusion works, or are they frustrated? If you find some students feeling frustrated, you might want to pair them with students who enjoy and understand the illusions.

The Opt Zoo, home of amazing animals

opt zoo

Faces within faces can be found—
20 if you just turn the book around.
Is the body of the royal pet shorter than its neck?
21 Is the height of the zookeeper's hat the same as

94

Activity

Cross Curricular: Social Studies

MONARCHIES Tell students that there are many countries that still have kings and queens. Their governments are called *monarchies*.

RESEARCH AND INQUIRY Tell students that some countries with monarchies are the United Kingdom, Sweden, the Netherlands, Belgium, and Denmark. Have students locate these countries on the map.

EUROPE

SWEDEN

DENMARK

UNITED KINGDOM

NETHERLANDS

BELGIUM

0   250   500 Miles
0   250   500 Kilometers

AFRICA

The Zookeeper and the Royal Pet hearing the news

the width of its brim?
For thirty seconds stare at the star that is blue.
Now look at white paper—a colorful change,
just for you.

22   **23**

95

Guided Instruction

22 **STEPS IN A PROCESS** Why is it important to follow the directions exactly? Why might you not see any color change? (because you didn't follow the steps carefully)

MODEL When I read page 95, I didn't see any color change. Let me reread the directions to make sure I followed them properly. Oh, I only stared at the blue star for a few seconds, and the jester tells me to stare at it for thirty seconds. I'll try again, this time following the steps exactly as I'm supposed to. Now I see the color change!

23 Look at the faces of the King, the zookeeper, and the royal pet. Do you think the news is good or bad? (The news is probably good, because they are smiling.) *Draw Conclusions*

LANGUAGE SUPPORT

ESL Write the words *look* and *stare* on the chalkboard. Have a volunteer explain the difference between the words. Review that the jester wants us to stare at the blue star. This means we must look at it very hard for a long time.

To reinforce the word *stare*, have partners play a "staring game." See which

partner can stare at the other the longest without smiling. To reinforce the word *look*, have partners play a game of "I Spy." Each partner says "I spy something with my eye that begins with the letter ___." Have the other partner look around the room and try to guess the word.

95

Guided Instruction

24 **STEPS IN A PROCESS** How can we find out if the color shades are the same or different? Who would like to show the class how to figure this one out? (One way might be to block out some of the background using self-stick notes.)

The Pavilion decorated with banners

Are the banners light green or dark green, light pink or dark pink?
Some say they're the same shade.
24 But what do *you* think?

96

Activity

Cross Curricular: Art

BACKGROUND COLORS Have students make their own pairs of optical-illusion banners like those shown on page 96. You will need colored construction paper, scissors, and glue.

Have each student choose three colors of construction paper—two for the banner's background and one for the design. Tell students the decorations must be identical. Then have students cut out and glue their decorations onto their banners. Hang pairs of completed banners around the class.

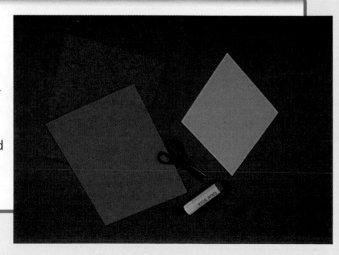

The Tower with guard spotting the guest

The guard marches up, stair by stair—
but is he getting anywhere?
He sees the guest.
Who can it be?
Turn the page and you will see! **25**

97

25 **MAKE PREDICTIONS** Can anyone predict who the guest might be? *(a fire-breathing dragon)* What clues do you see on this page that help you make that prediction? *(They all look surprised as they point up at the guest. There are some flames coming from where the guest is standing.)*

MULTIPLE-MEANING WORDS Read the words at the top of page 97. Is *spotting* a noun or a verb? *(verb)* What does the word mean here? *(seeing)*

PREVENTION/INTERVENTION

MULTIPLE-MEANING WORDS
Help students identify *spot* as the base word of *spotting*. Ask: Can you spot a spot on the board? Point out that, like many words, *spot* has more than one meaning. As a verb, it means "to see." As a noun, it means "a mark" or "a place." Discuss which meaning applies on page 97.

Explain that the words *spot*, *tower*, and

guard can be used as nouns as well as verbs. Group students in pairs. Have one student use these words as nouns in sentences and the other use them as verbs. Have students exchange papers and illustrate one of their partner's sentences. Then encourage students to brainstorm other words with multiple meanings. (Examples: *bank, charge*)

97

Guided Instruction

26 **MAKE PREDICTIONS** The guest has arrived! What is the narrator telling you about on this page? (The dragon arrives at the party with presents.) **What do you think will happen next?** (The dragon looks dangerous, but since he's bringing gifts and he's the guest, the party may be starting now.)

27 What is realistic in this illustration? (kites, presents) **What is fantasy?** (fire-breathing dragon) *Fantasy and Reality*

28 **STEPS IN A PROCESS** What optical illusion does the jester ask about? (He asks whether the ribbons on the gift are straight.) **What makes the ribbons look crooked?** (the lines on the present) **How can you prove that the lines are straight?** (use a ruler to line up along the ribbons)

26 The Guest is here!

The fire-snorting dragon now comes in.
Turn the book and his eyes will spin.
Arriving with presents—and none too late.
28 But did he tie the red ribbons on straight?

98

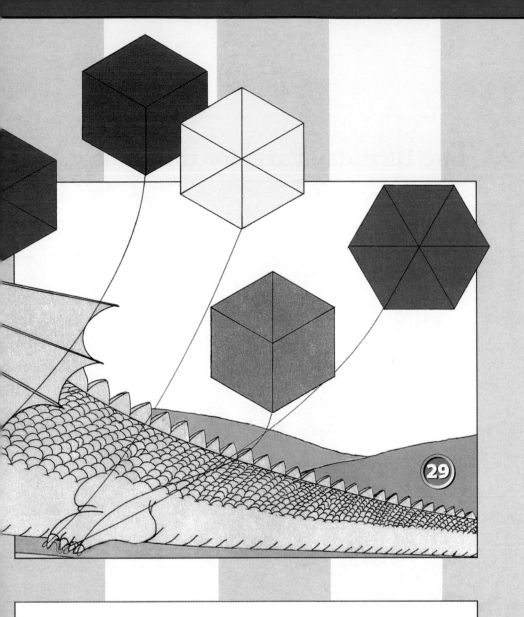

Look closely at the bright kites in the air.
Do flat kites or box kites float up there?

99

Guided Instruction

29 Look at the kites on pages 98 and 99. Study how they are drawn. How are the kites alike? How are they different? (At first glance, some of the kites appear to be box kites and others to be flat because they have different patterns of lines. However, when looked at more closely, the kites are alike in that each could be either a flat or box kite.) *Compare and Contrast*

Minilesson

REVIEW/MAINTAIN

Make Inferences

Tell students that a story's words and pictures can help them understand the different characters' emotions.

• Ask students: Based on what you have read and seen in this story so far, is the dragon a welcome or unwelcome guest? What words and pictures lead you to this conclusion?

Activity Ask students to go back and rewrite the story about the Prince's party; but to make the dragon an unwelcome guest in their version. Students may also want to illustrate the story, and students who need help with English may do a wordless picture book.

Guided Instruction

(30) STEPS IN A PROCESS How do six blocks turn into seven? (The jester tells us to stand on our heads to find out.) Is that a direction we can easily follow? What other steps could we take to get the same results? (turn the book upside down)

RETELL THE STORY Ask volunteers to tell what the selection was about. (There are two main ideas: It was a story about the Prince's birthday party, and it was also about optical illusions.) Then have partners write one or two sentences that summarize the main events in the story. Have them use their rulers and the illusions repeated here to remind them of the optical illusions in the story. *Summarize*

STUDENT SELF-ASSESSMENT

- How did using Steps in a Process help me understand what was happening in the selection?

- After I came to see what the story was about, what predictions could I make about illustrations I had yet to see?

TRANSFERRING THE STRATEGY

- When might I follow Steps in a Process again? What other kinds of information might this help me find?

The Birthday Party for the Prince

This gift, unwrapped, tells the Prince's age.
This is what the dragon said,
"Six blocks become seven if you stand on your head.
HAPPY BIRTHDAY!"

100

REREADING FOR *Fluency*

PARTNERS Have students choose a two-page spread from the selection to read and explain to a partner. Encourage students to pause briefly at commas and dashes, pause at the ends of sentences, and use their voices to express asking questions and making exclamations.

READING RATE You may want to evaluate an individual student's reading rate. Have the student read aloud from *Opt: An Illusionary Tale* for one minute. Ask the student to place a self-stick note after the last word read. Then count the number of words he or she has read.

A Running Record form provided in **Diagnostic/Placement Evaluation** will help you evaluate reading rate(s).

The Dragon saying good-bye

The dragon was a perfect guest.
The party was a great success.
But *you* don't have to go away,
come join me in Opt any day.

101

LITERARY RESPONSE

QUICK-WRITE Invite students to record their ideas about the story. These questions may help get them started:

- How important were the illustrations to the story?
- Was solving the optical illusions a challenge or a chore?

- What was your favorite optical illusion? Why?

ORAL RESPONSE Have students share their journal writings and discuss what they liked most and least about the story.

Guided Instruction

Return to Predictions and Purposes

Review with students their story predictions and reasons for reading the story. Were their predictions correct? Did they find out what they wanted to know?

PREDICTIONS	WHAT HAPPENED
The story is about a royal family.	Part of the story was about the Prince's birthday party.
The illustrations are clues.	The illustrations are the main reason for the story—it is all about optical illusions.

STEPS IN A PROCESS

HOW TO ASSESS

- Can students give at least one example of steps they took to find information about one of the optical illusions in this story?
- Can students find examples of Steps in a Process in the Jester's directions to them?

Students should know that they can find information by following Steps in a Process. They should also know that following directions means following Steps in a Process.

FOLLOW UP

If students have trouble understanding Steps in a Process, have them think of a task that requires directions to complete (for example: directions to a game, cooking directions, fire-drill directions, and so on). Ask volunteers to write the Steps in a Process on the chalkboard.

Story Questions

✤ TEKS ELA 3.9: F; H TAAS 3R3 (3.9: F) 3R4 (3.9: H)

Have students discuss or write answers to the questions on page 102.

Answers:

1. The story takes place in Opt, a make-believe kingdom. *Literal/Setting*

2. Answers will vary. *Literal/Steps in a Process*

3. The most important rule to follow is never to believe what you see at first glance. *Inferential/Judgments and Decisions*

4. The story is mainly about optical illusions. *Critical/Summarize*

5. Answers will vary. Possible answer: Phoebe would have fun with the optical illusions. *Critical/Reading Across Texts*

Write a Story For a full writing process lesson related to this suggestion, see page 105K.

✤ TEKS ELA 3.18: A,B,C,D,E,F
TAAS 4W2 (3.18: B) 4W3 (3.18: D) 4W4 (3.18: B,C) 4W5 (3.18: C) 4W7 (3.18: D)

Story Questions & Activities

1. Where does this story take place?

2. What is your favorite illusion in Opt? Explain how it works.

3. What is the most important rule to follow in the land of Opt?

4. What is this story mainly about?

5. What if Phoebe found herself in the land of Opt? What would she do?

Write a Story

Write a story about a time when something turned out to be different from what you expected. Maybe a scary sound was actually the wind. Be sure your story has a beginning, middle, and end.

Meeting Individual Needs

EASY	ON-LEVEL	CHALLENGE
Name___ Date___ Reteach **16**	Name___ Date___ Practice **17**	Name___ Date___ Extend **16**
Vocabulary	**Story Comprehension**	**Vocabulary**
Finish these sentences with words from the list.	Review the optical illusions shown in "Opt." Then list two of the illusions under each heading. Answers may vary. Sample answers are shown.	length / within / straighten / royal / guard / gift
gift guard length royal straighten within		Write a paragraph about a royal castle, using as many vocabulary words from the box as you can. Then erase those vocabulary words or cover them with tape. Exchange paragraphs with a partner and fill in the blanks.
1. Whenever the King was sleeping, a ___guard___ was ordered to stand outside the door of the ___royal___ bedroom.	**What Colors Do You See?** / **How Many Objects?**	
2. The pretty ___gift___ was wrapped with blue paper and bows.	1. White balloon appears green. / 3. Trident prongs change in number.	Extend **17**
3. A teddy bear was found ___within___ the box.	2. Gray dots appear where white lines cross. / 4. Six blocks become seven.	**Story Comprehension**
4. The Queen used a ruler to find the ___length___ of her hair.	**The Same Size?** / **Hidden Faces?**	Opt is a land where things don't always look as they really are. As you answer each question, explain how you decided your answer.
5. She decided to ___straighten___ her hair so that it would look longer.	5. Red tape appears longer than blue. / 7. Faces are hidden in portraits.	1. Which line is longer—A or B? How can you prove you are correct? Measure the lines.
Story Comprehension Reteach **17**	6. King appears taller than queen. / 8. Faces are hidden in zoo animals.	2. Is the shape you see here a perfect circle? How can you prove you are correct? Place a dime in the circle.
Write the answers to these questions about "Opt: An Illusionary Tale."	**Straight or Crooked?** / **Changing Shapes?**	
1. Why is Opt a strange place? What you think you see is not always what you really see.	9. Vertical lines on cloak appear crooked. / 11. Kites appear flat or box-shaped.	
2. What is strange about the sizes of things in Opt? Things that seem to be different sizes are really the same size.	10. Fishing rod appears crooked. / 12. The dragon's eyes seem to spin.	
Reteach, 17	**Practice, 17**	**Extend, 17**

Create an Optical Illusion

Follow these steps to make your own optical illusion.

1. Use a ruler to draw two parallel lines four inches long. Draw the lines about one inch apart.
2. On the top line, draw a V pointing inward at each end of the line.
3. On the bottom line, draw a V pointing outward at each end.
4. Ask a friend if one of the lines looks longer.

Make a Travel Brochure

Make a travel brochure for the land of Opt. Tell why people should visit there and describe some of the strange things they will see. Draw pictures to go along with your descriptions.

Find Out More

What would you like to know about real-life castles? Find out more. Share what you learn by creating castle fact cards and displaying them in your classroom.

103

Story Activities

Create an Optical Illusion

Materials: paper, rulers, pencils or felt-tipped markers

ONE When students have finished their illusions, discuss why the line with the V pointing outward looks longer. (The line looks longer because it draws your eyes outward like an arrow. It creates the illusion that the line continues in each direction farther than the other line.)

Make a Travel Brochure

Materials: paper, felt-tipped markers, stapler

GROUP Explain that travel brochures help people get an idea of different places they may visit. Present some brochures from a local travel agent for students to study. After groups make their brochures for Opt, display the brochures for the class to review.

Find Out More

RESEARCH AND INQUIRY Have partners **PARTNERS** write two or three questions about castles. They can find more information about castles by consulting encyclopedias, books, or the Internet.

Encourage them to use descriptive language and detailed illustrations on their fact cards. Have partners present their cards to the class.

 *inter*NET **CONNECTION** Go to **www.mhschool.com/ reading** for more information about castles.

FORMAL ASSESSMENT

After page 103, see the Selection Assessment.

103

Study Skills

PARTS OF A BOOK

OBJECTIVES

Students will:

- identify information from book covers.
- use a table of contents.

PREPARE Look at the covers and read the table of contents for *Ramona and Her Mother* with students. Display **Teaching Chart 15**.

TEACH Remind students that a book's cover and table of contents provide important information. Discuss what the book's cover can tell. Review how to use a table of contents.

PRACTICE Have students answer questions 1–5. Review the answers with them. **1.** *All About Optical Illusions* **2.** *All About Optical Illusions* **3.** 89 **4.** Made up; Ramona stories are fiction. **5.** Answers will vary.

ASSESS/CLOSE Have students create their own book covers and tables of contents for books they have read and enjoyed.

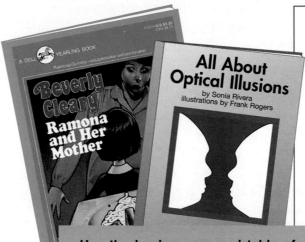

STUDY SKILLS

Use a Table of Contents

"Opt: An Illusionary Tale" blends science fact with fantasy in an unusual way. With most other books, it is easier to tell whether they are **fiction** or **nonfiction**. A book that tells about made-up characters and events is **fiction**. A book that tells about real people, places, and things is **nonfiction**.

Contents

1	A Present for Willa Jean	11
2	Slacks for Ella Funt	35
3	Nobody Likes Ramona	59
4	The Quarrel	89
5	The Great Hair Argument	115
6	Ramona's New Pajamas	150
7	The Telephone Call	175

Use the book covers and table of contents to answer these questions.

1 Which of these two books is nonfiction?

2 In which book would you find information about illusions?

3 If you finished chapter three of *Ramona and Her Mother* last night, what page should you turn to today?

4 Does the chapter "The Telephone Call" tell about a real or a made-up event? Explain.

5 What do you think a chapter title in *All About Optical Illusions* might be?

Meeting Individual Needs

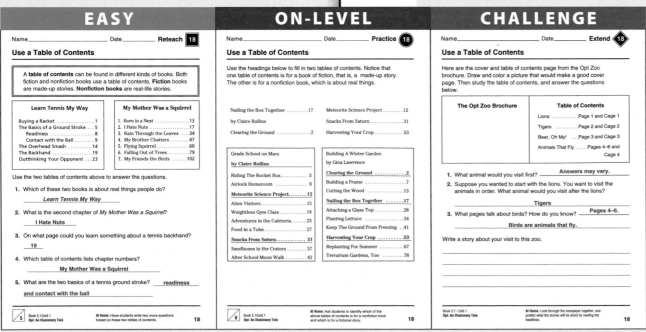

EASY

Name_____ Date_____ Reteach **18**

Use a Table of Contents

A **table of contents** can be found in different kinds of books. Both fiction and nonfiction books use a table of contents. **Fiction** books are made-up stories. **Nonfiction** books are real-life stories.

Learn Tennis My Way	My Mother Was a Squirrel
Buying a Racket 1	1. Born in a Nest 13
The Basics of a Ground Stroke. . . .5	2. I Hate Nuts 17
Readiness 8	3. Rain Through the Leaves . . .34
Contact with the Ball 9	4. My Brother Chatters 47
The Overhead Smash 14	5. Flying Squirrel 60
The Backhand 19	6. Falling Out of Trees 79
Outthinking Your Opponent . . .23	7. My Friends the Birds 102

Use the two tables of contents above to answer the questions.

1. Which of these two books is about real things people do?
   Learn Tennis My Way

2. What is the second chapter of *My Mother Was a Squirrel*?
   I Hate Nuts

3. On what page could you learn something about a tennis backhand?
   19

4. Which table of contents lists chapter numbers?
   My Mother Was a Squirrel

5. What are the two basics of a tennis ground stroke? **readiness and contact with the ball**

Book 3.1/Unit 1
Opt: An Illusionary Tale
At Home: Have students write two more questions based on these two tables of contents. **18**

Reteach, 18

ON-LEVEL

Name_____ Date_____ Practice **18**

Use a Table of Contents

Use the headings below to fill in two tables of contents. Notice that one table of contents is for a book of fiction, that is, a made-up story. The other is for a nonfiction book, which is about real things.

Nailing the Box Together 17	Meteorite Science Project 12
by Claire Rollins	Snacks From Saturn 31
Clearing the Ground 2	Harvesting Your Crop 53

Grade School on Mars	Building A Winter Garden
by Claire Rollins	by Gina Lawrence
Riding The Rocket Bus. 3	**Clearing the Ground** 2
Airlock Homeroom 8	Building a Frame 7
Meteorite Science Project. 12	Cutting the Wood 13
Alien Visitors. 15	**Nailing the Box Together** 17
Weightless Gym Class 19	Attaching a Glass Top 28
Adventures in the Cafeteria. 23	Planting Lettuce 34
Food in a Tube 27	Keep The Ground From Freezing . .41
Snacks From Saturn. 31	**Harvesting Your Crop** 53
Sandboxes in the Craters 37	Replanting For Summer 67
After School Moon Walk 42	Terrarium Gardens, Too 78

Book 3.1/Unit 1
Opt: An Illusionary Tale
At Home: Ask students to identify which of the above tables of contents is for a nonfiction book and which is for a fictional story. **18**

Practice, 18

CHALLENGE

Name_____ Date_____ Extend **18**

Use a Table of Contents

Here are the cover and table of contents page from the Opt Zoo brochure. Draw and color a picture that would make a good cover page. Then study the table of contents, and answer the questions below.

The Opt Zoo Brochure	Table of Contents
	Lions . . . . .Page 1 and Cage 1
	Tigers . . . . .Page 2 and Cage 2
	Bear, Oh My! . . .Page 3 and Cage 3
	Animals That Fly . . . .Pages 4–6 and Cage 4

1. What animal would you visit first? **Answers may vary.**

2. Suppose you wanted to start with the lions. You want to visit the animals in order. What animal would you visit after the lions?
   Tigers

3. What pages talk about birds? How do you know? **Pages 4–6.**
   Birds are animals that fly.

Write a story about your visit to this zoo.

_____

_____

_____

Book 3.1 / Unit 1
Opt: An Illusionary Tale
At Home: Look through the newspaper together, and predict what the stories will be about by reading the headlines. **18**

Extend, 18

TEST POWER

DIRECTIONS:
Read the story. Then read each question about the story.

SAMPLE

The Essay Contest

Arabella sat at the table and looked at a contest flyer.

Rules:
Write about a real person. The essay should be three pages long and your name should be on each page.

Schedule:
May 1 Essays turned in to teacher
May 2 Essays judged
May 8 Winners announced

Prizes:
All prizes will be given the last day of school.
First-prize essays will be entered in the State Fair.
Second-prize essays will receive a book.

1 To follow the rules, Arabella should—

○ write about an imaginary person

● write her name on every page of her essay

○ write an essay that is five pages long

○ write about a wild animal

2 To enter the contest, Arabella must turn in her essay by—

● May 1

○ May 2

○ May 5

○ May 8

Why are your answers correct?

105

Test Power

THE PRINCETON REVIEW

Read the Page

Have students read all of the information on the flyer. Instruct students to pay special attention to information under the bold titles.

Discuss the Questions

QUESTION 1: This question refers specifically to the rules (a heading on the flyer). Direct students to review the flyer. Have students read through all of the answer choices before choosing the best answer. Explain that students should eliminate answer choices that discuss things that were not mentioned on the flyer.

QUESTION 2: This question also requires students to locate information under a bold title. Teach students to work through the answer choices using process of elimination. Ask students: What happens on May 1?

ITBS/TEST PREPARATION

TERRANOVA/TEST PREPARATION

SAT 9/TEST PREPARATION

EASY

Answers to Story Questions

1. They went to Timbuktu to trade their goods at the market.

2. First, crossing the Atlas Mountains. Second, crossing the Sahara Desert.

3. They need things that aren't available where they live. They are able to trade what they have for those things in Timbuktu.

4. The story is about a young boy's first trip with his father across the desert and what he learned.

5. The mirage is a natural occurrence; the illusions in Opt are illusions drawn on paper. Both kinds of illusions play tricks on the eyes.

Story Questions and Writing Activity

1. Why did Ali and his father travel to Timbuktu?

2. What was the first part of their journey? What was the second?

3. Why do you think Ali and his father have to go to Marrakesh to trade?

4. What is the story mostly about?

5. Ali sees an illusion in the desert, and the Land of Opt is full of illusions. What is different about the illusion in the desert and the ones in *Opt*? What is the same about them?

Write About Your Solution

Suppose there were 50 camels in Ali's caravan. Thirty-one camels carried cloth and 19 camels carried spices. How many more camels carried cloth than carried spices? Write two or three sentences explaining how you determined the answer.

from Journey Across the Desert

Leveled Books

EASY

Journey Across the Desert

Long *i* and Long *o*

☑ Steps in a Process

☑ Instructional Vocabulary: *gift, guard, length, royal, straighten, within*

Guided Reading

PREVIEW AND PREDICT As you conduct a **picture walk**, ask: Why do the characters journey across the desert? What might the journey be like? Have students record their predictions.

SET PURPOSES Have students write down questions that they would like to have answered by the story. For example, they might want to know where Ali is going.

READ THE BOOK Use the questions to guide children's reading or after they have read the story independently.

Page 2: Who tells this story? (a boy named Ali who lives in Morocco) *Character*

Page 4: How does Ali's father prepare for his trip? (He loads and then ties packs on the camels.) *Steps in a Process*

Pages 6–7: How does the group begin its journey? (with a climb up the Atlas Mountains) What do they move toward? (the Sahara Desert) *Steps in a Process*

Page 8: What does a *guard* do? (protects someone or something from harm) How is the cloth around Ali's face like a guard? (It

protects his eyes, nose, and mouth.) *Vocabulary*

Page 9: Read the first paragraph. What words do you hear with the long *o* sound? *(blowing, robes)* Now read the second paragraph. What words have the long *i* sound? *(night, fire, shining)* Discuss the different spellings that make the /ō/ and /ī/ sounds. *Phonics and Decoding*

RETURN TO PREDICTIONS AND PURPOSES Review students' predictions and reasons for reading. Which predictions were accurate? Were their questions answered?

LITERARY RESPONSE Discuss these questions:

- What would be your favorite part of the journey? Why?

- What is something new you learned from reading this story?

Also see the story questions and activity in *Journey Across the Desert*.

See the **Phonics CD-ROM** for practice using words with long *i* and long *o*.

Leveled Books

PUPIL SELECTION

↓

INDEPENDENT

INDEPENDENT

Magical Illusions: Simple Tricks You Can Do!

☑ **Steps in a Process**

☑ **Instructional Vocabulary:**
gift, guard, length, royal, straighten, within

Magical Illusions: Simple Tricks You Can Do!

Written by Michael Teitelbaum
Illustrated by Jared Lee

Guided Reading

PREVIEW AND PREDICT Conduct a **picture walk** with students. Ask: Which trick do you think will be the best? Do you think you will be able to do the tricks?

SET PURPOSES Students should jot down a purpose for reading. For example, they may want to learn how to do the Vanishing Penny trick.

READ THE BOOK Have students read the story independently. After they have read the story, use the questions below to guide students' reading.

Pages 4–5: Read the third sentence. Does the word *straighten* mean that you should bend your fingers or make them straight? *Vocabulary*

Pages 6–7: What is the step you must do in order for the Disappearing Pencil trick to work? (You must use your index finger to hold the cloth as you cover the pencil with it.) *Steps in a Process*

Pages 12–13: What must you do before you begin the Vanishing Penny trick? Why? (Place a penny in the palm of your left hand and place a clear glass with a little bit

of water in it over the penny so it will look like the penny is in the glass) *Steps in a Process*

Pages 14–15: Which of the following sentences tells you the correct way to do the Royal Illusion?

1. Stare at a blank wall for one minute, then stare at the picture for one minute.

2. Stare at the picture for one minute, then stare at a blank wall for one minute.
(sentence 2) *Steps in a Process*

RETURN TO PREDICTIONS AND PURPOSES Review students' predictions and reasons for reading. Did they learn more about tricks? Were they able to perform a trick?

LITERARY RESPONSE Discuss these questions:

• Why do you think people are entertained by illusions?

• Which trick would they like to teach a friend or family member how to do?

Also see the story questions and activity in *Magical Illusions: Simple Tricks You Can Do!*

Answers to Story Questions

1. An illusion is something that appears to be one thing, but is really something else.

2. No, they can be done with simple, everyday materials.

3. Gather the materials, practice, and assemble the audience in front of a table.

4. Some magical illusions are simple to perform and are fun to learn. Illusions are sometimes just tricks that our eyes and brain play on us.

5. Answers will vary.

Story Questions and Writing Activity

1. What Is an Illusion?

2. Do the illusions require special materials?

3. What would you have to do to get ready to perform an illusion such as *The Disappearing Pencil* on page 6?

4. What is the main idea of this book?

5. If you were to perform some of the tricks in this book for the king and queen in the land of Opt, which tricks would you choose? Explain.

Come to a Magic Show!

Pretend you are a magician getting ready to put on a show. Create a poster for your magic show. Come up with a magician's name for yourself (like "The Great Houdini" or "Marvin the Magnificent"). Write that name on the poster. Also write the time and place of your magic show. Draw a picture of yourself in a magician's costume to put on your poster.

from *Magical Illusions*

105B

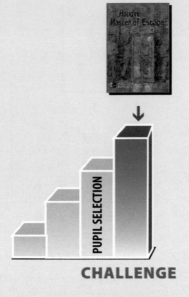

PUPIL SELECTION

CHALLENGE

from *Houdini: Master of Escape*

EXTEND

Have students imagine and draw an amazing escape. Share work.

Answers to Story Questions

1. His brother Theo, then his wife, Bess.
2. Houdini sounded more dramatic and reminded people of Robert Houdin.
3. Answers will vary.
4. The book tells about the life and career of Harry Houdini.
5. Answers will vary.

Story Questions and Writing Activity

1. Who helped Harry in his stage act?
2. Why do think Houdini changed his name from Ehrich Weiss?
3. Step by step, how might you go about becoming a magician?
4. What is the main idea of this book?
5. If, instead of the dragon, Houdini had been the guest in *Opt: An Illusionary Tale*, how might the story have been different?

Which Was the Best One?

Write about the Houdini trick that you liked the best. Why did you like it better than the others? Did you think that some tricks were harder to do? If you were going to do a magic act, which of Houdini's tricks would you like to try? Explain why.

Leveled Books

Houdini: Master of Escape

Written by Michael Teitelbaum
Illustrated by Mary Haverfield

CHALLENGE

Houdini: Master of Escape

- ☑ **Steps in a Process**
- ☑ **Instructional Vocabulary:** *gift, guard, length, royal, straighten, within*

Guided Reading

PREVIEW AND PREDICT Conduct a **picture walk.** Have students make predictions about the story based on the illustrations and title.

SET PURPOSES Students should write down questions that they would like to have answered by the story. For example, they may want to know if Houdini got hurt doing any tricks.

READ THE BOOK Have students read the story independently. Then use the questions below to guide their reading.

Pages 2–3: Who is this story about? (Harry Houdini) *Character*

Pages 4–5: How did reading the biography of the greatest French magician affect young Houdini? (It convinced Houdini to make magic his life's work; he took his stage name after the French magician, Houdin.) *Cause and Effect*

Page 7: How would the Houdini brothers begin their show? (Harry would do small stunts like pulling a handkerchief out of a candle flame.) How would they end it? (with the trunk trick) *Steps in a Process*

Pages 10–11: Find the word *guards* in the last sentence. What other words help you figure out what a guard is? (*jail cell*) What do you think a guard does? (watches over something or someone to prevent escape) *Vocabulary*

Pages 12–13: What did Houdini do so that he could free himself from a straightjacket while hanging from a crane? (He dislocated his shoulder.) *Steps in a Process*

RETURN TO PREDICTIONS AND PURPOSES Review students' predictions and reasons for reading. Were their predictions accurate? Were all their questions answered?

LITERARY RESPONSE Discuss these questions:

- Why was it important for Houdini to follow the steps of his tricks exactly? What might have happened if he hadn't?

- Why do you think people liked to see Houdini perform his tricks?

Also see the story questions and activity in *Houdini: Master of Escape.*

Activities
Anthology and Leveled Books

Connecting Texts

CLASS DISCUSSION
Lead a discussion of how the theme Illusions applies to each story. Ask questions such as these:

- What is an illusion?

- What are some examples of illusions?

- What parts of your body are fooled by illusions?

- Why is it necessary to follow steps when performing an illusion?

WORD WEB Have students create a web that contains general information about tricks and illusions.

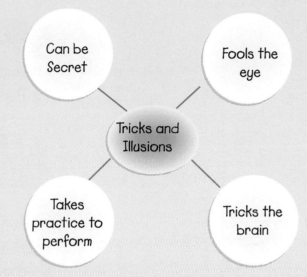

Viewing/Representing

GROUP PRESENTATIONS Divide the class into groups, one for each of the four books read in the lesson. (For *Opt: An Illusionary Tale*, combine students of different reading levels.) Have each group choose an illusion represented in their book. Have them explain or demonstrate how the trick or illusion is done.

AUDIENCE RESPONSE Ask students to pay attention to each group's presentation. Allow time for questions after each presentation.

Research and Inquiry

MORE ABOUT ILLUSIONS Have students ask themselves: Can I learn to use illusions in magic tricks? Invite students to do the following:

- Go to the library and find a book about magic tricks. (There are several listed in the back of *Magical Illusions: Simple Tricks You Can Do!*)

- Practice some of the tricks in the book.

- Research other famous magicians. Did each have a certain trick or kind of trick that was a specialty? Why do you think they did this?

 For more about illusions, students can visit **www.mhschool.com/reading.**

OBJECTIVES

Students will organize information as steps in a process.

Review Steps in a Process

PREPARE

Discuss Steps in a Process Review: Use steps in a process to help you find and organize information. Sometimes these steps are given in the form of directions, other times you must think of them yourself. Ask students how they used steps in a process while reading *Opt: An Illusionary Tale*.

TEACH

Read "Houdini" and Model the Skill Ask students to pay close attention to steps in a process as you read the **Teaching Chart 16** passage with them.

Houdini

William's favorite magician was named Harry Houdini. William decided that this would be a perfect subject for his school report.

First he needed to gather information about the magician. He went to the library to look for some books. He found three books and one encyclopedia article about Houdini's life. Next he took notes on the information he gathered. He even used his computer at home to find articles from the Internet.

Using an outline, he organized his information. Finally he was ready to write his report.

Teaching Chart 16

Discuss the steps William took to find the information he wanted.

MODEL William really wanted to write his report about Houdini. I can tell that he has put a lot of thought into his report. He followed many steps in order to gather information. He started by going to the library. That was the first step in the process.

PRACTICE

Identify Steps in a Process

GROUP

Have students identify and underline the steps William took to find the information he wanted for his report.

Next, ask students to explain how these steps compare to steps they took while writing reports of their own. ▶ **Logical/Interpersonal**

ASSESS/CLOSE

Write Directions for a Favorite Activity

Ask each student to think of an activity (for example, building paper airplanes). Then ask students to pretend they will teach that activity to someone who has never heard of that activity or seen that activity before. Ask each student to write down the directions, or the steps in the process, for the other person to follow. Remind students they need to write the steps clearly and completely so the other person will understand their directions.

ALTERNATE TEACHING STRATEGY

STEPS IN A PROCESS

For a different approach to teaching this skill, see page T66.

SELF-SELECTED Reading

Students may choose from the following titles:

ANTHOLOGY

• *Opt: An Illusionary Tale*

LEVELED BOOKS

• *Journey Across the Desert*

• *Magical Illusions: Simple Tricks You Can Do!*

• *Houdini: Master of Escape*

Bibliography, pages T76–T77

Meeting Individual Needs for Comprehension

EASY	ON-LEVEL	CHALLENGE	LANGUAGE SUPPORT

EASY

Name_____ Date_____ Reteach **19**

Steps in a Process

It is important to be able to follow the **steps in a process**. This is especially important in solving a problem.

Look back at the pictures from "Opt" described in the questions below. Then write the steps you followed to figure out what was really in the pictures. Answers may vary.

The King and Queen are waiting for a message. Who is taller?

1. First, I thought the King was _____ taller._____

2. Then, I _measured the height of each figure._

3. I discovered that _the King and the Queen were the same height._

How many ladies are framed in the Royal Art Gallery?

4. When I first looked at the drawing, I only saw _____ two _____ framed ladies.

5. As I looked at them longer, though, I saw _two more ladies'_ _portraits._

6. Then in the base of the table, I saw _two more faces._

7. Therefore, I counted a total of _____ six _____ faces.

The royal family stops at the sign. Which is the longer line, the bottom or the top?

8. First, I _measured the top line._

9. Then, I _measured the bottom line._

10. I found out that _the lines are the same length._

19   At Home: Have students choose their favorite picture from "Opt" and explain why they liked it.   Book 3.1/Unit 1 Opt: An Illusionary Tale **10**

ON-LEVEL

Name_____ Date_____ Practice **19**

Steps in a Process

Think about the steps you use when you solve a problem. Often you can use the same steps to solve other problems. Writing down the steps will help you remember them. A series of steps you follow in order are called **steps in a process**.

Read Problem 1 and the list of steps for solving it below. Then write a list of steps for solving Problem 2.

Problem 1

What steps will help you find out if the vertical lines of the messenger's cloak are crooked or straight?

Process

1. Measure the distance between two lines near the top.
2. Write down that number.
3. Measure the distance between the same two lines near the bottom.
4. Write down this number.
5. Compare your two measurements. If they are the same, the lines are straight.

Problem 2

In the picture of the Royal Pet at the zoo, what steps will help you decide if the body of the pet is shorter than its neck?

Process

1. Measure the length of the neck.
2. Write down that number.
3. Measure the length of the body.
4. Write down this number.
5. Compare the two measurements. If the second number is less, the body is shorter.

19   At Home: Have students follow the steps they wrote. What did they discover about the length of the Royal Pet's neck and body? Have them record the results.   Book 3.1/Unit 1 Opt: An Illusionary Tale **5**

CHALLENGE

Name_____ Date_____ Extend **19**

Steps in a Process

The following lists some things you might do if you are going to the zoo with the royal family. Two of these steps have nothing to do with going to the zoo. Mark an **X** beside those two steps. Then put the rest of the steps in order. Start with 1 for the first step. End with 5 for the last step.

_5_ 1. Say goodbye to the royal family and go home.

_1_ 2. Look at a map to find out how to get to the king's castle.

_X_ 3. Tie a ribbon around your bike.

_2_ 4. Greet the royal family at the castle.

_4_ 5. Have lunch with the royal family after seeing all of the animals.

_X_ 6. Rearrange your bedroom furniture.

_3_ 7. With the king's help, look at a map to find the zoo.

19   At Home: Plan the steps for running an everyday errand.   Book 3.1 / Unit 1 Opt: An Illusionary Tale

LANGUAGE SUPPORT

Name_____ Date_____

Make a Cake for a King

Show how the Jester made a cake. ▇▭▷ a number next to each picture. Show the steps in order. Start with the number 1.

Problem

Solution

22 Opt: An Illusionary Tale • Language Support/Blackline Master 10   Grade 3

Reteach, 19   **Practice, 19**   **Extend, 19**   **Language Support, 22**

OBJECTIVES

Students will analyze character and narrative point of view.

TEACHING TIP

INSTRUCTIONAL Tell students that a story's narrator may or may not be a character in the story. Discuss how the author's choice of narrator affects how we as readers see each character.

Review Story Elements

PREPARE

Discuss Characters and Point of View

Discuss a story the class recently read. Ask: From whose point of view was the story told? Choose a character from the story. Talk about what actions, thoughts, and words helped define him or her.

TEACH

Read "A Gift Fit for a Prince" and Model the Skill

Read "A Gift Fit for a Prince." Ask students: What do we learn about the characters of the narrator and the Prince from the passage?

A Gift Fit for a Prince

I wasn't sure what to get my friend the Prince for his birthday. What do you give a fun-loving boy who already has everything? Then I thought back to when I was six. That was many scales ago, but I still remember my favorite toy at that age was a set of wood blocks. I played with the blocks all the time, and would still have them if I hadn't accidentally breathed fire on them when I was eight. (I always was clumsy with fire.) I hope the Prince loves his wood blocks, too. Maybe he'll even let an old dragon like me play with them sometimes, if I promise to keep my mouth shut.

Teaching Chart 17

Ask students: Who or what is telling this story? What is the narrator like? What do we learn about the characters from this narrator? Have them circle clues to the narrator's identity.

MODEL The character telling the story is the dragon. I can tell because he mentions scales and breathing fire, and calls himself an "old dragon." From this passage we learn several things about the dragon's character—that he is friends with the Prince, clumsy with fire, and has a good sense of humor. We also learn that the Prince is fun-loving and, in the dragon's opinion, has everything.

PRACTICE

Create a Character Traits Chart

Have students create a Character Traits chart based on what they learned from the passage about the dragon's and Prince's characters.

▶ **Visual/Linguistic**

Dragon	Prince
friends with Prince	fun-loving
clumsy with fire	has everything
sense of humor	6 years old
old	it's his birthday

ASSESS/CLOSE

Create a Narrator's Point of View Chart

Have students create a Narrator's Point of View chart that lists the titles of several familiar books and stories and identifies the point of view from which the story is told.

ALTERNATE TEACHING STRATEGY

STORY ELEMENTS

For a different approach to teaching this skill, see page T60.

LOOKING AHEAD

Students will apply this skill as they read the next selection, *Max Malone.*

Meeting Individual Needs for Comprehension

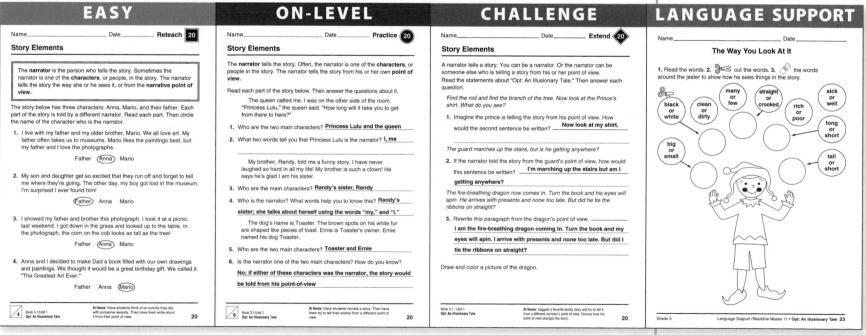

Reteach, 20   Practice, 20   Extend, 20   Language Support, 23

105H

OBJECTIVES

Students will identify the prefixes *un-* and *dis-* and recognize how prefixes change word meaning.

....

MATERIALS

- **Teaching Chart 18**
- prefix **Word Building Manipulative Cards**

TEACHING TIP

INSTRUCTIONAL The letters *un-* at the beginning of a word are not always a prefix. For example, in *uncle* and *under*, the letters *un-* are part of the base words.

Review Prefixes

PREPARE

Review Meaning of Prefixes *un-* and *dis-*

Review: A prefix is a word part added to the beginning of a base word. Prefixes have their own meanings. The prefixes *un-* and *dis-* both mean "not" or "the opposite of."

TEACH

Read the Passage and Model the Skill

Have students read the passage on **Teaching Chart 18**.

An Unusual Match

The Queen had a problem. She could not find any matches to light the unlit candles on the cake. The matches she bought had disappeared. She was unsure what to do when the dragon stepped forward.

"Allow me," he said.

The Queen felt uncomfortable as the huge dragon walked past her. The dragon blew gently on the cake. He lit every candle, but left everything else unharmed.

"Thanks!" said the Prince. He wished everyone could have a birthday as unforgettable as his.

Teaching Chart 18

Help students determine the meaning of *unlit*.

MODEL The word *unlit* in the second sentence begins with *un-*. The base word is *lit*. If *un-* means "not," then *unlit* means "not lit." Let me read that sentence again to see if that meaning makes sense.

Have students define *disappeared* in the third sentence, using the meaning of the prefix *dis-* with the base word. Ask them whether the word's meaning makes sense in the sentence.

PRACTICE

Identify Words with Prefixes

GROUP

Have volunteers underline each word in "An Unusual Match" that begins with the prefix *un-* or *dis-* and then circle the prefix. Have students discuss the meanings of the words. Have them focus on how the prefix changed the meaning of the base word.

▶ **Interpersonal/Linguistic**

ASSESS/CLOSE

Use Words with Prefixes

Have students write each of the words listed below on index cards. Then have them add the prefix *un-* or *dis-* (available from the Word Building Manipulative Cards) to each word. Ask partners to write a paragraph about the Prince's birthday party, using all the words. They may want to illustrate their paragraph.

wrap   tie   like   agree

ALTERNATE TEACHING STRATEGY
....

PREFIXES *un-* **AND** *dis-*
For a different approach to teaching this skill, see page T65.

Meeting Individual Needs for Vocabulary

EASY	ON-LEVEL	CHALLENGE	LANGUAGE SUPPORT

EASY — Reteach 21

Name_____ Date_____ Reteach **21**

Prefixes

A **prefix** is a word part or a group of letters that appears at the beginning of a word and changes the word's meaning. A prefix does not change the spelling of the base word. The prefix **dis-** means "opposite of" or "not." The prefix **un-** also means "not" or "opposite of."

dis- opposite of, not   dis + appear = disappear
un- opposite of, not   un + fair = unfair

Circle the prefix in each word. Then find the definition for each word in the list at the right. Write the definition of each word.

1. (un)lucky _____ not lucky _____   opposite of please
2. (dis)agree _____ to not agree _____   not locked
3. (un)happy _____ not happy _____   not true
4. (dis)obey _____ to not obey _____   opposite of appear
5. (un)usual _____ not usual _____   not like
6. (dis)appear _____ opposite of appear _____   not lucky
7. (un)locked _____ not locked _____   to not agree
8. (dis)please _____ opposite of please _____   not happy
9. (un)true _____ not true _____   not usual
10. (dis)like _____ not like _____   to not obey

21 **At Home:** Ask students to tell you the base word for each word listed on the left.   Book 3.1/Unit 1 Opt: An Illusionary Tale **20**

ON-LEVEL — Practice 21

Name_____ Date_____ Practice **21**

Prefixes

You can add the **prefixes un-** or **dis-** to the beginnings of some words to make new words. The prefix **un-** means "opposite of" or "not." The prefix **dis-** also means "opposite of."

Rewrite each sentence. Replace the underlined phrase with a word from the box that includes the prefix *un-* or *dis-*. Look at the following example:

Sean was not lucky flying the kite.
Sean was unlucky flying the kite.

unusual	unknown	displeased	disobeyed	unbelievable

1. The stranger was not known to the family.
   The stranger was unknown to the family.
2. Jeri did not please her science teacher.
   Jeri displeased her science teacher.
3. Quong's painting was not the same as everyone else's.
   Quong's painting was unusual.
4. My little brother can yell so loud it is not believable.
   My brother can yell so loud it is unbelievable.
5. Bruce did not obey the rule.
   Bruce disobeyed the rule.

21 **At Home:** Have students say a sentence that includes the word disagree.   Book 3.1/Unit 1 Opt: An Illusionary Tale **5**

CHALLENGE — Extend 21

Name_____ Date_____ Extend **21**

Prefixes

The prefixes *dis* and *un* can be added to some words to form their opposites. Read the sentences below. Add the prefix *un* or *dis* to a word in the first sentence to fill in the blank in the second sentence.

1. This is not your usual time. It is very _____ unusual _____ for you to be here now.
2. Do not agree with me! You must _____ disagree _____.
3. Flowers appear in the spring. They _____ disappear _____ when winter comes.
4. I was certain that I knew my words. However, now I'm really _____ uncertain _____.
5. Muffin did not obey my signals. I'm disappointed when he _____ disobeys _____.
6. That's not a real story. It is totally _____ unreal _____.

Imagine a visit to a museum or zoo. Use some words with the prefixes *dis* and *un* to tell a story about your imaginary visit.

_____
_____
_____
_____
_____

21 **At Home:** Try to have a conversation using only words with no prefixes. Talk about how much we use prefixes to make ourselves clear.   Book 3.1 / Unit 1 Opt: An Illusionary Tale

LANGUAGE SUPPORT

Name_____ Date_____

un- and dis- Words

1. Read the story. 2. Copy these words in the blanks to finish the story. 3. Draw a picture of the King and Queen's party.

wrap	true	announced	appears

The King and Queen gave such a strange party.

It was un_____ announced _____, but the guest showed up on time anyway.

The Queen was happy to un_____ wrap _____ all the beautiful gifts.

The cook said it was un_____ true _____ that the cake dis_____ appears _____ when the clock strikes twelve.

24 Opt: An Illusionary Tale • Language Support/Blackline Master 12   Grade 3

Reteach, 21   **Practice, 21**   **Extend, 21**   **Language Support, 24**

GRAMMAR/SPELLING
CONNECTIONS

See the 5-Day Grammar and Usage Plan on Subjects, pages 105M–105N.

See the 5-Day Spelling Plan on words with long *i* and long *o*, pages 105O–105P.

TECHNOLOGY TIP

A spell-checker won't tell you if you have used the correct punctuation. Always reread the story to check punctuation.

Personal Narrative

Prewrite

WRITE A STORY Present this writing assignment: Write a story about a time when something turned out different from what you had expected. Maybe a frightening sound turned out to be the wind. Be sure your story has a beginning, middle, and end.

VISUALIZING AND DRAWING Tell students that visualizing their story ideas will help them organize their thoughts. Have students draw one picture of what they thought they saw or heard and another of what it actually was.

Strategy: List Your Ideas Have students think of a main idea for their story and then brainstorm a list of details. Present the following suggestions:

- List details of the setting to tell when and where the event took place.
- List details of how you felt.
- List the steps you took to discover the truth.

Draft

USE THE LIST Have students free write a story line based on their idea lists. They can also use inspirations from their earlier descriptions and drawings. Remind them to include their personal feelings and important visual details.

Revise

SELF-QUESTIONING Ask students to assess their drafts.

- Does my story describe what I thought I saw or heard?
- Have I shown my experience?
- What sensory details or descriptive words would make my story more effective?

PARTNERS Have students trade stories with a peer to get another point of view on their work.

Edit/Proofread

CHECK FOR ERRORS Students should reread their stories for clarity, spelling, grammar, and punctuation.

Publish

SHARE THE STORIES Students can read their stories aloud. Encourage students to tell what they like best about each story.

THE DRAGON IN MY ROOM

By Catherine Sanderson

I woke up in the middle of the night. Moonlight coming through my bedroom window made everything look strange. Shadows lurked in corners. Bands of light fell across the dresser and the desk.

A small dragon was sitting on a chair in a corner of the room. It had pointed ears, a tail, and a long tongue. My heart pounded. Was it friendly or harmful?

Slowly, I put my hand out and put on the light. The dragon's tail turned into a strap. Its tongue was an open flap. The dragon was my backpack!

Presentation Ideas

MAKE A COVER Have students use their prewriting illustration to make a cover for their story. Display the stories and illustrations for the whole class to enjoy.

▶ **Viewing/Representing**

READ ALOUD Have students share their stories with students in other classes. Encourage the audience to let the reader know what works in the story.

▶ **Speaking/Listening**

Consider students' creative efforts, possibly adding a plus (+) for originality, wit, and imagination.

Scoring Rubric

Excellent	Good	Fair	Unsatisfactory
4: The writer	**3:** The writer	**2:** The writer	**1:** The writer
• writes a complete story using introduction, main, and concluding paragraphs. • includes a convincing account of her or his personal experience. • provides many rich details that bring the story to life.	• writes a complete story in paragraph form. • includes an adequate account of his or her personal experience. • presents some supporting details and descriptions.	• writes a story, but not in acceptable paragraph form. • doesn't mention his or her personal experience. • presents only a few details to the story.	• writes an incomplete, disorganized story. • doesn't include personal experience. • provides vague or few details.

0: The writer leaves the page blank or fails to respond to the writing task. The student does not address the topic or simply paraphrases the prompt. The response is illegible or incoherent.

Meeting Individual Needs for Writing

EASY

Caption Tell students to think about what an unusual place Opt was. Have students draw an illustration of a strange place. It could be Opt, or another imaginary place. Ask students to write a caption describing the drawing and write a name for their place.

ON-LEVEL

Directions Have students write directions telling a friend how to reach Opt. Encourage students to be creative by filling their directions with fun and silly landmarks. They may draw simple maps to go with their directions.

CHALLENGE

Thank-You Letter Ask students to imagine they have been to the Prince's party in Opt. Have them write a thank-you letter to the King telling him what they liked about their visit.

5Day Grammar and Usage Plan

LANGUAGE SUPPORT

ESL Ask students to act out action words such as *blink* and *sit*, saying sentences about what they or others do. *I blink; Maurice sits;* and so on. Explain that the person who does the action is the subject of the sentence.

DAILY LANGUAGE ACTIVITIES

Write the Daily Language Activities on the board each day, or use **Transparency 3**. For each item, have students orally identify the subject, or add a subject when it is missing.

Day 1
1. The balloon is green. The balloon
2. Some dots disappeared. Some dots
3. The king reads. The king

Day 2
1. The queen laughed. The queen
2. _came to the party. A lady
3. _goes fishing. The prince

Day 3
1. _are huge. Castles
2. _came to the castle. A messenger
3. Flowers grow in the sun. Flowers

Day 4
1. _is ready. The hall
2. A throne is a place to sit. A throne
3. The zookeeper heard the news. The zookeeper

Day 5
1. The blue star shines brightly. The blue star
2. _are many colors. The banners
3. A sign points the way. A sign

> **Daily Language Transparency 3**

105M *Opt: An Illusionary Tale*

DAY 1 — Introduce the Concept

Oral Warm-Up Read this sentence aloud: The queen was waiting. Ask students whom or what the sentence is about. (the queen)

Introduce Subjects Every complete sentence has two parts. There is an action—something that happens—and someone or something who does it. Present the following:

Subjects

- The **subject** of a sentence is whom or what the sentence is about.
- The subject can be one word or more than one word.

Present the Daily Language Activity. Then write the following sentences on the chalkboard. Ask students to underline the subject of each sentence.

Sarah wrote a story.
The dragon roared.

 WRITING Assign the daily Writing Prompt on page 78C.

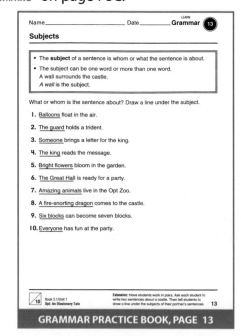

GRAMMAR PRACTICE BOOK, PAGE 13

DAY 2 — Teach the Concept

Review Subjects Remind students that a sentence is a group of words that tells a complete thought. Ask students how to identify a sentence's subject.

Introduce Sentence Fragments Sentences missing a subject are not complete sentences. They are called sentence fragments.

Sentence Fragments

- A **sentence fragment** is a group of words that does not express a complete thought.
- Some sentence fragments can be fixed by adding a subject.

Assign the Daily Language Activity. Then write two sentence fragments on the chalkboard and have students correct them by adding a subject to each: floated in the air. stood on his head.

 WRITING Assign the daily Writing Prompt on page 78C.

GRAMMAR PRACTICE BOOK, PAGE 14

Subjects

Learn from the Literature Review subjects and sentence fragments. Read the first two sentences on page 101 of *Opt: An Illusionary Tale*:

> **The dragon was a perfect guest.**
> **The party was a great success.**

Ask students whether each is a complete sentence or a sentence fragment. (Both are complete.) Have volunteers identify the subject of each sentence and explain how they found the subject.

Write Sentence Subjects Present the Daily Language Activity.

Ask each student to write two sentences about the land of Opt, leaving blanks where the subjects belong. Have students trade sentences with a partner and fill in the subjects. Ask students to read aloud their finished sentences.

 Assign the daily Writing Prompt on page 78D.

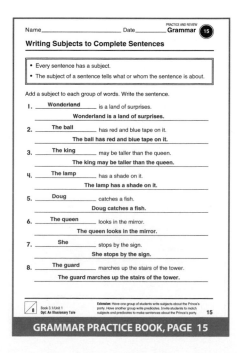

Review Subjects Write simple sentences on the board. Ask students to identify the subject in each. Then present the Daily Language Activity.

Mechanics and Usage Before presenting the daily Writing Prompt, review the parts of a letter. Display and discuss the following information about capitalization and punctuation in letters.

Letter Punctuation

- Begin the greeting and closing in a letter with a capital letter.
- Use a comma after the greeting and the closing in a letter.
- Use a comma between the names of a city and a state.
- Use a comma between the day and year in a date.

 Assign the daily Writing Prompt on page 78D.

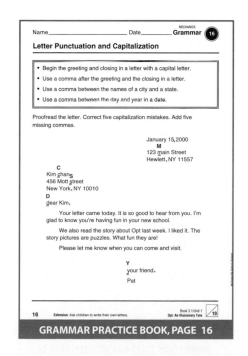

Assess Use the Daily Language Activity and page 17 of the **Grammar Practice Book** for assessment.

Reteach Write predicates from the Daily Language Activities on separate index cards. Put all of the cards in a pile. Ask each student to pull out a card and to write a complete sentence by adding a subject. Display the sentences in a word wall.

Use page 18 of the **Grammar Practice Book** for additional reteaching.

 Assign the daily Writing Prompt on page 78D.

5 Day Spelling Plan

ESL

Students may have trouble with the silent letters in some of these words. Write the Spelling Words, using a different color for the silent letters. Have students repeat each word as you say it.

DICTATION SENTENCES

Spelling Words

1. The child might take a bath.
2. The plant life in the park is green.
3. I rode my bike to the shore.
4. I own a blue toy plane.
5. Most of the children in the class are happy.
6. She has to tie her boots.
7. You can find the path past the brook.
8. I want to eat toast for breakfast.
9. He has to wipe the window.
10. Her plane flight was late.
11. The new bicycle made him happy.
12. Never tell a lie.
13. He spoke to the people.
14. She left home many years ago.
15. The cowboy was thrown to the ground.

Challenge Words

16. He was a guard at the bank.
17. The length of the speech was one hour.
18. That girl is the royal princess.
19. Straighten the clothes on the doll.
20. The pool is found within the park.

DAY 1 Pretest

Assess Prior Knowledge Use the Dictation Sentences at left and **Spelling Practice Book** page 13 for the pretest. Allow students to correct their own papers. If students have trouble, have partners give each other a midweek test on Day 3. Students who require a modified list may be tested on the first eight words.

	Spelling Words		Challenge Words
1.	might	9. wipe	16. **guard**
2.	life	10. flight	17. **length**
3.	**rode**	11. bicycle	18. **royal**
4.	**own**	12. lie	19. **straighten**
5.	most	13. spoke	20. **within**
6.	**tie**	14 ago	
7.	**find**	15. thrown	
8.	toast		

*Note: Words in **dark type** are from the story.*

Word Study On page 14 of the **Spelling Practice Book** are word study steps and an at-home activity.

DAY 2 Explore the Pattern

Sort and Spell Words Say *life* and *toast*. Ask students what vowel sounds they hear in each word. These words contain the long *i* and the long *o* sound.

Ask students to read aloud the 15 Spelling Words and sort them according to the spelling of long *i* or long *o*.

Words with long *i* spelled

i	*igh*	*i-e*	*ie*
find	might	life	tie
bicycle	flight	wipe	lie

Words with long *o* spelled

ow	*o-e*	*oa*	*o*
own	rode	toast	most
thrown	spoke		ago

Spelling Patterns Ask students which words have the pattern CVC*e* (consonant-vowel-consonant-*e*) *(life, wipe, rode, spoke)* Compare the vowel sounds in *rode* and *rod*. Ask: What does the silent *e* do to the vowel sound? Have students write more words with this pattern.

SPELLING PRACTICE BOOK, PAGE 13

WORD STUDY STEPS AND ACTIVITY, PAGE 14

SPELLING PRACTICE BOOK, PAGE 15

Words with Long *i* and Long *o*

DAY 3 — Practice and Extend

Word Meaning: Endings Explain to students that the ending -*ing* can be added to verb (action word) to tell what is happening right now—for example, *I am toasting the bread*. Explain that adding -*ing* to words such as *lie* and *wipe* means changing the *ie* to *y* or dropping the final *e*. Have students find the Spelling Words to which -*ing* can be added and spell the -*ing* forms. *(owning, tying, finding, toasting, wiping, lying)* Have them use the -*ing* forms in sentences.

Glossary Tell students that -*ed* and -*ing* forms of words may be shown at the end of a Glossary entry. Have students:

- write the Challenge Words.
- look up the words and find those with -*ed* and -*ing* forms.
- write the -*ed* and -*ing* forms.

DAY 4 — Proofread and Write

Proofread Sentences Write these sentences on the chalkboard, including the misspelled words. Ask students to proofread, crossing out incorrect spellings and writing the correct spellings. There are two spelling errors in each sentence.

> I (mite) find my (bycicle) at home. (might, bicycle)
>
> I ate (moste) of my (taost) for breakfast. (most, toast)
>
> He had (throan) up on the (flite.) (thrown, flight)

Have students create additional sentences with errors for partners to correct.

 Have students use as many **WRITING** Spelling Words as possible in the daily Writing Prompt on page 78D. Remind students to proofread their writing for errors in spelling, punctuation, and grammar.

DAY 5 — Assess

Assess Students' Knowledge Use page 18 of the **Spelling Practice Book** or the Dictation Sentences on page 105O for the posttest.

Personal Word List Students often forget that *igh* can make a long *i* sound as in *might*. Have them keep a list of *igh* words in their journals that they encounter in other texts and stories.

Students should refer to their lists during future writing activities.

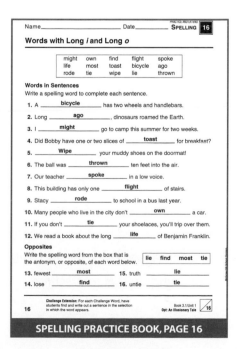

SPELLING PRACTICE BOOK, PAGE 16

SPELLING PRACTICE BOOK, PAGE 17

SPELLING PRACTICE BOOK, PAGE 18

Max Malone

Selection Summary Two boys figure out a clever way to earn money. When the boys buy a gift for a sick friend, they learn what their money is worth.

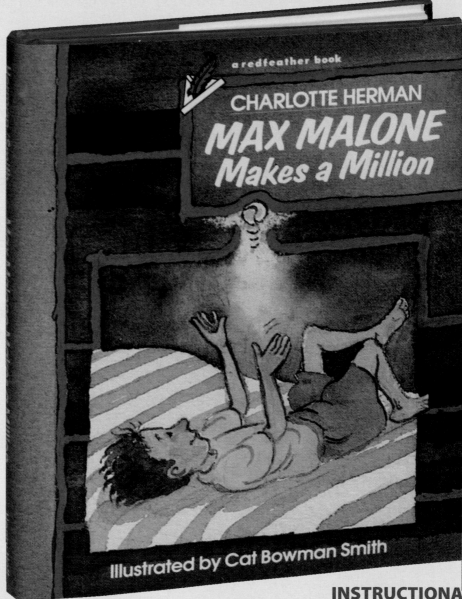

a redfeather book

CHARLOTTE HERMAN

MAX MALONE
Makes a Million

Illustrated by Cat Bowman Smith

**Listening
Library
Audiocassette**

INSTRUCTIONAL
Page 108–127

About the Author Charlotte Herman enjoys

bicycling around Lake Michigan and through the nearby forests. She says about her writing, "I want very much to write good books, books of value. That's always my intention. Young readers are the best people around, and I want to give them my best."

About the Illustrator B. B. Sams never thought he would be an artist. He studied English in college and then went into the Navy. Eventually he realized that art was what he did best. He has been an artist ever since. "I like things to be funny and a little weird," he says. "I put things in that interest me."

Resources for Meeting Individual Needs

Special Delivery

Written by
Illustrated by Kevin McGovern

EASY
Pages 127A, 127D

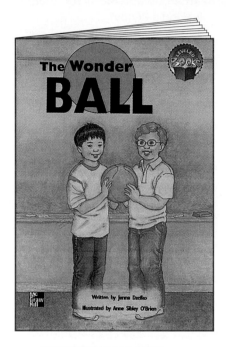

The Wonder BALL

Written by Jenna Dzello
Illustrated by Anne Sibley O'Brien

INDEPENDENT
Pages 127B, 127D

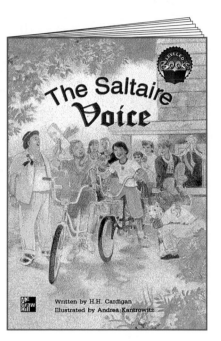

The Saltaire Voice

Written by H.H. Cardigan
Illustrated by Andrea Kantrowitz

CHALLENGE
Pages 127C, 127D

🏠 *Take-Home version available*

LEVELED PRACTICE

Reteach, 22–28
blackline masters with reteaching opportunities for each assessed skill

Practice, 22–28
workbook with Take-Home stories and practice opportunities for each assessed skill and story comprehension

Extend, 22–28
blackline masters that offer challenge activities for each assessed skill

ADDITIONAL RESOURCES

- **Language Support Book,** pp. 25–32
- **Take-Home Story, Practice** p. 23a
- **Alternate Teaching Strategies,** pp. T60–T66
- **Selected Quizzes Prepared by** 📖 Accelerated Reader

McGraw-Hill School
TECHNOLOGY

Phonics CD-ROM provides extra phonics support.

interNET CONNECTION Research & Inquiry ideas. Visit *www.mhschool.com/reading.*

READING AND LANGUAGE ARTS	DAY 1 *Focus on Reading and Skills*	DAY 2 *Read the Literature*
● **Comprehension** ● **Vocabulary** ● **Phonics/Decoding** ● **Study Skills** ● **Listening, Speaking, Viewing, Representing**	**Read Aloud and Motivate,** 106E "If I Find a Penny" **Develop Visual Literacy,** 106/107 ☑ **Review Problem and Solution,** 108A–108B **Teaching Chart 19** Reteach, Practice, Extend, 22	**Build Background,** 108C Develop Oral Language **Vocabulary,** 108D | ceiling	eager	scene
cents	including	section | **Teaching Chart 20** **Word Building Manipulative Cards** Reteach, Practice, Extend, 23 **Read the Selection,** 108–123 Guided Instruction ☑ Problem and Solution ☑ Story Elements **Minilessons,** 113, 115, 117, 119 **Cultural Perspectives,** 110
● **Curriculum Connections**	Fine Arts, 106/107	Math, 108C
● **Writing**	**Writing Prompt:** Write a short paragraph about a sport or other hobby you enjoy.	**Writing Prompt:** Imagine your town needs money to build a new sports center. Write a letter to the newspaper describing your plan to raise the money. **Journal Writing,** 123 Quick-Write
● **Grammar**	**Introduce the Concept: Predicates,** 127M Daily Language Activity 1. The boy is sad. 2. Gordy caught the ball. 3. Dusty autographed the ball. **Grammar Practice Book,** 19	**Teach the Concept: Predicates,** 127M Daily Language Activity 1. Max was a genius. 2. The boy went to the toy store. 3. The store manager was nice. **Grammar Practice Book,** 20
● **Spelling**	**Pretest: Words with /ū/ and /ü/,** 127O **Spelling Practice Book,** 19–20	**Explore the Pattern: Words with /ū/ and /ü/,** 127O **Spelling Practice Book,** 21

☑ = **Skill Assessed in Unit Test**

DAY 3 — Read the Literature

Rereading for Fluency, 122

Story Questions, 124
   Reteach, Practice, Extend, 24

Story Activities, 125

Study Skill, 126
   ☑ Parts of a Book
   Teaching Chart 21
   Reteach, Practice, Extend, 25

Test Power, 127
   TAAS Preparation and Practice Book, 26–27

 Read the Leveled Books,
   Guided Reading
   /ū/ and /ü/
   ☑ Problem and Solution
   ☑ Instructional Vocabulary
    CD-ROM

 Math, 112

 Writing Prompt: Think of someone you admire and would like to meet. Write a paragraph describing what you admire about this person.

Writing Process: Personal Narrative, 127K
   Prewrite, Draft

Review and Practice: Predicates, 127N
   Daily Language Activity
   1. The boys made a fortune.
   2. Baseball is my favorite sport.
   3. The girl watched the game.
   Grammar Practice Book, 21

Practice and Extend: Words with /ū/ and /ü/, 127P
   Spelling Practice Book, 22

DAY 4 — Build Skills

 Read the Leveled Books and Self-Selected Books

☑ **Review Problem and Solution,** 127E–127F
   Teaching Chart 22
   Reteach, Practice, Extend, 26
   Language Support, 30

☑ **Review Story Elements,** 127G–127H
   Teaching Chart 23
   Reteach, Practice, Extend, 27
   Language Support, 31

 Music, 116

 Writing Prompt: Write a conversation between two people. One person is playing baseball for the first time. The other is telling him or her how to use the bat.

Writing Process: Personal Narrative, 127K
   Revise

Meeting Individual Needs for Writing, 127L

Review and Practice: Predicates, 127N
   Daily Language Activity
   1. The first batter struck out.
   2. The pitcher threw a curve ball.
   3. The player hit a home run.
   Grammar Practice Book, 22

Proofread and Write: Words with /ū/ and /ü/, 127P
   Spelling Practice Book, 23

DAY 5 — Build Skills

 Read Self-Selected Books

☑ **Review Compound Words,** 127I–127J
   Teaching Chart 24
   Reteach, Practice, Extend, 28
   Language Support, 32

Listening, Speaking, Viewing, Representing, 127L
   Make a Magazine
   Broadcast a News Clip

Minilessons, 113, 115, 117

Phonics Review,
   /ū/ and /ü/, 119
   Phonics/Phonemic Awareness Practice Book, 57–60
    CD-ROM

 Science, 120

 Writing Prompt: Think about what makes a good friend, and write an essay about friendship.

Writing Process: Personal Narrative, 127K
   Edit/Proofread, Publish

Assess and Reteach: Predicates, 127N
   Daily Language Activity
   1. The two boys sold all the balls.
   2. The baseballs cost fifty cents.
   3. Austin received an autographed baseball.
   Grammar Practice Book, 23–24

Assess and Reteach: Words with /ū/ and /ü/, 127P
   Spelling Practice Book, 24

Read Aloud and Motivate

Language Arts

If I Find a Penny
a poem by Jeff Moss

If I find a penny
    And give it to you,
That means we'll both
Have a wish come true.
A penny is like magic
Lying on the ground.
It's like picking up a wish
That's waiting to be found.

So when I find one,
I'll give you a penny.
And if we're lucky,
I'll give you many.
I'll pick up your penny,
Won't let the trashman sweep it.
But if I find a dollar…
I'll probably keep it.

Oral Comprehension

LISTENING AND SPEAKING Motivate students to listen for rhyme by reading aloud this poem about pennies. Ask students to try and guess how the poem will end as you read it. When you have finished reading the poem, ask students, "Did you guess the way the poem was going to end?" Then ask, "Does the last word in every line rhyme?" What do you notice about the rhymes in this poem?

Activity Help students to make penny pictures. Remind them that in the poem, pennies could help wishes come true. Have students decide on a wish and then draw a picture about their wish, taping pennies to their work as part of the illustration. Pennies might be used as balloons, heads, flower centers, or other round objects.

▶ **Visual/Intrapersonal**

Develop **Visual Literacy**

Works of Art

An artist can tell a story. Sometimes you can almost hear what the people in the picture are saying.

Look at the picture. What do you think it is about? What do you think the boy holding the pitcher of lemonade is saying? How do you think the children could get more customers to buy their lemonade?

The artist made this picture many years ago. If the artist were to make it today, how might it look different?

Lemonade Stand
by Norman Rockwell
The Norman Rockwell Museum,
Stockbridge, Massachusetts

106

107

Objective: Identify Problem and Solution

VIEWING Norman Rockwell's paintings often show everyday situations and tell a story with a humorous twist. Discuss with students what they notice about the characters in this painting. What are the three children doing? Share with them that Rockwell was a famous illustrator whose work appeared in magazines and advertisements.

Read the page with students, encouraging individual interpretations of the painting.

Ask students how the children in the picture might increase their number of customers. For example:

• They could reduce the price.

• They could create a more interesting sign.

REPRESENTING Have students draw posters to advertise a lemonade stand. How would their signs attract customers? What would the signs say? What would they show? What price per glass would students charge?

OBJECTIVES

Students will analyze problem and solution.

TEACHING TIP

INSTRUCTIONAL Help students better understand problem and solution by asking them if they like to read mysteries or watch them on television.

Tell students that mystery stories have plots centered on problem and solution. The problem is usually not knowing who committed the crime. The solution is finding out who did it.

Review Problem and Solution

PREPARE

Discuss a Problem and Solution

Ask: Suppose you have been invited to two birthday parties on the same day. You want to go to both, but you cannot be in two places at once. How can you solve this problem?

TEACH

Explain to students that most stories involve problems. Recognizing the problems and trying to figure out the solutions makes a story more fun to read.

Birthday Problem

Gina knew her Dad's birthday was next Friday. She didn't know what to get him. Besides, she had spent all her money on a video game. When she told her friend Harry about the problem, he had an idea.

"Gina," said Harry, "no one else in the neighborhood has that video game. Just charge all the kids a quarter to play it. You'll have lots of money in no time." Gina thought that was a great idea—and it was. Gina also remembered that her Dad needed a new tie. He loved the one she got him for his birthday.

Teaching Chart 19

Read "Birthday Problem" and Model the Skill

Display **Teaching Chart 19**. Have students focus on the problems and solutions as you read the story.

MODEL I know Gina has to solve some problems. Otherwise she can't get her father a birthday gift. She needs to figure out how she can get money to buy him a present and what to buy him. Harry helps her solve one problem by suggesting a way to make the money.

Have students underline the problems and circle the solutions.

PRACTICE

Create a Problem/Solution Chart

Have students chart the problems and solutions in the story. Help them get started. ▶ **Logical/Visual**

GROUP

PROBLEM	SOLUTION
Gina doesn't have money to buy Dad a present.	She charges her friends money to play her video game.
Gina doesn't know what to buy Dad.	She remembers that he needs a new tie.

ASSESS/CLOSE

Identify Problems and Solutions

Ask students to create a Problem/Solution chart showing how they would solve a problem.

PROBLEM	SOLUTION
I borrowed my sister's favorite sweater and lost it.	I saved my allowance and bought her a new one.

ALTERNATE TEACHING
STRATEGY

PROBLEM AND SOLUTION
For a different approach to teaching this skill, see page T64.

Meeting Individual Needs for Comprehension

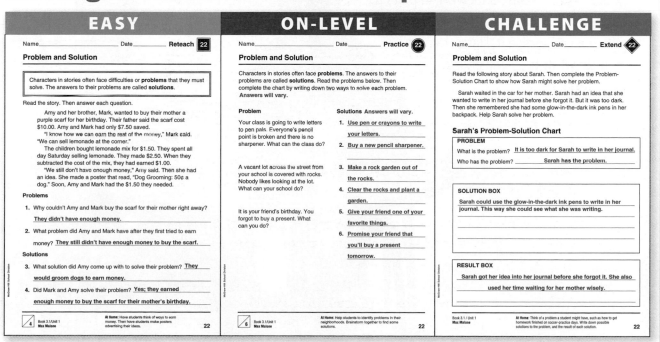

Reteach, 22   Practice, 22   Extend, 22

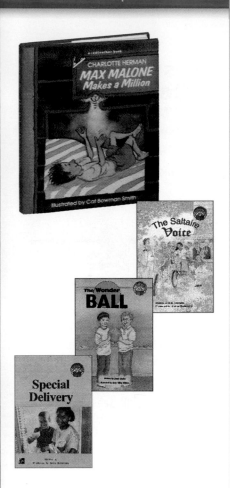

Build Background

 **Link**

Math

Anthology and Leveled Books

Evaluate Prior Knowledge

CONCEPT: MONEY–MAKING PROJECTS In these stories, the characters use their creativity to solve problems. Ask students who belong to sports teams and clubs how they have raised money for a project.

CATEGORIZE JOBS Explain that students can make money by selling a service or a product. Have students work together to create a chart of money-making projects.

▶ **Logical/Visual**

MONEY–MAKING PROJECTS	
SERVICES	**SELLING PRODUCTS**
Mow the lawn	Candy
Do the dishes	Magazines

Graphic Organizer 31

MAKE A FLYER Have students work in pairs to choose a service from the list and create a flyer to advertise it. Have them include what they will charge for their service.

PARTNERS WRITING

Develop Oral Language

PRACTICE A SALES PITCH Tell students that genuinely liking the product or service they are selling helps a salesperson to be more persuasive. Ask students to think of a food that they especially enjoy. Then have them work in pairs, taking turns with their partners describing what they like about the food. Try to pair students with lower English proficiencies with students of native or near-native fluency.

ESL

Have students:

- mention specific details about the taste and texture of the food.

- help their partner create a successful sales pitch by telling which details made the food sound the most appealing.

- present their advertisement to the class.

TEACHING TIP

MANAGEMENT When you are working with a small group, the rest of the class may stop doing their assigned task. To prevent this, do not sit down with the small group. Position the group so that you can stand and move between it and the rest of the class.

LANGUAGE SUPPORT

See the **Language Support Book, pages 25–28,** for teaching suggestions for Build Background and Vocabulary.

Vocabulary

Key Words

Max's Hero

1. Max has a poster of Dusty Field taped to the ⟨ceiling⟩ of his room over his bed. **2.** He also has the ⟨section⟩ of his wall near his closet covered with Dusty Field trading cards. **3.** Max paid 75 ⟨cents⟩ for a card showing Dusty sliding into first base. **4.** Now Max is ⟨eager⟩ to see Dusty play; he can hardly wait for tomorrow to come. **5.** Then he and his friends, ⟨including⟩ Gordy, will see Dusty Field in action. **6.** As Max goes to sleep, he imagines an exciting ⟨scene⟩ in which Dusty wins a tied game by hitting a home run.

Teaching Chart 20

Vocabulary in Context

IDENTIFY VOCABULARY WORDS Display **Teaching Chart 20** and read the passage with students. Have volunteers circle each vocabulary word and underline other words that are clues to its meaning.

DISCUSS MEANINGS Ask questions like these to help clarify word meanings:

- What color is the classroom ceiling?
- What is your favorite section in the toy store?
- How many cents are in a dime?
- Would you be eager to meet a famous athlete?
- What is the base word of *including*? What does it mean?
- Tell about a funny scene in a movie you saw recently.

Practice

DEMONSTRATE WORD MEANING Ask partners to write the words and their definitions on separate cards. Scramble the cards. Partners can take turns matching the words with their definitions.

▶ **Kinesthetic/Linguistic**

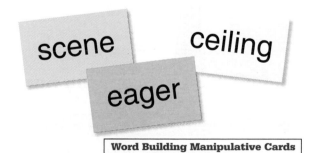

Word Building Manipulative Cards

USE THE VOCABULARY WORDS
WRITING Have students define each vocabulary word using their Glossary as needed. Divide the class into two teams and have a *definition bee*.

▶ **Logical/Linguistic**

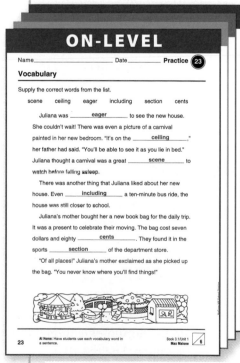

Take-Home Story 23a
Reteach 23
Practice 23 • Extend 23

Guided Instruction

Preview and Predict

Have students preview the story by reading the title and looking at the pictures.

- Why do you think this story is called *Max Malone*?
- What do the pictures tell you?
- What do you think this story will be about?
- Do you think this story will be a fantasy or a realistic one? Why? (I think it will be realistic because the events shown in the pictures look real.) *Genre*

Have students record their predictions about the story in a chart.

PREDICTIONS	WHAT HAPPENED
The story will be about a boy named Max.	
He will buy and sell baseballs.	

Set Purposes

What do students want to find out by reading this story? For example:

- Why do the boys buy and sell baseballs?
- Who is Dusty Field?

Meet CHARLOTTE HERMAN

Charlotte Herman has many happy memories of the Chicago neighborhood where she grew up in the 1940s. She especially remembers playing outdoors with her friends during the summer.

Herman often uses her childhood memories for ideas when she writes her books. She explains, "I have never completely grown up, it seems, and it's easy for me to become a child again, or an adolescent. I hope I'm a better writer because of this and can write about people that readers can identify with and believe in and care about."

Among Herman's books are two other books about Max, *Max Malone, the Magnificent* and *Max Malone and the Great Cereal Rip-Off*, and the award-winning *The House on Walenska Street*.

Meet B.B. SAMS

B.B. Sams never thought he would become an artist. He studied English in college and then went into the navy. But eventually, he realized that art was what he did best. He has been an illustrator ever since.

Sams didn't study art in school. He says he learned to draw at first by looking at other people's drawings. After a while, he came up with his own way of drawing. "I like things to be funny and also a little weird," he says. "I still consider myself a kid when I draw, so I put in things that interest me."

108

Meeting Individual Needs · Grouping Suggestions for Strategic Reading

EASY	ON-LEVEL	CHALLENGE
Read Together Read the story with students or have them use the **Listening Library Audiocassette**. Have students record problems and solutions on their charts. Guided Instruction and Prevention/Intervention prompts offer additional help with decoding and comprehension.	**Guided Reading** Preview the story words on page 109. You may want to have the students read the story first on their own. Then read the story together using selected Guided Instruction questions. Have students record problems and solutions on their charts.	**Read Independently** As students read the story on their own, have them record the problems and solutions on their charts. After reading, students can use their charts to summarize the story and check their predictions.

By Charlotte Herman

Illustrated by B.B. Sams

109

Guided Instruction

☑ **Problem and Solution**

☑ **Story Elements**

Strategic Reading Looking for story problems and their solutions will help you understand a story's plot. Before we begin reading, let's set up a Problem and Solution chart.

PROBLEM	SOLUTION

① **PROBLEM AND SOLUTION** In this story, Max and Gordy have a problem they want to solve. As you read, see if you can identify the problem and the boys' solution to it.

Story Words

The words below may be unfamiliar. Have students check their meanings and pronunciations in the Glossary on page 388.

- appendix, p. 110
- autograph, p. 110
- decimals, p. 112
- mobbed, p. 121

LANGUAGE SUPPORT

The blackline master on the right can be found in the **Language Support Book**.

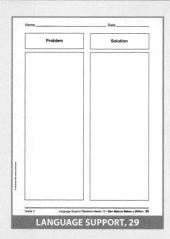

LANGUAGE SUPPORT, 29

109

Guided Instruction

 PROBLEM AND SOLUTION Max and Gordy want to make money. How do they plan to solve this problem? (They have $5. They decide to use it to buy rubber baseballs at 20 cents each. They can then sell them at a higher price.)

Baseballs for Sale

"Austin Healy is having his appendix out today," said Max.

"Yeah, I heard about that," said Gordy. "He threw up all his popcorn last night. Too bad he has to miss Dusty Field on Friday."

Max and Gordy were on their way to Toys for Less. They each had two dollars and fifty cents to spend at the store's Giant Summer Clearance Sale.

When they reached the store, they saw signs on all the windows:

SUMMER BLOWOUT!
PRICES SLASHED
25-50% OFF SELECTED ITEMS

"I hope we find some good stuff," said Max as they went inside. They walked past the first few counters, which displayed the inexpensive toys and prizes like the ones they'd bought for their carnival. They were looking for more expensive, quality items. Max hoped to find something worth five dollars for half off. Then he would have enough money. He didn't have to look far. The idea hit him the moment he saw them.

"That's it!" he cried out. "That's perfect."

"What's it? What's perfect?" asked Gordy.

 Max pointed to a box of rubber baseballs. A sign on the box read: 20 CENTS EACH.

 "Don't you see? We buy these baseballs for twenty cents each. Then we sell them at a higher price

 to people who want Dusty Field's autograph."

110

CULTURAL PERSPECTIVES

BASEBALL HALL OF FAME To learn about famous U.S. baseball players, you can visit the Baseball Hall of Fame. Did you know that Canada also has a Baseball Hall of Fame?

RESEARCH AND INQUIRY Have students research how popular baseball is in other countries. For example, how popular is it in Japan? They can combine their findings into a class book.

BASEBALLS 20¢ EACH

111

Guided Instruction

③ PROBLEM AND SOLUTION Buying the balls and selling them for more money involves a problem that the author doesn't mention directly. How are the boys going to make people want to buy the balls? (They're going to suggest that their customers ask Dusty Field to autograph the balls.) Let's write these problems and solutions on our chart.

PROBLEM	SOLUTION
Max and Gordy want to make money.	They will buy baseballs at 20 cents each and sell them at a higher price.
They need to think of how to make people want to buy the balls.	People will want to buy a ball so that Dusty Field will write his autograph on it.

④ CHARACTER, PLOT What does Max's plan for the baseballs show you about Max?

MODEL I see that Max has solved a problem. He realizes that people will need a reason to buy the rubber baseballs. He knows that if he tells people to use the balls instead of paper for Dusty Field to sign, they will want to buy them. Max's plan shows that he can think of a clever idea.

WORD STRUCTURE Read the second paragraph on page 110. What compound word do you see? (*popcorn*)

PREVENTION/INTERVENTION

WORD STRUCTURE Write the word *popcorn* on the chalkboard.

- Ask students which two smaller words make up the compound word. Have volunteers define the meaning of *pop* and *corn* and then give the definition of the entire word.

- Have students suggest other compound words for food, such as *applesauce, blueberry, pancake*.

- Write the words on the chalkboard and have volunteers draw circles around each word in the compound word.

- Ask other students to define each word making up the compound word and then give the meaning of the entire word.

Guided Instruction

(5) PROBLEM AND SOLUTION Max and Gordy are not sure how many 20-cent balls they can buy for $5. Before Max figures out the answer, however, he has a new idea. He asks the manager how much she'll charge for the balls if he buys all of them. Why is this a good idea?

MODEL I read that the balls were on sale. I know that one reason stores put things on sale is to make room for new merchandise. Max must have been hoping that the manager would sell the balls to him at an even lower price if he took all of them off her hands. He was right. She sold them all for only $5. There were 48 balls. This means that he paid only a little more than 10 cents a ball.

"You're a genius," said Gordy, slapping Max on the back. "That's a great idea. All we have to do is figure out how many balls we can buy for our five dollars." He looked up at the ceiling and concentrated. "Let's see now. If each ball costs twenty cents, and we have five dollars . . . I forget . . . Do we divide or multiply?"

"We divide," said Max, writing and erasing in the air. "Twenty cents into five dollars . . . "

Gordy was impressed. "How many can we buy, Max?"

"Hold your horses. I have to move the decimals."

Max continued writing, but he stopped suddenly in midair. "Wait. I have another idea. First we have to see the manager."

Max's eyes searched the store for someone who looked like a manager. He saw a young woman walking around, giving orders to the workers.

"That must be the manager," he said, walking toward her.

Gordy followed, and a few minutes later Max was asking, "Excuse me, but are you the manager?"

"Yes," said the young woman. "Can I help you?"

"I was wondering," said Max. "If we buy those rubber baseballs in quantity, how much will you sell them for?"

The manager looked up at the ceiling the way Gordy had done. Max waited nervously.

112

Activity

Cross Curricular: Math

DIVISION Max wants to know how many 20-cent balls they can buy for $5. Let students use play money to find out.

- Have students work in small groups.
- Give each group $5 in play dimes (50 dimes per group).
- Have students make two-dime piles.
- Ask: How many groups of 20 cents did you make? (25)
- Ask: How many balls could Max and Gordy buy with their money? (25)

▶ **Mathematical/Kinesthetic**

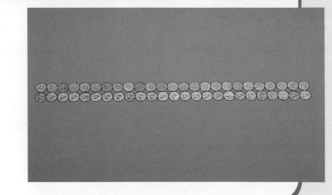

"How much do you want to spend?" she asked after a while.

"Five dollars—including tax," he answered.

"I'll tell you what. Summer's over. And I need the space more than I need the baseballs. For five dollars—including tax—you can have the whole box. There should be close to fifty balls in there."

"Fifty?" Max cried out. "It's a deal."

"Forty-eight baseballs at fifty cents apiece. We'll really make a fortune, almost," said Max.

"Forty-six," Gordy corrected. "We have to save two for ourselves."

Guided Instruction

6 **PROBLEM AND SOLUTION** Who helped Max and Gordy solve their problem with the baseballs? (the manager)

7 Max's idea of selling the baseballs at a higher price sounds good. But will people buy them? What do you think? *Make Predictions*

Minilesson

REVIEW/MAINTAIN

Analyze Character

Remind students that a character's actions and words help readers to understand what he or she is like.

- Have students reread the last paragraph on page 113. Ask: What does Gordy say? What does this tell you about him? (He suggests that they save two baseballs for themselves. This shows he is someone who thinks ahead.)

Activity Have students find a quote from Max. Then have them tell what Max's words tell about his character.

LANGUAGE SUPPORT

ESL Students who speak English as a second language may have difficulty thinking of words to describe specialized character traits. Help students work with native-English speakers to brainstorm a list of words that describe a good business person. Elicit descriptive words and phrases such as: *smart, honest, good* *with math*, and *fair*. You may wish to have students match each trait with an equivalent from their language. Then have students illustrate each of the words with drawings.

Guided Instruction

8 **PROBLEM AND SOLUTION** What problem did Max have when he arrived at the sporting goods store with Gordy? (He had trouble getting started selling the baseballs. His problem was that his legs felt like spaghetti.)

9 **CHARACTER, PLOT** Is Gordy having the same problem as Max? Why or why not? (No; Gordy has thought of a way to persuade people to buy the balls.)

It was Friday morning, and Max and Gordy, each carrying a bag of baseballs, were on their way to the sporting-goods store. It was only nine thirty, and the store didn't open until ten. But they wanted to get there early so they wouldn't miss a single person.

A long line of kids was already forming in front of the store. "Everyone wants to meet Dusty Field," said Max.

"My father said his autograph might become valuable some day," said Gordy. "A real collectible."

Some of the kids had come prepared with baseballs or mitts for autographing. Some had autograph books, and a few were holding scraps of paper. But most of them didn't have anything. Max was sure that lots of people would want the baseballs. Well, he was almost sure. He knew he should start selling right away, but he couldn't make himself move. His legs felt like spaghetti. Thinking about selling had been a lot easier than actually doing it. There were so many people. What if nobody wanted to buy any baseballs? What if he and Gordy got chased away by the store owner? Or the police?

Rosalie had warned him about that. She said that he and Gordy needed a license to sell the baseballs. Max didn't know if she knew what she was talking about. He had heard of a dog license. And a license to drive a car. But never a license to sell baseballs.

8

114

Activity

Cross Curricular: Social Studies

FOREIGN CURRENCY If Max and Gordy were in a foreign country, how might the money they used be different?

- Have students find the names of foreign currencies.
- Have them make posters showing a country's coins and bills.

RESEARCH AND INQUIRY Have students research a foreign currency.
▶ **Linguistic/Spatial**

inter NET CONNECTION Students can learn more about foreign currencies by visiting **www.mhschool.com/reading**.

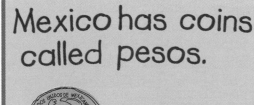

Mexico has coins called pesos.

"What are we waiting for?" asked Gordy.

"You go first," said Max.

"No, you first. It was your idea."

"We'll go together," said Max. He dipped his hand into the bag and pulled out two baseballs. He forced himself to walk along the line of kids and call out, "Baseballs for sale. Just fifty cents." He waved the balls around so everyone could see them. A few people glanced in Max's direction, but turned away.

Gordy, in the meantime, was calling out, "Get your baseballs autographed by Dusty Field. Just fifty cents. Sure to become a collectible."

To his surprise, Max saw that a few kids actually went over to buy some balls from Gordy.

Max then took up the call.

115

Guided Instruction

 10 The setting of a story is important to understanding the plot. Where does this part of the story take place? Why are the characters in this place? (They are at a sporting goods store because a famous baseball player is making an appearance there to sign autographs.) *Setting*

Minilesson

REVIEW/MAINTAIN

Suffixes

Review the definition of *suffix* with students. Ask:

• What base word and suffix can you find in the word *valuable*? (*value* and *-able*)

• How does *-able* change the meaning of *value*? (It makes it mean "having value.") How does it change its part of speech? (It changes it from a noun to an adjective.)

Activity Have students add the suffix *-able* to *break*, *read*, and *wash*. Ask them to define each new word and tell what part of speech it is.

LANGUAGE SUPPORT

ESL Students who speak English as a second language may not understand that *autograph* can be used as different parts of speech.

Explain that *autograph* can be a noun when it means a signature (get an autograph), a verb when it means to sign something (autograph the book), and an adjective when it describes

something (an autograph book).

Have English-proficient students give examples of other words that that can be used as different parts of speech without a spelling change, such as *wave*, *list*, and *drop*.

Explain that not all English words can be used as different parts of speech.

Guided Instruction

11 Max was worried that someone might make them stop selling the baseballs. Why? (He saw the store manager staring at him. Earlier, he had remembered that Rosalie had told him that he would need a license to sell his baseballs.) *Cause and Effect*

12 Do you think he will have to stop? Why or why not? *Make Predictions*

SELF-MONITORING

STRATEGY

RELATE TO PERSONAL EXPERIENCE
Comparing the way story characters feel to the way you might feel in a similar situation can sharpen your interest in a story.

MODEL I read that Max felt worried when he saw the manager looking at him. I read earlier that Rosalie said that he needed a license to sell things. When I try to do grown-up things, I'm always afraid I'll break a rule I didn't know about. In Max's place, I might also have worried that the manager would call the police.

"Get your baseballs autographed by Dusty. Just fifty cents. Sure to become valuable." He didn't want to copy Gordy exactly.

A girl with an autograph book came over to buy a ball. "A baseball is better than an autograph book," she said, handing him the money.

A mother with a small boy came by. "I didn't even think to bring anything that Dusty could sign. This is such a good idea."

Some kids with scraps of paper stuffed the papers into their pockets, or dumped them into trash cans. Then they bought baseballs from Max.

Max was having a great time. He could see that Gordy was too. The scene was just as he had pictured. He was selling what people wanted to buy. And the more he sold, the more confident he became. He even began singing "Take Me Out to the Ball Game." The crowd in front of the store joined in.

11 Suddenly Max stopped singing. Someone inside the store, the manager probably, was standing at the door, staring at Max. Max stared back, and then looked away. This was it! He and Gordy would be asked to leave. He should have known it was too good to last.

The manager opened the door, and the kids pushed their way in. But the manager disappeared. He was nowhere in sight. Neither were the police.

12 Max decided that if someone came and told him to stop, he would. But until then, he would keep on selling.

13

116

Activity

Cross Curricular: Music

SINGING Max sings an old song called "Take Me Out to the Ball Game" with the crowd. Teach the song to students, and let them sing it.

Activity Encourage students to brainstorm a list of songs they have heard or have sung at sporting events or school assemblies.

Organize students into groups. Let each group choose a song and perform it for the class.
▶ **Musical/Interpersonal**

Guided Instruction

13 **PROBLEM AND SOLUTION** At first, Max had a problem selling his baseballs. How does he solve this problem? (He tells people why they should buy the baseballs. He also entertains them by singing.)

Let's put this third problem and solution in our Problem and Solution chart.

PROBLEM	SOLUTION
Max and Gordy want to make money.	They will buy baseballs at 20 cents each and sell them at a higher price.
They need to think of how to make people buy the balls.	People will want to buy a ball so that Dusty Field will write his autograph on it.
Initially, no one wants to buy Max's baseballs.	He tells people why they should buy the baseballs.

Minilesson

REVIEW/MAINTAIN

Main Idea

Remind students that the main idea of a selection explains what the story or paragraph is about.

• Ask: What is the most important idea on this page? (Max is successful at selling baseballs.)

Activity Have partners work together to make a web showing the main idea of this page surrounded by its supporting details.

Guided Instruction

14 **PROBLEM AND SOLUTION** What problem do both Max and Gordy have when they meet Dusty? How do they solve their problem? (They don't know what to say to him. They just tell him their names.)

15 Do you think that the boys were satisfied just telling Dusty their names? Why or why not? (No; since they are baseball fans, they probably would have liked to have discussed baseball with him.) *Making Inferences*

16 **CHARACTER** Why do Max and Gordy have trouble thinking of what to say to Dusty? (They were shy when they first tried to sell the baseballs. They probably felt shy again when they met the famous ball player.)

Fluency

DRAMATIC READING

Have groups read pages 118–119 aloud dramatically. They should choose roles, including narrator. Remind students to pay attention to the following reading suggestions:

- Read clearly and slowly.
- Try to express the characters' emotions.
- Use the punctuation marks as clues to pausing and inflection.

He stopped customers before they went into the store. "Get your baseball for Dusty Field's autograph. Fifty cents." Or, "How about a baseball for Dusty's autograph?" Most people were eager to buy.

Dusty was going to be signing autographs until noon. But by eleven, Max and Gordy had sold all their baseballs. All except the two they had saved for themselves.

"I can't believe it," said Max when he and Gordy were waiting in line to meet Dusty. "We sold them all. I thought our goose was cooked when I saw the manager staring at me." Max's mother always used that expression—"my goose was cooked"—even though she had never cooked a goose in her life.

"I can't believe we're getting Dusty's autograph," said Gordy. "I wish the line would move faster. Dusty's hand will get all worn out from shaking hands before he even gets to us."

At last it was Max and Gordy's turn to meet Dusty. Dusty was tall and thin and had a friendly smile. He wasn't wearing a uniform. Just jeans and a T-shirt. But he looked like a ball player anyway.

Max and Dusty shook hands. Dusty said, "Nice to meet you."

 But Max couldn't think of anything to say except, "Would you sign this ball to Max?"

118

"Sure thing," said Dusty, and he signed the ball, *To my pal Max. Dusty Field.*

"Wow! Thanks, Dusty."

Gordy couldn't think of anything great to say either. So he handed Dusty his baseball and said, "I'm Gordy."

Dusty signed, *To my pal Gordy. Dusty Field.*

"Wow!" said Gordy.

"This was a great day," said Max.

(15)

(16)

(17)

119

Guided Instruction

(17) CHARACTER, PLOT As you may have noticed, Dusty doesn't say much. He just signs the balls and hands them back. What are some possible reasons for this? (Dusty may be shy, too. He might be tired from meeting so many people in one day. He is an athlete, and many athletes prefer to do something active rather than talk.)

PHONICS KIT
HANDS-ON ACTIVITIES AND PRACTICE

Minilesson

REVIEW/MAINTAIN

/ū/ and /ü/

Have students pronounce the words *noon*, *goose*, and *uniform* on page 118.

- Ask which two words have the same vowel sound. (*noon* and *goose*)
- Ask what makes the first vowel sound in *uniform* different from /ü/. (It is a long *u* sound.)
- Tell students these sounds can be represented by the letters *oo*, *u-e* (as in *use*), *ew*, *ui*, *ou* (as in *fruit* and *route*), and *u*.

Activity Have students list words with /ū/ and /ü/ sounds on the chalkboard according to their spelling.

Phonics CD-ROM Have students use the interactive phonics activities on the CD-ROM for more reinforcement.

119

Guided Instruction

PROBLEM AND SOLUTION What problem did Austin have? (Austin was ill and could not get Dusty Field's autograph.) How was Austin's problem solved? (Max and Gordy bought a ball for him and got Dusty to autograph it.)

"Let's go home and split up the money," said Gordy.

"We made a ton," said Max. "And all because we knew the market. We went where the people were. And we bought in quantity. Just like Austin . . . "

Austin. Max had forgotten all about him. Little Austin Healy, who was home with a scar where his appendix should have been. Austin, who was looking forward to meeting Dusty Field. Why, if it weren't for Austin, Max would never have known about Dusty. He and Gordy would never have bought the balls. They never would've made all that money.

"We can't go home yet," said Max. "There's something we have to do first." He led the way to the baseball section of the store. And there, in a bin, were baseballs. Real league baseballs. They cost three dollars, but Max didn't care. He picked one up and showed it to Gordy.

"For Austin," he said.

"We'll get it autographed by Dusty," said Gordy. They bought the ball and waited in line again.

"Let's see," said Gordy, looking up at the ceiling. "Not counting what we spent on Austin, if we sold forty-six balls at fifty cents each . . . "

"This time we multiply," said Max.

120

Cross Curricular: Science

THE APPENDIX Students have learned that Austin had his appendix out. Although humans do not need this organ to survive, other animals use their appendixes to digest food.

RESEARCH AND INQUIRY Have students find out more about the appendix. Then ask them to draw a diagram showing its location in the human body.

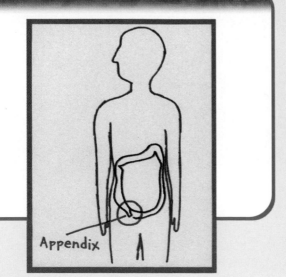

Appendix

Max Makes a Million

"How nice of you to come," said Austin Healy's mother. "Austin will be so happy to see you. He's been feeling a little low today. He had to miss Dusty Field."

"Maybe we can cheer him up," said Max. He thought of the baseball he had for Austin in his bag, and smiled as he went inside.

They found Austin in his room, feeding Newton some freeze-dried shrimp. Austin was wearing sweatpants and a Mickey Mouse sweatshirt.

"Hey, guys. I was thinking about you all day. Did you get to see Dusty?"

"We just came from there," said Max. "How are you feeling?"

"Okay. Do you want to see my scar?"

Max and Gordy shook their heads. "No thanks," said Max.

Austin fed Newton the last of the shrimp and climbed into bed. "I'm supposed to rest up for a few days. And I'm not supposed to laugh. So don't say anything funny. Just tell me about Dusty."

"The place was mobbed," said Max. "Everyone wanted to see him."

"I wanted to see him," said Austin.

"Yeah, that was too bad. Anyway, we got to shake his hand."

"Wow!" said Austin. "I wanted to shake his hand."

"That's rough," said Max.

"And we got his autograph too," Gordy added.

121

Guided Instruction

19 **CHARACTER, PLOT** What do Max and Gordy's actions show about their relationship with Austin? (They must like Austin because they buy him a real baseball and get it autographed. It also shows that Max and Gordy are generous.)

PHONICS AND DECODING Find the second word in the fourth line on page 120. Sound out the word. Do you hear a sound for each letter in the word? (No) Which letters do not make sounds? *(gh)*

p/i PREVENTION/INTERVENTION

PHONICS AND DECODING Write *brought* on the chalkboard. Ask students to suggest other words with the letters *ough*, such as *cough, rough, bough, ought,* and *though*. Have volunteers write the words on the chalkboard and circle the silent letters in each one. Then write the following words on the chalkboard: *talk, lamb, wrong*. Repeat the activity with the silent letter *l* in *talk; b* in *lamb; w* in *wrong*.

Guided Instruction

(20) PROBLEM AND SOLUTION Let's complete our charts. What can we add to them?

PROBLEM	SOLUTION
Max and Gordy want to make money.	They will buy baseballs at 20 cents each and sell them at a higher price.
They need to think of how to make people buy the balls.	People will want to buy a ball so that Dusty Field will autograph it.
Initially, no one wants to buy Max's baseballs.	He tells people why they should buy the baseballs.
Austin cannot get Dusty Field's autograph.	Max and Gordy give Austin an autographed ball.

RETELL THE STORY Ask volunteers to use their chart to retell the story. Have them explain what each event tells about the characters. *Summarize*

STUDENT SELF-ASSESSMENT

- How did analyzing problems and solutions help me understand the story?
- How did using the chart help me?

TRANSFERRING THE STRATEGY

- When might I use this strategy again?
- In what other kind of reading might I be able to use the chart?

"Wow! That's what I really wanted most. His autograph."

"Really rough," said Max, shaking his head.

"I might never get another chance to meet Dusty," said Austin, looking glum.

"You might not," said Max.

"I might have to wait forever to get his autograph." Now Austin was looking even more glum.

"I don't think you'll have to wait that long," Max told him. He turned to Gordy and winked. Then he reached into the bag and took out Austin's baseball.

(20) "From Dusty," he said, handing him the ball.

"For me?" asked Austin, turning the ball around so he could read the autograph. "'To my pal Austin. Dusty Field.' Oh, boy! This is great. This is the greatest." Austin was so excited, he practically jumped out of bed.

"Watch out for your stitches," said Max.

Austin turned to Max and Gordy and flashed them a smile. The widest smile they had ever seen on Austin's face. "Thanks, guys. Thanks a million."

"A million? Did you hear that, Gordy?" asked Max, slapping him on the back. "We made our million after all."

122

REREADING FOR *Fluency*

GROUP Ask students in groups of three to read the dialogue on pages 122 and 123. Tell them to read with expression, as if trying out for parts in a play.

READING RATE You may want to evaluate a student's reading rate. Have the student read aloud from *Max Malone* for one minute. Ask the student to place a self-stick note after the last word read. Then count the number of words he or she has read.

Alternatively, you could assess small groups or the whole class together by having students count words and record their own scores.

A Running Record form provided in **Diagnostic/Placement Evaluation** will help you evaluate reading rate(s).

123

Guided Instruction

Return to Predictions and Purposes

Review with students their story predictions and reasons for reading the story. Were their predictions correct? Did they find out what they wanted to know?

PREDICTIONS	WHAT HAPPENED
The story will be about a boy named Max.	The story was about Max and his friend Gordy.
He will buy and sell baseballs.	Max and Gordy made a lot of money selling the baseballs.

PROBLEM AND SOLUTION

HOW TO ASSESS

- Ask students what the most important problem and solution were.

- Have them tell how these events help them understand Max and Gordy.

Students should be able to identify Max and Gordy's problems and solutions and tell what they learned about Max and Gordy from the way they solved their problems.

FOLLOW UP

If students have trouble identifying the important problem, ask them which problem set off the story's events.

LITERARY RESPONSE

QUICK-WRITE Invite students to share their opinions about the solutions to the problems in this story. Have them choose a problem and solution from their chart and evaluate the solution. These questions may help get them started:

- Did the solution cover all parts of the problem?

- Did the solution help others?

ORAL RESPONSE Have students share their journal writings and discuss whether they liked the characters in the story.

Story Questions

Have students discuss or write answers to the questions on page 124.

Answers:

1. They sold them to people who were getting Dusty's autograph. *Literal/Plot*

2. She needed room to put out new items. *Inferential/Problem and Solution*

3. Possible answers: at school, at a playground, or at a baseball game *Critical/Problem and Solution*

4. Max's scheme to make money and to cheer up his friend Austin. *Critical/Summarize*

5. Possible answer: Phoebe is like Max. They both learned how to be supportive to friends. *Critical/Reading Across Texts*

Write an Article For a full writing-process lesson related to this suggestion, see pages 127K–127L.

Story Questions & Activities

1 What did Max and Gordy do with the baseballs that they bought?

2 Why did the store manager sell them all 48 baseballs for only five dollars?

3 Where else do you think the boys could have sold the baseballs?

4 What is this story mostly about?

5 Max was a good friend to Austin Healy. Think of another story about friendship that you know. How is the main character like Max?

Write an Article

Have you ever done something nice for a friend or relative? Or has someone ever done something really special for you? Write an article about what happened. Include details about how it made you feel.

Meeting Individual Needs

EASY	ON-LEVEL	CHALLENGE

EASY

Name _____ Date _____ Reteach 23

Vocabulary

Choose the word that matches the meaning. Then fill in the crossword puzzle.

ceiling   cents   eager   including   scene   section

Across
1. part _____ section
4. pennies _____ cents
5. wanting very much _____ eager

Down
1. a setting _____ scene
2. top part of a room _____ ceiling
3. containing _____ including

Story Comprehension Reteach 24

Circle the answer to each question about "Max Malone."

1. Why doesn't Austin go to see his baseball hero?
   He is too upset.   He is too young.   (He is recovering from surgery.)

2. What do Max and Gordy do at Toys for Less?
   sell baseballs   (buy baseballs)   autograph baseballs

3. What do Max and Gordy do at the sporting-goods store?
   autograph baseballs   buy baseballs   (sell baseballs)

4. What do Max and Gordy give to Austin?
   an appendix   46 baseballs   (an autographed baseball)

At Home: Have students create their own crossword puzzle using the words from the story.
23–24   Book 3.1/Unit 1 Max Malone 4

Reteach, 24

ON-LEVEL

Name _____ Date _____ Practice 24

Story Comprehension

Look back over "Max Malone." Then complete the chart below. Answers may vary.

1. Setting of story — Toys for Less, outside and inside the sporting-goods store, Austin's house
2. Main characters — Max, Gordy, Austin
3. Beginning of story — Max and Gordy figure out a way to make money by selling baseballs.
4. Middle of story — Max and Gordy sell all their baseballs to people who want Dusty Field's autograph. They also get autographs from Dusty Field for themselves and their sick friend, Austin.
5. End of Story — Max and Gordy visit Austin and give him a baseball autographed by Dusty Field.

Now match each detail.

6. __c__ sells all the baseballs for $5   a. Dusty Field
7. __e__ had his appendix taken out   b. Max
8. __a__ a baseball player   c. Toys are Less
9. __b__ gets idea to buy baseballs for $5   d. Gordy
10. __d__ helps Max sell the baseballs   e. Austin

At Home: Have students think of some ways to make money similar to the way Max and Gordy did.
24   Book 3.1/Unit 1 Max Malone 10

Practice, 24

CHALLENGE

Name _____ Date _____ Extend 23

Vocabulary

ceiling	cents	eager
including	scene	section

Write each word in the box on a card. Write definitions for each word on other cards. Play a matching game with a partner. Place the word cards face down on one side and the definitions face down on another side. Turn over two cards at a time, one from each side. If the word matches the definition, keep the cards. If not, turn them over and let your partner have a turn.

Extend 24

Story Comprehension

Imagine that you were at the sidewalk sale where Max and Gordy sold baseballs. On another sheet of paper, draw the sidewalk stands you would like to see there and label them. Put all the illustrations together into a booklet and gather them for the library corner. Or, organize your illustrations as a class and make one large book of sidewalk stands.

At Home: Look up entrepreneur together in the dictionary and discuss how Max and Gordy were entrepreneurs. Think of any other young people you know who are like Max.
23–24   Book 3.1/Unit 1 Max Malone

Extend, 24

Create a Bar Graph

Imagine that you have started your own lemonade stand. If you sell 10 cups on the first day, and 20 cups on the second day, how many cups would you need to sell on the third day to have sold 50 cups total? Create a bar graph to show your results.

Perform a Science Trick

You can change your dirty pennies into clean pennies. Put about an inch of vinegar in a cup. Stir in a teaspoon of salt. Put the dirty pennies in the cup. Leave them overnight. In the morning your pennies will look like new.

Find Out More

An autograph can make a baseball card much more valuable. Find out how much the average baseball card costs brand-new. Then find out how much a rare, autographed card might be worth. What cards are worth the most?

125

Story Activities

Create a Bar Graph

Materials: paper and pencils

ONE Guide students to see that they will need to sell 20 cups on the third day to have sold 50 cups total. Review bar graph form.

Perform a Science Trick

Materials: pennies, vinegar, plastic cups, salt

PARTNERS Let partners work together. Pairs can compare their coins the next day.

Find Out More

RESEARCH AND INQUIRY Have groups **GROUP** brainstorm a list of sources that will give them information about baseball cards. Each group member can pick a source and do the research. Group members can combine their findings. Sources may include books, sports magazines, sports stores, trading card shows, and the Internet.

interNET CONNECTION Have students go to **www.mhschool.com/reading** for more information about baseball cards.

FORMAL ASSESSMENT

After page 125, see the Selection Assessment.

Study Skills

PARTS OF A BOOK

OBJECTIVES

Students will use an index to locate information in a book.

PREPARE Preview the index with students. Display **Teaching Chart 21**.

TEACH Review that the purpose of an index is to locate specific details in a book. Review the use of alphabetical and numeric order and key words.

PRACTICE Have students answer questions 1–5. Review the answers: **1.** pages 7, 11, 12 **2.** pages 28, 48, 49, 54, 62, 63 **3.** in numerical order **4.** in alphabetical order **5.** They both tell you where to find information in a book. The table of contents shows chapter titles and page numbers. The index shows key words and page references, but not chapters.

ASSESS/CLOSE Have students write three questions they could answer using the index on this page, then find the answers.

STUDY SKILLS

Use an Index

You can learn about the different types of money used throughout the world by checking a nonfiction book such as *Money*. Part of the **index** from that book is below.

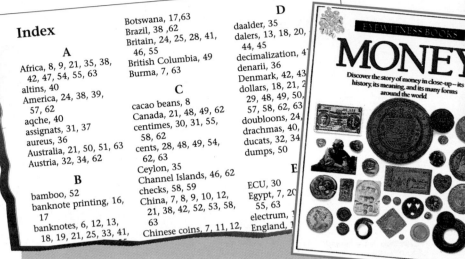

Index

A
Africa, 8, 9, 21, 35, 38, 42, 47, 54, 55, 63
altins, 40
America, 24, 38, 39, 57, 62
aqche, 40
assignats, 31, 37
aureus, 36
Australia, 21, 50, 51, 63
Austria, 32, 34, 62

B
bamboo, 52
banknote printing, 16, 17
banknotes, 6, 12, 13, 18, 19, 21, 25, 33, 41,

Botswana, 17, 63
Brazil, 38, 62
Britain, 24, 25, 28, 41, 46, 55
British Columbia, 49
Burma, 7, 63

C
cacao beans, 8
Canada, 21, 48, 49, 62
centimes, 30, 31, 55, 58, 62
cents, 28, 48, 49, 54, 62, 63
Ceylon, 35
Channel Islands, 46, 62
checks, 58, 59
China, 7, 8, 9, 10, 12, 21, 38, 42, 52, 53, 58, 63
Chinese coins, 7, 11, 12,

D
daalder, 35
dalers, 13, 18, 20, 44, 45
decimalization, 4?
denarii, 36
Denmark, 42, 43
dollars, 18, 21, 2?, 29, 48, 49, 50, 57, 58, 62, 63
doubloons, 24,
drachmas, 40,
ducats, 32, 34
dumps, 50

E
ECU, 30
Egypt, 7, 20, 55, 63
electrum,
England, 1

Use the index to answer these questions.

1 On what pages would you find information about Chinese coins?

2 On what pages should you look for facts about cents?

3 In what type of order do the page numbers in an index entry appear?

4 In what order do the key words in an index appear?

5 Compare this index with the Table of Contents shown on page 104. How are the two types of pages alike? How are they different?

Meeting Individual Needs

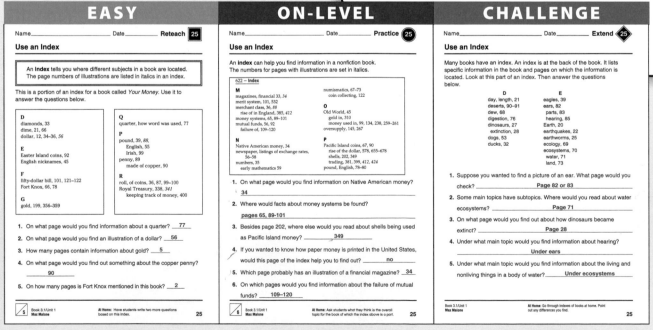

EASY	ON-LEVEL	CHALLENGE
Reteach, 25	Practice, 25	Extend, 25

TEST POWER

DIRECTIONS:

Read the story. Then read each question about the story.

SAMPLE

A Surprise for Benny

Cam wanted to help plan her cousin Benny's surprise birthday party. She started to make a list of games to play at the party.

"How about a piñata?" Cam's mom asked.

"What is a piñata?" Cam asked.

"A piñata is a container made of heavy paper that is usually shaped to look like an animal. It is stuffed with candy and prizes and hung from a tree. Everyone is blindfolded and hits the piñata with a stick. When the piñata breaks open, the candy and prizes fall out. Piñatas are always a lot of fun," Cam's mom said.

"What a great idea!" Cam said. "Benny will love that!"

1 How did Cam feel when her mother told her about the piñata?

● Excited
○ Angry
○ Sad
○ Worried

2 What will Cam probably do next?

● Make a piñata for the party
○ Cancel the party
○ Decide not to play games
○ Clean up after the party

Test Power

THE PRINCETON REVIEW

Read the Page

Direct students to read the story. Instruct students to pay special attention to how the characters react during the story. Ask: Are they reacting positively or negatively?

Discuss the Questions

QUESTION 1: This question requires students to understand Cam's feelings. Discuss what information in the story is a clue to how Cam feels. When Cam says, "What a great idea!" is Cam angry? If not, eliminate this choice. Work through the other choices.

QUESTION 2: This question requires students to determine what Cam will "probably do next." Remind students that Cam was excited about the piñata. Ask students: What is Cam likely to do next? Use process of elimination to choose the best answer.

ITBS Test Preparation and Practice
Grade 3

TERRANOVA Test Preparation and Practice
Grade 3

Stanford-9 Test Preparation and Practice
Grade 3

ITBS/TEST PREPARATION   TERRANOVA/TEST PREPARATION   SAT 9/TEST PREPARATION

EASY

Answers to Story Questions

1. Vanessa and Malik are the main characters.
2. It is hard for them to walk or carry things.
3. Possible answers include: Make a list or keep a chart of things to do. Keep track of tips.
4. Two kids start a delivery service to help elderly neighbors.
5. Max Malone would charge the people for deliveries.

Story Questions and Writing Activity

1. Who are the main characters in this story?
2. Why do Mrs. Green and the others need deliveries done for them?
3. How would you help Malik and Vanessa with their business?
4. What is the main idea of this story?
5. If Max Malone had started this business, how would it be different?

Nickels and Dimes

Vanessa and Malik gave Mrs. Green 50 cents change back from buying her groceries. If she had given them $10, what was the total of Mrs. Green's order?

from *Special Delivery*

Leveled Books

EASY

Special Delivery

/ū/ and /ü/

☑ **Problem and Solution**

☑ **Instructional Vocabulary:** *ceiling, cents, eager, including, scene, section*

Guided Reading

PREVIEW AND PREDICT Conduct a **picture walk**, discussing each illustration up to page 11. Ask: What might the story be about? What can you tell about the characters of this story based on its illustrations? Have students record their predictions in a journal.

SET PURPOSES Have students write down five questions they would like to have answered by the story. For example: Why are the kids helping Mrs. Green?

READ THE BOOK Use questions like these to guide students' reading or after they have read the story independently.

Page 1: Why hasn't Mrs. Green gotten her mail for a few days? (Her hip has been hurting.) *Cause and Effect*

Pages 6–7: What part of a dollar is fifty cents? (half) *Vocabulary*

Pages 10–11: Why wouldn't Vanessa's and Malik's mother let them help their neighbors? (She probably thought they were too young to go to different parts of the town alone.) What was the solution to this problem? (Their older sister offers to go with

them.) *Problem and Solution*

Page 11: What does the word *eager* mean? (enthusiastic) *Vocabulary*

Page 15: Look at the words *including* and *used* on this page. Say the sound represented by the letter *u* in both words. The sound in *including* is /ü/ and the sound in *used* is /ū/. Can you think of other words with these sounds? *Phonics and Decoding*

RETURN TO PREDICTIONS AND PURPOSES Review students' predictions and reasons for reading. Which predictions were correct?

LITERARY RESPONSE Discuss these questions:

- What would you have named the delivery service?
- Why do the kids want to start a service to help people?

Also see the story questions and activity in *Special Delivery*.

See the **Phonics CD-ROM** for practice using the /ū/ and /ü/ sounds.

Leveled Books

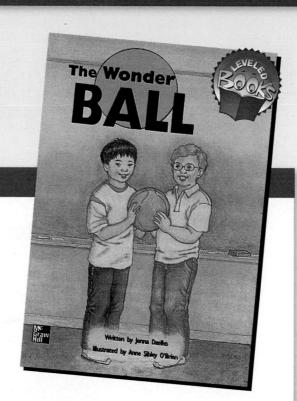

INDEPENDENT

The Wonder Ball

☑ **Problem and Solution**

☑ **Instructional Vocabulary:**
including, ceiling, section, eager, cents, scene

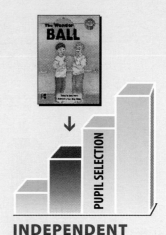

INDEPENDENT

Guided Reading

PREVIEW AND PREDICT Conduct a **picture walk**, discussing each illustration up to page 9. Ask: What might the story be about? What might the boys do with their special basketball?

SET PURPOSES Have students write down questions they would like to have answered by the story. For example: Why did Richie and Lee pour glue on the basketball?

READ THE BOOK Use questions like the following to guide students' reading.

Page 2: What does it mean when the author says that the boys had "two days left to finish, *including* today"? (The day on which the story opens was part of the boys' two-day time limit for completing their project.) *Vocabulary/Draw Conclusions*

Page 3: If the basketball bounced to the *ceiling*, how high in the room did it go? (to the top of the room) *Vocabulary*

Pages 4–5: When the boys discovered that the basketball bounced higher than other basketballs, what did they decide to do? (sell their invention) *Plot*

Pages 12–13: What problem arises during science class? (A girl claims that something besides the glue causes the basketball to bounce high. The children feel cheated.) What do the boys do? (They promise to give the money back.) *Problem and Solution*

Page 14–15: What caused the basketball to glow when the lights were turned off? (the glue) *Cause and Effect*

RETURN TO PREDICTIONS AND PURPOSES Review students' predictions and reasons for reading. Which predictions were correct? Which questions were answered?

LITERARY RESPONSE Discuss these questions:

• Why does the teacher believe that Richie and Lee didn't know the ball was a Wonderball Superball?

• Why didn't Richie's brother get mad?

Also see the story questions and activity in *The Wonder Ball*.

Story Questions and Writing Activity

1. What did Lee and Richie think they had invented?
2. Why were the kids in their class no longer angry at Richie and Lee, even after Victoria showed them that the ball was really a Wonderball Superball?
3. What would have probably happened if the boys hadn't dropped glue on the ball?
4. What is this story mostly about?
5. Imagine that Max Malone is Lee and Richie's friend. How do you think the story might have been different?

Invent Your Own Toy

Suppose your school is raising money to buy sports equipment. Think of a toy that kids might be interested in buying. Draw a picture of it, describe it, and give it a price. Then trade pictures with other kids and see who wants to buy it.

from The Wonder Ball

Leveled Books

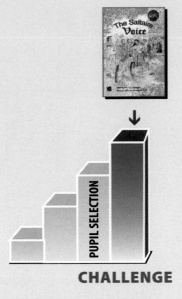

PUPIL SELECTION

CHALLENGE

Answers to Story Questions

1. Maura.
2. Tina thought it sounded like fun.
3. They had their friends deliver it.
4. The story is about two girls starting a newspaper.
5. Max and Gordy would have sold space.

Story Questions and Writing Activity

1. Who has the idea to make a community newspaper?
2. Why do you think Tina went along with it?
3. How did Maura and Tina solve the problem of getting their newspaper to as many people as possible?
4. What is the story mostly about?
5. If Max and Gordy from *Max Malone* had started the paper, what might they have done when people wanted to place ads?

Be a Reporter

You are on the staff of the *Saltaire Voice*. Draw a picture that shows the front page. What would you write about? What would the headline be? Would you include a picture with a caption?

from *The Saltaire Voice*

CHALLENGE

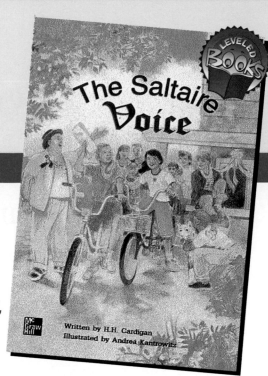

The Saltaire Voice

Written by H.H. Cardigan
Illustrated by Andrea Kantrowitz

The Saltaire Voice

☑ **Problem and Solution**
☑ **Instructional Vocabulary:** *scene, ceiling, eager, including, section, cents*

Guided Reading

PREVIEW AND PREDICT Conduct a **picture walk**, discussing each illustration up to page 6. Ask: What might the story be about? What are the girls doing? What can you tell about the characters of this story based on its illustrations? Have students record their predictions in a journal.

SET PURPOSES Have students write down five questions they would like to have answered from the story. For example, one question might be, "What is the Saltaire Voice?"

READ THE BOOK Use questions like these to guide students' reading or after they have read the story independently.

Page 2: What does the word *scene* mean as it is used on this page? (the place where something is happening) *Vocabulary*

Pages 3–4: What problem is posed when the newspaper closes down? (There's no newspaper.) How is this problem solved? (The girls start a paper; the office gets rebuilt.) Why did Maura and Tina shake hands? (to show that they had agreed to publish a newspaper) *Problem and Solution/Plot*

Page 12: What does the word *section* mean as it is used on this page? (part of a newspaper) *Vocabulary*

Page 16: Why do the girls think the reopening of the *Saltaire Star* is their last story? (They feel that no one will read their newspaper when the regular one comes back.) How is this problem solved? (Since the girls print a different kind of news, people will want to read both newspapers.) *Cause and Effect*

RETURN TO PREDICTIONS AND PURPOSES Review students' predictions and reasons for reading.

LITERARY RESPONSE Discuss these questions:

- What tools did the girls need to start their paper?
- Why do people like to read about local events?
- Do Maura and Tina have the qualities that reporters need? Explain.

Also see the story questions and activity in *The Saltaire Voice*.

Activities
Anthology and Leveled Books

Connecting Texts

PROBLEM/SOLUTION CHART
Write the story titles on a chart. Discuss with students the different projects taken on by the characters in each story. What problems motivated the characters? What did characters give and receive because of their projects? In what ways are the characters alike and different? Call on volunteers from each reading level and write their suggestions on the chart.

Max Malone	Special Delivery	The Wonder Ball	The Saltaire Voice
PROBLEM	*PROBLEM*	*PROBLEM*	*PROBLEM*
Max wants to make money.	The elderly people in this story have trouble going on errands.	The boys believe they've found a substance that gives balls "super bounce."	A town loses its newspaper when the newspaper office building burns down.
SOLUTION	*SOLUTION*	*SOLUTION*	*SOLUTION*
He buys balls cheaply , has them signed by a baseball player, then sells them at a profit.	The children help the elderly people by running their errands for them.	They discover that it makes the balls glow in the dark.	Two girls produce a newspaper about local events.

Viewing/Representing

GROUP PRESENTATIONS Divide the class into groups, one for each of the four books read in the lesson. For *Max Malone*, combine students of different reading levels. Have each group write short character profiles for each of the main characters in the group's story. Have them orally present their profiles to the class.

AUDIENCE RESPONSE Ask students to pay attention to each group's presentation. Allow time for questions after each presentation.

Research and Inquiry

MORE ABOUT MONEY-MAKING PROJECTS
Invite students to:

- List things they are good at. Can they use their talents to start a business?

- Interview a business person to find out how he or she got started in business.

- Do library research to discover how children can get involved in business. Ask the librarian to help you.

interNET CONNECTION Have students log on to **www.mhschool.com/reading** for links to Web pages about business.

OBJECTIVES

Students will identify problems and their solutions.

TEACHING TIP

INSTRUCTIONAL Explain that the most exciting part of a story is called the *climax*. The climax occurs just before the problem is solved. Ask students to tell the plot of a favorite movie or story. Help them identify its climax.

Review Problem and Solution

PREPARE

Discuss Problem and Solution

Review: The plot of a story is made up of problems and their solutions. Often a reader's main purpose in reading a story is to see how the characters solve their problems.

TEACH

Read "Baseballs for All" and Model the Skill

As you read **Teaching Chart 22** with students, ask them to focus on the problems and solutions in the passage.

Baseballs for All

At first, none of the people waiting in line wanted to buy the baseballs that Max and Gordy were selling. They didn't see any need to do so. However, when Gordy pointed out that they could use the baseballs for Dusty Field's autograph, everybody wanted one.

After they sold all of the baseballs, Max and Gordy realized they had none left for Austin. They wanted to get something special for Austin, who was sick at home. They decided to buy Austin a $3 baseball and get it autographed by Dusty Field.

Teaching Chart 22

Have students identify one problem in this passage, and its solution.

MODEL According to the first sentence, the problem is that no one wanted to buy the baseballs. As I continue reading, I look for the solution. How will the boys convince people to buy the baseballs? The third sentence states that Gordy solved the problem by telling everyone that the baseballs could be used for Dusty Field's autograph.

PRACTICE

Recognize Problems and Solutions

GROUP

Have students underline problems and circle solutions in the passage. Then ask students to explain why the solutions worked. (The solution that helped Max and Gordy sell the baseballs was a good one because it helped everyone. Getting a baseball signed by Dusty Field was a good solution because it made Austin feel better about not seeing Dusty in person.) ▶ **Visual/Logical**

ASSESS/CLOSE

Solve a Problem

Ask students what they would do if they wanted a video game that costs $50, when they had only $40.

Have students write three different solutions to this problem. (Possible responses: Wait and save another $10. Get a job to earn another $10. Borrow $10 from a friend. Get a less expensive game.)

SELF-SELECTED Reading

Students may choose from the following titles.

ANTHOLOGY

- *Max Malone*

LEVELED BOOKS

- *Special Delivery*
- *The Wonder Ball*
- *The Saltaire Voice*

Bibliography, pages T76–T77

Meeting Individual Needs for Comprehension

EASY	ON-LEVEL	CHALLENGE	LANGUAGE SUPPORT

EASY

Name_____ Date_____ Reteach 26

Problem and Solution

The **solution** is the way that a character solves his or her **problem**.

Max and Gordy solve a few problems in "Max Malone." Read each problem. Then circle the letter next to the solution that you read about in the story.

1. Max and Gordy want to know how many balls they can buy for $5.00.
   a. Gordy uses math to find out the answer.
   b. They talk to the store manager of Toys for Less.
   c. They make a deal with the owner of the sporting-goods store.
2. Max and Gordy want people to buy their baseballs.
   a. They call out to people on line at the sporting-goods store.
   b. They make a poster.
   c. They test out their ideas on Austin.
3. Max and Gordy need a baseball for Austin.
   a. The sporting-goods store owner gives them a free baseball.
   b. Dusty Field gives them a baseball of his own.
   c. Max and Gordy buy a baseball for Austin.
4. Austin is too sick to meet Dusty Field.
   a. Max and Gordy bring Austin an autographed baseball.
   b. Austin's mother gets an autographed baseball for her son.
   c. The sporting-goods store owner mails Austin some baseball cards.

At Home: Have students describe a problem that they helped to solve.
26   Book 3.1/Unit 1 Max Malone 4

ON-LEVEL

Name_____ Date_____ Practice 26

Problem and Solution

You can often find **solutions**, or answers, to even the most difficult **problems**. Finish the chart by writing down how Max and Gordy solved each of their problems.

Problem	Solution
1. Max and Gordy have $2.50 each and want to buy as many 20¢ baseballs as they can.	They talk to a store manager who sells them all the balls for $5.00.
2. Max and Gordy feel shy about selling their baseballs to people at the sporting-goods store.	They force themselves to call out to people to buy their baseballs for Dusty Field's autograph.
3. Max and Gordy both want their own Dusty Field-autographed baseballs.	They sell 46 baseballs and save 2 for themselves.
4. Max and Gordy forget to save a baseball for Austin.	They buy a baseball with the money they earned.
5. Max and Gordy know that Austin is sad about not seeing Dusty Field.	They give Austin a new baseball autographed by Dusty Field.

At Home: Have the students think of problems they might have if they were home sick from school. Then have them write down ways that friends could help them.
26   Book 3.1/Unit 1 Max Malone 5

CHALLENGE

Name_____ Date_____ Extend 26

Problem and Solution

There are solutions for most problems. Max and Gordy showed how to solve some problems. They also showed how to treat a good friend.

Suppose your school needs sports equipment. What ways can you think of to raise the money for your school to buy the equipment it needs?

_____
_____
_____
_____
_____
_____
_____
_____
_____
_____
_____
_____

At Home: Talk about daily problem/solution situations that students regularly face and deal with. Help them to see where they are adept at coming up with solutions and where they may need more practice.
26   Book 3.1/Unit 1 Max Malone

LANGUAGE SUPPORT

Name_____ Date_____

Finger Puppets

1. Act out what happened in the story to solve each problem below:
   Max and Gordy want to buy lots of baseballs with their money.
   Max and Gordy want to sell all their baseballs.
   Austin had an operation and could not get Dusty's autograph.

30 Max Malone Makes a Million • Language Support/Blackline Master 14   Grade 3

TEACHING TIP

INSTRUCTIONAL Have students identify two stories or movies that they like. Then ask them what happened to the main character in each story. Have them tell what they learned about the main character's personality from the way he or she reacted to the events in the story.

Review Story Elements

PREPARE

Discuss Character and Plot   Review: To analyze the characters and understand the plot in a story, it helps to focus on what the characters say and do.

TEACH

Read "Max's Idea" and Model the Skill   Have students read the passage about Max. To get an understanding of Max's character, suggest that they focus on his actions and what he says.

Max's Idea

Max had $5. He was hoping to find something at the Toys-R-Less sale. "Maybe they will have a $10 toy on sale for $5!" he said to Gordy. That's when he saw the baseballs. "I know how we can make a lot of money," he shouted to Gordy.

"What great money-making scheme do you have this time?" asked Gordy.

"We can buy the balls for 10¢ and sell them for 50¢," Max replied. Gordy shook his head. "Max, you've done it again!" he said.

Teaching Chart 23

Discuss how Max's and Gordy's personalities, or character traits, are shown in this passage. Have students underline words or actions that help them recognize these traits. Then have them summarize the plot.

MODEL   Max seems like a clever business person. He has a good idea about how to make money. His plan to buy baseballs for 10 cents and sell them for fifty cents shows that he is smart.

Create a Character/Plot Chart

PARTNERS

Have pairs of students record on a Character/Plot chart what the characters say and do in each important part of the plot. Have students use this information to analyze character traits. ▶**Logical/Visual**

Plot Events	Character's Words and Actions	Character Traits
Max is looking for an inexpensive toy.	"Maybe they will have a $10 toy on sale for $5!"	Max likes a bargain.
Max has a money-making idea.	"We can buy the balls for 10¢ and sell them for 50¢."	Max is smart.
Gordy likes the idea.	"Max, you've done it again!"	Gordy admires Max.

ASSESS/CLOSE

Analyze Character and Plot

Have students outline a favorite story or movie they have seen. Tell them to fill in details under the following headings: Title, Characters and Traits, Plot. (Plot might be subdivided into Beginning, Middle, and End.)

ALTERNATE TEACHING STRATEGY

STORY ELEMENTS

For a different approach to teaching this skill, see page T60.

Meeting Individual Needs for Comprehension

EASY	ON-LEVEL	CHALLENGE	LANGUAGE SUPPORT

EASY

Name_____ Date_____ Reteach **27**

Story Elements

> **Characters** are the people or animals that a story is about. The **plot** is what happens to those characters during the story.

Read the selections. Circle the letter that stands for the correct answer.

Kyle and Tipper spent the day fishing. There was not a cloud in the sky. The lake was calm and still. The two friends saw turtles and frogs swimming through the water. But they didn't see fish!
"Oh well," said Kyle, "we could try again tomorrow."
"Or we could go to the movies," said Tipper.

1. **CHARACTER:** Who are the main characters in the story?
   (a.) Kyle and Tipper   **b.** the fish   **c.** the turtles and frogs

2. **PLOT:** What is the plot of the story?
   a. The movie is playing.
   b. It is not cloudy.
   (c.) Kyle and Tipper didn't catch any fish.

It was Saturday. Genelle and Jackie were going to the mall by bus. Suddenly they heard a popping sound. The bus had a flat tire.
"How are we going to get to the store?" asked Genelle.
"I don't know," answered Jackie. "We'll have to wait until a tow truck comes."

3. **CHARACTER:** Who are the main characters in the story?
   a. the mall   **b.** the tow truck   (c.) Genelle and Jackie

4. **PLOT:** What is the plot of the story?
   a. Genelle and Jackie are bored.
   (b.) The girls' bus has a flat tire on the way to the mall.
   c. There is a sale at the mall.

Book 3.1/Unit 1
Max Malone   At Home: Have students discuss the characters and plot of a favorite children's book.   **27**

ON-LEVEL

Name_____ Date_____ Practice **27**

Story Elements

A **plot** is what happens in a story. The **characters** are who the story is about. Read the story before you answer each question.

Tippy was a small brown dog. Fluffy was a black cat with long hair. Both animals lived with their owner, Lisa. One day Lisa let her pets out into the backyard. Both animals wanted to see something new. Right away, Fluffy jumped over the fence. Tippy dug a hole under the fence and crawled through.
Fluffy and Tippy happily ran from yard to yard. Suddenly a big dog appeared. It was the largest, scariest dog Fluffy and Tippy had ever seen. The dog barked and growled. Fluffy and Tippy turned around and ran straight back to their yard.

1. Who are the main characters?   **Tippy, a dog and Fluffy, a cat**

2. What do the main characters want to do?   **see something new**

3. How are the characters able to do this?   **Fluffy jumps over the fence, and Tippy crawls under the fence to get out of the backyard.**

4. What problem do Tippy and Fluffy run into?   **They meet a large dog that growls at them.**

5. What do the animals do next?   **They run back to their own backyard.**

6. Do you think the animals learned anything from their experience?
   Answers may vary. Possible answer: Home is the best place to be.

Book 3.1/Unit 1
Max Malone   At Home: Have students draw pictures of other things that could have happened in the story.   **27**

CHALLENGE

Name_____ Date_____ Extend **27**

Story Elements

Complete the story map below. Tell what event in the story happened as a result of how the character felt. Under the character's name, draw a picture of the character's face showing how he felt.

CHARACTER	Character's Feelings	Story Event
Gordy	He wanted to start selling the baseballs.	Gordy started calling out, "Get your baseballs autographed by Dusty Field. Just fifty cents. Sure to become a collectable."
Max	Max had forgotten all about Austin.	Max and Gordy bought a three dollar real league baseball and asked Dusty to sign it for Austin.
Austin	Austin felt disappointed because he could not go to the sporting goods store to get Dusty's autograph.	Max and Gordy surprised Austin with a real league baseball signed by Dusty Field.

Book 3.1 / Unit 1
Max Malone   At Home: Ask students to draw a character they have read about, but have never seen in an illustration or on TV. Draw some conclusion about how easily readers picture their characters through the words they read.   **27**

LANGUAGE SUPPORT

Name_____ Date_____

Tell About Max

Good Friend

Great Ideas

Grade 3   Language Support/Blackline Master 15 • **Max Malone Makes a Million**   **31**

Reteach, 27   Practice, 27   Extend, 27   Language Support, 31

OBJECTIVES

Students will identify compound words.

....

MATERIALS

• Teaching Chart 24

TEACHING TIP

INSTRUCTIONAL Point out that the word *softhearted* literally means "having a soft heart." The way it is used, however, it means "sympathetic and generous." Have students give the meaning for the smaller words that make up *highway* and *cowhand.*

Then ask them to look up the compound words to see if their definitions match the combined meanings of the smaller words.

Review Compound Words

PREPARE

Discuss Meaning of Compound Words

Explain: A compound word is a word made up of two or more words. The meaning of a compound word is often a combination of the meanings of the smaller words it contains. Ask students: What does the word *baseball* mean? How do the two smaller words determine the meaning of the whole word?

TEACH

Read "At the Game" and Model the Skill

Have students read the passage on **Teaching Chart 24**. Before they begin, remind them to watch for compound words.

> **At the Game**
>
> Max and Gordy went to a <u>basketball</u> game after they sold all the <u>baseballs</u>. "Let's give <u>ourselves</u> a little treat," said Max.
>
> "And what will that be?" asked Gordy, as he took off his <u>sweatshirt</u>.
>
> "Let's save some money and buy a jumbo bag of <u>popcorn</u> and one large soda," said Max.
>
> Gordy thought Max's idea was perfect. "Max, you always know the best way to save money. I'm going to start calling you Mr. <u>Shopright</u>!"
>
> Teaching Chart 24

Have students underline the first compound word in the first sentence and tell which smaller words it contains.

MODEL The word *basketball* in the first sentence is made up of two smaller words: *basket* and *ball.* I can tell that the compound word *basketball* means a kind of ball that is used in a game with baskets.

Identify and Define Compound Words

GROUP

Have volunteers underline the remaining compound words in the passage and identify the smaller words in each. Have students explain how they can use these smaller words to figure out the meaning of each compound word. ▶ **Linguistic/Logical**

ASSESS/CLOSE

Create Compound Words

Have students match word parts from Column 1 to those in Column 2 to make up three compound words. Then have them use each word in a sentence.

COLUMN 1	COLUMN 2
them	shirt
mid	selves
sweat	air

ALTERNATE TEACHING STRATEGY

COMPOUND WORDS

For a different approach to teaching this skill, see page T63.

Meeting Individual Needs for Vocabulary

EASY

Name_____ Date_____ **Reteach** 28

Compound Words

A **compound word** is made by joining two smaller words. You can usually figure out the meaning of a compound word by looking at the two smaller words and putting their meanings together.

Make a compound word by joining a word in the list to the end of one of the words below. Then write the meaning of the compound word. You may use some words more than once. **Answers may vary.**

selves   boat   yard   balls   board   cloth   noon

1. sail ___sailboat___ ___a boat that has a sail___

2. after ___afternoon___ ___the time after 12 P.M., or noon___

3. table ___tablecloth___ ___a cloth that covers a table___

4. our ___ourselves___ ___us, our group___

5. base ___baseballs___ ___balls used for playing baseball___

6. house ___houseboat___ ___a boat that is also a house___

7. back ___backyard___ ___the yard in back___

8. floor ___floorboard___ ___a board in a floor___

At Home: Ask students to make compound words using each of the following words: rail, work, home, road.

28   Book 3.1/Unit 1 Max Malone   16

ON-LEVEL

Name_____ Date_____ **Practice** 28

Compound Words

A **compound word** is made by joining two smaller words. The meanings of the two smaller words can help you figure out the meaning of the compound word.

Look at each of the compound words. Write the two words that make up each compound word. Then use the meanings of the two smaller words to write the meaning of the compound word.

popcorn

1. ___pop___ + ___corn___

2. meaning = ___corn that can be popped___

homeland

3. ___home___ + ___land___

4. meaning = ___the land in which a person makes his or her home___

sweatshirt

5. ___sweat___ + ___shirt___

6. meaning = ___a shirt that absorbs sweat___

seacoast

7. ___sea___ + ___coast___

8. meaning = ___the place where the sea meets the land___

sandbox

9. ___sand___ + ___box___

10. meaning = ___a box that holds sand___

At Home: Ask students to name the short words in each of the following compound words: steamship, grandfather, goldfish.

28   Book 3.1/Unit 1 Max Malone   16

CHALLENGE

Name_____ Date_____ **Extend** 28

Compound Words

every	mid	base	air	balls
thing	them	selves	one	

Use the words in the box to make compound words you can use in the sentences below.

1. The outfielder caught the fly ball in ___midair___

2. Max and Gordy bought forty-six ___baseballs___

3. They wanted signatures for ___themselves___ , too.

4. In the end, ___everyone___ was happy.

Use some of the compound words that you built to write a story.

_____
_____
_____
_____
_____
_____
_____
_____
_____

At Home: Ask students to look at a newspaper for more compound words.

28   Book 3.1/Unit 1 Max Malone

LANGUAGE SUPPORT

Name_____ Date_____

Put It Together

pop + corn

midair

base + ball

themselves

them + selves

sweatshirt

sweat + shirt

popcorn

sweat + pants

baseball

mid + air

sweatpants

32   Max Malone Makes a Million • Language Support/Blackline Master 16   Grade 3

Reteach, 28   Practice, 28   Extend, 28   Language Support, 32

GRAMMAR/SPELLING CONNECTIONS

See the 5-Day Grammar and Usage Plan on predicates, pages 127M–127N.

See the 5-Day Spelling Plan on words with long /ū/ and /ü/, pages 127O–127P.

TECHNOLOGY TIP

Encourage students to experiment with fonts when publishing their writing. Suggest they keep their audience in mind when choosing a font. For example, a larger, darker font is better for work that will be displayed on a bulletin board.

Personal Narrative

Prewrite

WRITE AN ARTICLE Present this writing assignment: Have you ever done something nice for a friend or relative? Or has someone ever done something really special for you? Write an article about what happened, including a description of how it made you feel.

EXPLORING MEMORY LANE Encourage students to recall times when they helped someone or when someone helped them. Have them make a list of these events.

Strategy: Make a Chart Have students write about one act of kindness from their list. They can then make a chart listing details that answer who, what, where, when, why, and how questions. Help students get started by presenting a model like this:

QUESTIONS	ANSWERS
Who?	me
What?	made breakfast for Mom
Where?	in kitchen

Draft

FREE WRITE Encourage students to freely write about their experiences. Students can expand on the details from their chart and write them in a logical order.

Revise

SELF-QUESTIONING Ask students to assess their drafts.

- Did I put my events in a logical order?
- Are all of my details interesting and do they support the main topic?

PARTNERS Have students trade articles with a partner to get another point of view.

Edit/Proofread

CHECK FOR ERRORS Have students reread their articles and correct any errors in spelling, grammar, and punctuation.

Publish

READ IN GROUPS Have students read their articles to one another in small groups. Encourage group members to tell what interested them most about each article.

Helping Mom

    Last Saturday my mom was sick. She had the flu. She could not even get out of bed. I decided I would help her get better.

    So I made her breakfast. I put toast, jam, butter, milk, juice, and a crepe-paper flower on a tray. Then I brought the tray to her in bed.

    I could tell from the smile on her face that she liked her breakfast. By nighttime, she was really feeling better. I felt great!

Presentation Ideas

MAKE A MAGAZINE COVER Ask students to draw newsmagazine covers on folders. Have them put their articles in the folders and display them on a classroom table.

▶**Viewing/Representing**

BROADCAST A NEWS CLIP Have pairs of students pretend they are TV newscasters. They can take turns interviewing each other about their articles.

▶ **Speaking/Listening**

Consider students' creative efforts, possibly adding a plus (+) for originality, wit, and imagination.

Scoring Rubric

Excellent	Good	Fair	Unsatisfactory
4: The writer	**3:** The writer	**2:** The writer	**1:** The writer
• writes vividly.	• makes the point of the article clear.	• includes a topic sentence in each paragraph.	• does not include a topic sentence in each paragraph.
• includes a topic sentence in each paragraph.	• includes a topic sentence in each paragraph.	• includes details that answer *who* and *what* questions.	• may provide details, but paragraphs are not coherent.
• includes details that answer *who, what, where, why, how,* and *when* questions.	• includes details that answer *who, what,* and *when* questions.	• shows some sense of audience.	• shows inadequate sense of audience.
• has a good sense of audience.	• shows a sense of audience.		

0: The writer leaves the page blank or fails to respond to the writing task. The student does not address the topic or simply paraphrases the prompt. The response is illegible or incoherent.

Meeting Individual Needs for Writing

EASY	ON-LEVEL	CHALLENGE
Thank-You Card Have students design a thank-you card and write a brief note thanking someone who did something kind for them.	**Biographical Article** Have students write a brief article about a person they admire. Have them include details that describe the things this person has done. Suggest students include a picture of the person in their article.	**Citizen-of-the-Month Award** Have students write an article that describes a new award for citizens who perform exceptional acts of kindness. Instruct students to include details about what kind of acts will be considered, and what the award will be.

5 Day Grammar and Usage Plan

ESL Have volunteers pantomime the actions in the Daily Language Activities' predicates below.

DAILY LANGUAGE ACTIVITIES

Write the Daily Language Activities on the chalkboard each day or use **Transparency 4**. For each item, have students identify the predicate orally, or add a predicate.

Day 1

1. The boy is sad.
2. Gordy caught the ball.
3. Dusty autographed the ball.

Day 2

1. Max was a genius.
2. The boys. went to the toy store.
3. The store manager. was nice.

Day 3

1. The boys made a fortune.
2. Baseball. is my favorite sport.
3. The girl watched the game.

Day 4

1. The first batter. struck out.
2. The pitcher. threw a curve ball.
3. The player hit a home run.

Day 5

1. The two boys sold all the balls.
2. The baseballs. cost fifty cents.
3. Austin. received an autographed baseball.

Daily Language Transparency 4

DAY 1 — Introduce the Concept

Oral Warm-Up Read aloud the following sentence: The boys visited their sick friend. Have students identify the part of the sentence that tells what the boys did.

Introduce Predicates Every complete sentence has two parts—a subject and a predicate. Help students recall that the subject is whom or what the sentence is about. Present and discuss:

Predicates

The **predicate** of a sentence tells what the subject does or is.

Present the Daily Language Activity. Then have students write three new sentences, underlining the predicate in each.

 WRITING Assign the daily Writing Prompt on page 106C.

DAY 2 — Teach the Concept

Review Predicates Ask students to describe what a predicate tells about the subject of a sentence.

Say the Following: My favorite sport. Ask students whether this is a sentence or sentence fragment. Point out that it is a fragment that is missing a predicate. Present:

Sentence Fragments

- A **sentence fragment** is a group of words that does not express a complete thought.
- Some sentence fragments can be corrected by adding a predicate.

Present the Daily Language Activity. Then have students write two sentence fragments consisting only of subjects and exchange papers to complete them.

 WRITING Assign the daily Writing Prompt on page 106C.

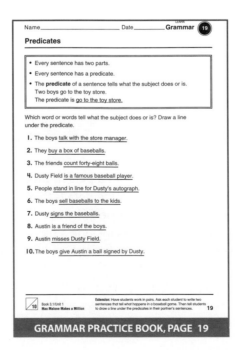

GRAMMAR PRACTICE BOOK, PAGE 19

GRAMMAR PRACTICE BOOK, PAGE 20

Predicates

Learn from the Literature Review predicates. Read aloud the following sentence from page 116 of *Max Malone:*

Max was having a great time.

Have students identify the predicate. Ask students to explain how they can identify the subject and the predicate of the sentence.

Identifying Predicates Present the Daily Language Activity and have students identify the predicate of each sentence orally. Then, have the class create a sentence web with the subject Max in the center of the web. Around it, ask volunteers to write predicates that connect to the subject to make complete sentences.

Assign the daily Writing Prompt on page 106D.

Review Predicates Write on the board the complete sentences from the Daily Language Activities for Days 1, 2, and 3. Have students identify the subjects and predicates. Next, present the Daily Language Activity for Day 4.

Mechanics and Usage Before students begin the daily Writing Prompt on page 106D, discuss the use of quotation marks in dialogue. Present:

> ### Quotation Marks
> Use **quotation marks** at the beginning and end of the speaker's exact words.

Assign the daily Writing Prompt on page 106D.

Assess Use the Daily Language Activity and page 23 of the **Grammar Practice Book** for assessment.

Reteach Ask students to write a definition for *complete sentence, sentence fragment, subject,* and *predicate.* Then ask students to work with a partner. Assign each pair three sentences based on the week's Daily Language Activities. Ask one partner to identify the predicate for every sentence, and the other to identify subjects. Have them write subjects and predicates on paper strips, and rejoin them to make complete sentences. Make a combined word wall of all partners' complete sentences.

Use page 24 of the **Grammar Practice Book** for additional reteaching.

Assign the daily Writing Prompt on page 106D.

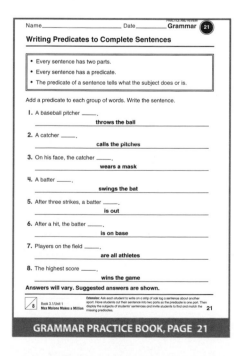

GRAMMAR PRACTICE BOOK, PAGE 21

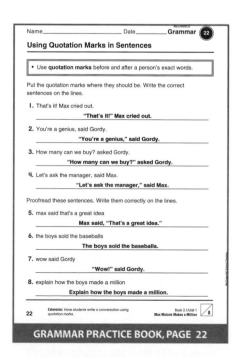

GRAMMAR PRACTICE BOOK, PAGE 22

GRAMMAR PRACTICE BOOK, PAGE 23

5 Day Spelling Plan

ESL To help students distinguish between the vowel sounds /ū/ and /ü/, repeat the two sounds aloud and then present contrasting pairs of words: *use, lose, mule, moon; cute, root; few, two.*

DICTATION SENTENCES

1. He likes to play loud <u>music</u>.
2. He has a new <u>broom</u> made of straw.
3. There is more <u>soup</u> for the children.
4. Do you have <u>fruit</u> with breakfast?
5. She had a <u>huge</u> bite of her sandwich.
6. The children <u>drew</u> on their papers.
7. Tell me the <u>truth</u>.
8. The <u>pool</u> is filled with water.
9. A <u>goose</u> is a large bird.
10. A cold is no <u>excuse</u> to miss a day.
11. <u>Dew</u> covers the lawn when the day starts.
12. Do you have more <u>juice</u>?
13. The <u>crew</u> works on the road.
14. That <u>group</u> likes to dance.
15. The insects can <u>produce</u> many eggs.

Challenge Words

16. There is a hole in the <u>ceiling</u>.
17. The team is <u>eager</u> to play.
18. She had a party <u>including</u> the children.
19. He saw a pretty beach <u>scene</u>.
20. Stay in this <u>section</u> of the house.

DAY 1 Pretest

Assess Prior Knowledge Use the Dictation Sentences at left and **Spelling Practice Book** page 19 for the pretest. Allow students to correct their own papers. If students have trouble, have partners give each other a midweek test on Day 3. Students who require a modified list may be tested on the first eight words.

Spelling Words		Challenge Words
1. music	9. **goose**	16. **ceiling**
2. broom	10. **excuse**	17. **eager**
3. soup	11. dew	18. **including**
4. fruit	12. juice	19. **scene**
5. huge	13. crew	20. **section**
6. drew	14. group	
7. truth	15. produce	
8. pool		

*Note: Words in **dark type** are from the story.*

Word Study On page 20 of the **Spelling Practice Book** are word study steps and an at-home activity.

DAY 2 Explore the Pattern

Sort and Spell Words Say *use* and *do*. Ask students what vowel sound they hear in each word. These words contain similar vowel sounds, /ū/ and /ü/.

Ask students to read aloud the 15 Spelling Words before sorting them according to the spelling pattern.

Words with /ū/ and /ü/ spelled

u-e	ew	ou
huge	drew	soup
excuse	dew	group
produce	crew	

oo	ui	u
pool	fruit	music
broom	juice	truth
goose		

Word Wall As students read other stories and texts, have them look for new words with the sound /ū/ or /ü/ and add them to a classroom word wall, underlining the spelling pattern in each word.

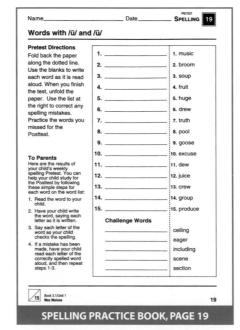

SPELLING PRACTICE BOOK, PAGE 19

WORD STUDY STEPS AND ACTIVITY, PAGE 20

SPELLING PRACTICE BOOK, PAGE 21

Words with /ū/ and /ü/

DAY 3 Practice and Extend

Word Meaning: Definitions Have students write the spelling words on index cards, then write definitions chosen from the cards as others try to guess what word is being defined. When the correct word is guessed, have others share, compare, and agree on one class definition. List the word and the class definition on chart paper. Continue with all words on the list.

Glossary Have students write a sentence using as many of the Challenge Words as they can. Then have them look up the meaning of the words in the Glossary and rewrite the sentence inserting the definitions. Example: I am *eager* to paint a *section* of the *ceiling*. I *want very much* to paint *part of an area* of the *inside overhead surface*.

DAY 4 Proofread and Write

Proofread Sentences Write these sentences on the chalkboard, including the misspelled words. Ask students to proofread, circling incorrect spellings and writing the correct spellings. There are two spelling errors in each sentence.

> I like ⟨frute⟩ and ⟨jooce⟩ for breakfast.
> (fruit, juice)
>
> The ⟨groop⟩ can ⟨produice⟩ great music.
> (group, produce)
>
> A ⟨guoose⟩ went into the ⟨poole.⟩ (goose, pool)

Have students create additional sentences with errors for partners to correct.

 Have students use as many Spelling Words as possible in the daily Writing Prompt on page 106D. Remind students to proofread their writing for errors in spelling, grammar, and punctuation.

DAY 5 Assess and Reteach

Assess Students' Knowledge Use page 24 of the Spelling Practice Book or the Dictation Sentences on page 127O for the posttest.

Personal Word List Students often misspell *ew* words with *u-e*, such as *crue* for *crew*. Have students keep a list in their journal of both categories of words as well as homophones. (*blew, blue; do, dew*) Encourage them to add words they come across in the reading.

Students should refer to their lists during future writing activities.

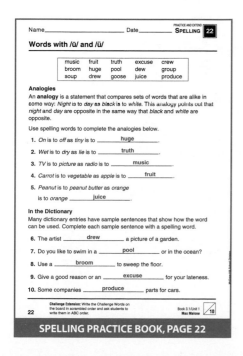

SPELLING PRACTICE BOOK, PAGE 22

SPELLING PRACTICE BOOK, PAGE 23

SPELLING PRACTICE BOOK, PAGE 24

127P

Champions
of the World

Selection Summary Chris Cardone will never forget the day he took the place of another Little League player and then hit a home run. His Toms River, New Jersey, team won the Little League World Series.

Listening
Library
Audiocassette

INSTRUCTIONAL
Pages 130–137

Resources for Meeting Individual Needs

EASY
Pages 137A–137D

INDEPENDENT
Pages 137B–137D

CHALLENGE
Pages 137C–137D

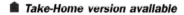 *Take-Home version available*

LEVELED PRACTICE

Reteach, 29–35
blackline masters with reteaching opportunities for each assessed skill

Practice, 29–35
workbook with Take-Home stories and practice opportunities for each assessed skill and story comprehension

Extend, 29–35
blackline masters that offer challenge activities for each assessed skill

ADDITIONAL RESOURCES

- **Language Support Book,** pp. 33–40
- **Take-Home Story, Practice** p. 30a
- **Alternate Teaching Strategies,** pp. T60–T66
- **Selected Quizzes Prepared by** Accelerated Reader

McGraw-Hill School **TECHNOLOGY**

Phonics CD-ROM provides extra phonics support.

interNET CONNECTION Research & Inquiry ideas. Visit **www.mhschool.com/reading.**

Suggested
Lesson Planner

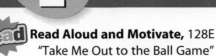

🔵 **Available on CD-ROM**

READING AND LANGUAGE ARTS

 DAY 1 *Focus on Reading and Skills*

DAY 2 *Read the Literature*

- ⬤ **Comprehension**
- ⬤ **Vocabulary**
- ⬤ **Phonics/Decoding**
- ⬤ **Study Skills**
- ⬤ **Listening, Speaking, Viewing, Representing**

DAY 1

 Read Aloud and Motivate, 128E
"Take Me Out to the Ball Game"

Develop Visual Literacy, 128/129

☑ **Review Make Predictions,** 130A–130B
Teaching Chart 25
Reteach, Practice, Extend, 29

DAY 2

Build Background, 130C
Develop Oral Language

Vocabulary, 130D

celebrated	fans	score
cork	pitcher	wrap

Teaching Chart 26
Word Building Manipulative Cards
Reteach, Practice, Extend, 30

 Read the Selection, 130–133
Guided Instruction
☑ Make Predictions
☑ Problem and Solution

⬤ **Curriculum Connections**

 Link Fine Arts, 128/129

 Link Social Studies, 130C

⬤ **Writing**

 Writing Prompt: Think of a group or team you belong to. What does your group do? How many people are in it? When did you join? Write your answers in a paragraph.

 Writing Prompt: Do you think everyone who belongs to a team or group has to like everyone else? Why or why not? Write a paragraph to explain.

Journal Writing, 133
Quick-Write

⬤ **Grammar**

Introduce the Concept: Sentence Combining, 137M
Daily Language Activity
1. Mike throws the ball. Chris swings.
   Mike throws the ball, and Chris swings.
2. The ball goes far. The crowd cheers.
   The ball goes far, and the crowd cheers.
3. The team won. The players were happy.
   The team won and the players were happy.
Grammar Practice Book, 25

Teach the Concept: Sentence Combining, 137O
Daily Language Activity
1. Ed hit the ball. Todd stole a base.
2. Joey pitched well. Sally hit hard.
3. The parade was long. The boys were tired.
Grammar Practice Book, 26

⬤ **Spelling**

Pretest: Words from Physical Education, 137O
Spelling Practice Book, 25–26

Explore the Pattern: Words from Physical Education, 137O
Spelling Practice Book, 27

Meeting Individual Needs

 = Skill Assessed in Unit Test

DAY 3 — Read the Literature

Rereading for Fluency, 132

Story Questions, 134
Reteach, Practice, Extend, 31
Story Activities, 135

Study Skill, 136
☑ Technology
Teaching Chart 27
Reteach, Practice, Extend, 32

 Read the Leveled Books,
Guided Reading
Phonics Review
☑ Comprehension Review
☑ Instructional Vocabulary
 CD-ROM

 Social Studies, 135

 Writing Prompt: What would you like most to excel at? Explain in a paragraph.

Writing Process: Personal Narrative, 137K
Prewrite, Draft

Review and Practice: Sentence Combining, 137N
Daily Language Activity
1. The team waved. The people shouted.
2. I drove the car. She honked the horn.
3. The game was tied. Cardone ran fast.
Grammar Practice Book, 27

Practice and Extend: Words from Physical Education, 137P
Spelling Practice Book, 28

DAY 4 — Build and Review Skills

 Read the Leveled Books and Self-Selected Books

☑ **Review Steps in a Process,** 137E–137F
Teaching Chart 28
Reteach, Practice, Extend, 33
Language Support, 38

☑ **Review Compound Words,** 137G–137H
Teaching Chart 29
Reteach, Practice, Extend, 34
Language Support, 39

 Writing Prompt: Write a paragraph explaining how different members of a team work together. For example, write about a pitcher and catcher.

Writing Process: Personal Narrative, 137K
Revise

Meeting Individual Needs for Writing, 137L

Review and Practice: Sentence Combining, 137N
Daily Language Activity
1. Jim hit a home run. Todd cheered.
2. Sara was up at bat. The crowd was silent.
3. Mark broke the record. His son was proud.
Grammar Practice Book, 28

Proofread and Write: Words from Physical Education, 137P
Spelling Practice Book, 29

DAY 5 — Build and Review Skills

Read Self-Selected Books

☑ **Review Prefixes,** 137I–137J
Teaching Chart 30
Reteach, Practice, Extend, 35
Language Support, 40

Listening, Speaking, Viewing, Representing, 137L
Make an Exhibition
A Talk Show

Writing Prompt: Think about one positive and one negative thing that happens to people on a team or in a group. Discuss both things in a brief essay.

Writing Process: Personal Narrative, 137K
Edit/Proofread, Publish

Assess and Reteach: Sentence Combining, 137N
Daily Language Activity
1. The race was on. We went to watch.
2. Sammy hits hard. The ball goes far.
3. Todd was safe. The game was over.
Grammar Practice Book, 29–30

Assess and Reteach: Words from Physical Education, 137P
Spelling Practice Book, 30

Music

Read Aloud and Motivate

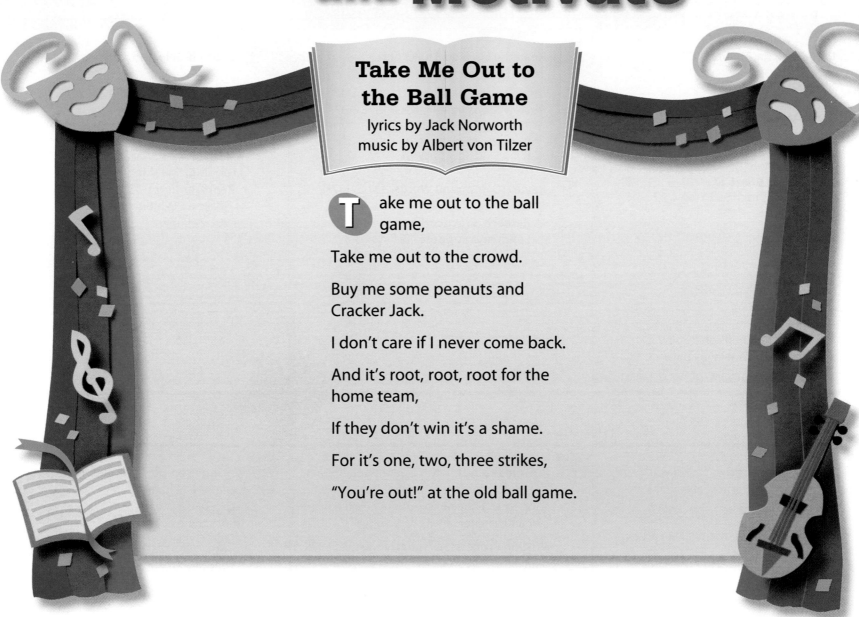

Take Me Out to the Ball Game

lyrics by Jack Norworth
music by Albert von Tilzer

Take me out to the ball game,

Take me out to the crowd.

Buy me some peanuts and Cracker Jack.

I don't care if I never come back.

And it's root, root, root for the home team,

If they don't win it's a shame.

For it's one, two, three strikes,

"You're out!" at the old ball game.

Oral Comprehension

LISTENING AND SPEAKING Sing or read aloud the lyrics to the song. Invite students to listen to the rhythm of the song. Repeat the song and have students join in and clap out it's rhythm. Ask students how the song-writer feels about going to a baseball game. Encourage students who have been to a baseball game to share their experiences with the rest of the class.

Activity Have students make up their own dance to the song "Take Me Out to the Ball Game." Encourage them to base their movements on the movements of baseball players and baseball fans during a game. Have them perform their dances in small groups as the rest of the class sings the song.

▶ **Kinesthetic/Interpersonal**

Develop Visual Literacy

Anthology pages 128–129

This painting almost makes you feel like you can step into the picture. You are closer to the players than the people who are watching them.

~

Look at this painting. What do you think is happening? What do you think the blue team will try to do? Look at the sky. Do you think it will rain? Why or why not?

~

Look at the painting again. What other details do you notice about it?

Hockey at Malvern Girls College
by Henry Deykin

128

129

Objective: Make Predictions

VIEWING This painting depicts a girls' field hockey game. Invite students to notice the spectators in the background and to tell why the artist gave "front row" seats to the people viewing the painting. What else do students find interesting about the perspective of this painting? Why do they think the closest player partially disappears from the canvas? Discuss with students how the colors in the landscape seem to reflect the hues of the uniforms. What other details do they notice?

Read the page with students, encouraging individual interpretations of the painting.

Review with students their predictions about what might happen next in the game. For example:

- The blue team will probably try to score a point.
- It will rain before the goal is made.

REPRESENTING Have students choose a sport and draw or paint a scene from a typical game. How do the colors they use set the mood or tone of the game?

OBJECTIVES

Students will predict outcomes in stories and articles.

TEACHING TIP

INSTRUCTIONAL Tell students that at the end of each unit they will read a short magazine article. Discuss some differences between stories found in books and articles found in magazines.

Review Make Predictions

PREPARE

Discuss Making Predictions   Tell students that people can find out what a book is about by skimming through it. Ask them what parts of a book they could look at to get an idea of what it will be about.

TEACH

Find Clues   Remind students that the title of a book or article often tells what it's about. Chapter and paragraph headings, illustrations, and the captions for the illustrations are also helpful. Look for key phrases that suggest the final outcome or conclusion of the book or article.

Robins Surprise Pumas

The Robins, the women's basketball team of Brad High, amazed everyone in last night's game against the Cott Pumas. Cott High fans expected to see their team beat the Robins. The Robins were behind until the final two minutes when Lori Metzler scored three baskets to make the score 38–37. Kay Gibbs made two free throws with three seconds left and the Robins had their first win over Cott!

Teaching Chart 25

Read the Story Aloud and Model the Skill   Display **Teaching Chart 25**. As the story is read, have students pay attention to clues about its outcome.

> **MODEL** The title tells me that the Robins surprised the Pumas, so I predict that they won the game. Reading that they had amazed everyone, and that the Pumas had expected to beat them tells me that they must have won.

PRACTICE

Create a Clues and Predictions Chart Have students underline the parts of the passage that helped them make their prediction. Then help students set up a Clues and Predictions chart. Ask volunteers to record the clues and the predictions suggested by the clues. ► **Logical/Spatial**

CLUE	PREDICTIONS
Robins Surprise Pumas	The Robins beat the Pumas.
The Robins amazed everyone.	The Robins won unexpectedly.
Fans expected to see the Robins lose.	The Robins broke a losing streak.

ASSESS/CLOSE

Give More Examples of Clues Ask students to replace the clues in the story with clues that suggest other predictions. For example, instead of "Robins Surprise Pumas," retitle the story, "Robins Routed—Again!"

SELECTION
Connection

Students will make predictions when they read *Champions of the World* and the Leveled Books.

ALTERNATE TEACHING
STRATEGY

MAKE PREDICTIONS
For a different approach to teaching this skill, see page T62.

Meeting Individual Needs for Comprehension

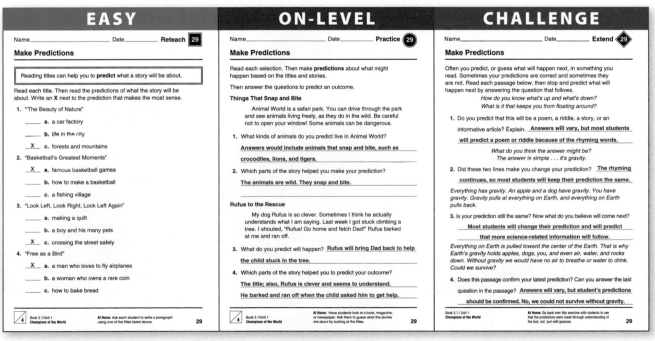

Reteach, 29   **Practice, 29**   **Extend, 29**

Build Background

Social Studies

Evaluate Prior Knowledge

CONCEPT: TEAM SPORTS Bring pictures of team sports and individual sports to class. Have students identify the sports and share experiences they have had with them. Discuss how working together as a team in a game can help people learn to work together on other types of projects or jobs.

COMPARE INDIVIDUAL AND TEAM SPORTS Have students compare and contrast team and individual sports. Then have them display their similarities and differences in a Venn diagram. ▶ **Logical/Visual**

INDIVIDUAL SPORTS		TEAM SPORTS
Different	**Alike**	**Different**

performed alone — Both are exciting. — performed in a group

Both require

focus is inward — concentration. — focus both inward and on team members

Both require

competitive with self — physical skill. — competitive with others

Graphic Organizer 14

INTERVIEW A SPORTS FAN Ask pairs
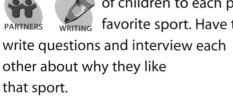 of children to each pick a
favorite sport. Have them
PARTNERS   WRITING
write questions and interview each
other about why they like
that sport.

Develop Oral Language

ATTEND AN IMAGINARY SPORTS EVENT

ESL Show students the sports pictures you showed earlier. Have them vote on a sports event they would most enjoy watching. Then have students discuss what they might see if they attended a professional performance of that sport. Write the names of the sport's equipment, uniforms, and so forth on the chalkboard. Have students make sketches of the listed items. Display and discuss the completed drawings. Encourage ESL students to ask questions about any aspects of the game they don't understand and invite English-fluent students to answer.

TEACHING TIP

INSTRUCTIONAL Encourage students to talk about playing team sports. Ask them what they like and dislike about them. Have them compare these other activities with team sports.

LANGUAGE SUPPORT

See **Language Support Book, pages 33–36,** for teaching suggestions for Build Background and Vocabulary.

Vocabulary

Key Words

Our Team Won!

1. Many (fans) turned out to cheer their favorite Little League baseball team. **2.** They (celebrated) their team's statewide victory by holding a parade. **3.** The hometown team won by a final (score) of 12 to 0. **4.** The winning (pitcher) in the game had thrown six innings of shutout ball. **5.** The baseball he used had a round, springy piece of light (cork) wood in its center. **6.** After the game he had to (wrap) some soft, warm cloths around his arm to keep it from getting stiff.

Teaching Chart 26

Vocabulary in Context

IDENTIFY VOCABULARY WORDS
Display **Teaching Chart 26** and read the passage with students. Have volunteers circle the vocabulary words and underline clues to their meaning.

DISCUSS MEANINGS Ask questions like these to help clarify word meanings.

- If you're a fan of something, do you like or dislike it?

- When you celebrated something, were you glad it happened or sad?

- Does the pitcher throw a ball or catch it?

- If you win a game, is your score higher or lower than the other team's?

- Is cork a heavy stone or light wood?

- If you wrap something, are you covering or uncovering it?

Practice

BASEBALL TALK Have pairs of students take turns choosing vocabulary words from a pile. The chooser must use his or her word in a statement about baseball.

▶ **Kinesthetic/Linguistic**

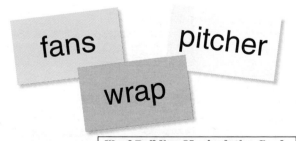

Word Building Manipulative Cards

SHOW AND TELL Have volunteers illustrate a vocabulary word on the chalkboard. Have other volunteers write the word's definition under its picture. Students can refer to their Glossary as needed. ▶ **Linguistic/Spatial**

fans (p. 132) people who admire a famous individual or group or an activity

celebrated (p. 132) gave special notice to a happy occasion

score (p. 131) the number of points made in a game

pitcher (p. 131) the player who throws the ball to the batter in baseball

cork (p. 133) the light, springy wood of a certain tree

wrap (p. 133) to cover something by winding something around it or folding something over it

SPELLING/VOCABULARY CONNECTIONS

See Spelling Challenge Words, pages 137O–137P.

Take-Home Story 30a
Reteach 30
Practice 30 • Extend 30

Guided Instruction

Preview and Predict

Have students preview the selection, looking for headings, pictures, and captions that give clues about the article's contents.

- What is the article likely to be about?
- What subject do the pictures, headings, and captions all have in common? (baseball)
- Is this article nonfiction or a fable? How can you tell? (The photographs are of real people. It's about a real event.) *Genre*

Have students record their predictions.

PREDICTIONS	WHAT HAPPENED
A Little League team wins a championship game.	
The article gives extra information about baseball.	

Set Purposes

What do students want to find out by reading the selection? For example:

- Was it easy or hard to win the game?
- What new things can I learn about baseball?

TIME FOR KIDS
SPECIAL REPORT

CHAMPIONS of the World

Meeting Individual Needs • Grouping Suggestions for Strategic Reading

EASY	ON-LEVEL	CHALLENGE
Read Together Read the article together with students or have them first use the **Listening Library Audiocassette**. Have students use a Clues and Predictions chart as on page 131 to record important information about what is likely to happen. Guided Instruction prompts offer additional help with comprehension strategies.	**Guided Reading** Display the story words listed on page 131. Use the Guided Instruction questions as you read the article with students or after they have played the **Listening Library Audiocassette**. Have them use the Clues and Predictions chart to record meaningful information as they read.	**Read Independently** Encourage students to make predictions about the outcome of the article. Have students set up a Clues and Predictions chart. After reading, they can use their charts to help them summarize the article.

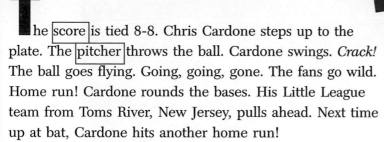

On the Ball
A Winning Little League Team ①

The score is tied 8-8. Chris Cardone steps up to the plate. The pitcher throws the ball. Cardone swings. *Crack!* The ball goes flying. Going, going, gone. The fans go wild. Home run! Cardone rounds the bases. His Little League team from Toms River, New Jersey, pulls ahead. Next time up at bat, Cardone hits another home run!

② "When the ball hit the bat, I knew it was gone," says Chris. And get this: It was Cardone's first time up at bat. He was taking the place of another player.

The Toms River team was playing against a team from Japan. Nicknamed the "Beast from the East," Cardone's team won the 1998 Little League World Series. It was the first time since 1993 that a U.S. team had won the series.

"You're out!" A player for the team from Japan gets tagged by Toms River's Brad Frank.

"Way to go!" Todd Frazier's team wins the Little League championship, 12 to 9.

131

Guided Instruction

☑ **Make Predictions**
☑ **Problem and Solution**

Strategic Reading Making predictions can help us focus on information in the article. Before we begin reading, let's prepare Clues and Predictions charts.

CLUES	PREDICTIONS

① **MAKE PREDICTIONS** Read the title and headings of this article. What do the words *Champions*, *On the Ball*, and *Winning* tell you? (The article is about a winning team.)

② **PROBLEM AND SOLUTION** What problem is mentioned in the first paragraph on page 131? (The score is tied.) How was it solved? (The batter hits a home run.)

Story Words

The words below may be unfamiliar. Have students check their meanings and pronunciations in the Glossary beginning on page 388.

- Little League, p. 131
- souvenir, p. 132
- Mark McGwire, p. 133
- Sammy Sosa, p. 133
- season, p. 133

LANGUAGE SUPPORT

This chart is available as a blackline master in the **Language Support Book.**

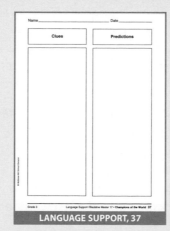

LANGUAGE SUPPORT, 37

Guided Instruction

③ MAKE PREDICTIONS The heading on this page reads "Parade Time." Who do you think will hold the parade and why? (The people in Toms River will have a parade for the team.) Let's add this to our Clues and Predictions charts.

CLUES	PREDICTIONS
Champions of the World, winning	The article will be about a champion Little League team.
Parade Time	A parade will be held for the champions.

④ PROBLEM AND SOLUTION What do you think the 108 stitches do for a baseball? (hold the cowhide cover on)

ORGANIZE INFORMATION Tell students to summarize what they learned in a chart with the headings: *Champion Little League Team* and *General Information About Baseball.* *Summarize*

The team proudly carries the Little League Championship banner.

"I thought we had it in us," says Todd Frazier. Todd was the star pitcher in the game. He also hit a home run. After the final game, Frazier said he was holding on to a souvenir. "I got my home-run ball right here," he said. "It just means everything to me."

③ PARADE TIME

After the game, the boys headed back to Toms River. Then it was time for a parade. About 2,000 people came out to cheer them. A plane circled overhead carrying a sign that said, "Welcome Home Toms River East Champs." Signs on homes and cars also celebrated the big win.

The team rode on top of a fire truck and waved to their fans. The kids knew their team was Number One!

132

Boys and girls both play Little League baseball.

REREADING FOR *Fluency*

PARTNERS Have partners take turns reading page 131 aloud as if they were sportscasters. Encourage students to reread any difficult parts.

READING RATE You may want to evaluate a student's reading rate. Have the student read aloud from *Champions of the World* for one minute. Ask the student to place a self-stick note after the last word read.

Then count the number of words he or she has read.

Alternatively, you could assess small groups or the whole class together by having students count words and record their own scores.

A Running Record form provided in **Diagnostic/Placement Evaluation** will help you evaluate reading rate(s).

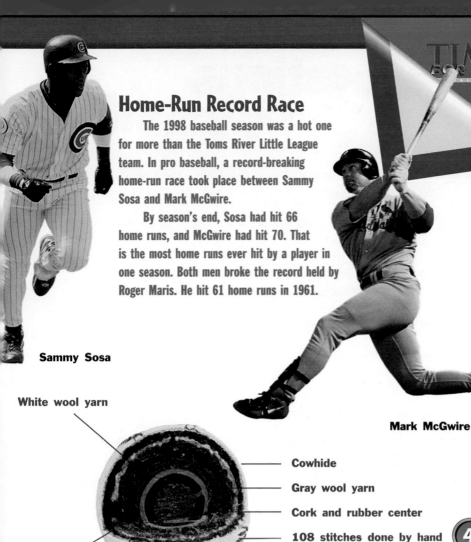

Home-Run Record Race

The 1998 baseball season was a hot one for more than the Toms River Little League team. In pro baseball, a record-breaking home-run race took place between Sammy Sosa and Mark McGwire.

By season's end, Sosa had hit 66 home runs, and McGwire had hit 70. That is the most home runs ever hit by a player in one season. Both men broke the record held by Roger Maris. He hit 61 home runs in 1961.

Sammy Sosa

Mark McGwire

White wool yarn

Cowhide

Gray wool yarn

Cork and rubber center

108 stitches done by hand ④

Cotton yarn

Want to Make a Baseball?

Wrap a round piece of cork with 150 yards of cotton yarn and 219 yards of wool yarn. Cover it with cowhide. Sew it with 108 stitches. You've got yourself a baseball!

FIND OUT MORE
Visit our website:
www.mhschool.com/reading

*inter*NET
CONNECTION

Based on an article in *TIME FOR KIDS*.

133

Guided Instruction

Return to Predictions and Purposes

Review with students their predictions about the article. Were they correct? Did they find out what they wanted to know?

PREDICTIONS	WHAT HAPPENED
A Little League team wins a championship game.	The Toms River team won the championship game of the Little League World Series.
The article gives extra information about baseball.	The article describes the 1998 race to break the home-run record and tells how to make a baseball.

INFORMAL ASSESSMENT

MAKE PREDICTIONS

HOW TO ASSESS

- Have students give examples of clues that helped them predict the outcome of this article.

Students should understand that titles, headings, pictures, and captions contain clues about the content and outcome of stories and articles.

FOLLOW UP If students have trouble understanding how to make predictions, have them think about the title of this article, "Champions of the World." If students do not see the connection between this title and the contents of the article, ask them to make up a title that they think gives clearer clues.

LITERARY RESPONSE

QUICK-WRITE Invite students to record their thoughts about whether they would like to play in a Little League World Series.

ORAL RESPONSE Have students share their journal writings and discuss what part of the article they enjoyed most.

*inter*NET
CONNECTION For more information on how long the Little League World Series has been played and what teams have been winners have students visit *www.mhschool.com/reading.* Have them show the information they find in chart form.

133

Story Questions

Have students discuss or write answers to the questions on page 134.

Answers:

1. Toms River, New Jersey *Literal/Setting*

2. happy, proud *Inferential/Character*

3. They probably focused mainly on the entire team because baseball is a team sport and all players are important. *Inferential/Make Predictions*

4. The Toms River Little League team won the 1998 Little League World Series. *Critical/Summarize*

5. Austin got a ball signed by his hero, while Todd got a ball he himself had hit to help his team win. *Critical/Reading Across Texts*

Write an Essay For a full writing process lesson on personal narrative, see pages 137K–137L.

Story Questions & Activities

1. Where was the team that won the 1998 Little League World Series from?

2. How do you think Chris Cardone felt when he hit his second home run?

3. Do you think the town celebration focused on the heroes of the final game or on the entire team? Explain.

4. What is the main idea of this selection?

5. Austin Healy and Todd Frazier both got souvenir baseballs. What makes their baseballs so special to them?

Write an Essay

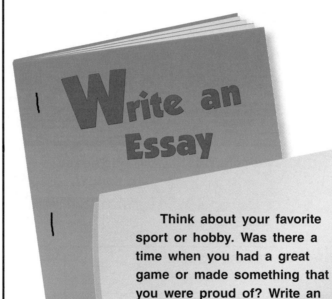

Think about your favorite sport or hobby. Was there a time when you had a great game or made something that you were proud of? Write an essay telling what you did and why it made you feel good.

Meeting Individual Needs

EASY	ON-LEVEL	CHALLENGE
Reteach, 31	Practice, 31	Extend, 31

Make a Bar Graph

Borrow a baseball or a softball. In a clear area outside, throw the ball underhand three times. Stand at the same spot each time. Measure and record the distance you were able to throw the ball each time. Make a bar graph to show your data.

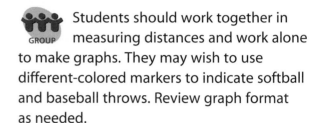

Draw a Map

In 1998, Sammy Sosa hit 66 home runs. He is from the Dominican Republic, an island in the Caribbean. Make a map of the Dominican Republic and include some facts about the island.

Find Out More

Who invented baseball? Basketball? Soccer? Pick your favorite sport and find out when and where people first began playing it. Make a poster about your sport.

135

Story Activities

Make a Bar Graph

Materials: baseball or softball, measuring tapes, rulers, graph paper

GROUP Students should work together in measuring distances and work alone to make graphs. They may wish to use different-colored markers to indicate softball and baseball throws. Review graph format as needed.

Draw a Map

Materials: drawing materials, world maps, atlas, encyclopedia, or Internet

ONE Have students show on their maps that the Dominican Republic is located on the island of Hispaniola in the Caribbean. Encourage them to draw small symbols on the map to show some of the island's products.

Find Out More

RESEARCH AND INQUIRY Encourage

ONE students to use encyclopedias, books about sports, and the Internet to find out more about their favorite sport. Have them make up a list of questions they would like to answer before they start their research.

*inter***NET** **CONNECTION** For more information on sports, have students go to *www.mhschool.com/reading.*

FORMAL ASSESSMENT

After page 135, see Selection and Unit Assessments.

Study Skills

TECHNOLOGY

 OBJECTIVES

Students will search for and use information on the Internet.

PREPARE Discuss possible topics for Internet searches. Display **Teaching Chart 27.**

TEACH Model an Internet search. Then have students try it themselves. Explain that they may have to think of several different key words for their topic.

PRACTICE Have students answer questions **1–5**. Review the answers with them.
1. Fact Hunt **2.** Little League **3.** five **4.** Little League statistics **5.** possible answer: type in "Little League World Series, 1998."

ASSESS/CLOSE Have students perform an Internet search for information on Sammy Sosa and print out some of their results.

STUDY SKILLS

Use a Search Engine

The Internet can be used to search for almost anything. After connecting to the Internet, click on **Search** in the toolbar. Select a **search engine** by typing the name of one. Then type the key words for the subject you are researching.

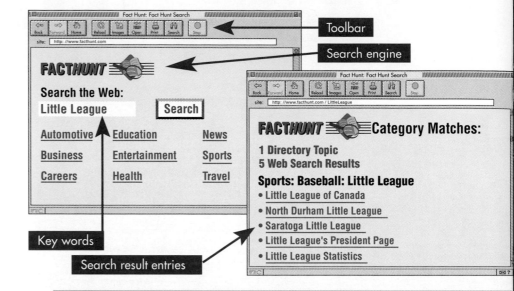

Use the computer screens to answer these questions.

1 Which search engine was chosen?

2 What key words were used for the search?

3 How many search result entries were found?

4 Which search result entry might you click on to find out more about the Little League batting averages?

5 How could you change the search to find information on the winners of the 1998 Little League World Series?

Meeting Individual Needs

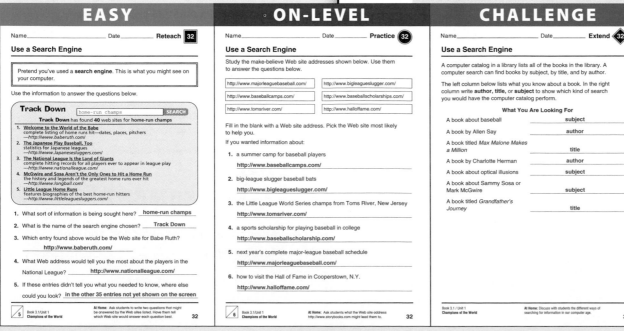

Reteach, 32	Practice, 32	Extend, 32

TEST POWER

Test Power

THE PRINCETON REVIEW

Test Tip

Read the story slowly and carefully.

DIRECTIONS:

Read the story. Then read each question about the story.

SAMPLE

The Talent Show

June and her parents looked at the program that they got in the mail.

Churchill Elementary School presents
THE SECOND GRADE TALENT SHOW

Saturday afternoon, March 23
3:30 PM, in the Gym

Performances:
Taka Smith—Piano Playing
James Mason—Poem
Alesha Botts—Tap Dance
Chorus—America the Beautiful
Cookies and juice will be served in the Cafeteria after the performance.

Special thanks to:
Mr. George Mendez, our teacher
Lisa Miller, school custodian
All of our family and friends

1 Where will June go if she wants cookies and juice after the show?

  ○ To the Gym

  ● To the Cafeteria

  ○ To the Main Office

  ○ To the Chorus Room

2 The Talent Show will take place in—

  ● the Gym

  ○ the Cafeteria

  ○ the Main Office

  ○ the Chorus Room

Why are your answers correct?

137

Read the Page

Have students read all of the information on the program. Instruct students to note the description above the flier and information under the headings. Remind students to read all answer choices.

Discuss the Questions

QUESTION 1: This question requires students to locate information on the program. Direct students back to that portion of the flier. Explain to students that they must refer back to the flier before choosing an answer. Remind students that it is important to double-check details.

QUESTION 2: This question also requires students to refer back to the flier. Ask: Where can you find the information about where the talent show will take place?

ITBS
Test Preparation and Practice

Grade 3

ITBS/TEST PREPERATION

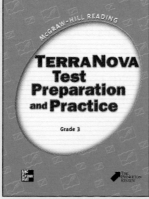

TERRANOVA
Test Preparation and Practice

Grade 3

TERRANOVA/TEST PREPERATION

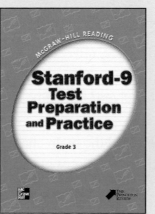

Stanford-9
Test Preparation and Practice

Grade 3

SAT 9/TEST PREPERATION

EASY

☑ **Comprehension**

• story elements

• problem and solution

• steps in a process

• make predictions

Phonics

• short vowels

• long *a* and long *e*

• long *i* and long *o* /ū/ and /ü/

Answers will vary. Have students cite examples from the story to support their answers.

EASY

Story Questions for Selected Reading

1. What was a problem in this story?

2. How did the characters in the story face the problem?

3. What was your favorite part of the story?

4. Would you have acted as the story characters acted?

5. How would you describe the characters?

Draw a Picture

Draw a picture of one scene from the book.

Self-Selected Reading
Leveled Books

EASY

UNIT SKILLS REVIEW

Phonics

☑ **Comprehension**

Help students self-select an Easy Book to read and apply phonics and comprehension skills.

Guided Reading

PREVIEW AND PREDICT Discuss the illustrations in the beginning of the book. As you take the **picture walk**, have students predict what the story will be about. List their ideas. If the book has chapter headings, ask students to use the headings to predict what happened in the first chapter.

SET PURPOSES Have students write why they want to read the book. Have them share their purposes.

READ THE BOOK Use items like the following to guide students' reading or after they have read the story independently. Model blending and other phonics and decoding strategies for students who need help.

• How did you think the story would end? *Make Predictions*

• What is the main problem of the story? How is the problem solved? *Problem and Solution*

• What particular steps did the main characters take to reach a goal? *Steps in a Process*

• Look back through the story. Can you find any examples of words with the long *e* or long *a* sound? *Phonics and Decoding*

RETURN TO PREDICTIONS AND PURPOSES Discuss students' predictions. Ask which were close to the book's contents and why. Have students review their purposes for reading. Did they find out what they wanted to know?

LITERARY RESPONSE Have students discuss questions like the following:

• What did you like about the setting of the book? Why?

• Which was your favorite character in the story?

• What would be another good title for this book?

See the **Phonics** CD-ROM for practice with long *a, e, i,* and *o* words, and words with the /ū/ and /ü/ sounds.

Self-Selected Reading
Leveled Books

INDEPENDENT

INDEPENDENT

UNIT SKILLS REVIEW

☑ **Comprehension**

Help students self-select an Independent Book to read and apply comprehension skills.

☑ **Comprehension**

- story elements
- problem and solution
- steps in a process
- make predictions

Guided Reading

PREVIEW AND PREDICT Discuss the illustrations in the beginning of the book. As you take the **picture walk**, have students predict what the story will be about. List their ideas. If the book has chapter headings, ask students to use the headings to predict what will happen.

SET PURPOSES Have students write why they want to read the book. Have them share their purposes.

READ THE BOOK Use items like the following to guide students' reading or after they have read the story independently.

- What is the main idea in the first four pages of the story? *Main Idea*
- Identify a problem in the book and discuss several different potential solutions. *Problem and Solution*
- Explain what steps a story character took to solve a problem. *Steps in Process*
- What can you tell about the main character of the story? *Character*

RETURN TO PREDICTIONS AND PURPOSES Have students review their predictions. Students can talk about whether their purposes were met, and if they have any questions the story left unanswered. For books with chapter headings, were the headings useful? How?

LITERARY RESPONSE The following questions will help focus students' responses:

- If you were to meet the author of this story, what would you say to him or her?
- How would you describe this story to someone who was about to read it?
- Can you think of a different way in which the story could have ended?

Answers will vary. Have students cite examples from the story to support their answers.

INDEPENDENT

Story Questions for Selected Reading

1. How does this story begin?
2. Where does the story take place?
3. What do you think is the purpose of the story?
4. Can you name the main events in the story from beginning to end?
5. Would you find it exciting to be a character in this story?

Write a Review

Write a review of the book telling why you liked or disliked it.

PUPIL SELECTION

CHALLENGE

Self-Selected Reading
Leveled Books

☑ **Comprehension**

- story elements
- problem and solution
- steps in a process
- make predictions

Answers will vary. Have students cite examples from the story to support their answers.

CHALLENGE

Story Questions for Selected Reading

1. Did you think the main character was going to overcome all his/her challenges?

2. What were some of his/her problems?

3. What was your favorite part of this story?

4. What did you learn from this book?

5. Do you think all the events in this story could really happen?

Make a Poster

Have students make a poster that tells about the book.

UNIT SKILLS REVIEW

☑ **Comprehension**

Help students self-select a Challenge Book to read and apply comprehension skills.

Guided Reading

PREVIEW AND PREDICT Discuss the illustrations in the beginning of the book. As you take the **picture walk**, have students predict what the story will be about. List their ideas. If the book has chapter headings, ask students to use the headings to predict what happened in the first chapter.

SET PURPOSES Have students write or draw why they want to read the book. Have them share their purposes.

READ THE BOOK Use items like the following to guide students' reading or after they have read the story independently.

- What was a problem in the story? How was it solved? *Problem and Solution*

- Did you think that the ending of the story would be different? Why? *Make Predictions*

- What steps did the story's main character take to accomplish a goal? *Steps in a Process*

- Where does the story take place? *Setting*

RETURN TO PREDICTIONS AND PURPOSES Discuss students' predictions. Ask which were close to the book's contents and why. For books with chapter headings, were the headings useful? How? Have students review their purposes for reading. Did they find out what they wanted to know?

LITERARY RESPONSE Have students discuss questions like the following:

- Did you admire the main character in the story? Why?

- If you were to give this book a new title, what would it be?

- Can you compare the main character you may have read about or seen in a movie?

Activities
Anthology and Leveled Books

Connecting Texts

PROBLEM-SOLVING CHARTS Have students discuss connections between the stories. For example, write these story titles horizontally across the top of two separate charts: *Journey Across the Desert, Journey to America, Jason and the Argonauts,* and *Ruthie Rides the Trolley.* Label one chart: Problems. Label the second chart: Solutions. Talk with students about problems the characters faced in the stories and the way they "figured out" solutions to these problems or issues. Write students' suggestions on the chart.

PROBLEMS

Journey Across the Desert	Journey to America	Jason and the Argonauts	Ruthie Rides the Trolley
• Falling snow slows the journey.	• Lena starts to cry.	• Jason does not know where the golden fleece is.	• The family needs to make the trolley stop.

SOLUTIONS

Journey Across the Desert	Journey to America	Jason and the Argonauts	Ruthie Rides the Trolley
• The caravan keeps going.	• Marco makes Lena feel better.	• King Phineas tells him where to go.	• Ruthie's father lights a newspaper to signal.

Viewing/Representing

GROUP PRESENTATIONS Have students break into groups in which students have all read some of the same titles. Students in each group can choose their favorite book and suggest it is going to be made into a movie. Have each group create a poster advertising such a film and illustrate it with an exciting scene from the book.

AUDIENCE RESPONSE Give students time to study all posters. Encourage them to ask questions about each group's poster, for example: why the group thought the story would make a good movie, why group members chose that particular scene to illustrate.

Research and Inquiry

CHOOSE A TOPIC Have students choose a topic to research. Then have them:

- list a few questions about their topics.

- think about ways to find information: encyclopedia, library books, magazines, or organizations.

- make notes as they gather information.

- create a class encyclopedia with their findings.

 *inter*NET CONNECTION Have students log on to **www.mhschool.com/reading** for links to Web pages.

Review **Steps in a Process**

TEACHING TIP

INSTRUCTIONAL Encourage students to think about steps in a process by remembering the steps they take to do an everyday routine, such as making the bed.

PREPARE

Discuss Steps in a Process

Tell students that sometimes the steps in a process are given in the form of directions, but at other times they must be figured out. Ask students to list the steps they used in predicting the contents of *Champions of the World*.

TEACH

Read "How to Make a Baseball" and Model the Skill

Ask students to pay attention to the order of the steps in the process as you read **Teaching Chart 28** with them.

How to Make a Baseball

Although the steps in making a baseball are few and simple, the actual work takes a lot of skill.

1. First you must get a round piece of cork. **2.** Wrap a piece of red rubber and a piece of black rubber around the cork. **3.** Next, wind 150 yards of cotton yarn and 219 yards of wool yarn around the layers of cork and rubber. **4.** Then cover the whole thing with cowhide and, **5.** finally, stitch the cowhide closed with 108 stitches of tough thread.

Teaching Chart 28

Read "How to Make a Baseball" and Model the Skill

Display **Teaching Chart 28**. Discuss how to recognize steps in a process.

MODEL I need to identify the steps in making a baseball. I know that, in this case, the steps will be directions listed in the order in which they're supposed to be done. I will look for such words as *first, next,* and *finally.* Now I see that the first step is to get a piece of cork.

PRACTICE

Identify Steps in a Process

GROUP

Have students identify and number the steps in the process of making a baseball. Have them discuss why it is important to notice the sequence of the steps. ▶ **Logical/Interpersonal**

ASSESS/CLOSE

List Steps in a Process

Ask students to choose a skill that they have recently learned, such as how to play a new game or make cookies. Then have them write a list of directions. Encourage them to illustrate their directions with sketches and diagrams. Display their illustrated lists on the bulletin board.

ALTERNATE TEACHING STRATEGY

....

STEPS IN A PROCESS

For a different approach to teaching this skill, see page T66.

SELF-SELECTED Reading

....

Students may choose from the following titles.

ANTHOLOGY

• *Champions of the World*

LEVELED BOOKS

All titles for the unit.

Bibliography, pages T76–T77

Meeting Individual Needs for Comprehension

EASY	ON-LEVEL	CHALLENGE	LANGUAGE SUPPORT

EASY

Name_____ Date_____ Reteach **33**

Steps in a Process

A series of steps you follow in order is called **steps in a process.** Writing down steps in the correct order will help you remember them.

In "Champions of the World," you learned how to make a baseball. The steps are written below, but they are out of order. Next to each step, write a number from 1 to 4 to show the order. Use the story if you need help.

Process: Make a Baseball

Step __2__ Put 219 yards of wool around the yarn.

Step __4__ Sew the ball closed with 108 stitches.

Step __3__ Cover the wool with a piece of cowhide.

Step __1__ Put 150 yards of cotton yarn around a piece of cork.

Now write down four steps that you would use to make a sandwich for lunch. **Answers may vary.**

Process: Make a Sandwich

Step 1: Take out two pieces of bread.

Step 2: Slice cheese and a tomato.

Step 3: Spread mustard on the bread.

Step 4: Put the cheese and tomato between the slices of bread.

At Home: Have students write the steps they follow when getting ready for bed each night.
33   Book 3.1/Unit 1 **Champions of the World** /8

Reteach, 33

ON-LEVEL

Name_____ Date_____ Practice **33**

Steps in a Process

Steps that you follow in order are called **steps in a process.** Writing down the steps in order will help you to remember them.

Think about the following activities. Each of them has several steps that need to be followed. Write down the steps in the process for each activity below. **Answers will vary. Possible examples follow.**

Find a book at the library.

1. Look up the number for the book.

2. Write down the number of the book.

3. Find the floor and bookshelf.

4. Locate the book that has the number.

Make a cup of chocolate milk.

1. Take the milk out of the refrigerator.

2. Take chocolate syrup from the cupboard.

3. Pour chocolate syrup into a glass.

4. Fill the rest of the glass with milk.

5. Stir it until it is mixed.

Make a costume for a costume party.

1. Decide which character you want to be.

2. Draw a picture of your costume.

3. Gather or buy materials and supplies.

4. Cut out the materials to be sewn together.

5. Sew your costume together.

At Home: Have students write down five steps that they follow when they do their homework.
33   Book 3.1/Unit 1 **Champions of the World** /14

Practice, 33

CHALLENGE

Name_____ Date_____ Extend ◈**33**

Steps in a Process

In "Champions of the World," you read about how to make a baseball. Think about how you would make your own sports card.

Choose the size of card or paper you want to use.

Decide on the sport you want to be good at.

Draw a picture of yourself playing this sport.

Add color to the picture.

Decide on the information that belongs on the back.

List your name, where you were born, and the year.

List all the other important information.

What other finishing touches do you want to add?

Share the sports cards with classmates.

At Home: Look through a newspaper to find pictures or statistics on favorite sports figures.
33   Book 3.1/Unit 1 **Champions of the World**

Extend, 33

LANGUAGE SUPPORT

Name_____ Date_____

It's a Home Run!

38 Champions of the World • Language Support/Blackline Master 18   Grade 3

Language Support, 38

137F

OBJECTIVES

Students will identify compound words and use structural clues to determine their meaning.

....

MATERIALS

- **Teaching Chart 29**

TEACHING TIP

MANAGEMENT Turn magnetic photo albums into learning centers. Mount worksheets, workbook pages, and activity cards in the books. Students can take albums to their desk and work with wipe-off crayons.

Place answer keys at the back of each book for self-checking.

Review Compound Words

PREPARE

Discuss Compound Words
Explain to students that compound words are long words made from two or more shorter words. You can often guess the meaning of compound words by looking at the meaning of each of the shorter words.

TEACH

Read "Darnell's Dream" and Model the Skill
Ask students to look for compound words as they read "Darnell's Dream."

Darnell's Dream

    Darnell had a favorite daydream in which he helped his team win the Little League World Series. The people in his town would give him and his teammates a big homecoming parade after their victory.

    In the summer, Darnell played baseball every day. Sometimes he got up at sunrise to practice hitting and throwing.

Teaching Chart 29

Help students figure out the meanings of compound words.

MODEL I know that compound words are made up of smaller words. Let me find the first compound word in the passage. It's *daydream*, which is made from *day* and *dream*. So, it means a dream you have when you're awake.

PRACTICE

Identify and Understand Compound Words

ONE

Have students find and circle all the compound words in the passage. Then help students create a Compound Word chart. Model the analysis of *daydream* in the chart. Then have students use the chart to analyze the other compound words in "Darnell's Dream." ▶**Visual/Logical**

COMPOUND WORD	SHORTER WORDS	MEANING
daydream	day + dream	a waking dream or wish

ASSESS/CLOSE

Write Compound Words

Give students a list of words like those below. Challenge them to make at least three compound words from the smaller words and to use each in a sentence.

light   house   boat   fire   side   ways

ALTERNATE TEACHING STRATEGY

COMPOUND WORDS

For a different approach to teaching this skill, see page T63.

Meeting Individual Needs for Vocabulary

EASY	ON-LEVEL	CHALLENGE	LANGUAGE SUPPORT

EASY

Name_____ Date_____ Reteach **34**

Compound Words

> When two words are put together to make one word, the new word is called a **compound word**.

Circle the compound words in each sentence below. Write the two words that make up each compound word. Then write the meaning of the compound word.

After the game, Willy got a big sack and put all the (baseballs) in it.

1. **Word parts:** __base__ + __balls__

2. **Meaning:** __the balls that are used to play the game of baseball__

Gina spread the new (tablecloth) on the picnic table.

3. **Word parts:** __table__ + __cloth__

4. **Meaning:** __cloth that goes over a table__

Eduardo was unable to turn the (doorknob.)

5. **Word parts:** __door__ + __knob__

6. **Meaning:** __the knob on a door that opens it__

They put up their tent in the (campground) and got some water from the stream.

7. **Word parts:** __camp__ + __ground__

8. **Meaning:** __a place where people go camping in tents or vans__

The whole class went out to the (playground) to run and jump.

9. **Word parts:** __play__ + __ground__

10. **Meaning:** __a place where children go to play__

Book 3.1/Unit 1
Champions of the World   **At Home:** Ask students to name the compound word in this sentence: Let's go to the park this afternoon.   **34**

Reteach, 34

ON-LEVEL

Name_____ Date_____ Practice **34**

Compound Words

You can figure out the meaning of a compound word by looking at the two smaller words within it and putting the two meanings together.

Below are definitions of some compound words. Complete the chart.

Definition	Compound Word	Two Words	
1. the town where a person makes his or her home	hometown	home	town
2. balls that are used to play the game of basketball	basketballs	basket	balls
3. made at home, not at a factory or a store	homemade	home	made
4. the place made for walking at the side of a road	sidewalk	side	walk
5. the days at the end of the school or work week	weekend	week	end
6. case to store books	bookcase	book	case

Book 3.1/Unit 1
Champions of the World   **At Home:** Ask students to name the compound word that means the work that you do at school.   **34**

Practice, 34

CHALLENGE

Name_____ Date_____ Extend **34**

Compound Words

In each sentence, there are two words that you can put together to make a compound word listed in the Word Box. Write the compound word on the line.

overhead	basketball	baseball	afternoon
airplane	grandfather	something	sunshine

1. The plane flew over my head. __overhead__
2. The plane is in the air. __airplane__
3. Please meet me at noon or after. __afternoon__
4. The waves seem to shine in the sun. __sunshine__
5. The ball went in the basket. __basketball__
6. Some days I can't think of a thing to do. __something__
7. Juan's father plays a grand piano. __grandfather__
8. The ball just missed me at first base. __baseball__

Book 3.1 / Unit 1
Champions of the World   **At Home:** Make a word box together of items in the room that can be put together to make a compound word.   **34**

Extend, 34

LANGUAGE SUPPORT

Name_____ Date_____

Compound Word Match

over	town
home	ball
short	hide
base	thing
cow	head
every	stop

Grade 3   Language Support/Blackline Master 19 • Champions of the World **39**

Language Support, 39

OBJECTIVES

Students will review how the prefixes *un-* and *dis-* change word meaning.

MATERIALS

- **Teaching Chart 30**
- prefix **Word Building Manipulative Cards**
- index cards

TEACHING TIP

INSTRUCTIONAL Not all words can be changed into their opposite meaning by adding the prefix *un-*. The opposite of *good* is *bad*, not *ungood*.

Review Prefixes

PREPARE

Review Meaning of the Prefixes *un-* and *dis-*

Review: A prefix is a group of letters added to the beginning of a base word. Prefixes have their own meaning. The prefix *un-* usually means "the opposite of." The prefix *dis-* usually means "not" or "opposite." A prefix changes the meaning of the word to which it is added.

TEACH

Read the Passage and Model the Skill

Have students read the passage on **Teaching Chart 30**.

Going, Going, Gone

As soon as Chris hit the ball, she knew she'd hit a home run. As she ran to first base, the other team looked very (dis)pleased. Chris's hit changed the score from 8-8 to 9-8.

The victory by Chris's team was not (un)expected. They had gone through the season (un)beaten. Their record (dis)proved the complaint that they were just lucky.

Teaching Chart 30

Have students define the word *displeased* by analyzing its prefix and base.

MODEL The word *displeased* in the second sentence has the prefix *dis-*. The base word is *pleased*. Since *dis-* means not or opposite, *displeased* means "not pleased", or "not happy."

PRACTICE

Identify Words with Prefixes

GROUP

Have volunteers underline each word in "Going, Going, Gone" that begins with the prefix *un-* or *dis-*. Then have them circle the prefix. Have students discuss the meanings of the words.

▶ **Linguistic/Interpersonal**

ASSESS/CLOSE

Form Words with Prefixes and Use Them in a Paragraph

Direct students to write the words *equal, real, order,* and *obey* on index cards. Have them add the prefix card *un-* to *equal* and *real,* and *dis-* to *order* and *obey* to make new words. Ask students to work in pairs to write a paragraph using all the words. They may want to draw a picture to illustrate their paragraph.

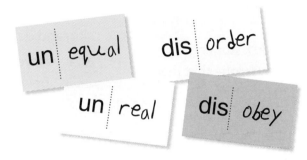

ALTERNATE TEACHING STRATEGY

PREFIXES

For a different approach to teaching this skill, see page T65.

Meeting Individual Needs for Vocabulary

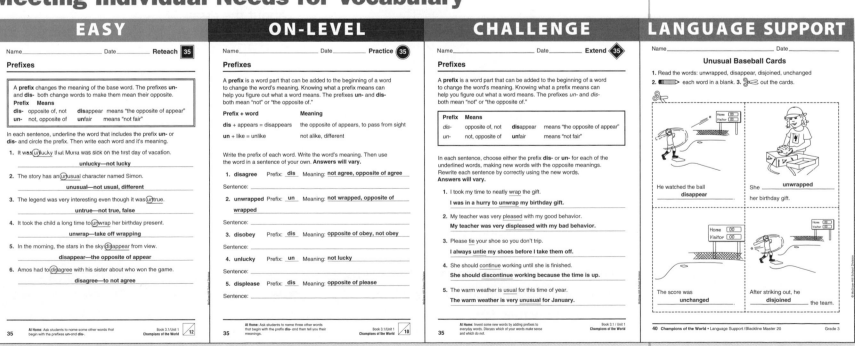

EASY	ON-LEVEL	CHALLENGE	LANGUAGE SUPPORT
Reteach, 35	Practice, 35	Extend, 35	Language Support, 40

Personal Narrative

GRAMMAR/SPELLING CONNECTIONS

See the 5-Day Grammar and Usage Plan on sentence combining, pages 137M–137N.

See the 5-Day Spelling Plan on pages 137O–137P.

TECHNOLOGY TIP

When students begin revising, have them rename their documents using the Save As feature. If they change their minds about revisions, they can cut and paste text from the original.

Prewrite

WRITE AN ESSAY Present this writing assignment: Think about your favorite sport or hobby. Was there a time when you played a great game, or made something that you were proud of? Write an essay telling what you did and why it made you feel good.

BRAINSTORM IDEAS Ask students to brainstorm things they have done that made them feel good about themselves. List their suggestions on the chalkboard. Then have each student think about what activity made him or her feel proud. What gave them more confidence? Encourage them to choose the event that they feel best about.

Strategy: Make a Word Web Have students create word webs of details.

Graphic Organizer 29

Draft

FREE WRITE Guide students to write without self-editing. Encourage them to elaborate on the information in their webs. They should use rich sensory details to describe how they felt .

Revise

LOOK AT THE BIG PICTURE Ask students to assess their drafts.

- Did I clearly explain what I did during the event or project?
- Did I keep my audience in mind as I wrote?
- Did I bring my experience to life with feeling and details?

PARTNERS Have students trade reports with a peer and ask for suggestions.

Edit/Proofread

CHECK FOR ERRORS Have students reread their essays and correct any errors in spelling, grammar, and punctuation.

Publish

READ IT OUT LOUD Have each student read his or her essay aloud. Other students can ask questions and tell what they liked about the essay.

How I Trained Sam

by Mike Camizzi

I found out that I could train a puppy. This happened when we got a new puppy named Sam. Sam ran around like crazy and grabbed people's things. Dad said I could help train Sam. So everyday I trained him in the backyard.

I can get Sam to sit. I tell him to sit. When he sits, I give him a treat. I tell him, "Good sit, Sam." Now he sits whenever I tell him to.

I throw the ball. When Sam brings it back, I give him a treat. I tell him he is a good dog.

I feel very happy because I love Sam. Dad says that I am doing a good job. I am proud that I can help train Sam.

Presentation Ideas

MAKE AN EXHIBITION Have students design a bulletin board display with illustrations that represents all the activities and hobbies the class wrote about.

▶ **Viewing/Representing**

A TALK SHOW Have students present their accomplishments on a radio or TV talk show. One student can play the host, and the members of the audience can ask questions.

▶ **Speaking/Listening**

Consider students' creative efforts, possibly adding a plus (+) for originality, wit, and imagination.

Scoring Rubric

Excellent	Good	Fair	Unsatisfactory
4: The writer	**3:** The writer	**2:** The writer	**1:** The writer
• vividly shares an important accomplishment from her or his own life.	• clearly outlines an accomplishment from her or his own life.	• attempts to tell about an accomplishment from her or his own life.	• may not focus on an accomplishment from her or his life.
• richly describes the experience, in a logical sequence.	• uses some detail to elaborate on the experience in a logical sequence.	• gives a basic idea of what happened.	• may not clearly state a series of events.
• clearly expresses her or his feelings about the experience, and why she or he is proud of it.	• gives a good sense of how she or he feels about the experience.	• may have some gaps in sequence of events.	• may not connect the experience with her or his personal feelings.
		• may not clearly express how she or he feels about the experience.	• may exhibit problems with language use or grammar.

0: The writer leaves the page blank or fails to respond to the writing task. The student does not address the topic or simply paraphrases the prompt. The response is illegible or incoherent.

Meeting Individual Needs for Writing

EASY

Make a Cartoon Have students draw a cartoon illustrating a positive experience they recently had at school or at home. Have them write dialogue bubbles and captions. Encourage them to use humor in their cartoons.

ON-LEVEL

Goals and Needs Have students write about a hobby they have or would like to become involved in, describing what is needed for this hobby. For example, to train pets one needs a pet, time, patience, treats, and so forth.

CHALLENGE

Sammy's Story Have students research Sammy Sosa's life and write a short essay telling about his life in the Dominican Republic.

ESL Write the following sentences on the board: *Mario walked. Pam struck out.* Have students combine the sentences, using colored chalk for the comma and *and.*

DAILY LANGUAGE ACTIVITIES

Write each day's activity on the chalkboard or use **Transparency 5.** Have students combine sentences orally. Answers are given for Day 1; remaining answers follow the same pattern.

Day 1
1. Mike throws the ball. Chris swings.
   Mike throws the ball, and Chris swings.
2. The ball goes far. The crowd cheers.
   The ball goes far, and the crowd cheers.
3. The team won. The players were happy.
   The team won, and the players were happy.

Day 2
1. Ed hit the ball. Todd stole a base.
2. Joey pitched well. Sally hit hard.
3. The parade was long. The boys were tired.

Day 3
1. The team waved. The people shouted.
2. I drove the car. She honked the horn.
3. The game was tied. Cardone ran fast.

Day 4
1. Jim hit a home run. Todd cheered.
2. Sara was up at bat. The crowd was silent.
3. Mark broke the record. His son was proud.

Day 5
1. The race was on. We went to watch.
2. Sammy hits hard. The ball goes far.
3. Todd was safe. The game was over.

Daily Language Transparency 5

DAY 1 Introduce the Concept

Oral Warm-Up Review the definition of a sentence. Then read aloud this sentence: *Robert loves to play baseball, and he is part of a winning team.* Ask students what two ideas about Robert are in the sentence, and which word joins the two ideas. (and)

Introduce Sentence Combining Explain that two sentences about the same topic can be combined into one. Present the following:

> **Sentence Combining**
>
> Two related sentences can be joined with a comma and *and.*

Present the Daily Language Activity. Then have students write two related sentences about a favorite sport, and then combine the sentences using *and.* Have students share their combined sentences.

 WRITING Assign the daily Writing Prompt on page 128C.

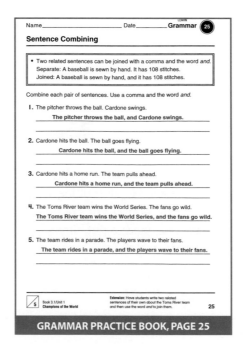

GRAMMAR PRACTICE BOOK, PAGE 25

DAY 2 Teach the Concept

Review Sentence Combining Have students explain how to combine sentences. Ask for some oral examples.

Introduce Compound Sentences Present the following:

> **Compound Sentences**
>
> A sentence that contains two sentences joined by *and* is called a **compound sentence**.

Present the Daily Language Activity. Then have students take turns writing sentences about baseball on the chalkboard. When several sentences are written, have each student choose two related sentences to combine into a compound sentence. Have volunteers share their compound sentences with the rest of the class.

 WRITING Assign the daily Writing Prompt on page 128C.

GRAMMAR PRACTICE BOOK, PAGE 26

Sentence Combining

DAY 3 Review and Practice

Learn from the Literature Review compound sentences. Read the first sentence in the second paragraph on page 133 of *Champions of the World*.

> **By season's end, Sosa had hit 66 home runs, and McGwire had hit 70.**

Ask students to identify which two parts of the sentence might have been combined. (By season's end, Sosa had hit 66 home runs. McGwire had hit 70.)

Form Compound Sentences Present the Daily Language Activity.

Then have students look at the first four sentences on page 131 of *Champions of the World*. Have students find pairs of related sentences to combine into compound sentences. Example: *The pitcher throws the ball, and Cardone swings.* Ask volunteers to write their compound sentences on the chalkboard.

Assign the daily Writing Prompt on page 128D.

DAY 4 Review and Practice

Review Compound Sentences Ask students to find the verbs from the Daily Language Activities for Days 1 through 3, and to use them to write their own compound sentences. Introduce the Daily Language Activity for Day 4.

Mechanics and Usage Review punctuation of compound sentences.

Compound Sentences

- Use a comma before *and* when you join two sentences to form a compound sentence.
- Begin each sentence with a capital letter.

Assign the daily Writing Prompt on page 128D.

DAY 5 Assess and Reteach

Assess Use the Daily Language Activity and page 29 of the **Grammar Practice Book** for assessment.

Reteach Have students write rules about combining sentences and punctuating compound sentences. Then play a sentence-combining game. Have one student say a simple sentence and then call on another student to combine it with another sentence, using *and*. Repeat until all students have made up a sentence.

Then have students create a classroom word wall with compound sentences from the game.

Use page 30 of the **Grammar Practice Book** for additional reteaching.

Assign the daily Writing Prompt on page 128D.

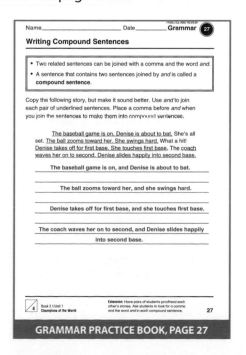

GRAMMAR PRACTICE BOOK, PAGE 27

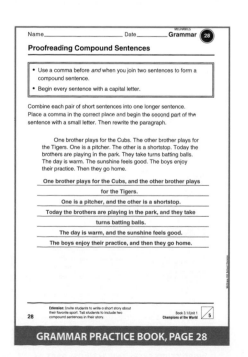

GRAMMAR PRACTICE BOOK, PAGE 28

GRAMMAR PRACTICE BOOK, PAGE 29

GRAMMAR PRACTICE BOOK, PAGE 30

137N

5 Day Spelling Plan

LANGUAGE SUPPORT

ESL To help students find the number of syllables in a word, have them tap out the number of vowel sounds they hear. Point out the difference between vowels, which may be silent, and vowel sounds, which correlate with the number of syllables.

DICTATION SENTENCES

1. The player was in the field.
2. The pitch was a strike.
3. He went to see the parade.
4. Can you catch with the new mitt?
5. The batter rubs on his hands.
6. She slides past the bases.
7. Her glove was brown.
8. The team was in action by the park.
9. The crowd was loud.
10. Do you like to play baseball?
11. She stood on the mound to pitch.
12. The season is over.
13. They did not like foul weather.
14. She was in the outfield.
15. He broke an old record.

Challenge Words

16. We celebrated her birthday with a party.
17. Push the cork into the hole.
18. The pitcher left the team.
19. What was the score?
20. Wrap the sandwich in paper.

DAY 1 Pretest

Assess Prior Knowledge Use the Dictation Sentences at left and **Spelling Practice Book** page 25 for the pretest. Allow students to correct their own papers. If students have trouble, have partners give each other a midweek test on Day 3. Students who require a modified list may be tested on the first eight words.

Spelling Words		Challenge Words
1. **player**	9. crowd	16. **celebrated**
2. strike	10. **baseball**	17. **cork**
3. **parade**	11. mound	18. **pitcher**
4. mitt	12. **season**	19. **score**
5. batter	13. foul	20. **wrap**
6. bases	14. outfield	
7. glove	15. **record**	
8. action		

*Note: Words in **dark type** are from the story.*

Word Study On page 26 of the **Spelling Practice Book** are word study steps and an at-home activity.

DAY 2 Explore the Pattern

Sort and Spell Words Say the words *strike* and *baseball*. Ask students the number of syllables they hear in each word. Continue reading each word. Ask students to repeat the words aloud before sorting them by the number of syllables.

Words with one syllable	Words with two syllables
strike	player
mitt	parade
glove	batter
crowd	bases
mound	action
foul	baseball
	season
	outfield
	record

Word Wall Have students search through magazines or books for other sports words. Have them add the words to a word wall, sorting by one, two, or more than two syllables.

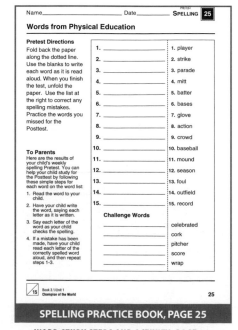

SPELLING PRACTICE BOOK, PAGE 25

WORD STUDY STEPS AND ACTIVITY, PAGE 26

SPELLING PRACTICE BOOK, PAGE 27

... Words from Physical Education

Word Meaning: Suffixes Explain to students that adding the ending *-er* to a word changes it to mean "one who." Have students find the words on the list with the *-er* suffixes and explain the meaning. (player, batter) Ask them to find a word on the list to which *-er* can be added. (outfield) Ask them to think of other words of people involved in baseball or other sports—catcher, runner, kicker.

Glossary Review the way words are divided into syllables in the Glossary. Ask students to look up each Challenge Word. Explain that *celebrated* is listed in its base word form, *celebrate*. Have students:

- write each Challenge Word or its base word (as listed in the Glossary).

- write the number of syllables each contains.

- draw lines between syllables in words with two or more syllables.

Proofread Sentences Write these sentences on the chalkboard, including the misspelled words. Ask students to proofread, circling incorrect spellings and writing the correct spellings. There are two spelling errors in each sentence.

> The (croud) in (fowl) ground made noise.
> (crowd, foul)
>
> The (bater) walked to the (mownd).
> (batter, mound)
>
> A (playar) stood in the (outfeild) (player, outfield)

Have students create additional sentences with errors for partners to correct.

 Have students use as many **WRITING** Spelling Words as possible in the daily Writing Prompt on page 128D. Remind students to proofread their writing for errors in spelling, punctuation, and grammar.

Assess Students' Knowledge Use page 30 of the **Spelling Practice Book** or the Dictation Sentences on page 137O for the posttest.

Personal Word List Have students set aside space in their **JOURNAL** journals for sports terms. The ones that they can spell correctly can be called "home runs." The tough-to-spell words could be "strikeouts."

Students should refer to their lists during future writing activities.

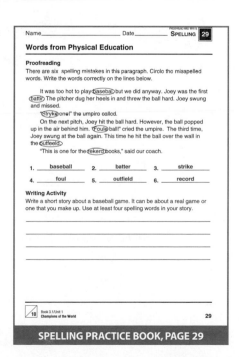

Wrap Up the Theme

Great Adventures

Life is made up of big and small experiences.

REVIEW THE THEME Remind students that all the selections in this unit relate to the theme Great Adventures. If students could be characters within one of the selections, which would they choose? Ask students to share a personal experience that they think could be called a Great Adventure, whether large or small.

READ THE POEM Explain that the Spanish word *Abuelita*, like *Nana* or *Nonnie*, refers to Grandmother. Then read aloud "Abuelita's Lap" by Pat Mora. Ask students to think why, to a child, a grownup's lap can be a favorite place. Ask how the speaker of the poem feels. How is the speaker's experience soothing like a lullaby? Reread the poem, having students listen for the repetition of lines.

LISTENING LIBRARY
AUDIOCASSETTE

MAKE CONNECTIONS Have students work in small groups to brainstorm a list of ways that the stories, poems, and the *Time for Kids* magazine article relate to the theme Great Adventures.

Groups can then compare their lists as they share them with the class.

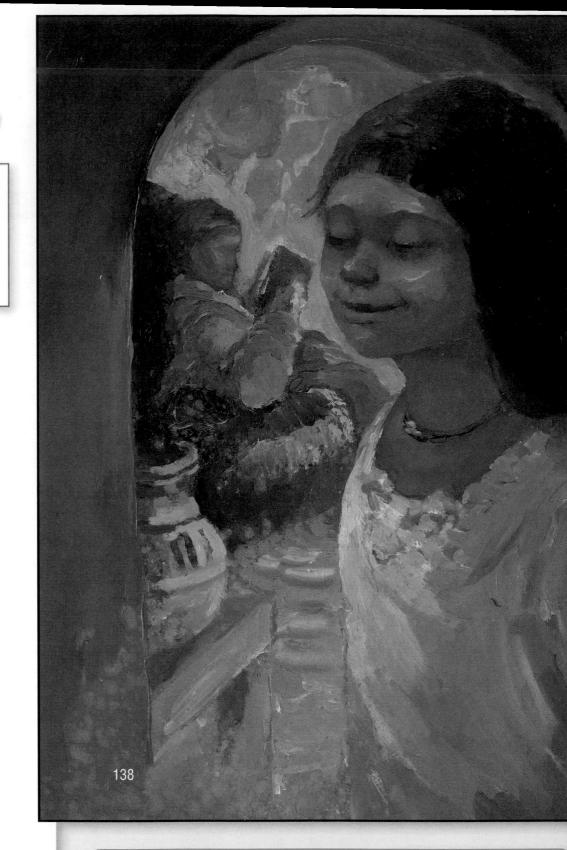
138

LOOKING AT GENRE

Have students review *Opt: An Illusionary Tale* and *Max Malone*. What makes *Opt: An Illusionary Tale* a fantasy? What makes *Max Malone* realistic fiction?

FANTASY *Opt: An Illusionary Tale*	REALISTIC FICTION *Max Malone*
• There are imaginary creatures.	• Characters seem real.
• Events could not happen in real life.	• Events could happen in real life.
• Setting does not look real.	• Setting looks and sounds real.

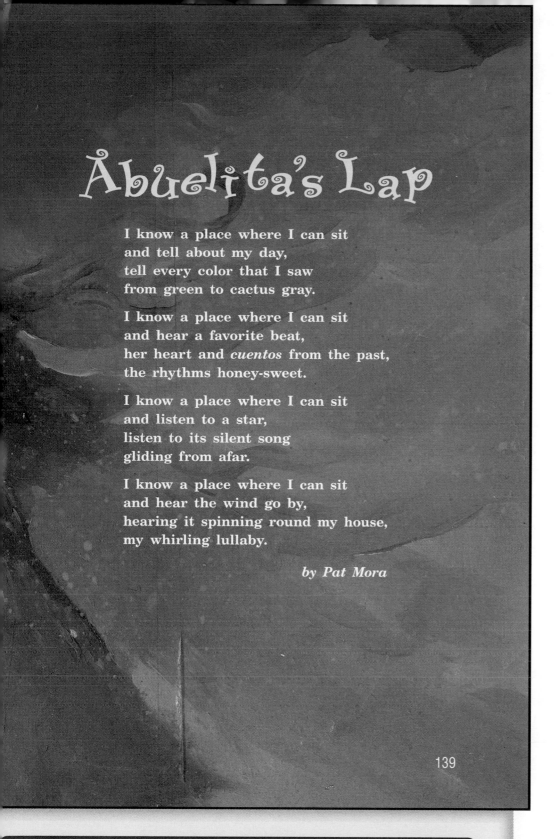

Abuelita's Lap

I know a place where I can sit
and tell about my day,
tell every color that I saw
from green to cactus gray.

I know a place where I can sit
and hear a favorite beat,
her heart and *cuentos* from the past,
the rhythms honey-sweet.

I know a place where I can sit
and listen to a star,
listen to its silent song
gliding from afar.

I know a place where I can sit
and hear the wind go by,
hearing it spinning round my house,
my whirling lullaby.

by Pat Mora

139

LEARNING ABOUT POETRY

Literary Devices: Repetition and Rhyme Point out the repetition in the first line of each stanza. Discuss how repetition emphasizes the importance of Abuelita's lap to the child. Abuelita's lap serves a different purpose in each stanza.

Reread the poem, having students echo the last word in each line. Encourage students to listen for the rhymes.

Poetry Activity Help students understand and interpret the poem through music. Lead them in singing a lullaby (such as "Hush, Little Baby") and an upbeat song (such as "If You're Happy"). Ask which seems closer in feeling to the poem. Have students name other songs that remind them of the poem and tell why. Ask students to "sing" the poem.

Research and Inquiry

Complete the Theme Project Have students work in teams to complete their group project. Remind students that people may experience the same event in different ways. Ask them to incorporate different points of view in their production. Encourage students to share the tasks of making props, painting scenery, writing scripts, and performing so that each member of the team contributes to the play project.

Make a Classroom Presentation Have teams take turns presenting their projects. Be sure to include time for questions from the audience.

Draw Conclusions Have students draw conclusions about what they have learned from researching and preparing their projects. Was their list of questions helpful? Did they find additional resources? What did they learn about using the Internet for research? Was their presentation effective? What did students discover about their topic that gave them a new point of view? Has doing the research changed their opinions of the people involved? Of what have they gained a deeper understanding?

Ask More Questions What additional questions do students now have? What else would students like to find out? Do students have questions about different kinds of journeys or experiences? You might encourage groups to continue their "What Was It Like?" investigations by researching different countries, periods of history, or kinds of adventures.

Personal Narrative

CONNECT TO LITERATURE In *Grandfather's Journey*, Allen Say writes about events in his grandfather's life as well as his own life. Engage students in a brainstorming session, and make a chalkboard list of their suggested words describing Grandfather's travels and his feelings about the places in the story.

GROUP

Dear Bobby,
    I just got back from San Antonio.
My family goes there every year to see
the Thanksgiving Float Parade.
    We got to the parade early and
found a good spot to watch the riverboat show. Thousands of people had
lined up along the Riverwalk. Each boat
was full of people in fancy costumes.
Many boats had bands or singers.
Trees along the river were decorated
with blazing colored lights and bright
paper flowers.
    What a great time we had! By the
end of the day I felt like I had been
floating in the parade, too.
                        Your friend,
                        John Jaramillo

Prewrite

PURPOSE AND AUDIENCE Tell students that they will write letters describing an important or interesting event from their lives. Explain that the purpose of the letter is to entertain the person who will receive it.

STRATEGIES: CHOOSING AND EXPLORING TOPICS Have students bring in snapshots or objects that remind them of a memorable experience they have had, such as a family trip or party. Each student can show the photo or object and briefly tell what event it reminds them of. From this exercise, students can identify the topic for their letters.

Use **Writing Process Transparency 1A** as a model.

PREWRITE TRANSPARENCY

My letter is to:

Jen
40 Pine Street
Cove, Oregon 99999

My letter is about:

fixing up our house

What Happened

heard about clean-up
took off wallpaper
painted rooms
finished clean-up

How I Felt

surprised, nervous
tired
pleased
proud

McGraw-Hill School Division

Book 3.1/Unit 1: Personal Narrative / Prewriting 1A

Draft

STRATEGY: FREE WRITING Invite students to choose a strong memory as their letter's starting point. Using their prewriting charts as a foundation, students can begin drafting. From there, encourage them to pour their thoughts freely onto the page without editing. During this stage, students should focus on ideas and not be concerned with spelling or punctuation.

Use **Writing Process Transparency 1B** as a model for discussion.

LANGUAGE CONTROL Have students circle colorful words in their charts and use them to begin making word banks. This exercise will give the students an opportunity to explore richer vocabulary choices for the assignment. You can make this a group activity by asking students to write selections from their word banks on the chalkboard, so that class-mates can share each other's vocabulary development.

LANGUAGE SUPPORT

Some students may need indi-vidual coaching to establish a specific anecdote for their per-sonal narrative. You can invite the student to close her or his eyes for a moment and visually recall a special day or experi-ence such as celebrating a birthday, riding horseback, or learning to swim. Help the stu-dent to elaborate visual details and feelings of the experience.

DRAFT TRANSPARENCY

40 Pine Street
Cove, Oregon 99999
October 22, 1999

Dear Jen,

    Did I ever tell you what happened when my family moved three years ago? Before we could sell our house, we had to fix it up. Our mother told that all the wallpaper had to come off, the inside of the house had to be painted, and a new bathtubb had to be put in. I couldn't believe it. This was to much! But my mom said we would all work together, and it might be fun.

    The first week we pealed the wallpaper off and smoothed the walls. The second week we painted seven rooms and half of a cat—sorry, sheba. The third week my brother Mike got to show how strong he was by—oops—almost lifting a bathtub. We finished it all It felt nice to do a good job. But was it fun. are you kidding?

Your friend,
Sue

McGraw-Hill School Division

Book 3.1/Unit 1: Personal Narrative / Drafting 1B

Revise

Have students review their personal narratives for clarity and expressiveness. Ask them to check the sequence of their thoughts on the page and to see if the story's events are clear.

Use **Writing Process Transparency 1C** for classroom discussion on the revision process. Ask students to comment on how revisions may have improved this writing example.

STRATEGY: ELABORATION Have students compare first drafts with their prewriting charts, to decide if they should add information or sensory details to make the text clearer and richer. Encourage students to ask themselves these questions:

- Does my letter sound like it's written by me, not just anybody?
- Have I used colorful words?
- Have I described what made the event fun or important?

REVISE TRANSPARENCY

40 Pine Street
Cove, Oregon 99999
October 22, 1999

Dear Jen,

   Did I ever tell you what happened when my family moved three years ago? Before we could sell our house, we had to fix it up. Our mother told that all the wallpaper had to come off, the ^whole inside of the house had to be painted, and a new bathtubb had to be put in. I couldn't believe it. ~~This was to much!~~ But my mom said we would all work together, and it might be fun.

   The first week we pealed the wallpaper off and ~~smoothed~~ ^sanded the walls. The second week we painted seven rooms and half of a cat—sorry, sheba! The third week my brother Mike got to show how strong he was by—oops—almost lifting a bathtub. We finished it all It felt ~~nice~~ ^great to do a good job. But was it fun. are you kidding?

Your friend,

Sue

Book 3.1/Unit 1: Personal Narrative / Revising 1C

McGraw-Hill School Division

Personal Narrative

Edit/Proofread

After students finish making their revisions, have them proofread for final corrections to the text.

GRAMMAR/SPELLING CONNECTIONS

See the 5-Day Grammar and Usage Plans on Sentences, pp. 47M–47N, 77M–77N, 105M–105N, 127M–127N, and 137M–137N.

See the 5-Day Spelling Plans, pp. 47O–47P, 77O–77P, 105O–105P, 127O–127P, and 137O–137P.

GRAMMAR, MECHANICS, USAGE

- Begin sentences with a capital letter.
- Use periods, exclamation, and question marks correctly.
- Use commas correctly when combining sentences.

Publish

SHARE THE LETTERS Students can mail their letters. Instruct them on addressing and invite them to apply stamps and decorative stickers to their envelopes.

Use **Writing Process Transparency 1D** as a proofreading model and **Writing Process Transparency 1E** to discuss presentation ideas for their writing.

PROOFREAD TRANSPARENCY

40 Pine Street
Cove, Oregon 99999
October 22, 1999

Dear Jen,

Did I ever tell you what happened when my family moved three years ago? Before we could sell our house, we had to fix it up. Our mother told ᵘˢthat all the wallpaper had to come off, the ᵂʰᵒˡᵉinside of the house had to be painted, and a new bathtub had to be put in. I couldn't believe it. ~~This was to much!~~ But my mom said we would all work together, and it might be fun.

The first week we peᵉled the wallpaper off and ˢᵃⁿᵈᵉᵈsmoothed the walls. The second week we painted seven rooms and half of a cat—sorry, sheba! The third week my brother Mike got to show how strong he was by—oops—almost lifting a bathtub. We finished it allˡt ᵍʳᵉᵃᵗfelt ~~nice~~ to do a good job. But was it fun? are you kidding?

Your friend,
Sue

Book 3.1/Unit 1: Personal Narrative / Proofreading 1D

PUBLISH TRANSPARENCY

40 Pine Street
Cove, Oregon 99999
October 22, 1999

Dear Jen,

Did I ever tell you what happened when my family moved three years ago? Before we could sell our house, we had to fix it up. Our mother told us that all the wallpaper had to come off, the whole inside of the house had to be painted, and a new bathtub had to be put in. I couldn't believe it. But my mom said we would all work together, and it might be fun.

The first week we peeled the wallpaper off and sanded the walls. The second week we painted seven rooms and half of a cat—sorry, Sheba! The third week my brother Mike got to show how strong he was by—oops—almost lifting a bathtub. We finished it all. It felt great to do a good job. But was it fun? Are you kidding?

Your friend,
Sue

Book 3.1/Unit 1: Personal Narrative / Publishing 1E

Presentation Ideas

MAKE A DISPLAY Help students to create a portable display of their letters, with collages illustrating each story. They can visit other classes with the display and read their letters. ▶ **Representing/Speaking**

MAKE A BOOK Have students create a class book to showcase their letters. Engage them in a discussion of each other's work. Distribute the book to other classes and the school library. ▶ **Viewing/Speaking**

Assessment

SCORING RUBRIC When using the rubric, please consider students' creative efforts, possibly adding a plus (+) for originality, wit, and imagination.

SELF-ASSESSMENT Present the Features of Personal Narrative Writing from page 139B in question form. Have students use these questions.

Scoring Rubric: 6-Trait Writing

4 Excellent	**3** Good	**2** Fair	**1** Unsatisfactory
Ideas & Content • creates a cohesive, focused picture of an event, with an extensive set of features; shows a keen sense of audience.	**Ideas & Content** • crafts a solid, clear description of an event; details help convey key ideas to the reader.	**Ideas & Content** • has some control of the narrative, but may not elaborate clearly or may lose control of the story line.	**Ideas & Content** • does not tell a personal story; may go off in several directions.
Organization • unfolds a consistent, carefully-organized narrative, in a sequence that moves the reader smoothly through the text.	**Organization** • shows a well-planned narrative strategy; story is easy to follow; ideas are evenly tied together.	**Organization** • may not have a clear story structure, or may show trouble tying ideas together; reader may be confused by vague details.	**Organization** • extreme lack of organization interferes with understanding the text; sequence, if shown, is disorganized or incomplete.
Voice • shows originality, reflectiveness, and a strong personal message that speaks directly to the reader.	**Voice** • makes a strong effort to share an authentic personal message directly with the reader.	**Voice** • may not connect with telling a personal story; may get the basic message across, without a sense of involvement with an audience.	**Voice** • is not involved in sharing an experience; does not focus on anything of personal importance or interest.
Word Choice • makes inventive use of both figurative and everyday language in a natural way; makes sophisticated choices that create a clear, striking picture in the reader's mind.	**Word Choice** • shows an overall clarity of expression, and an effective control of both new and everyday words that bring the story to life.	**Word Choice** • may not experiment with words that express a strong feeling; may not use words that create a vivid picture for the reader.	**Word Choice** • does not use words that fit the topic; some word choices may detract from the meaning of the text.
Sentence Fluency • creative, effective sentences flow with a smooth rhythm; dialogue, if used, sounds natural and strengthens the story.	**Sentence Fluency** • crafts careful, easy-to-follow sentences; may effectively use fragments and/or dialogue to strengthen and enhance the story.	**Sentence Fluency** • may have trouble with complex sentences; sentences are understandable, but may be choppy, rambling, or awkward.	**Sentence Fluency** • constructs incomplete, rambling, or confusing sentences; may have trouble understanding how words and sentences fit together.
Conventions • is skilled in most writing conventions; proper use of the rules of English enhances clarity and narrative style.	**Conventions** • has some errors in spelling, capitalization, punctuation or usage which do not interfere with understanding the text; some editing may be needed.	**Conventions** • makes noticeable mistakes which interfere with a smooth reading of the story.	**Conventions** • makes repeated errors in spelling, word choice, punctuation and usage; sentence structures may be confused; few explicit connections made between ideas.

0: This piece is either blank, or fails to respond to the writing task. The topic is not addressed, or the student simply paraphrases the prompt. The response may be illegible or incoherent.

VOCABULARY

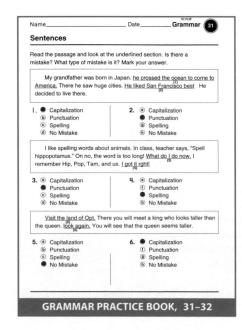

GROUP Divide the class into five groups. Give each group the vocabulary words for one selection. Tell each group to select a word and pantomime its meaning. Then have the other groups try to guess the word.

Unit Review

Grandfather's Journey

astonished	journey	surrounded
enormous	scattered	towering

Phoebe and the Spelling Bee

continue	embarrass	legend
correct	groaning	unusual

Opt: An Illusionary Tale

gift	length	straighten
guard	royal	within

Max Malone

ceiling	eager	scene
cents	including	section

Champions of the World

celebrated	fans	score
cork	pitcher	wrap

Name_____ Date_____ **Practice** (36)

Unit 1 Vocabulary Review

A. Read each word in Column 1. Then find a word in Column 2 that means the opposite. Write the letter of the word on the line.

_c_ 1. ceiling   a. wrong

_d_ 2. enormous   b. stop

_a_ 3. correct   c. floor

_e_ 4. within   d. tiny

_b_ 5. continue   e. outside

B. Supply the correct vocabulary word.

scene	journey	celebrated	gift
fans	cents	guard	

1. The _____fans_____ roared when Cora hit the home run.

2. Denny bought a _____gift_____ for his grandmother.

3. The _____journey_____ across the mountains took three days.

4. The large ball cost 75 _____cents_____ more than the small one.

5. The class _____celebrated_____ Leo's birthday by giving him a party.

6. When Jane saw the lovely _____scene_____, she wanted to paint a picture of it.

7. Harry and Jim stood _____guard_____ around the campfire.

PRACTICE BOOK, 36–37

GRAMMAR

PARTNERS To review the skills covered in the grammar lessons, have students write a short essay about a family or friend's pet. Have them circle the punctuation mark at the end of each sentence. Then ask them to underline the subject in each sentence. Have partners check each other's work.

Unit Review

Grandfather's Journey
Statements and Questions

Phoebe and the Spelling Bee
Commands and Exclamations

Opt: An Illusionary Tale
Subjects

Max Malone
Predicates

Champions of the World
Sentence Combining

Name_____ Date_____ **Grammar** (31)

Sentences

Read the passage and look at the underlined section. Is there a mistake? What type of mistake is it? Mark your answer.

> My grandfather was born in Japan. he crossed the ocean to come to America. There he saw huge cities. He liked San Francisco best   He decided to live there.

1. ● Capitalization
   ⓑ Punctuation
   ⓒ Spelling
   ⓓ No Mistake

2. ⓔ Capitalization
   ● Punctuation
   ⓖ Spelling
   ⓗ No Mistake

> I like spelling words about animals. In class, teacher says, "Spell hippopotamus." On no, the word is too long! What do I do now, I remember Hip, Pop, Tam, and us. I got it rght!

3. ⓐ Capitalization
   ● Punctuation
   ⓒ Spelling
   ⓓ No Mistake

4. ⓔ Capitalization
   ⓕ Punctuation
   ● Spelling
   ⓗ No Mistake

> Visit the land of Opt. There you will meet a king who looks taller than the queen. look again. You will see that the queen seems taller.

5. ⓐ Capitalization
   ⓑ Punctuation
   ⓒ Spelling
   ● No Mistake

6. ⓔ Capitalization
   ⓕ Punctuation
   ⓖ Spelling
   ● No Mistake

GRAMMAR PRACTICE BOOK, 31–32

SPELLING

Have students select and write a review word. Then have them write each letter on a separate piece of paper and put them in a bag. Explain that one person from each group selects letters and reads them aloud while the others cross out the letters in their words as they are read. Teams get one point for each completed word.

Unit Review

Short Vowels
black
rocks
kept
rub
thing

/ū/ and /ü/
broom
soup
truth
excuse
juice

Long *a* and Long *e*
breeze
paper
weigh
thief
awake

Physical Education Words
strike
parade
glove
season
record

Long *i* and Long *o*
might   ago
life   thrown
toast
bicycle

Name_____ Date_____ UNIT TEST SPELLING 31

Book 3.1/Unit 1 Review Test

Read each sentence. If an underlined word is spelled wrong, fill in the circle that goes with that word. If no word is spelled wrong, fill in the circle below NONE. Read Sample A, and do Sample B.

A. I <u>like</u> the <u>nayght</u> <u>owl</u> in the room.   A. Ⓐ ● Ⓒ Ⓓ

B. Her <u>brume</u> was <u>thrown</u> on the <u>rocks</u>.   B. ● Ⓕ Ⓖ Ⓗ

1. I <u>might</u> see the <u>parade</u> on my <u>bicycle</u>.   1. Ⓐ Ⓑ Ⓒ ●

2. They <u>strike</u> <u>truth</u> from the <u>record</u>.   2. Ⓔ Ⓕ Ⓖ ●

3. A good <u>thief</u> <u>might</u> not tell the <u>trueth</u>.   3. Ⓐ Ⓑ ● Ⓓ

4. The <u>black</u> <u>toast</u> is on the <u>paper</u>.   4. Ⓔ Ⓕ Ⓖ ●

5. She wore that <u>glove</u> to a <u>parade</u> a long time <u>ago</u>.   5. Ⓐ Ⓑ Ⓒ ●

6. Does the <u>rock</u> <u>whay</u> more than the <u>paper</u>?   6. Ⓔ ● Ⓖ Ⓗ

7. The <u>thief</u> will <u>rubb</u> the <u>rocks</u> for luck.   7. Ⓐ ● Ⓒ Ⓓ

8. I will <u>rub</u> the <u>brume</u> on this <u>paper</u>.   8. Ⓔ ● Ⓖ Ⓗ

9. She <u>kept</u> the <u>black</u> <u>glube</u> there.   9. Ⓐ Ⓑ ● Ⓓ

10. We <u>myght</u> have a new <u>excuse</u> from the <u>parade</u>.   10. ● Ⓕ Ⓖ Ⓗ

SPELLING PRACTICE BOOK, 31-32

☑ SKILLS & STRATEGIES

Comprehension
☑ Story Elements
☑ Make Predictions
☑ Problem and Solution
☑ Steps in a Process

Vocabulary Strategy
☑ Compound Words
☑ Prefixes

Study Skills
☑ Parts of a Book

Writing
☑ Personal Narrative

MCGRAW-HILL READING

Unit Test

Student Name: _____

Date: _____

Grade 3 • Book 1 • Unit 1

McGraw Hill

UNIT 1 TEST

Assessment
Follow-Up

Use the results of the informal and formal assessment opportunities in the unit to help you make decisions about future instruction.

SKILLS AND STRATEGIES	Reteaching Blackline Masters	Alternate Teaching Strategies
Comprehension		
Story Elements	1, 5, 20, 27	T60
Make Predictions	6, 13, 29	T62
Problem and Solution	8, 12, 22, 26	T64
Steps in a Process	15, 19, 33	T66
Vocabulary Strategy		
Compound Words	7, 28, 34	T63
Prefixes	14, 21, 35	T65
Study Skills		
Parts of a Book	4, 11, 18, 25, 32	T61

Writing	Alternate Writing Project–Easy	Unit Writing Process Lesson
Personal Narrative	47L, 77L, 105L, 127L, 137L	139A–139F

McGraw-Hill School
TECHNOLOGY

 CD-ROM provides extra phonics support.

 Research & Inquiry ideas. Visit **www.mhschool.com/reading.**

Glossary

Introduce students to the Glossary by reading through the introduction and looking over the pages with them. Encourage the class to talk about what they see.

Words in a glossary, like words in a dictionary, are listed in **alphabetical order.** Point out the **guide words** at the top of each page that tell the first and last words appearing on that page.

Point out examples of **entries** and **main entries.** Read through a simple entry with the class, identifying each part. Have students note the order in which information is given: entry words(s), definition(s), example sentence, syllable division, pronunciation respelling, part of speech, plural/verb/adjective forms.

Note that if more than one definition is given for a word, the definitions are numbered. Note also the format used for a word that is more than one part of speech.

Review the parts of speech by identifying each in a sentence:

inter.	*adj.*	*n.*	*conj.*	*adj.*	*n.*
Wow!	A	dictionary	and	a	glossary

v.	*adv.*	*pron.*	*prep.*	*n.*
tell	almost	everything	about	words!

Explain the use of the **pronunciation key** (either the **short key,** at the bottom of every other page, or the **long key,** at the beginning of the glossary). Demonstrate the difference between **primary** stress and **secondary** stress by pronouncing a word with both.

Point out an example of the small triangle signaling a homophone. **Homophones** are words with different spellings and meanings but with the same pronunciation. Explain that a pair of words with the superscripts **1** and **2** are **homographs**—words that have the same spelling, but different origins and meanings, and in some cases, different pronunciations.

The **Word History** feature tells what language a word comes from and what changes have occurred in its spelling and/or meaning. Many everyday words have interesting and surprising stories behind them. Note that word histories can help us remember the meanings of difficult words.

Allow time for students to further explore the Glossary and make their own discoveries.

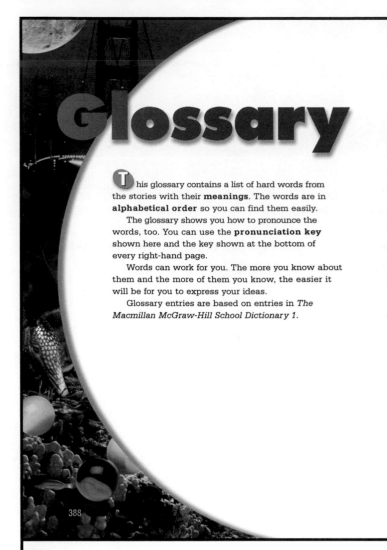

Glossary

This glossary contains a list of hard words from the stories with their **meanings**. The words are in **alphabetical order** so you can find them easily.

The glossary shows you how to pronounce the words, too. You can use the **pronunciation key** shown here and the key shown at the bottom of every right-hand page.

Words can work for you. The more you know about them and the more of them you know, the easier it will be for you to express your ideas.

Glossary entries are based on entries in *The Macmillan McGraw-Hill School Dictionary 1.*

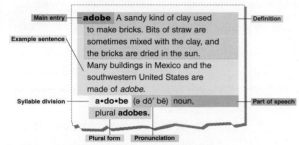

adobe/banner

First word on the page | Last word on the page

Sample Entry

Main entry — **adobe** A sandy kind of clay used to make bricks. Bits of straw are sometimes mixed with the clay, and the bricks are dried in the sun. Many buildings in Mexico and the southwestern United States are made of *adobe.* — Definition

Example sentence

Syllable division — **a•do•be** (ə dō′ bē) *noun,* plural **adobes.** — Part of speech

Plural form | Pronunciation

a	at, bad	d	dear, soda, bad
ā	ape, pain, day, break	f	five, defend, leaf, off, cough, elephant.
ä	father, car, heart		
âr	care, pair, bear, their, where	g	game, ago, fog, egg
e	end, pet, said, heaven, friend	h	hat, ahead
ē	equal, me, feet, team, piece, key	hw	white, whether, which
i	it, big, English, hymn	j	joke, enjoy, gem, page, edge
ī	ice, fine, lie, my	k	kite, bakery, seek, tack, cat
îr	ear, deer, here, pierce	l	lid, sailor, feel, ball, allow
o	odd, hot, watch	m	man, family, dream
ō	old, oat, toe, low	n	not, final, pan, knife
ô	coffee, all, taught, law, fought	ng	long, singer, pink
ôr	order, fork, horse, story, pour	p	pail, repair, soap, happy
oi	oil, toy	r	ride, parent, wear, more, marry
ou	out, now	s	sit, aside, pets, cent, pass
u	up, mud, love, double	sh	shoe, washer, fish, mission, nation
ū	use, mule, cue, feud, few	t	tag, pretend, fat, button, dressed
ü	rule, true, food	th	thin, panther, both,
u̇	put, wood, should	<u>th</u>	this, mother, smooth
ûr	burn, hurry, term, bird, word, courage	v	very, favor, wave
ə	about, taken, pencil, lemon, circus	w	wet, weather, reward
		y	yes, onion
b	bat, above, job	z	zoo, lazy, jazz, rose, dogs, houses
ch	chin, such, match	zh	vision, treasure, seizure

Aa

adobe A sandy kind of clay used to make bricks. Bits of straw are sometimes mixed with the clay, and the bricks are dried in the sun. Many buildings in Mexico and the southwestern United States are made of *adobe.*
a•do•be (ə dō′ bē) *noun,* plural **adobes.**

Word History
The word **adobe** comes from the Spanish word of the same spelling, meaning "sun-dried brick." But the Spanish got this word from an even earlier Arabic word, *at-tob,* meaning "the brick."

anxious 1. Wanting very much; eager. I was *anxious* to make friends at my new school. **2.** Nervous, worried or fearful about what may happen. My cousin was *anxious* about driving on the slippery roads.
anx•ious (angk′ shəs or ang′ shəs) *adjective.*

390

appendix A short, hollow pouch that is attached to the large intestine.
ap•pen•dix (ə pen′ diks) *noun,* plural **appendixes.**

applaud To show approval or enjoyment of something by clapping the hands. The children *applauded* the clown's funny tricks.
ap•plaud (ə plôd′) *verb,* **applauded, applauding.**

arachnid Any of a large group of small animals without a backbone. The body of an arachnid is divided into two parts. Arachnids have four pairs of legs and no antennae or wings. Spiders, scorpions, mites, and ticks are *arachnids.*
ar•ach•nid (ə rak′ nid) *noun,* plural **arachnids.**

area A particular space, region, or section. We moved from the city to a rural *area.*
ar•e•a (âr′ ē ə) *noun,* plural **areas.**

astonish To surprise very much; amaze. The news that I had won the contest *astonished* me.
▲Synonym: astound
as•ton•ish (ə ston′ ish) *verb,* **astonished, astonishing.**

Language Note
A **synonym** is a word that can be used for another word. A synonym for *astonish* is *surprise.*

attic The space just below the roof of a house. We use our *attic* to store trunks of old clothes.
at•tic (at′ ik) noun, plural **attics.**

autograph To write one's name in one's own handwriting. Will you *autograph* a copy of your book for me? *Verb.* —A person's signature written in that person's own handwriting. *Noun.*
au•to•graph (ô′ tə graf′) *verb,* **autographed, autographing;** *noun,* plural **autographs.**

Word History
The word **autograph** comes from the Greek words *autos,* meaning "self," and *graphein,* meaning "to write."

Bb

banner A flag or other piece of cloth that has a design and sometimes writing on it. The fans at the baseball game held up a *banner.*
ban•ner (ban′ ər) *noun,* plural **banners.**

beauty A quality that makes a person or a thing pleasing to look at, hear, or think about. The garden is a place of *beauty.*
beau•ty (bū′ tē) *noun,* plural **beauties.**

bewilder To confuse or puzzle; mix up. The student was *bewildered* by the math problem.
be•wil•der (bi wil′ dər) *verb,* **bewildered, bewildering.**

black widow A black spider. The female black widow is poisonous and has a red mark on her body. The female black widow is larger than the male.
black wi•dow (blak wid′ ō) *noun,* plural **black widows.**

blossom The flower of a plant or tree, especially one that produces fruit. We gathered *blossoms* from the apple trees. *Noun.*—To have flowers or blossoms; bloom. The peach trees *blossom* in the spring. *Verb.*
blos•som (blos′ əm) *noun,* plural **blossoms;** *verb,* **blossomed, blossoming.**

at; āpe; fär; câre; end; mē; it; īce; pîerce; hot; ōld; sông; fôrk; oil; out; up; ūse; rüle; pu̇ll; tûrn; chin; sing; shop; thin; <u>th</u>is; hw in white; zh in treasure. The symbol ə stands for the unstressed vowel sound in about, taken, pencil, lemon, and circus.

bronco busting The act of taming and training wild horses. The cowboys spent part of each day *bronco busting*.
bron•co bust•ing (brong′ kō bust′ ing) *noun.*

buffalo 1. A large North American animal that has a big shaggy head with short horns and a hump on its back; bison. 2. Any of various oxen of Europe, Asia, and Africa.
buf•fa•lo (buf′ ə lō′) *noun, plural* **buffaloes** *or* **buffalos** *or* **buffalo.**

Cc

canyon A deep valley with very high, steep sides. A *canyon* often has a stream running through it.
can•yon (kan′ yən) *noun, plural* **canyons.**

capture To catch and hold a person, animal, or thing. The explorers *captured* the tiger in a large net. ▲**Synonyms:** take, seize
cap•ture (kap′ chər) *verb* **captured, capturing.**

392

ceiling The inside overhead surface of a room. The tall guest reached up and almost touched the *ceiling*.
ceil•ing (sē′ ling) *noun, plural* **ceilings.**

celebrate To observe or honor a special day or event with ceremonies and other activities. We *celebrated* Grandma's birthday with a big party.
cel•e•brate (sel′ ə brāt′) *verb,* **celebrated, celebrating.**

cent A coin of the United States and Canada. One hundred *cents* is equal to one dollar. ▲Other words that sound like this are **scent** and **sent.**
▲**Synonym:** penny
cent (sent) *noun, plural,* **cents.**

Language Note
A *homonym* is a word that sounds like another word but has a different meaning. A homonym for *cent* is *sent*.
---

combine To cause to mix together; blend. We *combined* eggs, flour, and milk to make the batter for the pancakes.
▲**Synonyms:** blend, mix
com•bine (kəm bīn′) *verb,* **combined, combining.**

---

concert A performance, usually a musical performance by a number of musicians. We went to a *concert* in the park.
▲**Synonyms:** show, recital, symphony
con•cert (kon′ sərt) *noun, plural* **concerts.**

conductor 1. A person who leads a group of musicians. Our music teacher is also the *conductor* of the school orchestra. 2. A person on a train or bus who collects fares and assists passengers. The *conductor* walked down the aisle and called out the name of the next stop.
con•duc•tor (kən duk′ tər) *noun, plural* **conductors.**

consonant A letter of the alphabet that is not a vowel. *Consonants* include the letters *b, d, f, g, m, p, t,* and others.
con•so•nant (kon′ sə nənt) *noun, plural* **consonants.**

continue 1. To go on or do after stopping. We will *continue* the meeting after lunch. 2. To keep on happening, being, or doing; go on without stopping. The rain had *continued* for two days.
con•tin•ue (kən tin′ ū) *verb,* **continued, continuing.**

cork The light, thick outer bark of a kind of oak tree. *Cork* is used for such things as bottle stoppers, insulation, and floats for rafts.
cork (kôrk) *noun, plural* **corks.**

correct Not having any mistakes; accurate. This is the *correct* answer to the arithmetic problem. *Adjective.*
—To mark the mistakes in; change to make right. The teacher *corrected* our spelling tests. *Verb.*
cor•rect (kə rekt′) *adjective; verb,* **corrected, correcting.**

costume Clothes worn in order to look like someone or something else. I wore a cowboy *costume* to the Halloween party.
cos•tume (kos′ tūm *or* kos′ tūm) *noun, plural* **costumes.**

---
at; āpe; fär; câre; end; mē; it; īce; pîerce; hot; ōld; sông; fôrk; oil; out; up; ūse; rüle; pùll; tûrn; chin; sing; shop; thin; this; hw in white; zh in treasure. The symbol ə stands for the unstressed vowel sound in about, taken, pencil, lemon, and circus.

393

---

creep To move slowly along the ground or over a surface. The wind *creeps* in through the window.
creep (krēp) *verb,* **crept, creeping.**

crooked Not straight; bent or curving. The path through the woods was very *crooked*.
▲**Synonyms:** bent, winding
crook•ed (krûk′ id) *adjective.*

crop Plants that are grown to be used as a food or to be sold for profit. Wheat and corn are two *crops* grown in the Midwest.
crop (krop) *noun, plural* **crops.**

crumble 1. To break into small pieces. The muffin *crumbled* when I tried to butter it. 2. To fall apart or be destroyed. The old house is slowly *crumbling*.
crum•ble (krum′ bəl) *verb,* **crumbled, crumbling.**

Dd

daddy-longlegs A kind of bug that looks like a spider. A daddy-longlegs has a small, round body and eight very long, thin legs.
dad•dy long•legs (dad′ē lông′ legz′) *noun, plural* **daddy-longlegs.**

394

darkness A partial or total absence of light; the result of a light going out. The sun dipped behind the hilltops and *darkness* fell.
dark•ness (därk′ nis) *noun.*

dawn The first light that appears in the morning. We left our house before *dawn*.
▲**Synonym:** daybreak
dawn (dôn) *noun, plural* **dawns.**

deaf Not able to hear, or not able to hear well. The *deaf* children were using sign language to speak to one another
deaf (def) *adjective,* **deafer, deafest.**

decimal 1. A period put before a decimal fraction. The periods in .5, .30, and .052 are *decimals*. 2. A fraction with a denominator of 10, or a multiple of 10 such as 100 or 1,000. The *decimal* .5 is another way of writing $\frac{5}{10}$.
dec•i•mal (des′ ə məl) *noun, plural* **decimals.**

---

den A place where wild animals rest or sleep. The bear uses a cave as a *den* during its long winter sleep.
den (den) *noun, plural* **dens.**

disaster An event that causes much suffering or loss. The flood was a *disaster*.
▲**Synonyms:** tragedy, trouble
dis•as•ter (di zas′ tər) *noun, plural* **disasters.**

Word History
The word **disaster** comes from the Latin *dis*, meaning "away," and *astrum*, meaning "star."
---

dragonfly An insect that has a long, thin body and two pairs of wings. *Dragonflies* eat mosquitoes and live near fresh water.
drag•on•fly (drag′ ən flī′) *noun, plural* **dragonflies.**

Ee

eager Wanting very much to do something. A person who is *eager* is full of interest and enthusiasm.
▲**Synonym:** excited
ea•ger (ē′ gər) *adjective.*

earthquake A shaking or trembling of the ground. *Earthquakes* are caused by rock, lava, or hot gases moving deep inside the earth. Some *earthquakes* are so powerful that they cause the ground to split.
earth•quake (ûrth′ kwāk′) *noun, plural* **earthquakes.**

echo The repeating of a sound. *Echoes* are caused when sound waves bounce off a surface. We shouted "hello" and soon heard the *echo* of our voices.
ech•o (ek′ ō) *noun, plural* **echoes.**

embarrass To make someone feel shy, uncomfortable, or ashamed. My foolish mistake *embarrassed* me.
em•bar•rass (em bar′ əs) *verb,* **embarrassed, embarrassing.**

enormous Much greater than the usual size or amount; very large. The flood caused an *enormous* amount of damage.
▲**Synonyms:** large, gigantic
e•nor•mous (i nôr′ məs) *adjective.*

---
at; āpe; fär; câre; end; mē; it; īce; pîerce; hot; ōld; sông; fôrk; oil; out; up; ūse; rüle; pùll; tûrn; chin; sing; shop; thin; this; hw in white; zh in treasure. The symbol ə stands for the unstressed vowel sound in about, taken, pencil, lemon, and circus.

395

eon A very long period of time. That deposit of coal was formed *eons* ago.
e•on (ē′ ən *or* ē′ on) *noun, plural* **eons.**

Espino, Fernando
(es pē′ nō, fûr nän′ dō)

examine 1. To look at closely and carefully; check. We *examined* the baseball bat to be sure it wasn't cracked. **2.** To question in a careful way or test, usually to discover what a person knows. The lawyer *examined* the witness during the trial.
▲Synonyms: inspect, study
ex•am•ine (eg zam′ in) *verb,* **examined, examining.**

excitement The condition of being excited. We could hardly sleep because of our *excitement* about starting the trip tomorrow.
ex•cite•ment (ek sīt′ mənt) *noun.*

Ff

fade 1. To lose freshness; wither. The flowers *faded* after three days. **2.** To lose or cause to lose color or brightness. Blue jeans may *fade* when they are washed.
fade (fād) *verb,* **faded, fading.**

fan A person who is very interested in or enthusiastic about something. The *fans* ran up to the movie star.
▲Synonym: admirer
fan (fan) *noun, plural* **fans.**

feelers A part of an animal's body that is used for touching things. Many insects have *feelers* on their heads.
feel•er (fē′ lər) *noun, plural* **feelers.**

flex To bend. If your arm is tired, *flex* it to keep it loose.
flex (fleks) *verb,* **flexed, flexing.**

flow To move along steadily in a stream. Water *flows* through these pipes.
flow (flō) *verb,* **flowed, flowing.**

furniture Tables, chairs, beds, and other movable articles used in a home or office. Our living room is full of *furniture.*
fur•ni•ture (fûr′ ni chər) *noun.*

396

Gg

gaze To look at something a long time. We all *gazed* at the beautiful sunset. *Verb.*—A long steady look. Our *gaze* rested on the bear and its two playful cubs. *Noun.*
gaze (gāz) *verb,* **gazed, gazing;** *noun, plural* **gazes.**

Genghis Khan
(geng′ gis kän′)

gift 1. Something given; a present. This basketball was a *gift* from my parents. **2.** Talent; ability. That student has a *gift* for dancing.
gift (gift) *noun, plural* **gifts.**

grain 1. A tiny, hard piece of something. *Grains* of sand fell from the beach towel. **2.** The seed of wheat, corn, rice, oats, and other cereal plants. Breakfast cereal is made from *grains.*
grain (grān) *noun, plural* **grains.**

groan To make a deep, sad sound. I *groaned* when the doctors touched my injured ankle.
▲Synonym: moan ▲ Another word that sounds like this is **grown.**
groan (grōn) *verb,* **groaned, groaning.**

guard A person who is assigned to watch over things. The museum *guard* collected our tickets at the door. *Noun.*—To keep safe from harm or danger; protect. The dog *guarded* the house. *Verb.*
guard (gärd) *noun, plural* **guards;** *verb,* **guarded, guarding.**

Hh

halfway To or at half the distance; midway. We climbed *halfway* up the mountain.
half•way (haf′ wā) *adverb.*

handful 1. The amount the hand can hold at one time. Each child took a *handful* of peanuts. **2.** A small number. Only a *handful* of people showed up.
hand•ful (hand′ fool′) *noun, plural* **handfuls.**

at; āpe; fär; câre; end; mē; it; īce; pîerce; hot; ōld; sông; fôrk; oil; out; up; ūse; rūle; pull; tûrn; chin; sing; shop; thin; this; hw in white; zh in treasure. The symbol ə stands for the unstressed vowel sound in about, taken, pencil, lemon, and circus.

397

---

hatch To come from an egg. We are waiting for these chicks to *hatch.*
hatch (hach) *verb,* **hatched, hatching.**

haunch A part of the body of a person or animal including the hip and upper thigh. The lion sat on its *haunches.*
haunch (hônch) *noun, plural* **haunches.**

heap A collection of things piled together. We left a *heap* of peanut shells on the kitchen table.
▲Synonyms: pile, load, mound
heap (hēp) *noun, plural* **heaps.**

herd A group of animals that live or travel together. A *herd* of cattle grazed in the pasture.
▲Another word that sounds like this is **heard.**
herd (hûrd) *noun, plural* **herds;** *verb,* **herded, herding.**

Ii

ill Not healthy or well; sick. Many children in our class were *ill.*
ill (il) *adjective.*

imaginary Existing only in the mind; unreal. Most people believe that elves are *imaginary.*
▲Synonyms: unreal, fictional
i•mag•i•nary (i maj′ə ner′ē) *adjective.*

include To have as part of the whole; contain. You don't have to buy batteries for that toy because they are already *included* in the box.
in•clude (in klüd′) *verb,* **included, including.**

instrument 1. A device for producing musical sounds. Our music teacher plays the guitar, flute, and several other *instruments.* **2.** A device used for doing a certain kind of work; tool. The dental hygienist used a sharp *instrument* to scrape my teeth.
in•stru•ment (in′strə mənt) *noun, plural* **instruments.**

invent 1. To make or think of for the first time; create. Do you know who *invented* the phonograph? **2.** To make up. I'm ashamed to say I *invented* an excuse for being late.
in•vent (in vent′) *verb,* **invented, inventing.**

398

Word History
The word **invent** comes from a Latin word meaning "to come upon" or "find." The word *invent* was originally used to describe the finding of an answer, the solution to a problem, or the means to do something.

Jj

jagged Having sharp points that stick out. Some eagles build nests on *jagged* cliffs.
jag•ged (jag′ id) *adjective.*

jingle To make or cause to make a tinkling or ringing sound. When the bell moved, it *jingled.*
jingle (jing′gəl) *verb,* **jingled, jingling.**

journey A long trip. The Pilgrims crossed the Atlantic on their *journey* to the New World.
jour•ney (jûr′ nē) *noun, plural* **journeys.**

Kk

kinship A relationship or close connection. There has always been a *kinship* between the two villages.
kin•ship (kin′ ship′) *noun, plural* **kinships.**

Ll

lasso A long rope with a loop. A *lasso* is used to catch animals. *Noun.*
—To catch with a lasso. The cowhands will *lasso* the steer. *Verb.*
las•so (la′sō *or* lasü′) *noun, plural* **lassos** *or* **lassoes;** *verb,* **lassoed, lassoing.**

lease To rent. The family *leased* a cabin for the summer. *Verb.*
—A written agreement for renting a house, apartment, or land. My parents signed a new *lease. Noun.*
lease (lēs) *verb,* **leased, leasing;** *noun, plural* **leases.**

at; āpe; fär; câre; end; mē; it; īce; pîerce; hot; ōld; sông; fôrk; oil; out; up; ūse; rūle; pull; tûrn; chin; sing; shop; thin; this; hw in white; zh in treasure. The symbol ə stands for the unstressed vowel sound in about, taken, pencil, lemon, and circus.

399

Glossary

legend A story passed down through the years that many people believe, but that is not entirely true. There are many *legends* about the knights of the Middle Ages.
leg•end (lej'end) *noun, plural* **legends.**

length The distance from one end to the other end. The *length* of a football field is 100 yards.
▲Synonym: measure
length (lengkth *or* length) *noun, plural* **lengths.**

liquid A form of matter that is not a solid or a gas. A liquid can flow easily. It can take on the shape of any container into which it is poured. Milk is a *liquid*.
liq•uid (lik'wid) *noun, plural* **liquids.**

Little League A baseball league for children under thirteen years of age. We play for the West Side *Little League* on Saturday.
Lit•tle League (lit' el lēg) *noun.*

locate 1. To put or settle in a particular place. The baker *located* the bakery in the shopping mall. 2. To find the place or position of. He could not *locate* his glasses.
lo•cate (lō'kāt) *verb,* **located, locating.**

longhorn A breed of cattle with very long horns. *Longhorns* were once common in the southwestern United States.
long•horn (lông' hôrn) *noun, plural* **longhorns.**

Mm

marvel To feel wonder and astonishment. We *marveled* at the acrobat's skill.
mar•vel (mär'vel) *verb,* **marveled, marveling.**

McGwire, Mark (me gwīr', märk)

mischievous Playful but naughty. That *mischievous* child hid my slippers again.
mis•chie•vous (mis'che ves) *adjective.*

400

---

miserable 1. Very unhappy; wretched. We all felt *miserable* about losing our dog. 2. Causing discomfort or unhappiness. I had a *miserable* cold.
▲Synonyms: sad, horrible, unpleasant
mis•er•a•ble (miz' er e bel) *adjective.*

mob To crowd around in excitement or anger. Shoppers *mobbed* the store during the big sale. *Verb.* —A large number of people; crowd. A *mob* is sometimes made up of people who are so angry or upset about something that they break the law and cause damage. *Noun.*
mob (mob) *verb,* **mobbed, mobbing;** *noun, plural* **mobs.**

mock Not real; imitation. In history class we had a *mock* battle with cardboard shields. *Adjective.*—To make fun of in a mean way. Instead of helping, they laughed and *mocked* me when I fell off my bike. *Verb.*
mock (mok) *adjective; verb,* **mocked, mocking.**

musician A person who is skilled in playing a musical instrument, composing music, or singing. My brother studied piano for years and became a talented *musician*.
mu•si•cian (mū zish' en) *noun, plural* **musicians.**

mustang A wild horse that lives on the American plains; bronco. We watched the *mustangs* go down to the river for a cool drink of water.
mus•tang (mus'tang) *noun, plural* **mustangs.**

Nn

New World North and South America; the Western Hemisphere.
New World (nü wûrld)

Nilsson, Kerstin (Nil'sen, Kûr'stin)

northern lights Shining bands of light that can be seen in the night sky in the Northern Hemisphere. In the winter, you can see the *northern lights* in Alaska.
north•ern lights (nôr'thern līts) *noun.*

at; āpe; fär; câre; end; mē; it; īce; pîerce; hot; ōld; sông; fôrk; oil; out; up; ūse; rūle; pùll; tûrn; chin; sing; shop; thin; this; hw in white; zh in treasure. The symbol ə stands for the unstressed vowel sound in about, taken, pencil, lemon, and circus.

401

Oo

orchestra 1. A group of musicians playing together on various instruments. 2. The area just in front of a stage in which the orchestra plays.
▲Synonyms: symphony, band
or•ches•tra (ôr' ke strə) *noun, plural* **orchestras.**

Word History
The word **orchestra** comes from a Greek word meaning "dance area." In the theater of ancient Greece, one section of the stage was called the *orchestra*. It was there that a chorus of performers danced and sang during a performance.

Pp

palace A very large, grand building where a king, queen, or other ruler usually lives. In London, we got to visit Buckingham *Palace*.
pal•ace (pal' is) *noun, plural* **palaces.**

Panama A country in Central America.
Pan•a•ma (pan' e mä) *noun.*

pattern The way in which colors, shapes, or lines are arranged or repeated in some order. The wallpaper was printed with a pretty flower *pattern*.
▲Synonym: design
pat•tern (pat' ern) *noun, plural* **patterns.**

peak 1. A high mountain, or the pointed top of a high mountain. We could see the snowy *peaks* in the distance. 2. A sharp or pointed end or top. If you stand on the *peak* of our roof, you can see the ocean.
▲Synonyms: mountain top, crest, summit
peak (pēk) *noun, plural* **peaks.**

pedestrian A person who travels on foot; walker. Sidewalks are for *pedestrians*.
ped•es•tri•an (pe des'trē ən) *noun, plural* **pedestrians.**

402

Word History
The word **pedestrian** comes to us from the Latin root *pedis*, meaning "on foot."

percussionist One who is skilled in playing percussion instruments, such as the drum, cymbal, xylophone, and piano. The *percussionist* in the orchestra played the bass drum and cymbals.
per•cus•sion•ist (pər kush' ən ist) *noun, plural* **percussionists.**

petition A formal request that is made to a person in authority. All the people on our street signed a *petition* asking the city to put a stop sign on the corner. *Noun.*—To make a formal request to. The students in our school *petitioned* the principal to keep the library open on weekends. *Verb.*
pe•ti•tion (pe tish' en) *noun, plural* **petitions;** *verb,* **petitioned, petitioning.**

pitcher A baseball player who throws the ball to the batter. The *pitcher* stands near the middle of the diamond facing home place.
pitch•er (pich' er) *noun, plural* **pitchers.**

pitcher

prairie Flat or rolling land covered with grass. A *prairie* has few trees.
▲Synonym: plains
prai•rie (prâr' ē) *noun, plural* **prairies.**

prey An animal that is hunted by another animal for food. Rabbits and birds are the *prey* of foxes.
prey (prā) *noun, plural* **prey.**

prong One of the pointed ends of an antler or of a fork or other tool. My grandmother's forks have only three *prongs*.
▲Synonym: point
prong (prông *or* prong) *noun, plural* **prongs.**

at; āpe; fär; câre; end; mē; it; īce; pîerce; hot; ōld; sông; fôrk; oil; out; up; ūse; rūle; pùll; tûrn; chin; sing; shop; thin; this; hw in white; zh in treasure. The symbol ə stands for the unstressed vowel sound in about, taken, pencil, lemon, and circus.

403

Glossary

pure 1. Nothing but. We won that game with *pure* luck. **2.** Not mixed with anything else. This bracelet is made of *pure* silver.
▲Synonyms: true, actual
pure (pyür) *adjective,* **purer, purest.**

Rr

respect High regard or consideration. We show *respect* for our teacher. *Noun.*—To have or show honor or consideration for. I *respect* your opinion. *Verb.*
▲Synonyms: admiration, esteem
re•spect (ri spekt′) *noun; verb,* **respected, respecting.**

ripe Fully grown and ready to be eaten. The tomatoes in the garden are *ripe* now.
ripe (rīp) *adjective,* **riper, ripest.**

royal Of or pertaining to a king or queen or their family. The *royal* family lives in the palace.
roy•al (roi′ əl) *adjective.*

rubble Rough, broken pieces of stone, rock, or other solid material. The rescue workers searched through the *rubble* of the collapsed building.
rub•ble (rub′ əl) *noun.*

ruin Harm or damage greatly. The earthquake *ruined* the town. *Verb.*—Destruction, damage, or collapse. The storekeeper faced financial *ruin*. *Noun.*
▲Synonym: destroy
ru•in (rü′ in) *verb,* **ruined, ruining;** *noun, plural* **ruins.**

Ss

Sabana Grande
(sə bän′ə grän′ dä)

scatter 1. To spread or throw about in various places. The wind *scattered* the leaves all over the yard. **2.** To separate or cause to separate and go in different directions. The loud thunder *scattered* the cattle.
▲Synonyms: cast, fling, sprinkle
scat•ter (skat′ ər) *verb,* **scattered, scattering.**

404

---

scene 1. The place where something happens. The police arrived on the *scene* just as the thieves were escaping. **2.** A part of an act in a play or movie.
▲Another word that sounds like this is **seen.**
scene (sēn) *noun, plural* **scenes.**

schedule The time at which something is supposed to happen. The train was running behind *schedule* because of the weather.
sched•ule (skej′ ül) *noun, plural* **schedules.**

score The points or a record of the points made in a game or on a test. The final *score* of the game was 5 to 4. *Noun.*—To make a point or points in a game or test. She *scored* 10 points for her basketball team. *Verb.*
score (skôr) *noun, plural* **scores;** *verb,* **scored, scoring.**

season 1. Any special part of the year. There is almost no rain during the dry *season*. **2.** One of the four parts of the year: spring, summer, fall, or winter.
sea•son (sē′ zən) *noun, plural* **seasons.**

season

> **Word History**
> The word **season** comes from a French word that originally meant, "the season of spring," or "planting time."

section 1. A part of an area or group. We visited the old *section* of the city. **2.** A part taken from a whole; portion. Please cut the apple into four *sections*.
▲Synonym: quarter
sec•tion (sek′ shən) *noun, plural* **sections.**

serious 1. Dangerous. Sam risked *serious* injury when he drove so fast on that icy road. **2.** Not joking; sincere. Were you *serious* about taking piano lessons?
▲Synonyms: grave, critical
se•ri•ous (sîr′ ē əs) *adjective.*

at; āpe; fär; câre; end; mē; it; īce; pîerce; hot; ōld; sông; fôrk; oil; out; up; ūse; rüle; pùll; tûrn; chin; sing; shop; thin; this; hw in white; zh in treasure. The symbol ə stands for the unstressed vowel sound in about, taken, pencil, lemon, and circus.

405

---

shallow Not deep. The water in the pond is *shallow*.
shallow (shal′ ō) *adjective,* **shallower, shallowest.**

shelter 1. To find or take refuge. It is not safe to take *shelter* under a tree during an electrical storm. **2.** To give shelter to. The umbrella *sheltered* us from the rain. *Verb.*—Something that covers or protects. The hikers used a cave as *shelter* during the thunderstorm. *Noun.*
shel•ter (shel′ tər) *verb,* **sheltered, sheltering;** *noun, plural* **shelters.**

skill The power or ability to do something. Swimming is an important *skill* to know when you are out on a boat.
▲Synonym: talent
skill (skil) *noun, plural* **skills.**

sloth A slow-moving animal that lives in the forests of South America. *Sloths* use their long arms and legs and their curved claws to hang upside down from trees.
sloth (slôth *or* slōth) *noun, plural* **sloths.**

snipping The act or sound of cutting with scissors in short, quick strokes. *Snipping* coupons from the newspaper is a way to save money on groceries.
snip•ping (snip′ ing) *noun.*

soldier A person who is a member of an army. The *soldiers* marched in a parade.
sol•dier (sōl′ jər) *noun, plural* **soldiers.**

Sosa, Sammy
(sō′ sə, sam′ mē)

souvenir Something that is kept because it reminds one of a person, place, or event. I kept my ticket as a *souvenir* of my first play.
▲Synonym: keepsake, memento
sou•ve•nir (sü′ və nîr′ *or* sü′ və nîr′) *noun, plural* **souvenirs.**

steamship A large ship that is powered by steam.
steam•ship (stēm′ ship) *noun, plural* **steamships.**

406

---

stem The main part of a plant that supports the leaves and flowers. Water and food travel through the *stem* to all parts of the plant.
▲Synonym: stalk
stem (stem) *noun, plural* **stems.**

straighten 1. To make or become straight. The picture on the wall slanted to the left, so I *straightened* it. **2.** To put into proper order. I asked you to *straighten* your room.
straight•en (strā′ tən) *verb,* **straightened, straightening.**

struggle To make a great effort. The children *struggled* through the heavy snow.
strug•gle (strug′ əl) *verb,* **struggled, struggling.**

stumble To lose one's balance; trip. I *stumbled* over the rake.
stum•ble (stum′ bəl) *verb,* **stumbled, stumbling.**

surround To be on all sides of; form a circle around. A fence *surrounds* our yard.
▲Synonym: enclose
sur•round (sə round′) *verb,* **surrounded, surrounding.**

Sweden A country in northern Europe.
Swe•den (swē′ dən) *noun.*

Tt

tall tale A made-up or exaggerated story; a tale too fantastic to believe.
tall tale (tôl tāl) *noun, plural* **tall tales.**

Tanksi
(tawnk′ shē)

tarantula A hairy spider that is found in warm areas. The *tarantula* has a painful bite.
ta•ran•tu•la (tə ran′ chə lə) *noun, plural* **tarantulas.**

Tiblo
(tē′ blo)

toucan A bird that has a heavy body, a very large beak, and colorful feathers. *Toucans* are found in Central America.
tou•can (tü′ kan) *noun, plural* **toucans.**

at; āpe; fär; câre; end; mē; it; īce; pîerce; hot; ōld; sông; fôrk; oil; out; up; ūse; rüle; pùll; tûrn; chin; sing; shop; thin; this; hw in white; zh in treasure. The symbol ə stands for the unstressed vowel sound in about, taken, pencil, lemon, and circus.

407

---

towering Very tall; lofty. *Towering* palm trees lined the beach.
tow•er•ing (tou′ ər ing) *adjective.*

trade To give one thing in return for something else. I'll *trade* you two of my cards for one of yours.
▲Synonyms: exchange, swap
trade (trād) *verb,* **traded, trading.**

triangle 1. A musical instrument made of a metal bar bent in the shape of a triangle. A *triangle* sounds like a bell when it is hit. 2. A figure or object with three sides and three angles.
tri•an•gle (trī′ang′əl) *noun, plural* **triangles.**

trim To cut away or remove parts to make something neat and orderly. Please *trim* the hedge evenly.
trim (trim) *verb,* **trimmed, trimming.**

unusual Not usual, common, or ordinary. It is very *unusual* for them not to want to go to a movie.
un•u•su•al (un ū′ zhü əl) *adjective.*

vibration Rapid movement back and forth or up and down. People many miles away could feel the *vibration* of the earthquake.
▲Synonym: shaking
vi•bra•tion (vī brā′ shən) *noun, plural* **vibrations.**

visitor A person who visits. I have to clean my room because we're having *visitors* this afternoon.
▲Synonym: guest
vis•i•tor (viz′ i tər) *noun, plural* **visitors.**

wilderness A natural place where no people live. In a *wilderness* there may be a dense forest and wild animals.
wil•der•ness (wil′ dər nis) *noun, plural* **wildernesses.**

within In or into the inner part or parts of. The troops camped *within* the walls of the fort.
with•in (with in′ *or* with in′) *preposition.*

Woutilainen, Johan
(woo ti lā′ nən, yō′ han)

woven Formed or made by lacing together thread, yarn, or strips of straw or other material. Gold thread had been *woven* into the blouse.
wo•ven (wō′ vən) *past participle of* **weave.**

wrap To cover by putting something around. Please help me *wrap* these presents.
wrap (rap) *verb,* **wrapped, wrapping.**

zinnia A garden plant that has rounded, brightly colored flowers.
zin•ni•a (zin′ ē ə) *noun, plural* **zinnias.**

at; āpe; fär; câre; end; mē; it; īce; pîerce; hot; ōld; sông; fôrk; oil; out; up; ūse; rūle; pùll; tûrn; chin; sing; shop; thin; this; hw in white; zh in treasure. The symbol ə stands for the unstressed vowel sound in about, taken, pencil, lemon, and circus.

Acknowledgments

Cover Illustration: Lori Lohstoeter

The publisher gratefully acknowledges permission to reprint the following copyrighted material:

"The Ants" from BEAST FEAST by Douglas Florian. Copyright © 1994 by Douglas Florian. Used by permission of Harcourt Brace & Company.

"Arachne the Spinner" from GREEK MYTHS retold by Geraldine McCaughrean. Text copyright © 1992 by Geraldine McCaughrean. Illustrations copyright © 1992 by Emma Chichester Clark. Used by permission of Margaret K. McElderry Books, Macmillan Publishing Company.

"Arkansas Traveler" from GONNA SING MY HEAD OFF! Used by permission of Alfred A. Knopf.

"At the Flick of a Switch" from EARTH LINES, POEMS FOR THE GREEN AGE by Pat Moon. Copyright © 1991 by Pat Moon. Used by permission of Greenwillow Books, a division of William Morrow & Company, Inc.

"Basket" from WORLDS I KNOW AND OTHER POEMS by Myra Cohn Livingston. Copyright © 1985 by Myra Cohn Livingston. Used by permission of Marian Reiner for the author.

"Frog and Locust" from A HEART FULL OF TURQUOISE by Joe Hayes. Copyright © 1988 by Joe Hayes. Used by permission of Mariposa Publishing.

"From the Bellybutton of the Moon/Del ombligo de la luna" from FROM THE BELLY-BUTTON OF THE MOON AND OTHER SUMMER POEMS by Francisco X. Alarcón. Poems copyright © 1998 by Francisco X. Alarcón. Illustrations copyright © 1998 by Maya Christina Gonzalez. Used by permission of Children's Book Press.

"A Garden" from ALWAYS WONDERING by Aileen Fisher. Text copyright © 1991 by Aileen Fisher. Illustrations copyright © 1991 by Joan Sandin. Used by permission of HarperCollins Publishers.

"The Hen and the Apple Tree" from FABLES by Arnold Lobel. Copyright © 1980 by Arnold Lobel. Used by permission of HarperCollins Publishers.

"The Hurricane" from SING TO THE SUN by Ashley Bryan. Copyright © 1992 by Ashley Bryan. Used by permission of HarperCollins.

"Ice Cycle" from ONCE UPON ICE AND OTHER FROZEN POEMS by Mary Ann Hoberman. Copyright © 1997 by Mary Ann Hoberman. Used by permission of Wordsong/Boyds Mills Press, Inc.

"If I Find a Penny" from THE BUTTERFLY JAR by Jeff Moss. Text copyright © 1988 by Jeff Moss. Illustrations copyright © 1988 by Chris Demarest. Used by permission of Bantam Doubleday Dell Publishing Group.

"In Daddy's Arms" from IN DADDY'S ARMS I AM TALL, AFRICAN AMERICANS CELEBRATING FATHERS by Folami Abiade. Text copyright © 1997 by Folami Abiade. Illustrations copyright © 1997 by Javaka Steptoe. Used by permission of Lee & Low Books, Inc.

ACKNOWLEDGMENTS

The publisher gratefully acknowledges permission to reprint the following copyrighted material:

"Abuelita's Lap" by Pat Mora from CONFETTI: POEMS FOR CHILDREN by Pat Mora. Text copyright © 1996 by Pat Mora. Reprinted by permission of Lee & Low Books Inc.

"Baseballs for Sale" from MAX MALONE MAKES A MILLION by Charlotte Herman. Text copyright © 1991 by Charlotte Herman. Illustrations copyright © 1991 by Catherine Bowman Smith. Reprinted by permission of Henry Holt and Company, Inc.

Entire text and art and cover of CITY GREEN by DyAnne DiSalvo-Ryan. Copyright © 1994 by DyAnne DiSalvo-Ryan. By permission of Morrow Junior Books, a division of William Morrow and Company, Inc.

"Closed, I am a mystery" by Myra Cohn Livingston from A PLACE TO DREAM. From My Head is Red and Other Riddle Rhymes by Myra Cohn Livingston. Copyright © 1990 by Myra Cohn Livingston (Published by Holliday House, NY) by pressmission of Marian Reiner.

"Different Drum" by Joe Scruggs from ANTS by Joe Scuggs. (Produced by Gary Powell.) Copyright © 1994 by Educational Graphics Press, Inc.

"Dream Wolf" is from DREAM WOLF by Paul Goble. Copyright © 1990 by Paul Goble. Reprinted with the permission of Simon & Schuster Books For Young Readers.

"Fog" by Carl Sandburg from CHICAGO POEMS by Carl Sandburg. Copyright © 1916 by Holt Reinhart & Winston Inc.; renewed 1944 by Carl Sandburg. Reprinted by permission of Harcourt Brace Jovanovich, Inc.

Cover permission for THE GIRL WHO LOVED WILD HORSES by Paul Goble. Copyright © 1978 by Paul Goble. Reprinted by permission of Simon & Schuster Books for Young Readers.

"Grandfather's Journey" by Allen Say. Copyright © 1993 by Allen Say. Reprinted with the permission of Houghton Mifflin Company. All rights reserved.

"The Little Painter of Sabana Grande" by Patricia Maloney Markun, illustrated by Robert Casilla. Text copyright © 1993 by Patricia Maloney Markun. Illustrations copyright © 1993 by Robert Casilla. Published by Simon & Schuster Books for Young Readers. Reprinted by permission.

"Moses Goes to a Concert" by Issac Millman. Copyright © 1998 by Isaac Millman. Reprinted by permission of Frances Foster Books/Farrar, Straus and Giroux.

"My Pencil" by Shirley R. Williams from POETRY PLACE ANTHOLOGY by Instructor Publications, Inc. Text copyright © 1983 by Instructor Publications, Inc.

"Opt: An Illusionary Tale" from OPT: AN ILLUSIONARY TALE by Arline and Joseph Baum. Copyright © 1987 by Arline and Joseph Baum. Used by permission of Viking Penguin, a division of Penguin Putnam, Inc.

"The Patchwork Quilt" from THE PATCHWORK QUILT by Valerie Flournoy, illustrations by Jerry Pinkney. Text copyright © 1985 by Valerie Flournoy. Illustrations copyright © 1985 by Jerry Pinkney. Published by arrangment Dial Books for Young Readers, a division of Penguin Putnam, Inc.

"Phoebe and the Spelling Bee" by Barney Saltzberg. Text and illustrations © 1996 by Barney Saltzberg. Reprinted by permission of Hyperion Books for Children.

Cover permission for RABBIT MAKES A MONKEY OUT OF LION by Verna Aardema; pictures by Jerry Pinkney. Pictures copyright © 1989 by Jerry Pinkney. Reprinted with the permission of Dial Books for Young Readers, a division of Penguin Books USA, Inc.

"The Sun, the Wind and the Rain" from THE SUN, THE WIND AND THE RAIN by Lisa Westberg Peters. Text copyright © 1988 by Lisa Westberg Peters. Illustrations copyright © 1988 by Ted Rand. Reprinted by permission of Henry Holt and Co., Inc.

Cover permission for TURTLE IN JULY by Marilyn Singer; illustrated by Jerry Pinckney. Illustrations copyright © 1989 by Jerry Pinckney. Reprinted with the permission of Atheneum Books for Young Readers, an imprint of Simon & Schuster.

"Who Am I?" by Felice Holman. Copyright © Felice Holman from AT THE TOP OF MY VOICE AND OTHER POEMS. Published by Charles Scribner's Sons, 1970.

"My Pencil" by Shirley R. Williams in POETRY PLACE ANTHOLOGY, published by Scholastic Professional Books. Copyright © 1983 by Edgell Communications, Inc. Reprinted with premission of Scholastic Inc.

Illustration

Myron Grossman, 105; B.B. Sams, 108–123; Pat Rasch, 107; Andy Levine, 171; Pat Rasch, 224; Vilma Ortiz–Dillon, 231, 234, 236; Mike DiGiorgio, 232, 237, 242; Andy Levine, 243; Mike DiGiorgio, 288; John Kanzler, 352–371; Leonor Glynn, 374; Tom Foty, 10–11 Marni Backer, 138–139 Greg Couch, 140–141 Christopher Zacharow, 254–255 Steve Barbaria, 256–257 Peter M. Fiore, 386–387; Rodica Prato, 391, 396, 407; George Thompson, 399.

Photography

12–13: The Bridgeman Art Library International/Christopher Wood Gallery, London UK. 48–49: Jane Wooster Scott/Superstock. 78–79: Art Resource, Inc./Herscovici. 50: t.l. Courtesy of Hyperion Press/Barry E. Levine, Inc. 106–107: The Norman Rockwell Museum at Stockbridge. 128–129: The Bridgeman Art Library International/Wingfield Sporting Gallery, London, UK. 135: Duomo./William Sallaz. 142–143: The Image Works/Cameramann. 172–173: The Bridgeman Art Library International/Bonhams, London, UK. 204–205: Art Resource, Inc./K.S. Art. 226–227: Madison Press Books. 228: m.l. Courtesy of Diane Hoyt–Goldsmith/Lawrence Migdale. 228–229: DRK Photo/(c) Tom Bean 1990. 230: DRK Photo/(c) Larry Ulrich. 231: Animals Animals/(c) Bill Beatty. 233: DRK Photo/(c) Stephen J. Kraseman. 236: Photo Researchers, Inc./(c) Scott Camazine. 238: ENP Images/(c) Gerry Ellis. 239: Photo Researchers, Inc./(c) Jewel Craig. 244–245: The Bridgeman Art Library International/Kathryn Kooyahoema/Jerry Jacka Photography. 250: b. Photo Researchers, Inc.. m. Photo Researchers, Inc. 258–259: Superstock/Gil Mayers. 260: t.r. reprinted by permission of Farrar, Straus and Giroux Books for Young Readers/(c) Daniel Lee. 318–319: Photo by William C.L. Weintraub for the Georgia Quilt Project, Inc. . 350–351: Gerald Peters Gallery, Santa Fe, New Mexico. . 376–377: Superstock. 383: Peter Arnold, Inc./(c) Kim Heacox.

"Paul Bunyan, the Mightiest Logger of Them All" from AMERICAN TALL TALES by Mary Pope Osborne. Copyright © 1991 by Mary Pope Osborne. Used by permission of Alfred A. Knopf, Inc.

"Pincushion Cactus" from WHISPERS AND OTHER POEMS by Myra Cohn Livingston. Copyright © 1958, 1986 by Myra Cohn Livingston. Used by permission of Marian Reiner for the author.

"The Rabbit's Tale" from THE DRAGON'S TALE AND OTHER ANIMAL FABLES OF THE CHINESE ZODIAC by Demi. Copyright © 1996 by Demi. Used by permission of Henry Holt and Company, Inc.

"Seeing the Animals" from NATIVE AMERI-CAN ANIMAL STORIES by Joseph Bruchac. Copyright © 1992 by Joseph Bruchac. Used by permission of Fulcrum Publishing.

"The Song of the World's Last Whale" words and music by Pete Seeger. Copyright © 1970, 1994 by Stormking Music Inc.

"Spider on the Floor" from RAFFI'S TOP 10 SONGS TO READ. Words and music by Bill Russell. Text copyright © 1976 by Egos Anonymous (PRO). Illustrations copyright © 1993 by True Kelley. Used by permission of Crown Publishers, Inc., a Random House company.

"Take a Bite Out of Music" from TAKE A BITE OUT OF MUSIC, IT'S YUMMY by Mary Ann Hall. Copyright © 1986 by Mary Ann Hall's Music for Children.

"Take Me Out to the Ballgame" words by Jack Norworth, music by Albert von Tilzer from GONNA SING MY HEAD OFF! Used by permission of Alfred A. Knopf.

"Toad's Trick" from TO RIDE A BUTTERFLY by Verna Aardema. Text copyright © 1991 by Verna Aardema. Illustrations copyright © 1991 by Will Hillenbrand. Used by permission of Bantam Doubleday Dell Publishing Group, Inc.

"Using Your Head" from JATAKA TALES edited by Nancy DeRoin. Text copyright © 1975 by Nancy DeRoin. Drawings copyright © 1975 by Ellen Lanyon. Used by permission of Houghton Mifflin Company.

"Whale" from THE RAUCOUS AUK by Mary Ann Hoberman. Copyright © 1973 by Mary Ann Hoberman. Used by permission of The Viking Press.

"Why Bears Have Short Tails" from AND IT IS STILL THAT WAY by Byrd Baylor. Copyright © 1976 by Byrd Baylor. Used by permission of Trails West Press.

"The Wind and the Sun" told by Margaret Hughes from AESOP'S FABLES. Copyright © 1979 by Albany Books. Used by permission of Chartwell Books Inc., a division of Book Sales Inc.

"The Wolf and His Shadow" from THE BEST OF AESOP'S FABLES retold by Margaret Clark. Text copyright © 1990 by Margaret Clark. Illustrations copyright © 1990 by Charlotte Voake. Used by permission of Little, Brown and Company.

Notes

Backmatter Contents

From the Bellybutton of the Moon
Del ombligo de la luna

Francisco X. Alarcón

1. cuando
digo
"México"

siento
en la cara
el mismo viento

que sentía
al abrir
la ventanilla

en mi primer
viaje al sur
en coche

veo
otra vez
Atoyac

el pueblo
donde se crió
mi madre

y yo pasé
vacaciones
de verano

oigo
voces
familiares

risas
saludos
despedidas

huelo
las gardenias
de mi abuela

whenever
I say
"Mexico"

I feel
the same wind
on my face

I felt when
I would open
the window

on my first
trip south
by car

I see
Atoyac
again

the town
where my mother
was raised

and I spent
summer
vacations

I hear
familiar
voices

laughter
greetings
farewells

I smell
my grandma's
gardenias

2. cuando
digo
"México"

oigo
a mi abuela
hablándome

de los aztecas
y de la ciudad
que fundaron

en una isla
en medio
de un lago

"México"
me dice
mi abuela

"significa:
del ombligo
de la luna"

"no olvides
tu origen
mijo"

quizás
por eso
mismo

cuando
ahora digo
"México"

quiero
tocarme
el ombligo

whenever
I say
"Mexico"

I hear
my grandma
telling me

about the Aztecs
and the city
they built

on an island
in the middle
of a lake

"Mexico"
says
my grandma

"means: from
the bellybutton
of the moon"

"don't forget
your origin
my son"

maybe
that's
why

whenver
I now say
"Mexico"

I feel
like touching
my bellybutton

The Wind and the Sun

a fable by Aesop
told by Margaret Hughes

The wind and the sun were arguing as to who was the stronger.

"I am," said the wind, blowing out his cheeks so hard that all the trees bent before him and men turned up the collars of their overcoats.

"There," he said to the sun, "I can make the trees bend. You can't do that. You just shine and people lie down and bask in the warmth."

"Well, then," said the sun, "if you're so sure, why don't we arrange a contest, then everyone will know which of us is the stronger."

"Good idea," said the wind. "See the traveller down below. Let's see which of us can make him take off his coat."

The sun agreed to the contest and told the wind to try first. The wind took a deep breath and blew and blew. A great storm came up and everything shook. But the traveller didn't take off his coat. Instead he drew it closer round him, gripping it tightly, trying to shut out the wind.

At last the wind was exhausted with blowing and he had to give up. Now it was the sun's turn. He appeared in the sky behind the storm clouds and slowly they drifted away, leaving the sky bright blue. The air grew warmer and warmer. The flowers opened up their blossoms. The birds hopped about the branches and the traveller loosened his coat, glad of the warmth of the sun. Higher and higher the sun rose, throwing out his heat, until the traveller found it too hot to walk. So he flung off his coat and carried it over his arm.

"There," said the sun to the wind, "admit I am stronger than you."

And the wind, knowing he was the loser, crept away to hide.

Moral: *Gentleness is more effective than force.*

The Wolf and His Shadow

a fable by Aesop
retold by Margaret Clark and Charlotte Voake

One day, when the sun was low in the sky, a wolf caught sight of an enormous shadow on the ground beside him. He looked all round, but there was no one else about.

"Why, that's *my* shadow," said the wolf. "What a wonderful animal I must be! I've never even seen another animal as big as that. The lion calls himself king, but he's not nearly as big as I am. I'm going to be king from now on."

So the wolf strutted about, thinking of all the things he would do now he was king. He was so busy thinking about himself, he didn't even notice the lion, who suddenly sprang on him and swallowed him whole.

As the lion licked his lips, he said, "What a silly wolf! Everyone knows that sometimes your shadow is big, sometimes it's small, and sometimes you have no shadow at all."

If I Find a Penny
Jeff Moss

If I find a penny
And give it to you,
That means we'll both
Have a wish come true.
A penny is like magic
Lying on the ground.
It's like picking up a wish
That's waiting to be found.

So when I find one,
I'll give you a penny.
And if we're lucky,
I'll give you many.
I'll pick up your penny,
Won't let the trashman sweep it.
But if I find a dollar . . .
I'll probably keep it.

Take Me Out to the Ball Game

Take me out to the ball game,
Take me out to the crowd.
Buy me some peanuts and Cracker Jack,
I don't care if I never come back.
And it's root, root, root for the home team,
If they don't win it's a shame.
For it's one, two, three strikes, "You're out!" at the
  old ball game.

Annotated Workbooks (vertical, left margin)

Practice 1

Name_____ Date_____

Story Elements

The **setting** is where and when a story takes place. The **characters** are the people the story is about.

Read the story. Then answer each question.

My name is Dawn. I live on a farm in New Jersey. Our farm has hills with apple trees. Every fall, the apples on our trees are ready to be picked.

Every fall, Grandmother María comes from Texas to visit us. Together, we make apple juice and apple pies. She tells me stories. My favorite stories are about my father when he was a boy.

"When your father was the same age as you, he rode horses," Grandmother María said.

"Where did he ride?" I asked.

"All over our ranch," Grandmother María said.

Then she told me that Texas was so big that a boy could ride all day and never see a house or a person. She said that instead of apple trees, my father saw cactus plants.

1. Where does Dawn live? **on a farm where apple trees grow**

2. Where is the farm? **in New Jersey**

3. When does Dawn pick apples? **in the fall**

4. Who are the three characters in the story? **Dawn, Grandmother María, Dawn's father**

5. Who is Grandmother María's story about? **Dawn's father when he was a boy**

6. Where is Grandmother María's story set? **on a ranch in Texas**

At Home: Have students make up a story about someone visiting them. Have them identify their story's characters and settings.
1

Practice 2

Name_____ Date_____

Vocabulary

Supply the correct words from the list.

scattered   enormous   towering   journey   surrounded   astonished

The long **journey** to the center of the desert was well worth it. Everything we saw there **astonished** us. It was all so different!

Wonders of nature **surrounded** our campsite in every direction. There were **enormous** sand drifts that seemed to sweep across the desert floor like huge tidal waves. Overhead were **towering** cliffs made of red and black sandstone.

The most amazing thing we saw was the tumbleweed **scattered** about the desert for miles and miles. Strong, warm winds whipped them into action. We marveled as they danced across the horizon.

At Home: Have students read the dictionary definitions for each of the vocabulary words.
Book 3.1/Unit 1
Grandfather's Journey 6

THE DREAM

I always remember my dreams. Usually they are about a *journey*. In last night's dream my journey was very strange. It *astonished* and amazed me.

In my dream, my bed was as *enormous* as a swimming pool. While I was in it, it rolled out of the house and onto the sidewalk. On the sidewalk there were many toys *scattered* under tall, *towering* trees.

I stopped my huge bed from rolling by grabbing one of the trees. Then I climbed down a giant ladder to get off my bed. On the ground, I was *surrounded* by the greatest toys I had ever seen in my life. What a dream!

1. How did the author feel about the dream?
   astonished, amazed
2. What types of dreams does the author best remember?
   dreams about a journey
3. What things are *scattered* in the dream?
   toys
4. What two words describe the size of things in this dream?
   towering, enormous
5. Why might the dreamer have been happy the bed rolled outside?
   There were great toys outside to play with.

At Home: Have students draw a picture of two things at home that are enormous.
 2A

Practice 3

Name_____ Date_____

Story Comprehension

Read each statement. Write **T** if the statement describes "Grandfather's Journey." Write **F** if the statement does not correctly describe "Grandfather's Journey."

1. **F** The grandfather first left Japan when he was an old man.

2. **T** Grandfather traveled to North America on his journey.

3. **T** Grandfather saw the desert on his trip to the New World.

4. **F** The grandfather explored North America by covered wagon.

5. **T** For part of his journey, Grandfather traveled by steamship.

6. **F** The grandfather liked Florida best.

7. **T** Grandfather returned to Japan to get married and because he was homesick.

8. **T** The grandson went to California because his grandfather had told him stories about the place.

9. **T** The grandfather, his new wife, and baby daughter lived in San Francisco.

10. **F** The grandson now lives in China.

At Home: Have students imagine a faraway place that they would like to visit. Have them write down reasons why they would like to go and things they would expect to find there.
Book 3.1/Unit 1
Grandfather's Journey 10

Grandfather's Journey • PRACTICE

Use Book Parts

The **author** and the **title** of a book appear on both the front cover and the side of the book, or **spine**.

Old Friends	Joe Parker
Victorian Porches	Selma Davidson
Painting Easter Eggs	Paula Brunst
COMPUTER REPAIR	Kathy Verang
Wigs and Hats	Rhonda Newcomb

Cooking with Woks	Li Woo
Kindergarten Art	Harry Waters
JUMP ROPE	Rhonda Newcomb
Bonsai Trees	Larry Larsen
Scary Stories	Paula Arnot

Use the stacks of books to answer these questions.

1. Who wrote a book about art in kindergarten? **Harry Waters**

2. What is the title of the book written by Joe Parker? **Old Friends**

3. If your computer was broken, which book would you need? **Computer Repair**

4. Who wrote more than one book in these piles? **Rhonda Newcomb**

5. What is the title of the book about cooking? **Cooking with Woks**

6. Who wrote Scary Stories? **Paula Arnot**

7. What is the name of the book that Larry Larsen wrote? **Bonsai Trees**

8. Which book did Paula Brunst write? **Painting Easter Eggs**

Story Elements

Grandfather is the main **character** in "Grandfather's Journey." Japan and North America are the **settings**, or places where the story happens. Answer the questions about the main character and settings in the chart below.

CHARACTER:	SETTINGS:
Grandfather	North America
1. Why does Grandfather leave Japan? **to see the world**	4. What does Grandfather like best about California? **sun, seacoast, mountains**
	Japan
2. What does Grandfather like best when he returns to Japan? **seeing old friends, seeing mountains and rivers**	5. Why does Grandfather decide not to build a house in his village? **He thinks a city is a better place for his daughter to grow up.**
3. What does Grandfather tell his grandson stories about? Why? **California; he misses it even though he is happy at home in Japan.**	6. Why does Grandfather spend the end of his life in his village? **War destroyed his home in the city.**

Make Predictions

You can use what you have learned about a character in a story to **predict** what this character might do. Read each story. Then answer the questions.

Tanisha is good at solving problems. She also likes taking care of her little brother. Last summer, Tanisha and her family went on a camping trip. One afternoon, Tanisha and her little brother got lost on the way from their tent to the car. Tanisha's brother became scared and started to cry.

1. Will the children find their way back to the tent? How do you know?

Yes; Tanisha is good at solving problems.

Tonight, Jerry has to finish a science project for school. Tomorrow is the science fair. They are giving prizes for the best project. Jerry would really like to win a prize. Tonight, Jerry's favorite TV show is on from eight o'clock to eight-thirty. Jerry has to go to bed at eight-thirty.

2. Will Jerry finish his science project? Why? **Yes; he wants to win a prize.**

3. When will Jerry work on his science project? **before his TV show**

Wendy lives in the country. The ocean is far away. Her favorite books are about boats. She dreams of sailing far and fast across the ocean.
Last summer, Wendy's father asked her to choose what they would do on their next summer trip.

4. What will Wendy and her father do on their next summer trip?

They will go sailing.

Compound Words

A **compound word** is a word that is made up of two smaller words. Each word in a compound word can stand alone.

brake + man = brakeman

Use the picture clues to write the compound word. The first part of the compound word appears below.

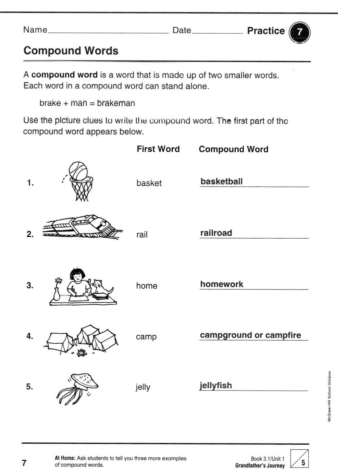

		First Word	Compound Word
1.		basket	**basketball**
2.		rail	**railroad**
3.		home	**homework**
4.		camp	**campground or campfire**
5.		jelly	**jellyfish**

Grandfather's Journey • RETEACH

Story Elements

> The main **character** is the person that a story is about. Identifying the **setting**, where and when a story takes place, will help you to understand what you are reading.

Read the stories below. Then write the name of the main character and the setting for each story.

> Pam was so happy. Her teacher, Mrs. Johnson, had asked her to be in the school play. Pam had always dreamed of being in a play. The whole school liked the play.

1. Main Character: Pam

2. Setting: Pam's school

> James wants to bake a birthday cake for his little sister. James goes to the store with his mother. They look for all the things James needs, such as eggs, sugar, butter, and apples.

3. Main Character: James

4. Setting: a store

> At home last night, my mom asked me, "What would you like to be when you grow up?"
> I told her, "I like painting best of all. One day I want to be a great artist, just like Grandfather. His paintings are even in museums!"

5. Main Character: the author

6. Setting: at home last night

Book 3.1/Unit 1
Grandfather's Journey

At Home: Have students make up names for two or three characters. Have them think of settings for stories involving these characters.

1

Name_____ Date_____ **Reteach** 2

Vocabulary

Read each clue. Then find the vocabulary word in the row of letters and circle it.

astonished   enormous   journey   scattered   surrounded   towering

1. surprised   p a s t o n i s h e d m z

2. spread out   s c a t t e r e d y w o s

3. trip   b s y j o u r n e y y j i

4. large   v i c p s e n o r m o u s

5. tall   i t o w e r i n g o a t s

6. circled   b e s u r r o u n d e d z

6

Story Comprehension   **Reteach** 3

Write a ✔ next to every sentence that tells about "Grandfather's Journey."

✔ 1. Grandfather leaves Japan to see the world.

___ 2. Grandfather wants to live near farms and factories in North America.

✔ 3. Grandfather brings his wife and daughter to live in Japan.

✔ 4. The grandson learns about California from Grandfather.

✔ 5. A war prevents Grandfather from visiting California again.

✔ 6. California and Japan both feel like home to the grandson.

2–3
At Home: Have students make up two more sentences that describe "Grandfather's Journey."

Book 3.1/Unit 1
Grandfather's Journey
6

Name_____ Date_____ **Reteach** 4

Use Book Parts

> A **table of contents** is a guide to what is inside a book. Most books are broken down into chapters. The table of contents also shows you the page numbers of the chapters.

In a book about a trip, the table of contents could show you where the author has traveled.

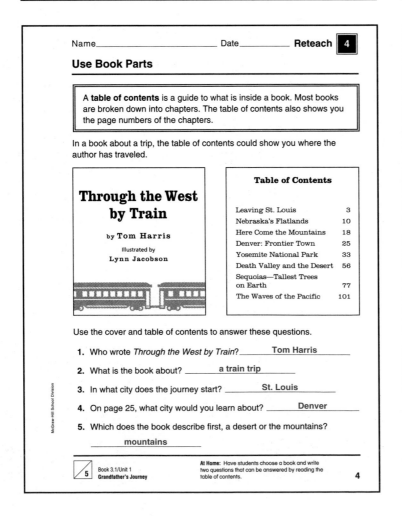

Through the West by Train

by Tom Harris

Illustrated by Lynn Jacobson

Table of Contents

Use the cover and table of contents to answer these questions.

1. Who wrote *Through the West by Train*? Tom Harris

2. What is the book about? a train trip

3. In what city does the journey start? St. Louis

4. On page 25, what city would you learn about? Denver

5. Which does the book describe first, a desert or the mountains?
   mountains

Book 3.1/Unit 1
Grandfather's Journey

At Home: Have students choose a book and write two questions that can be answered by reading the table of contents.

4

Name_____ Date_____ **Reteach** 5

Story Elements

> **Characters** are *who* a story is about. The **setting** tells *where* and *when* a story happens.

Here are some of the settings from "Grandfather's Journey." Put things that Grandfather saw in Japan in the left box. Put things that he saw in North America in the right box. Put things that he saw in both Japan and North America in the middle.

villages   rivers   mountains   deserts   cities   farm fields

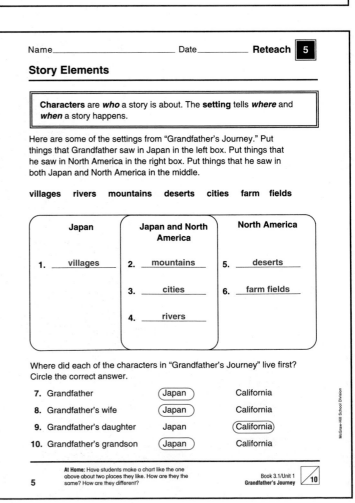

Japan	Japan and North America	North America
1. villages	2. mountains	5. deserts
	3. cities	6. farm fields
	4. rivers	

Where did each of the characters in "Grandfather's Journey" live first? Circle the correct answer.

7. Grandfather   (Japan)   California

8. Grandfather's wife   (Japan)   California

9. Grandfather's daughter   Japan   (California)

10. Grandfather's grandson   (Japan)   California

5
At Home: Have students make a chart like the one above about two places they like. How are they the same? How are they different?

Book 3.1/Unit 1
Grandfather's Journey
10

T8   *Annotated Workbooks*

Grandfather's Journey • RETEACH

Make Predictions

> You can use what you know about story characters to **predict** what the characters would do in other situations.

Read the story below. Then make predictions about what will happen next. Write your answers on the lines. **Answers will vary.**

> Cassie liked helping her mother take care of the yard. Her mother knew that Cassie shared her love of yard work. Today, though, Cassie had to help her brother James finish his geography project. Cassie looked out the window and could see her mother weeding. She wanted to be outside. James was becoming impatient. Cassie wasn't paying attention.
>
> Just then, their father came home from work. "Hi, kids!" he said. "What's that you're doing? Do you need any help?"

1. How do you think Cassie will answer her father's question?

She will probably ask her father if he would help James.

2. How do you think James will answer his father's question?

He will probably ask his father to help him.

3. Do you think that Cassie will stay inside and continue to help James? Explain why or why not. **Since she likes to work in the yard, she will probably let her father help James while she goes outside.**

4. How do you think the yard will look after Cassie's mother is finished working? Explain your answer. **It will look neat and pretty because Cassie's mother takes pride in her yard.**

5. Do you think James and his father will help with the yard work? Why or why not? **No; James needs help on his project.**

At Home: Have students make another prediction about the story.

Compound Words

> When two words are put together to make one word, the bigger word is called a **compound word**. Use the meaning of each of the smaller words to help you figure out the meaning of the compound word.

Look at the compound words below. Write the two smaller words that make up each compound word. Then write the meaning of the compound word.

backyard

1. _____back_____   **2.** _____yard_____

3. the yard in the back

sunlight

4. _____sun_____   **5.** _____light_____

6. light from the sun

grandfather

7. _____grand_____   **8.** _____father_____

9. the father of one's father or mother

riverboat

10. _____river_____   **11.** _____boat_____

12. a boat that travels on a river

homesick

13. _____home_____   **14.** _____sick_____

15. missing home

16. Now write a compound word that you know. **Answers will vary.**

At Home: Ask students to name the words in the compound words *baseball, blueberry,* and *homemade.*

T9

Grandfather's Journey • EXTEND

Story Elements

Think about one of your favorite stories. What character do you remember the most? (*Characters* are the people in a story.) **Where did the story take place?** (The *setting* is where and when the story takes place.)

Write a paragraph about your favorite character. How did the character look? What important action did he or she perform in the story? What makes your character special? What did your character do to make it a good story? Where and when did the story take place? Did the time or place matter? Why or why not?

_____

_____

_____

_____

_____

Act out your character to see if your classmates can guess who the character is and where the story happens. (To do this activity, remember to act out a well-known story and character.) Take a cat stuck in a tree for example. How would you act out the ways it gets into mischief? (Obviously, it is because the cat is curious, but how would you show its actions?) What if your character is feeling fear or anger? How would you show these feelings?

_____

_____

_____

_____

Book 3.1/Unit 1
Grandfather's Journey

At Home: Take a favorite story or stories and discuss the illustrations that best show the characters acting in important settings.

1

Vocabulary

astonished	enormous	journey
scattered	surrounded	towering

Imagine you're far from home in a place of your choice. Write a letter home using some of the words in the box. Remember to include details about the places you are seeing.

Extend 3

Story Comprehension

Grandfather's Journey

Work with a partner. Choose a setting from "Grandfather's Journey." Draw one detail about the setting. Then choose a title for your illustration.

At Home: Draw a timeline together tracing some of the main events in Grandfather's life.

2–3

Book 3.1/Unit 1
Grandfather's Journey

Use Book Parts

Suppose you wanted to write a book about holidays in the United States. There are several ways you could organize your book into chapters. One way would be to have a chapter for each holiday. Think of other ways your book could be organized, and write them below.

_____**Answers will vary. Some possibilities are by season, by month, by**_____

_____**national holidays and state holidays.**_____

Now use your method of organization to make a sample table of contents for your book. Use another sheet of paper if you need more room.

Holidays in the United States
Table of Contents

_____

_____

_____

_____

_____

_____

_____

_____

Book 3.1/Unit 1
Grandfather's Journey

At Home: Read through the table of contents of a book. Then quiz each other on the information that can be found in the book, and how that information is organized.

4

Story Elements

The author wrote about his grandfather as if he had interviewed him for a long time. He had many details to put into his story.

Interview three people who you know and who have traveled. Ask each person to name a place and tell you something each remembers about the trip. Take notes on each person in the space provided below.

_____ _____ _____

_____ _____ _____

_____ _____ _____

_____ _____ _____

_____ _____ _____

_____ _____ _____

_____ _____ _____

Write about one of these places that you would also like to visit and tell why.

_____

_____

_____

_____

_____

5

At Home: Discuss the difference in reading books in a series and watching a weekly TV show. Ask: How do you get to know the characters? Are they always the same? How do the authors and producers make them different in each book or show?

Book 3.1/Unit 1
Grandfather's Journey

Grandfather's Journey • EXTEND

Make Predictions

Some things that happen can change everyone's life. In "Grandfather's Journey," the war started. "Bombs fell from the sky and scattered our lives like leaves in a storm." Write what you think might have happened to the author and his grandfather if the war had not started.

_____

Answers will vary. Some students may predict that Allen Say and his

grandfather journeyed to California again.

Would you guess that the author of the story would feel the same way about journeys that his grandfather did? Why or why not?

_____

_____

Some may indicate that because they both took a trip away from their

homeland, they would feel the same way.

Book 3.1/Unit 1
Grandfather's Journey

At Home: Have students make predictions about what they might do next Saturday.

6

Compound Words

Compound words are made by putting two words together. The words *basket* and *ball* make the word basketball.

Use the words below to write as many new compound words as you can.

grand	steam	sick	river	sea	father	ship
boat	coast	land	end	parent	home	week

Suggested responses:

grandfather	homeland
steamship	weekend
riverboat	grandparent
seacoast	homesick
	steamboat

Choose some of these compound words and write a story about someone you know who has gone on a journey.

_____

_____

_____

_____

_____

Create a class compound word chart. Display it in the classroom. Add words to the chart during the year.

At Home: Ask students to think of compound words that will have something to do with what they will do that day.

7

Book 3.1/Unit 1
Grandfather's Journey

Grandfather's Journey • GRAMMAR

What Is a Sentence?

> • A **sentence** is a group of words that tells a complete thought.
> • Every sentence begins with a capital letter.
> Sentence: *My grandfather walked for days.*
> Not a sentence: *Walked for days.*

Write **yes** if the words make a sentence. Write **no** if they do not.

1. My grandfather was born in Japan. _____yes_____
2. He came to America on a ship. _____yes_____
3. He married and lived in California. _____yes_____
4. Land of sunlight and sea. _____no_____
5. Homesick for Japan. _____no_____
6. He moved his family to Japan. _____yes_____
7. Mountains and rivers of his childhood. _____no_____
8. Laughed with old friends. _____no_____
9. He raised songbirds. _____yes_____
10. Missed California. _____no_____

Extension: Have students write three sentences about their family.

1

Statements and Questions

> • A **statement** is a sentence that tells something. It ends with a period.
> • A **question** is a sentence that asks something. It ends with a question mark.
> Statement: *My grandfather liked to travel.*
> Question: *Do you like to travel?*

Write **statement** if the sentence tells something. Write **question** if the sentence asks something. Put the correct end mark at the end of the sentence.

1. My grandfather's ship crossed an ocean. _____statement_____
2. Have you seen an ocean? _____question_____
3. Is an ocean deep? _____question_____
4. My grandfather explored America. _____statement_____
5. He saw huge cities. _____statement_____
6. Do you know how many people live in cities? _____question_____
7. Where is San Francisco Bay? _____question_____
8. My grandfather missed Japan. _____statement_____
9. There are rivers in Japan. _____statement_____
10. Are there mountains in Japan? _____question_____

Extension: Have students work in pairs. Ask each student to write a question about the story. Then have them write a statement to answer each other's question.

Writing Statements and Questions

> • A **statement** is a sentence that tells something. It ends with a period.
> • A **question** is a sentence that asks something. It ends with a question mark.
> Statement: *My grandfather liked to travel.*
> Question: *Do you like to travel?*

After each sentence, write **statement** or **question** for the kind of sentence it is. Then write the sentence correctly. Use capital letters and end marks.

1. many people live in cities _____statement_____
   Many people live in cities.
2. the cities are run by electricity _____statement_____
   The cities are run by electricity.
3. electricity lights houses and streets _____statement_____
   Electricity lights houses and streets.
4. what is it like when the electricity goes out _____question_____
   What is it like when the electricity goes out?
5. if it's at night, the whole city is dark _____statement_____
   If it's at night, the whole city is dark.
6. your home seems like a different place _____statement_____
   Your home seems like a different place.
7. has that ever happened to you _____question_____
   Has that ever happened to you?
8. were you ever in a city with no lights at night _____question_____
   Were you ever in a city with no lights at night?

Extension: Have pairs of students choose a subject and take turns making up statements and questions about it. The student who is listening tells what kind of sentence is given.

3

Using Capital Letters and End Marks

> • Every sentence begins with a capital letter.
> • A statement ends with a period.
> • A question ends with a question mark.

Correct each sentence. Write the capital letter over the small letter. Add the end mark.

1. i think our country is beautiful _.__ (I)
2. would you like to travel across our country _?__ (W)
3. i've never seen a desert _.__ (I)
4. have you ever seen one _?__ (H)
5. a desert is cold at night _.__ (A)
6. is it cold during the day _?__ (I)
7. where are the mountains in our country _?__ (W)
8. some mountains have snow on the top _.__ (S)
9. our country has many rivers _.__ (O)
10. do you live near a river _?__ (D)

Extension: Have pairs of students look through magazines to find examples of the two kinds of end marks. Have students copy an example of each.

T12 *Annotated Workbooks*

Grandfather's Journey • GRAMMAR

Statements and Questions

A. Read each group of words. Write **yes** if the group of words forms a sentence. Write **no** if it does not form a sentence.

1. I like to visit my grandfather. ____yes____

2. Raised warblers and silvereyes. ____no____

3. He could not forget California. ____yes____

4. Never returned to California. ____no____

B. Decide if the sentence is a statement or a question. Write your answer on the line.

5. My grandfather moved back to Japan ____statement____

6. Where did he buy a house ____question____

7. When did his daughter marry ____question____

8. There was a war ____statement____

9. After the war, his house was gone ____statement____

10. Did Grandfather get another songbird ____question____

Statements and Questions

- A sentence is a group of words that tells a complete thought.
- A statement is a sentence that tells something.
- A question is a sentence that asks something.

Mechanics:
- Begin every sentence with a capital letter.
- End a statement with a period.
- End a question with a question mark.

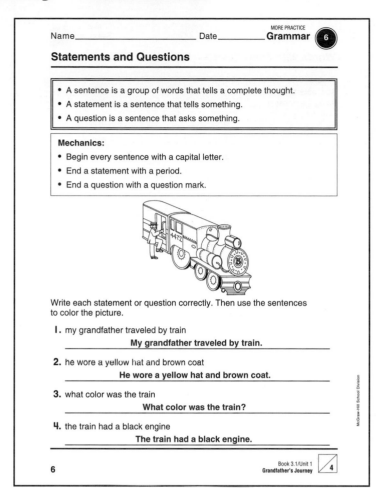

Write each statement or question correctly. Then use the sentences to color the picture.

1. my grandfather traveled by train

    My grandfather traveled by train.

2. he wore a yellow hat and brown coat

    He wore a yellow hat and brown coat.

3. what color was the train

    What color was the train?

4. the train had a black engine

    The train had a black engine.

Grandfather's Journey • SPELLING

Words with Short Vowels

Pretest Directions

Fold back the paper along the dotted line. Use the blanks to write each word as it is read aloud. When you finish the test, unfold the paper. Use the list at the right to correct any spelling mistakes. Practice the words you missed for the Posttest.

To Parents

Here are the results of your child's weekly spelling Pretest. You can help your child study for the Posttest by following these simple steps for each word on the word list:

1. Read the word to your child.
2. Have your child write the word, saying each letter as it is written.
3. Say each letter of the word as your child checks the spelling.
4. If a mistake has been made, have your child read each letter of the correctly spelled word aloud, and then repeat steps 1-3.

1. _____	1. leg
2. _____	2. black
3. _____	3. much
4. _____	4. bag
5. _____	5. rocks
6. _____	6. kept
7. _____	7. hid
8. _____	8. window
9. _____	9. van
10. _____	10. mix
11. _____	11. rub
12. _____	12. ever
13. _____	13. buzz
14. _____	14. body
15. _____	15. thing

Challenge Words

_____ astonished
_____ enormous
_____ journey
_____ scattered
_____ surrounded

Words with Short Vowels

Using the Word Study Steps

1. LOOK at the word.
2. SAY the word aloud.
3. STUDY the letters in the word.
4. WRITE the word.
5. CHECK the word.
   Did you spell the word right? If not, go back to step 1.

Spelling Tip

Short vowel sounds are usually spelled with one letter.
Examples:
beg   sag   lid

Find Rhyming Words

Circle the word in each row that rhymes with the word in dark type.

1.	beg	rag	(leg)	bog
2.	rack	sick	block	(black)
3.	such	each	(much)	lunch
4.	sag	sat	big	(bag)
5.	clocks	(rocks)	cracks	clucks
6.	wept	wiped	left	(kept)
7.	lid	lad	lied	(hid)
8.	window	(doe)	do	drew
9.	man	men	(van)	vend
10.	six	sit	box	(mix)
11.	scrub	(rub)	rob	describe
12.	clever	deer	(ever)	clover
13.	fuzz	furs	fizz	(buzz)
14.	anybody	(nobody)	copy	anyone
15.	ring	rang	(thing)	clung

To Parents or Helpers:

Using the Word Study Steps above as your child comes across any new words will help him or her spell well. Review the steps as you both go over this week's spelling words.

Go over the Spelling Tip with your child. Ask him or her to find words with short vowel sounds and point out the letter that makes the vowel sound in each word. Help your child complete the spelling activity.

Words with Short Vowels

leg	bag	hid	mix	buzz
black	rocks	window	rub	body
much	kept	van	ever	thing

Rhyme Time

Write the spelling words that rhyme with the words below. Then circle the letter that spells the short-vowel sound in each word.

1. did ___hid___
2. slept ___kept___
3. fix ___mix___
4. fuzz ___buzz___
5. peg ___leg___
6. swing ___thing___
7. tag ___bag___
8. shrub ___rub___
9. tack ___black___
10. can ___van___

Vowel Power

Write the spelling words that contain each short vowel sound below.

Short a

11. ___black___   12. ___bag___   13. ___van___

Short e

14. ___leg___   15. ___kept___   16. ___ever___

Short i

17. ___hid___   18. ___window___   19. ___mix___
20. ___thing___

Short o

21. ___rocks___   22. ___body___

Short u

23. ___much___   24. ___rub___   25. ___buzz___

Words with Short Vowels

leg	bag	hid	mix	buzz
black	rocks	window	rub	body
much	kept	van	ever	thing

What's the Word?

Complete each sentence with a spelling word.

1. The ___black___ spider crawled slowly along the wall.
2. Crickets ___rub___ their front wings together to chirp.
3. The humming sound of a bee is a ___buzz___.
4. Dad hurt his ___leg___ and could not walk.
5. When our dog ___hid___ the bone, I found it under a pillow.
6. I opened a ___bag___ of chips for the party.
7. I can't do one more ___thing___ today.
8. The dress didn't fit the doll's ___body___.
9. Mom ___kept___ our drawings in a box.
10. We washed the ___window___ with a glass cleaner.

Define It!

Write the spelling words that have the same meanings as the words or phrases below.

11. a kind of truck ___van___
12. always ___ever___
13. a great amount ___much___
14. stir together ___mix___
15. stones ___rocks___

Grandfather's Journey • SPELLING

Words with Short Vowels

Proofreading

There are six spelling mistakes in this visitor's guide to the zoo. Circle the misspelled words. Write the words correctly on the lines below.

A zoo is a (winndow) to the animal kingdom. If you wonder how wild animals live, visit the zoo. Come by bus, car, (vann,) or train. Remember this: these animals are not pets.

Follow these safety rules. Don't throw (roks) at the birds. Don't put your arm or (legg) through a bar of a cage. A dangerous animal might be (cept) there. Don't pet the animals.

There is a lot you can do at the zoo. Watch the seals play in the water. See a (blak) bear. Have fun!

1.	window	2.	van	3.	rocks
4.	leg	5.	kept	6.	black

Writing Activity

Write a postcard to a friend describing the zoo. Use at least four spelling words in your description.

_____

_____

_____

_____

_____

_____

Words with Short Vowels

Look at the words in each set. One word in each set is spelled correctly. Use a pencil to color in the circle in front of that word. Before you begin, look at the sample sets of words. Sample A has been done for you. Do Sample B by yourself. When you are sure you know what to do, you may go on with the rest of the page.

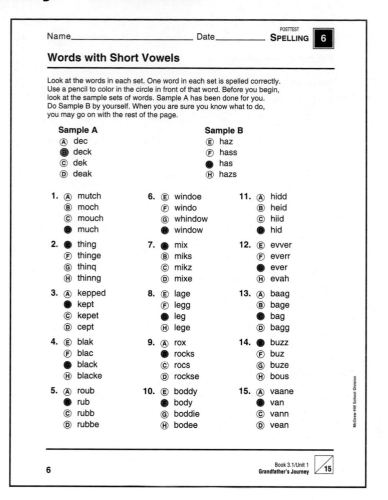

Sample A
- Ⓐ dec
- ● deck
- Ⓒ dek
- Ⓓ deak

Sample B
- Ⓔ haz
- Ⓕ hass
- ● has
- Ⓗ hazs

1.
- Ⓐ mutch
- Ⓑ moch
- Ⓒ mouch
- ● much

2.
- ● thing
- Ⓕ thinge
- Ⓖ thinq
- Ⓗ thinng

3.
- Ⓐ kepped
- ● kept
- Ⓒ kepet
- Ⓓ cept

4.
- Ⓔ blak
- Ⓕ blac
- ● black
- Ⓗ blacke

5.
- Ⓐ roub
- ● rub
- Ⓒ rubb
- Ⓓ rubbe

6.
- Ⓔ windoe
- Ⓕ windo
- Ⓖ whindow
- ● window

7.
- ● mix
- Ⓑ miks
- Ⓒ mikz
- Ⓓ mixe

8.
- Ⓔ lage
- Ⓕ legg
- ● leg
- Ⓗ lege

9.
- Ⓐ rox
- ● rocks
- Ⓒ rocs
- Ⓓ rockse

10.
- Ⓔ boddy
- ● body
- Ⓖ boddie
- Ⓗ bodee

11.
- Ⓐ hidd
- Ⓑ heid
- Ⓒ hiid
- ● hid

12.
- Ⓔ evver
- Ⓕ everr
- ● ever
- Ⓗ evah

13.
- Ⓐ baag
- Ⓑ bage
- ● bag
- Ⓓ bagg

14.
- ● buzz
- Ⓕ buz
- Ⓖ buze
- Ⓗ bous

15.
- Ⓐ vaane
- ● van
- Ⓒ vann
- Ⓓ vean

Phoebe and the Spelling Bee • PRACTICE

Problem and Solution

The answer you find to a **problem** is called the **solution**.

Draw a line between the problem and its matching solution.

Problem	Solution

1. There is a lot of snow on the ground.

a. My mother will bring the bike to a bike shop.

2. My baby sister was crying.

b. My dad bought a big umbrella for us to sit under.

3. My bike has a flat tire.

c. I wear my boots to school.

4. Our babysitter is on a trip, and my parents are going out on Friday night.

d. Mom helps me get dressed in the morning.

5. My dad has no time to paint the house.

e. We replaced the glass.

6. We can't sit in our backyard because it's too hot.

f. I rocked the baby to sleep.

7. I broke my arm, and I can't button my shirt.

g. My grandparents offer to spend the weekend.

8. My brother broke a window.

h. He hires a painter.

At Home: Have students write another problem and solution pair.

Vocabulary

Write a vocabulary word from the list that means almost the same thing as the underlined words.

> legend   correct   groaning   unusual   continue   embarrass

1. Do you think an octopus is a <u>strange</u> and ____**unusual**____ animal?

2. We were <u>right</u>, she gave us the ____**correct**____ answer.

3. Spilling milk in front of twenty people might <u>shame</u> or ____**embarrass**____ you.

4. A ____**legend**____ and a <u>folk tale</u> are similar kinds of stories.

5. The bear held its injured paw and started <u>moaning</u> and ____**groaning**____ in pain.

6. Keep going, ____**continue**____ to the next green light.

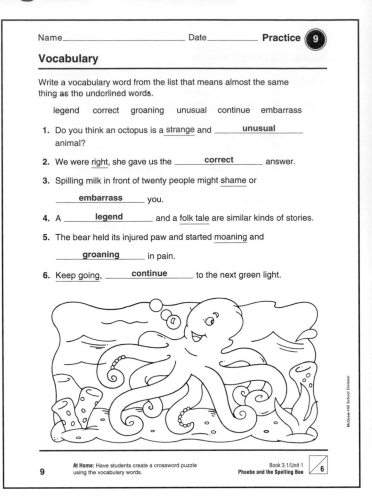

At Home: Have students create a crossword puzzle using the vocabulary words.

Eric and the Happy Answer

Once there was a boy named Eric. Eric liked to be *correct*. If his teacher said he was doing something the wrong way, Eric would still *continue*. "I would *embarrass* myself if I said I had been wrong," he thought.

One day Eric's teacher heard him *groaning* at his desk. "Why are you making such an *unusual* sound?" she asked. "You sound like a strange creature in a *legend* or tall tale."

"I don't want to think I'm always right," Eric said. "Next time I'm doing something wrong will you help me do it right?"

"Of course!" the teacher replied.

From that day on, things changed for Eric.

1. Who always thought he had to be *correct*?

   <u>Eric</u>

2. What was Eric afraid he would do if he said he was wrong?

   <u>embarrass himself</u>

3. What *unusual* thing did his teacher hear Eric doing?

   <u>groaning</u>

4. What did Eric sound like when he was *groaning*?

   <u>a creature in a legend</u>

5. Why did things change for Eric?

   <u>He decided he would ask his teacher for help.</u>

At Home: Have students write about a time they asked for help. Were they afraid to ask? Were they happy they did?

Story Comprehension

Answer the questions about "Phoebe and the Spelling Bee."

1. Why is Phoebe afraid of Friday? <u>Phoebe is afraid because Mrs. Ravioli has planned a spelling bee.</u>

2. Why does Phoebe pretend to be sick at school? <u>She hasn't studied her spelling words.</u>

3. How is Katie different from her friend Phoebe? <u>Katie likes spelling, and she is not afraid of the spelling bee.</u>

4. How does Phoebe upset Katie? <u>Phoebe lied to her and the class.</u>

5. How does Phoebe make up for what she does to Katie? <u>She gives Katie a tulip and studies hard for the spelling bee.</u>

6. Why do Phoebe and Katie get certificates? <u>Katie gets her certificate for good spelling. Phoebe gets hers for good imagination.</u>

At Home: Have students choose a word they find difficult to spell. Then have them make a sign that gives a spelling tip for that word. Post the signs in a place where everyone can see them.

Phoebe and the Spelling Bee • PRACTICE

Use a Glossary

A **glossary** is a list of words and definitions for a specific book.

124 Shetland pony–Stomp

Shetland pony (noun) 1. a small-built pony of a breed that came from the Shetland Islands
shortchange (verb) 1. to give less money back than is owed 2. to cheat or trick
shoe (noun) 1. a covering for the foot 2. a piece of metal for a horse's foot
slouch (verb) 1. to sit with an awkward, drooping posture
snake oil (noun) 1. a worthless preparation sold as medicine
sofa bed (noun) 1. a couch that unfolds into a bed
son (noun) 1. a male child
springer spaniel (noun) 1. a dog having drooping ears and a silky brown and white coat
stomachache (noun) 1. a pain in the belly

Use the part of a glossary page above to answer these questions.

1. Is *stomachache* a noun, verb, adverb, or adjective? __noun__

2. What word comes after *shoe* in this glossary? __slouch__

3. To find the definition of the word *stories*, would you look before or after this page in the glossary? Explain. __after — "story" comes after__ __"stomp" (the second guide word for this page) in alphabetical order.__

4. What are the guide words for the page on which *son* appears?
   __Shetland pony, stomp__

5. Pretend you saw the word *shoe* in a story about an animal who can't walk because of sore feet. Which of the two definitions shown in the glossary would apply? Write that definition. __2. a piece of metal__ __for a horse's foot__

5 Book 3.1/Unit 1
Phoebe and the Spelling Bee

At Home: Ask students to think of another word that would fall between the guide words on this glossary page.

11

Problem and Solution

One subject in school presents **problems** for the main character in "Phoebe and the Spelling Bee." Read each problem in the chart below. Then write the solution Phoebe finds for the problem.

Problem	Solution
1. Phoebe needs to learn how to spell **actor** correctly.	1. **She thinks of the word act and or in a sentence.**
2. On Tuesday, Mrs. Ravioli asks Phoebe if she's looked at the spelling list yet. Phoebe has not spent a lot of time on spelling.	2. **Phoebe shares a sentence with the class that shows that she has at least read the words.**
3. Mrs. Ravioli gives a practice spelling bee, and Phoebe is not ready for it.	3. **Phoebe pretends she is sick and goes to the nurse's office.**
4. Katie is mad at Phoebe for lying to her.	4. **Phoebe brings Katie a tulip and says she is sorry.**
5. Phoebe wants to learn how to spell the word **method**.	5. **She makes up a story about a caveman whose name is Me, Thod.**
6. Phoebe misspells the word **brontosaurus**.	6. **She shares her spelling stories with the class, and everyone enjoys them.**

12 At Home: Have students use Phoebe's spelling techniques. Have them write stories to help them remember this week's spelling words.

Book 3.1/Unit 1
Phoebe and the Spelling Bee 6

Make Predictions

What you learn in a story can help you **predict** what will happen next. Read each story. Then answer the questions.

Mrs. Miller is ninety years old. She lives alone in a small house. Three children live next door to Mrs. Miller. Every Saturday they visit her. Sometimes they help her do things around the house. Lately, Mrs. Miller has been feeling a little tired. She has not been able to rake the leaves or weed her garden.

1. What might happen the next time the children visit Mrs. Miller?
   They will help her take care of her yard.

2. What parts of the story helped you make your prediction? **The children live next door; they visit Mrs. Miller; they help her do things around the house.**

Elaine and Michael found soda cans all over the sidewalk. They thought the cans made the street look messy. So they began collecting the cans. Elaine's father told the children about a new store down the block that bought soda cans for a nickel each.

3. What do you think might happen next in the story? **Elaine and Michael will take the cans they collected, bring them to the store, and earn money.**

4. What parts of the story helped you make your prediction? **The children were collecting the cans. A store down the street buys soda cans.**

4 Book 3.1/Unit 1
Phoebe and the Spelling Bee

At Home: The next time students begin a TV program or a book, ask them to predict an outcome. Have them write down their prediction, and then check it when they find out the outcome.

13

Prefixes

A **prefix** is a word part that can be added to the beginning of a word. It creates a new word with its own meaning. The prefix **un-** means "not," or "opposite of." For example, the word **unfair** means "not fair" or "the opposite of fair."

Below each sentence, write the word that includes the prefix **un-**. Then write the meaning of the word.

1. It was unlucky that Mona was sick on the first day of vacation.
   unlucky—not lucky

2. The story has an unusual character named Simon.
   unusual—not usual, different

3. The movie was very interesting, even though it was untrue.
   untrue—not true, false

4. It took the child a long time to unwrap her birthday present.
   unwrap—take off wrapping

5. The number of stars in the sky is unknown.
   unknown—not known

6. Jack was unhappy that he did not get a better score in the game.
   unhappy—not happy

14 At Home: Ask students to name three other words that begin with the prefix un-.

Book 3.1/Unit 1
Phoebe and the Spelling Bee 6

Phoebe and the Spelling Bee • RETEACH

Problem and Solution

Sometimes a character in a story has some trouble, or a question that needs to be answered. This is called a **problem**. The answer to the problem is called the **solution**.

Read the story below. Then answer the questions.

Margo had a problem. She had one day to get things ready for her party. There was not enough time for her to do everything herself.

Margo thought about what she needed to do. She began by making a list. Her finished list had ten things on it.

Then she called nine of her friends who would be at the party. She asked each person to help her. Everyone said "Yes!" Now all Margo had to do for her party was bake a cake.

1. What is the problem? **Margo has too much to do and not enough time to do it.**

2. What does Margo do first to solve her problem? **She makes a list of all the things she needs to do.**

3. What does Margo do next to solve her problem? **She calls nine friends and asks each of them to do one thing for her.**

4. How is the problem finally solved? **Each friend agrees to do one thing.**

5. Do you think Margo's solution was a good one? **Possible answer: Yes, it gave her time to bake a cake.**

At Home: Have students draw pictures of a character, and make up a story in which the character has a problem. Then challenge students to think of solutions to this problem.

Vocabulary

Use the correct word from the list.

continue   correct   embarrass   groaning   legend   unusual

1. The story was very ___unusual___. But it wasn't a tall tale or a ___legend___. It was a true story!

2. I don't know the ___correct___ way to spell your name. Let me ___continue___ thinking about it.

3. My little cousin kept making these ___groaning___ sounds. Everyone was laughing! I told him that he didn't ___embarrass___ me at all!

/6

Story Comprehension   Reteach 10

1. How does Phoebe avoid studying for the spelling bee? **Possible answers: by pretending to be sick, hiding, playing**

2. How does Phoebe remember the spelling of difficult words? **She breaks up the words and makes up stories about them.**

3. How does Phoebe remember how to spell *legend*? **She thinks of a leg and end.**

4. How does Phoebe probably feel after the spelling bee? **Possible answers: She is proud of herself; she is happy.**

At Home: Have students write a paragraph about the way they remember how to spell a word.

Use a Glossary

A **glossary** is like a dictionary in the back of a book. It gives definitions for words in that book.

Komodo dragon (noun) A large monitor lizard that lives on islands off the coast of Indonesia. A full-grown Komodo dragon is more than 10 feet long. Komodo dragons dig caves that they spend the night in. A female Komodo dragon can lay about 28 eggs at one time.

Use the sample glossary to help you answer the questions below.

1. If you need to know what a Komodo dragon is, would you look in the book's glossary or the table of contents? ___glossary___

2. Is **Komodo dragon** a noun or a verb? ___noun___

3. How many words make up the name of this animal? What are the words? ___two: Komodo and dragon___

4. What kind of a lizard is a Komodo dragon? ___monitor___

5. Where do Komodo dragons spend the night? ___in caves that they have dug___

6. How many eggs can a female Komodo dragon lay at one time? ___about 28___

At Home: Have students copy two glossary listings from a book of their choice. Then have them write one question about the glossary listings.

Problem and Solution

A **problem** is the difficulty or challenge that a character in a story faces. The **solution** is the way in which a character solves his or her problem.

Read the stories below. Then write the problem and the solution for each of the stories.

Three friends are at a picnic. Josie has only one piece of cake. Kim and Rosa didn't bring dessert to the picnic. Josie has an idea. She breaks her cake into three pieces. Now everyone can have dessert!

PROBLEM: **There is only one piece of cake.**

SOLUTION: **Josie breaks the cake into three pieces, so everyone can have dessert.**

There are twelve students. All of them want to be on the tennis team. Mr. Danforth needs only six players on the team. He would like everyone to get the chance to play. Finally, he decides to create two teams.

PROBLEM: **Mr. Danforth needs only six players on the tennis team. Twelve students want to be on the team.**

SOLUTION: **Mr. Danforth decides to create two tennis teams.**

At Home: Invite students to name an important problem a character faces in a movie they know. Have them explain how the problem is solved.

Phoebe and the Spelling Bee • RETEACH

Make Predictions

When you guess what happens next, you are making a **prediction**.

Read the sentences. Then circle the prediction you think is most likely to happen.

1. Jill is hungry. What do you think Jill will do when she gets home?

    a. take a nap

    (b.) make herself something to eat

    c. watch TV

2. The store had been busy all week. By Friday night there was nothing left in the store to sell. What do you think the store might do on Saturday?

    (a.) stay closed

    b. have a sale

    c. give away free gifts

3. Phillip and Steven are brothers. The boys will have to share a bedroom. But the room is too small for two beds. What do you think the boys' parents will do?

    a. buy a different house

    b. have the brothers take turns sleeping

    (c.) buy bunk beds for the brothers

4. Carol loves milk. She also likes anything that is made with milk. On Tuesday morning, Carol's mother asked her what she wanted for breakfast. What do you think Carol chose?

    (a.) yogurt   **b.** toast   **c.** fresh fruit

At Home: Have students draw a comic strip. Then have them ask a family member to predict what might happen next in their comic.

Prefixes

A **prefix** is a word part that can be added to the beginning of a word. It makes a new word with its own meaning. The prefix **un-** means "not" or "opposite of." For example, the word **unhappy** means "not happy."

prefix + base word = new word

un + **happy** = **unhappy**

Fill in the list below by writing the prefix and base word or the new word. Then write the meaning of the new word. The first one is done for you.

Prefix +	Base Word	= New Word	Meaning
1. un	usual	unusual	not usual
2. un	clear	unclear	not clear
3. un	fair	unfair	not fair
4. un	true	untrue	not true
5. un	folded	unfolded	not folded
6. un	known	unknown	not known
7. un	kind	unkind	not kind
8. un	wrap	unwrap	opposite of wrap
9. un	wanted	unwanted	not wanted
10. un	tie	untie	opposite of tie

At Home: Ask students to think of some other words that begin with the prefix **un-**.

Phoebe and the Spelling Bee • EXTEND

Problem and Solution

For most problems there are solutions. Some solutions are simple and predictable. Other solutions can be part of a plot, or plan, of a story. Read each of the problems below and choose the solution that you think would make the best story. Explain why. Then choose one problem and solution and write a paragraph about it.

Problem

1. A new student just moved into the school. The new student is sitting on the playground alone.

Solution

1. **(A)** A high flying ball comes sailing at her and she catches it. The others swarm around her.

1. **(B)** A girl asks the child to play.

2. A friend is coming over to play, but your room is a terrible mess.

2. **(A)** First, you have to find the missing baseball card your friend expects you to return.

2. **(B)** You quickly clean your room so you can play.

3. You will have a spelling bee tomorrow, but you have not studied for it yet.

3. **(A)** You start studying and ask your sister for help.

3. **(B)** You take your spelling list to a spelling owl who lives in a tree down the street.

At Home: Discuss ways of solving problems. Suggest that, in stories, solutions are not always practical. Talk about some stories that solve a problem creatively.

Vocabulary

The correct spelling of some words is difficult to remember. Make up a short and funny story using these words and illustrate it.

| continue | correct | legend | unusual | embarrass | groaning |

Do you find these words difficult to spell? Tell how you can remember them.

Answers will vary. For example, some students might say that they

remember there are 3 u's in *unusual*.

Story Comprehension

Phoebe had a special way of studying her spelling words. Turn Phoebe's solution into a play. Have each person in your group take a character. First, find lines from the story for your character. Then predict what your character might say, and write some lines on your own. Act out the play you have written. Give the play a new ending.

At Home: Ask students to cut challenging spelling words out of magazines. Discuss how you can remember these words.

Use a Glossary

A glossary is a small dictionary in the back of a book.

As in a dictionary, words are defined in the glossary. An example sentence is usually given for each word. Some glossaries show the page where the word can be found. Use the sample glossary below to answer each of the questions.

Earth The only planet known in our solar system to have all the conditions and materials needed for human life. There are many forms of plant and animal life on *Earth*. (Page 18)

endangered A living thing that may become extinct. The manatee is an *endangered* animal. (Page 43)

erosion The washing away of the land. The roots of trees can help stop *erosion*. (Page 25)

evaporate To change from a liquid to a gas. Water *evaporates* to form water vapor. (Page 22)

extinct When all animals of one kind die. There are no dinosaurs, such as brontosauruses, today, because these animals are *extinct*. (Page 44)

F

flat teeth Teeth that are good for grinding food. Many plant-eating dinosaurs had *flat teeth*. (Page 42)

fossil Remains or imprint of a once-living thing. Brontosaurus footprints in rock are one kind of *fossil*. (Page 45)

1. Look up the word *endangered* and write another example sentence for it. **Answers will vary.**

2. Look up the word *fossil* and write another example sentence for it.

3. If you decided to add the word *everglade* to this glossary, between what two words would it be placed? **evaporate and extinct**

4. Where do you think you might find out more about a brontosaurus?

Answers will vary, but students may infer the pages 42, 44 and 45 since brontosauruses are mentioned in the definitions.

At Home: Start a journal of third grade words. Have students put in words worth remembering from anything they study in class. Write definitions and, later, put the words in A-B-C order.

Problem and Solution

Most problems have solutions. Some solutions are good. Other solutions are not so good. For each problem Phoebe had, write her solution. Then tell whether the solution was good or not so good.

Answers may vary.

1. Katie tried to help Phoebe spell brontosaurus.

   Solution: Phoebe fell to the ground, blamed the brontosaurus, and raced Katie back to class. This was not a good solution.

2. Katie called Phoebe to find out how she was doing with her spelling list.

   Solution: Phoebe said "great," but she was really folding the spelling list into paper airplanes. This was not a good solution.

3. Ms. Ravioli announced a mock spelling bee. Phoebe was nervous.

   Phoebe pretended she was sick, went to the nurse's office, and lied to Katie. This was not a good solution.

4. Phoebe felt very bad about lying to Katie.

   Solution: Phoebe studied her spelling list, brought Katie a tulip, and told Katie that she was sorry for lying. This was a good solution.

5. Ms. Ravioli started the spelling bee.

   Solution: Phoebe started to raise her hand to go to the nurse's office, but she decided not to have the flu. This was a good solution.

At Home: Debate Phoebe's and Katie's ways of learning spelling. Which works better?

Phoebe and the Spelling Bee • EXTEND

Make Predictions

A prediction is a good guess about what will happen in the future. You need some good information to make good predictions. Think about what Phoebe did in "Phoebe and the Spelling Bee." Then make a prediction for each question below.

1. Do you predict that Katie will do well in future spelling bees?

Katie won this spelling bee and thinks that spelling is a "breeze."

She will probably continue to do well.

2. Do you predict that Phoebe will continue to put off studying her

spelling? _____ Answers will vary.

Phoebe seems to put off chores and imagine ways to get out of

them. She probably will not change just because of this one

spelling bee.

3. Do you predict that Phoebe and Katie will continue to be friends?

They will probably continue to be friends, because they made up.

4. Do you predict that some of the class will use Phoebe's method for

learning spelling words? Some classmates may learn spelling

words the way Phoebe did, as she spelled most of the words

correctly, and won a certificate.

Book 3.1/Unit 1
Phoebe and the Spelling Bee

At Home: Make up two prediction questions about another story or TV show.

13

Prefixes

Word parts, such as *un* and *re* are called prefixes. The prefixes *un* and *re* can change the meaning of words. For example, *un* means "not" as in unable, or "opposite" as in uncover. The word part *re* means "again," as in refill, or "back" as in replay.

Use *un* or *re* to change the meaning of the words below. Then write sentences using the words you created.

1. __un__ lucky

_____

2. __un__ usual

_____

3. __un__ happy

_____

4. __re__ check

_____

5. __re__ fill

_____

6. __re__ play

_____

7. __un__ fair

_____

8. __re__ paint

_____

14

At Home: Put up a list on the refrigerator with two columns- one for words with the prefix *un* and the other for words with the prefix *re*. Everyone should add words as they think of them. Keep the list up for several days.

Book 3.1/Unit 1
Phoebe and the Spelling Bee

T21

Phoebe and the Spelling Bee • GRAMMAR

Name_____ Date_____ **Grammar** 7

Commands

> • A **command** is a sentence that tells or asks someone to do something.
> • It ends with a period.
>   Command: *Go to the nurse's office.*

Make each group of words a command. Add a word from the box.
Then write the sentence correctly.

break	call	raise	sound	stand	take	tell

1. ____**Take**____ the spelling list home
   Take the spelling list home.

2. ____**Call**____ me on the phone
   Call me on the phone.

3. ____**Tell**____ me the truth
   Tell me the truth.

4. ____**Sound**____ out the word
   Sound out the word.

5. ____**Break**____ the word into two parts
   Break the word into two parts.

6. ____**Sound**____ each part
   Sound each part.

7. ____**Raise**____ your hand
   Raise your hand.

8. ____**Stand**____ in line, please
   Stand in line, please.

8 Book 3.1/Unit 1
Phoebe and the Spelling Bee

Extension: Have students work in pairs. Tell students to take turns giving a command for their partner to act out.

7

Name_____ Date_____ **Grammar** 8

Exclamations

> • An **exclamation** shows strong feeling.
> • It ends with an exclamation mark.
>   Exclamation: *What hard work this is!*

Make each group of words an exclamation. Add a word from the box.
Then write the sentence correctly.

great	how	oh	ouch	what	wonderful	wow	watch

1. ____**Oh**____ no, the spelling bee is in three days
   Oh no, the spelling bee is in three days!

2. ____**What**____ a problem this is
   What a problem this is!

3. ____**Ouch**____ , I think my leg is broken
   Ouch, I think my leg is broken!

4. ____**Wow**____ , Katie won the spelling bee
   Wow, Katie won the spelling bee!

5. That's ____**wonderful**____
   That's wonderful!

6. ____**How**____ exciting to get a certificate
   How exciting to get a certificate!

7. My certificate said ____**what**____ IMAGINATION
   My certificate said what IMAGINATION!

8. ____**Watch**____ out
   Watch out!

8 **Extension:** Invite students to write two exclamations about an exciting event in their school.

Book 3.1/Unit 1
Phoebe and the Spelling Bee 8

Name_____ Date_____ **Grammar** 9

Commands and Exclamations

> • A command tells or asks someone to do something. It ends with a period.
> • An exclamation shows strong feeling. It ends with an exclamation point.

After each sentence, write **command** or **exclamation** for the kind of
sentence it is. Then write the sentence correctly. Use capital letters
and end marks.

1. study the words ____**command**____
   Study the words.

2. try to spell each word ____**command**____
   Try to spell each word.

3. what a long list this is ____**exclamation**____
   What a long list this is!

4. oh no, I think I have the chicken pox ____**exclamation**____
   Oh no, I think I have the chicken pox!

5. listen to the sounds ____**command**____
   Listen to the sounds.

6. how hard this is ____**exclamation**____
   How hard this is!

7. please learn the words by Friday ____**command**____
   Please learn the words by Friday.

8. oh dear, Friday is here ____**exclamation**____
   Oh dear, Friday is here!

16 Book 3.1/Unit 1
Phoebe and the Spelling Bee

Extension: Ask students to write a command and an exclamation about spelling or another school subject.

9

Name_____ Date_____ **Grammar** 10

Sentence Capitalization and Punctuation

> • Every sentence begins with a capital letter.
> • A **command** ends with a period.
> • An **exclamation** ends with an exclamation mark.

Proofread the sentences. Write them correctly.

1. wow, that's my favorite food
   Wow, that's my favorite food!

2. tell it to me
   Tell it to me.

3. what a terrific word that is
   What a terrific word that is!

4. spell your word
   Spell your word.

5. oh no, the word is too long
   Oh no, the word is too long!

6. i like words that describe animals
   I like words that describe animals.

7. listen to my list
   Listen to my list.

8. i'm learning to spell my words
   I'm learning to spell my words.

10 **Extension:** Have students write two commands and two exclamations to tell about some kind of emergency situation.

Book 3.1/Unit 1
Phoebe and the Spelling Bee 8

Phoebe and the Spelling Bee • GRAMMAR

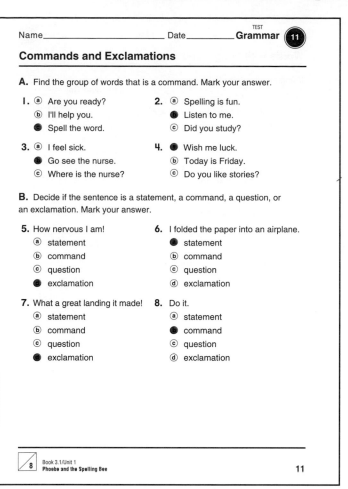

Name_____ Date_____ **Grammar** (11)

Commands and Exclamations

A. Find the group of words that is a command. Mark your answer.

1. ⓐ Are you ready?
   ⓑ I'll help you.
   ● Spell the word.

2. ⓐ Spelling is fun.
   ● Listen to me.
   ⓒ Did you study?

3. ⓐ I feel sick.
   ● Go see the nurse.
   ⓒ Where is the nurse?

4. ● Wish me luck.
   ⓑ Today is Friday.
   ⓒ Do you like stories?

B. Decide if the sentence is a statement, a command, a question, or an exclamation. Mark your answer.

5. How nervous I am!
   ⓐ statement
   ⓑ command
   ⓒ question
   ● exclamation

6. I folded the paper into an airplane.
   ● statement
   ⓑ command
   ⓒ question
   ⓓ exclamation

7. What a great landing it made!
   ⓐ statement
   ⓑ command
   ⓒ question
   ● exclamation

8. Do it.
   ⓐ statement
   ● command
   ⓒ question
   ⓓ exclamation

8 | Book 3.1/Unit 1
Phoebe and the Spelling Bee

11

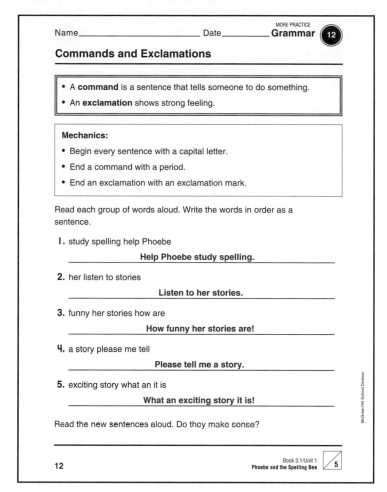

Name_____ Date_____ **Grammar** (12)

Commands and Exclamations

- A **command** is a sentence that tells someone to do something.
- An **exclamation** shows strong feeling.

Mechanics:
- Begin every sentence with a capital letter.
- End a command with a period.
- End an exclamation with an exclamation mark.

Read each group of words aloud. Write the words in order as a sentence.

1. study spelling help Phoebe
   _____**Help Phoebe study spelling.**_____

2. her listen to stories
   _____**Listen to her stories.**_____

3. funny her stories how are
   _____**How funny her stories are!**_____

4. a story please me tell
   _____**Please tell me a story.**_____

5. exciting story what an it is
   _____**What an exciting story it is!**_____

Read the new sentences aloud. Do they make sense?

12

Book 3.1/Unit 1
Phoebe and the Spelling Bee | 5

T23

Phoebe and the Spelling Bee • SPELLING

Words with Long *a* and Long *e*

Pretest Directions

Fold back the paper along the dotted line. Use the blanks to write each word as it is read aloud. When you finish the test, unfold the paper. Use the list at the right to correct any spelling mistakes. Practice the words you missed for the Posttest.

1. _____	1. plane
2. _____	2. team
3. _____	3. raise
4. _____	4. breeze
5. _____	5. paper
6. _____	6. marry
7. _____	7. weigh
8. _____	8. thief
9. _____	9. cream
10. _____	10. awake
11. _____	11. grade
12. _____	12. creek
13. _____	13. carry
14. _____	14. sail
15. _____	15. neighbor

To Parents

Here are the results of your child's weekly spelling Pretest. You can help your child study for the Posttest by following these simple steps for each word on the word list:

1. Read the word to your child.
2. Have your child write the word, saying each letter as it is written.
3. Say each letter of the word as your child checks the spelling.
4. If a mistake has been made, have your child read each letter of the correctly spelled word aloud, and then repeat steps 1-3.

Challenge Words

_____ continue
_____ correct
_____ embarrass
_____ legend
_____ unusual

Words with Long *a* and Long *e*

Using the Word Study Steps

1. LOOK at the word.
2. SAY the word aloud.
3. STUDY the letters in the word.
4. WRITE the word.
5. CHECK the word.
   Did you spell the word right?
   If not, go back to step 1.

Spelling Tip

Words with **i** and **e** can be tricky. This rhyme gives a tip.
i before **e**
except after **c**
or when sounded like /ā/
as in *neighbor* and *weigh*

Crossword Puzzle

Solve the crossword puzzle with spelling words that complete the sentences.

ACROSS
2. You need a pen and ___ to draw.
5. He plays on the baseball ___ .
7. I'm wide ___ after my nap.
8. Did you get a good ___ on the test?
10. The flag blew in the ___.
11. He will ___ his boat on the lake.
12. I help Mom ___ the heavy bags.
13. My next door ___ is coming over.

DOWN
1. The water in the ___ is cold.
2. The pilot flew the ___.
3. I ___ ninety pounds.
4. Do you like ___ in your coffee?
5. The ___ stole her purse.
6. I'll have a big wedding when I ___.
9. I will ___ my right hand to answer.

To Parents or Helpers:
Using the Word Study Steps above as your child comes across any new words will help him or her spell well. Review the steps as you both go over this week's spelling words.
Go over the Spelling Tip with your child. Help him or her find other words that contain i and e. Use the rhyme to explain the spelling pattern.
Help your child complete the crossword puzzle.

Words with Long *a* and Long *e*

plane	breeze	weigh	awake	carry
team	paper	thief	grade	sail
raise	marry	cream	creek	neighbor

Write the spelling words that contain the matching spelling of the long **a** sound.

long *a* spelled *a*   **long *a* spelled *a-e***

1. __paper__   4. __plane__
                      5. __awake__
                      6. __grade__

long *a* spelled *ai*   **long *a* spelled *eigh***

2. __raise__   7. __weigh__
3. __sail__   8. __neighbor__

Write the spelling words that contain the matching spelling of the long **e** sound.

long *e* spelled *ea*   **long *e* spelled *y***

9. __team__   13. __marry__
10. __cream__   14. __carry__

long *e* spelled *ee*   **long *e* spelled *ie***

11. __breeze__   15. __thief__
12. __creek__

Words with Long *a* and Long *e*

plane	breeze	weigh	awake	carry
team	paper	thief	grade	sail
raise	marry	cream	creek	neighbor

It Takes Three

Write a spelling word that goes with the other two words.

1. group, club, __team__   2. river, pond, __creek__
3. robber, crook, __thief__   4. measure, balance, __weigh__

What Does It Mean?

Write a spelling word that matches each clue below.

5. Not asleep   __awake__
6. A flying machine   __plane__
7. Thin sheet used for writing   __paper__
8. The person who lives next door   __neighbor__
9. A class or year in school   __grade__
10. Heavy, thick milk   __cream__
11. A gentle wind   __breeze__

Past Tense

To form the past tense of a verb you usually add *-ed* . If there is a y at the end of the word, it changes to *i*. If there is an *e* at the end it is dropped. Put these words in the past tense:

12. raise __raised__   13. marry __married__
14. sail __sailed__   15. carry __carried__

Challenge Extension: Have students draw a picture to illustrate each Challenge Word, then exchange papers with a partner and label each other's pictures.

Phoebe and the Spelling Bee • SPELLING

Words with Long *a* and Long *e*

Proofreading

There are six spelling mistakes in this letter. Circle the misspelled words. Write the words correctly on the lines below.

Dear Laura,

Our camping trip was so much fun. We fished in a creak I caught a fish but let it go. Mom said that the fish didn't whay enough.

We all worked as a teem Everyone helped to put up the tents. I also helped raze the sail on the rented boat.

The first night, I lay awayk watching the stars. We went on hikes, but I didn't like to cary my own backpack.

Write soon!
Your friend,
Melissa

1. _____creek_____   2. _____weigh_____

3. _____team_____   4. _____raise_____

5. _____awake_____   6. _____carry_____

Writing Activity

Write a letter to a friend describing a fun event. Use at least four spelling words in your description.

_____

_____

_____

_____

Words with Long *a* and Long *e*

Look at the words in each set. One word in each set is spelled correctly. Use a pencil to color in the circle in front of that word. Before you begin, look at the sample sets of words. Sample A has been done for you. Do Sample B by yourself. When you are sure you know what to do, you may go on with the rest of the page.

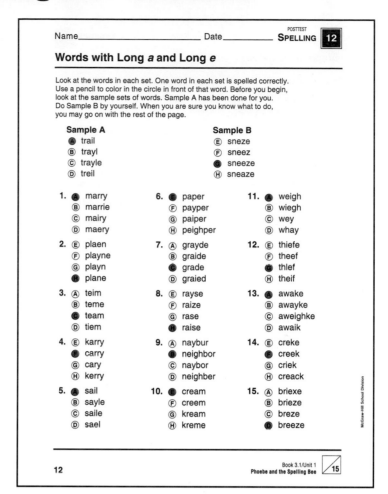

Sample A
- Ⓐ trail ●
- Ⓑ trayl
- Ⓒ trayle
- Ⓓ treil

Sample B
- Ⓔ sneze
- Ⓕ sneez
- Ⓖ sneeze ●
- Ⓗ sneaze

1.
- Ⓐ marry ●
- Ⓑ marrie
- Ⓒ mairy
- Ⓓ maery

2.
- Ⓔ plaen
- Ⓕ playne
- Ⓖ playn
- Ⓗ plane ●

3.
- Ⓐ teim
- Ⓑ teme
- Ⓒ team ●
- Ⓓ tiem

4.
- Ⓔ karry
- Ⓕ carry ●
- Ⓖ cary
- Ⓗ kerry

5.
- Ⓐ sail ●
- Ⓑ sayle
- Ⓒ saile
- Ⓓ sael

6.
- Ⓔ paper ●
- Ⓕ payper
- Ⓖ paiper
- Ⓗ peighper

7.
- Ⓐ grayde
- Ⓑ graide
- Ⓒ grade ●
- Ⓓ graied

8.
- Ⓔ rayse
- Ⓕ raize
- Ⓖ rase
- Ⓗ raise ●

9.
- Ⓐ naybur
- Ⓑ neighbor ●
- Ⓒ naybor
- Ⓓ neigher

10.
- Ⓔ cream ●
- Ⓕ creem
- Ⓖ kream
- Ⓗ kreme

11.
- Ⓐ weigh ●
- Ⓑ wiegh
- Ⓒ wey
- Ⓓ whay

12.
- Ⓔ thiefe
- Ⓕ theef
- Ⓖ thief ●
- Ⓗ theif

13.
- Ⓐ awake ●
- Ⓑ awayke
- Ⓒ aweighke
- Ⓓ awaik

14.
- Ⓔ creke
- Ⓕ creek ●
- Ⓖ criek
- Ⓗ creack

15.
- Ⓐ briexe
- Ⓑ brieze
- Ⓒ breze
- Ⓓ breeze ●

Name_____ Date_____ Practice **15**

Steps in a Process

A series of steps you follow in order are called **steps in a process**.

The steps below in each set are not in order. Write numbers 1 through 4 on the lines to show the order.

Shop for Spaghetti

___3___ Put noodles in shopping cart.

___1___ Go to the store.

___2___ Choose a shopping cart.

___4___ Pay for the noodles.

Cook Spaghetti

___4___ Put the cooked noodles on a plate.

___1___ Go to the kitchen.

___2___ Open the box of noodles.

___3___ Cook the noodles in a pan.

Go Skating with a Friend

___4___ Skate down the street together.

___1___ Find skates in closet.

___2___ Put on right and left skates.

___3___ Skate to friend's house.

Go to School

___4___ Walk out the door.

___3___ Pick up the school books.

___1___ Wake up on time.

___2___ Get dressed.

16 Book 3.1/Unit 1
Opt: An Illusionary Tale

At Home: Help students to identify a step-by-step process that they follow at home. Have them write down the steps in order.

15

Name_____ Date_____ Practice **16**

Vocabulary

Supply the correct words from the list:

length   guard   royal   within   gift   straighten

Once a prince and a princess lived happily in an underground castle. There was one problem, though. The _____royal_____ kingdom always looked boring and dull. So the prince had an idea. As a birthday _____gift_____ he bought the princess some paintings to decorate the castle walls.

The princess was thrilled! Her favorite painting showed a small face tucked _____within_____ a larger face. She hung this one on the castle door, next to the _____guard_____ who protected them. Another painting showed a group of bent and slanted lines. If you looked at the lines long enough, they seemed to _____straighten_____ out. Looking at this will keep people busy, she thought.

After three days all of the paintings were hung, except one. This last painting is shown below. Do you think the lines are the same _____length_____ ?

16   **At Home:** Use each of the vocabulary words in a sentence.

Book 3.1/Unit 1
Opt: An Illusionary Tale   6

Anything Can Happen!

I used to visit the land of make-believe very often. *Within* the land of make-believe, anything can happen! Once, an old woman offered me a ring as a *gift*. The ring changed shape as fast as I could say "one, two, three." Then I made it *straighten* out into a long magic wand.

With my magic wand I knew I could become anyone and anything I wished. I decided to become a *guard* for a *royal* family. I marched up and down the *length* of their long hallway. Then I marched right into the royal kitchen. You can find all kinds of cookies and cakes in the land of make-believe!

1. What kind of family lived in the castle?

   royal

2. What did the speaker have to do to change the ring to a wand?

   straighten it

3. What kind of person watches over *royal* families?

   a guard

4. When you measure from one end to the other of the castle hall, what do you learn?

   its length

5. What is special about the land of make-believe?

   Anything can happen there.

5 Book 3.1/Unit 1
Opt: An Illusionary Tale

At Home: Encourage students to write about what they would like to find within the world of make-believe.

16A

Name_____ Date_____ Practice **17**

Story Comprehension

Review the optical illusions shown in "Opt." Then list two of the illusions under each heading. **Answers may vary. Sample answers are shown.**

What Colors Do You See?	How Many Objects?
1. White balloon appears green.	3. Trident prongs change in number.
2. Gray dots appear where white lines cross.	4. Six blocks become seven.

The Same Size?	Hidden Faces?
5. Red tape appears longer than blue.	7. Faces are hidden in portraits.
6. King appears taller than queen.	8. Faces are hidden in zoo animals.

Straight or Crooked?	Changing Shapes?
9. Vertical lines on cloak appear crooked.	11. Kites appear flat or box-shaped.
10. Fishing rod appears crooked.	12. The dragon's eyes seem to spin.

17   **At Home:** Ask students to circle the two optical illusions that they enjoyed the most.

Book 3.1/Unit 1
Opt: An Illusionary Tale   12

Opt: An Illusionary Tale • PRACTICE

Name_____ Date_____ **Practice 18**

Use a Table of Contents

Use the headings below to fill in two tables of contents. Notice that one table of contents is for a book of fiction, that is, a made-up story. The other is for a nonfiction book, which is about real things.

At Home: Ask students to identify which of the above tables of contents is for a nonfiction book and which is for a fictional story.

18

Name_____ Date_____ **Practice 19**

Steps in a Process

Think about the steps you use when you solve a problem. Often you can use the same steps to solve other problems. Writing down the steps will help you remember them. A series of steps you follow in order are called **steps in a process**.

Read Problem 1 and the list of steps for solving it below. Then write a list of steps for solving Problem 2.

Problem 1

What steps will help you find out if the vertical lines of the messenger's cloak are crooked or straight?

Process

1. Measure the distance between two lines near the top.
2. Write down that number.
3. Measure the distance between the same two lines near the bottom.
4. Write down this number.
5. Compare your two measurements. If they are the same, the lines are straight.

Problem 2

In the picture of the Royal Pet at the zoo, what steps will help you decide if the body of the pet is shorter than its neck?

Process

1. Measure the length of the neck.
2. Write down that number.
3. Measure the length of the body.
4. Write down this number.
5. Compare the two measurements. If the second number is less, the body is shorter.

At Home: Have students follow the steps they wrote. What did they discover about the length of the Royal Pet's neck and body? Have them record the results.

Name_____ Date_____ **Practice 20**

Story Elements

The **narrator** tells the story. Often, the narrator is one of the **characters**, or people in the story. The narrator tells the story from his or her own **point of view**.

Read each part of the story below. Then answer the questions about it.

> The queen called me. I was on the other side of the room. "Princess Lulu," the queen said. "How long will it take you to get from there to here?"

1. Who are the two main characters? **Princess Lulu and the queen**

2. What two words tell you that Princess Lulu is the narrator? **I, me**

> My brother, Randy, told me a funny story. I have never laughed so hard in all my life! My brother is such a clown! He says he's glad I am his sister.

3. Who are the main characters? **Randy's sister, Randy**

4. Who is the narrator? What words help you to know this? **Randy's sister; she talks about herself using the words "my," and "I."**

> The dog's name is Toaster. The brown spots on his white fur are shaped like pieces of toast. Ernie is Toaster's owner. Ernie named his dog Toaster.

5. Who are the two main characters? **Toaster and Ernie**

6. Is the narrator one of the two main characters? How do you know? **No; if either of these characters was the narrator, the story would be told from his point-of-view**

At Home: Have students narrate a story. Then have them try to tell their stories from a different point of view.

20

Name_____ Date_____ **Practice 21**

Prefixes

You can add the **prefixes un-** or **dis-** to the beginnings of some words to make new words. The prefix **un-** means "opposite of" or "not." The prefix **dis-** also means "opposite of" or "not."

Rewrite each sentence. Replace the underlined phrase with a word from the box that includes the prefix **un-** or **dis-**. Look at the following example:

Sean was <u>not lucky</u> flying the kite.

Sean was **un**lucky flying the kite.

unusual	unknown	displeased	disobeyed	unbelievable

1. The stranger was <u>not known</u> to the family.

   The stranger was unknown to the family.

2. Jeri <u>did not please</u> her science teacher.

   Jeri displeased her science teacher.

3. Quong's painting was <u>not the same as everyone else's.</u>

   Quong's painting was unusual.

4. My little brother can yell so loud it is <u>not believable.</u>

   My brother can yell so loud it is unbelievable.

5. Bruce <u>did not obey</u> the rule.

   Bruce disobeyed the rule.

At Home: Have students say a sentence that includes the word **disagree**.

Name_____ Date_____ **Reteach** 15

Steps in a Process

Steps you follow in order are called **steps in a process**.

Read the list of what Tom will do on Friday. Then put the list in the correct order.

eat breakfast	1.	wake up
go to sleep	2.	eat breakfast
have dinner in a restaurant	3.	take the bus to school
say the Pledge of Allegiance at school	4.	say the Pledge of Allegiance at school
wake up	5.	take a math test
take a math test	6.	have dinner in a restaurant
put on pajamas	7.	put on pajamas
take the bus to school	8.	go to sleep

At Home: Have students write six things they do every day in the order that they do them.

Name_____ Date_____ **Reteach** 16

Vocabulary

Finish these sentences with words from the list.

gift   guard   length   royal   straighten   within

1. Whenever the King was sleeping, a ___**guard**___ was ordered to stand outside the door of the ___**royal**___ bedroom.
2. The pretty ___**gift**___ was wrapped with blue paper and bows.
3. A teddy bear was found ___**within**___ the box.
4. The Queen used a ruler to find the ___**length**___ of her hair.
5. She decided to ___**straighten**___ her hair so that it would look longer.

6

Story Comprehension

Reteach 17

Write the answers to these questions about "Opt: An Illusionary Tale."

1. Why is Opt a strange place? **What you think you see is not always what you really see.**

2. What is strange about the sizes of things in Opt? **Things that seem to be different sizes are really the same size.**

At Home: Have students measure the length of three things at home that seem to be the same length. Have them explain the results.

Name_____ Date_____ **Reteach** 18

Use a Table of Contents

A **table of contents** can be found in different kinds of books. Both fiction and nonfiction books use a table of contents. **Fiction** books are made-up stories. **Nonfiction books** are real-life stories.

Use the two tables of contents above to answer the questions.

1. Which of these two books is about real things people do?
   Learn Tennis My Way

2. What is the second chapter of *My Mother Was a Squirrel*?
   I Hate Nuts

3. On what page could you learn something about a tennis backhand?
   19

4. Which table of contents lists chapter numbers?
   My Mother Was a Squirrel

5. What are the two basics of a tennis ground stroke? **readiness and contact with the ball**

At Home: Have students write two more questions based on these two tables of contents.

Name_____ Date_____ **Reteach** 19

Steps in a Process

It is important to be able to follow the **steps in a process**. This is especially important in solving a problem.

Look back at the pictures from "Opt" described in the questions below. Then write the steps you followed to figure out what was really in the pictures. **Answers may vary.**

The King and Queen are waiting for a message. Who is taller?

1. First, I thought the King was ___**taller.**___
2. Then, I **measured the height of each figure.**
3. I discovered that **the King and the Queen were the same height.**

How many ladies are framed in the Royal Art Gallery?

4. When I first looked at the drawing, I only saw ___**two**___ framed ladies.
5. As I looked at them longer, though, I saw **two more ladies' portraits.**
6. Then in the base of the table, I saw **two more faces.**
7. Therefore, I counted a total of ___**six**___ faces.

The royal family stops at the sign. Which is the longer line, the bottom or the top?

8. First, I **measured the top line.**
9. Then, I **measured the bottom line.**
10. I found out that **the lines are the same length.**

At Home: Have students choose their favorite picture from "Opt" and explain why they liked it.

Opt: An Illusionary Tale • RETEACH

Story Elements

> The **narrator** is the person who tells the story. Sometimes the narrator is one of the **characters**, or people, in the story. The narrator tells the story the way she or he sees it, or from the **narrative point of view.**

The story below has three characters: Anna, Mario, and their father. Each part of the story is told by a different narrator. Read each part. Then circle the name of the character who is the narrator.

1. I live with my father and my older brother, Mario. We all love art. My father often takes us to museums. Mario likes the paintings best, but my father and I love the photographs.

   Father   (Anna)   Mario

2. My son and daughter get so excited that they run off and forget to tell me where they're going. The other day, my boy got lost in the museum. I'm surprised I ever found him!

   (Father)   Anna   Mario

3. I showed my father and brother this photograph. I took it at a picnic last weekend. I got down in the grass and looked up to the table. In the photograph, the corn on the cob looks as tall as the tree!

   Father   (Anna)   Marlo

4. Anna and I decided to make Dad a book filled with our own drawings and paintings. We thought it would be a great birthday gift. We called it "The Greatest Art Ever."

   Father   Anna   (Mario)

Book 3.1/Unit 1
Opt: An Illusionary Tale   4

At Home: Have students think of an activity they did with someone recently. Then have them write about it from their point of view.   20

Prefixes

> A **prefix** is a word part or a group of letters that appears at the beginning of a word and changes the word's meaning. A prefix does not change the spelling of the base word. The prefix **dis-** means "opposite of" or "not." The prefix **un-** also means "not" or "opposite of."
>
> **dis-**   opposite of, not   **dis + appear = disappear**
> **un-**   opposite of, not   **un + fair = unfair**

Circle the prefix in each word. Then find the definition for each word in the list at the right. Write the definition of each word.

1. (un)lucky   _____not lucky_____   opposite of please

2. (dis)agree   _____to not agree_____   not locked

3. (un)happy   _____not happy_____   not true

4. (dis)obey   _____to not obey_____   opposite of appear

5. (un)usual   _____not usual_____   not like

6. (dis)appear   ____opposite of appear____   not lucky

7. (un)locked   _____not locked_____   to not agree

8. (dis)please   ____opposite of please____   not happy

9. (un)true   _____not true_____   not usual

10. (dis)like   _____not like_____   to not obey

T29

Opt: An Illusionary Tale • EXTEND

Steps in a Process

Make an upside-down face! You could draw the face of an animal, or draw a silly person. In the drawings above, a hairdo turns into a beard, a bow tie is also a hair bow, and a mouth becomes a wrinkle.

What steps must you follow to complete your upside-down face? Write them below your picture.

_____
_____
_____
_____
_____

Book 3.1/Unit 1
Opt: An Illusionary Tale

At Home: Think of other activities you do at home and create a list of steps for each activity.

15

Vocabulary

length	within	straighten
royal	guard	gift

Write a paragraph about a royal castle, using as many vocabulary words from the box as you can. Then erase those vocabulary words or cover them with tape. Exchange paragraphs with a partner and fill in the blanks.

Extend 17

Story Comprehension

Opt is a land where things don't always look as they really are. As you answer each question, explain how you decided your answer.

1. Which line is longer—A or B? How can you prove you are correct?

   Measure the lines.

2. Is the shape you see here a perfect circle? How can you prove you are correct? _____ **Place a dime in the circle.**

At Home: Students can draw their own characters who could live in Opt and label their drawings.

16–17

Book 3.1 / Unit 1
Opt: An Illusionary Tale

Use a Table of Contents

Here are the cover and table of contents page from the Opt Zoo brochure. Draw and color a picture that would make a good cover page. Then study the table of contents, and answer the questions below.

The Opt Zoo Brochure	Table of Contents
	Lions . . . . .Page 1 and Cage 1
	Tigers . . . . .Page 2 and Cage 2
	Bear, Oh My! . . .Page 3 and Cage 3
	Animals That Fly . . . . .Pages 4–6 and Cage 4

1. What animal would you visit first? ___ **Answers may vary.**

2. Suppose you wanted to start with the lions. You want to visit the animals in order. What animal would you visit after the lions?

   _____ **Tigers** _____

3. What pages talk about birds? How do you know? ___ **Pages 4–6.**

   _____ **Birds are animals that fly.** _____

Write a story about your visit to this zoo.

_____
_____
_____
_____

Book 3.1 / Unit 1
Opt: An Illusionary Tale

At Home: Look through the newspaper together, and predict what the stories will be about by reading the headlines.

18

Steps in a Process

The following lists some things you might do if you are going to the zoo with the royal family. Two of these steps have nothing to do with going to the zoo. Mark an **X** beside those two steps. Then put the rest of the steps in order. Start with 1 for the first step. End with 5 for the last step.

____5____ 1. Say goodbye to the royal family and go home.

____1____ 2. Look at a map to find out how to get to the king's castle.

____X____ 3. Tie a ribbon around your bike.

____2____ 4. Greet the royal family at the castle.

____4____ 5. Have lunch with the royal family after seeing all of the animals.

____X____ 6. Rearrange your bedroom furniture.

____3____ 7. With the king's help, look at a map to find the zoo.

Opt: An Illusionary Tale • EXTEND

Story Elements

A narrator tells a story. You can be a narrator. Or the narrator can be someone else who is telling a story from his or her point of view.
Read the statements about "Opt: An Illusionary Tale." Then answer each question.

Find the rod and find the branch of the tree. Now look at the Prince's shirt. What do you see?

1. Imagine the prince is telling the story from his point of view. How would the second sentence be written? __Now look at my shirt.__

_____

The guard marches up the stairs, but is he getting anywhere?

2. If the narrator told the story from the guard's point of view, how would this sentence be written? __I'm marching up the stairs but am I getting anywhere?__

The fire-breathing dragon now comes in. Turn the book and his eyes will spin. He arrives with presents and none too late. But did he tie the ribbons on straight?

3. Rewrite this paragraph from the dragon's point of view. _____
__I am the fire-breathing dragon coming in. Turn the book and my eyes will spin. I arrive with presents and none too late. But did I tie the ribbons on straight?__

Draw and color a picture of the dragon.

At Home: Suggest a favorite family story and try to tell it from a different narrator's point of view. Discuss how the point of view changes the story.

20

Prefixes

The prefixes *dis* and *un* can be added to some words to form their opposites. Read the sentences below. Add the prefix *un* or *dis* to a word in the first sentence to fill in the blank in the second sentence.

1. This is not your usual time. It is very ___unusual___ for you to be here now.

2. Do not agree with me! You must ___disagree___.

3. Flowers appear in the spring. They ___disappear___ when winter comes.

4. I was certain that I knew my words. However, now I'm really ___uncertain___.

5. Muffin did not obey my signals. I'm disappointed when he ___disobeys___.

6. That's not a real story. It is totally ___unreal___.

Imagine a visit to a museum or zoo. Use some words with the prefixes *dis* and *un* to tell a story about your imaginary visit.

_____
_____
_____
_____
_____
_____
_____
_____

21

At Home: Try to have a conversation using only words with no prefixes. Talk about how much we use prefixes to make ourselves clear.

Book 3.1 / Unit 1
Opt: An Illusionary Tale

Worksheet 13

Name_____ Date_____ **Grammar** 13
LEARN

Subjects

- The **subject** of a sentence is whom or what the sentence is about.
- The subject can be one word or more than one word.
  A wall surrounds the castle.
  A wall is the subject.

What or whom is the sentence about? Draw a line under the subject.

1. <u>Balloons</u> float in the air.
2. <u>The guard</u> holds a trident.
3. <u>Someone</u> brings a letter for the king.
4. <u>The king</u> reads the message.
5. <u>Bright flowers</u> bloom in the garden.
6. <u>The Great Hall</u> is ready for a party.
7. <u>Amazing animals</u> live in the Opt Zoo.
8. <u>A fire-snorting dragon</u> comes to the castle.
9. <u>Six blocks</u> can become seven blocks.
10. <u>Everyone</u> has fun at the party.

10 | Book 3.1/Unit 1
Opt: An Illusionary Tale

Extension: Have students work in pairs. Ask each student to write two sentences about a castle. Then tell students to draw a line under the subjects of their partner's sentences.

13

Worksheet 14

Name_____ Date_____ **Grammar** 14
LEARN AND PRACTICE

Fixing Fragments by Adding Subjects

- A **sentence fragment** is a group of words that does not express a complete thought.
- Some sentence fragments can be fixed by adding a subject.

Fix each fragment in the first column by adding a subject from the second column. Write the subject.

1. The wall has white lines on it.	Gray dots
2. Gray dots disappear from the wall.	A clue
3. The king waits for a letter.	The prince
4. A clue makes the message clear.	The wall
5. Two pictures hang on the wall.	A sign
6. The prince fishes with his new rod.	The king
7. The princess picks flowers.	Two pictures
8. Flower centers are black and white.	Many kites
9. A sign points the way to the zoo.	Flower centers
10. Many kites float in the air.	The princess

Extension: Invite students to take turns finding subjects from the story Opt: An Illusionary Tale. Then have them make a sentence about each subject.

14 | Book 3.1/Unit 1
Opt: An Illusionary Tale | 10

Worksheet 15

Name_____ Date_____ **Grammar** 15
PRACTICE AND REVIEW

Writing Subjects to Complete Sentences

- Every sentence has a subject.
- The subject of a sentence tells what or whom the sentence is about.

Add a subject to each group of words. Write the sentence.

1. Wonderland is a land of surprises.
   Wonderland is a land of surprises.

2. The ball has red and blue tape on it.
   The ball has red and blue tape on it.

3. The king may be taller than the queen.
   The king may be taller than the queen.

4. The lamp has a shade on it.
   The lamp has a shade on it.

5. Doug catches a fish.
   Doug catches a fish.

6. The queen looks in the mirror.
   The queen looks in the mirror.

7. She stops by the sign.
   She stops by the sign.

8. The guard marches up the stairs of the tower.
   The guard marches up the stairs of the tower.

8 | Book 3.1/Unit 1
Opt: An Illusionary Tale

Extension: Have one group of students write subjects about the Prince's party. Have another group write predicates. Invite students to match subjects and predicates to make sentences about the Prince's party.

15

Worksheet 16

Name_____ Date_____ **Grammar** 16
MECHANICS

Letter Punctuation and Capitalization

- Begin the greeting and closing in a letter with a capital letter.
- Use a comma after the greeting and the closing in a letter.
- Use a comma between the names of a city and a state.
- Use a comma between the day and year in a date.

Proofread the letter. Correct five capitalization mistakes. Add five missing commas.

January 15,2000

M
123 main Street
Hewlett,NY 11557

C
Kim chanS
456 Mott street
New York,NY 10010

D
dear Kim,

Your letter came today. It is so good to hear from you. I'm glad to know you're having fun in your new school.

We also read the story about Opt last week. I liked it. The story pictures are puzzles. What fun they are!

Please let me know when you can come and visit.

Y
your friend,

Pat

16 | **Extension:** Ask children to write their own letters. | Book 3.1/Unit 1
Opt: An Illusionary Tale | 10

Page 17

Subjects

A. Write the subject of each sentence.

1. The queen dusts the room. _____The queen_____

2. Four banners hang from the ceiling. _____Four banners_____

3. The Opt sign has lines on it. _____The Opt sign_____

4. A guest arrives in Opt. _____A guest_____

B. Choose a subject from the box that best completes each sentence. Write it on the line.

A guard	Opt	A messenger	The castle

5. _____Opt_____ is an unusual place.

6. _____The castle_____ is surrounded by a wall.

7. _____A guard_____ stands in front of the castle.

8. _____A messenger_____ brings a letter.

Page 18

Subjects

- The subject of a sentence tells what or whom the sentence is about.

Mechanics:
- Begin every sentence with a capital letter.
- End every sentence with a special mark.

Look at the picture. Read the paragraph and look at the underlined parts. What should you do to correct each part? Rewrite the sentences on the lines.

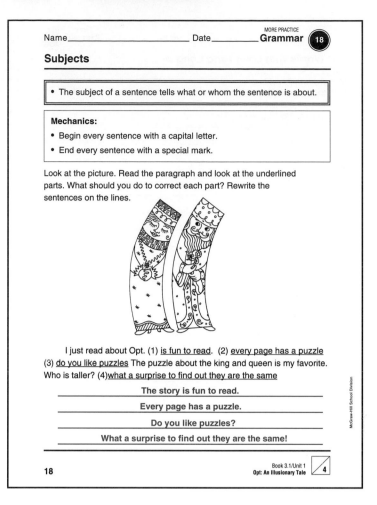

I just read about Opt. (1) is fun to read. (2) every page has a puzzle (3) do you like puzzles The puzzle about the king and queen is my favorite. Who is taller? (4)what a surprise to find out they are the same

_____The story is fun to read._____

_____Every page has a puzzle._____

_____Do you like puzzles?_____

_____What a surprise to find out they are the same!_____

Opt: An Illusionary Tale • SPELLING

Words with Long *i* and Long *o*

Pretest Directions

Fold back the paper along the dotted line. Use the blanks to write each word as it is read aloud. When you finish the test, unfold the paper. Use the list at the right to correct any spelling mistakes. Practice the words you missed for the Posttest.

1. _____	1. might
2. _____	2. life
3. _____	3. rode
4. _____	4. own
5. _____	5. most
6. _____	6. tie
7. _____	7. find
8. _____	8. toast
9. _____	9. wipe
10. _____	10. flight
11. _____	11. bicycle
12. _____	12. lie
13. _____	13. spoke
14. _____	14. ago
15. _____	15. thrown

To Parents

Here are the results of your child's weekly spelling Pretest. You can help your child study for the Posttest by following these simple steps for each word on the word list:

1. Read the word to your child.
2. Have your child write the word, saying each letter as it is written.
3. Say each letter of the word as your child checks the spelling.
4. If a mistake has been made, have your child read each letter of the correctly spelled word aloud, and then repeat steps 1-3.

Challenge Words

_____ guard
_____ length
_____ royal
_____ straighten
_____ within

Words with Long *i* and Long *o*

Using the Word Study Steps

1. LOOK at the word.
2. SAY the word aloud.
3. STUDY the letters in the word.
4. WRITE the word.
5. CHECK the word.
   Did you spell the word right? If not, go back to step 1.

Spelling Tip

When there is a long vowel sound at the beginning or in the middle of a one syllable word, it usually has two vowels. How many spelling words follow this rule?

life **own** **toast**

Find and Circle

Where are the spelling words?

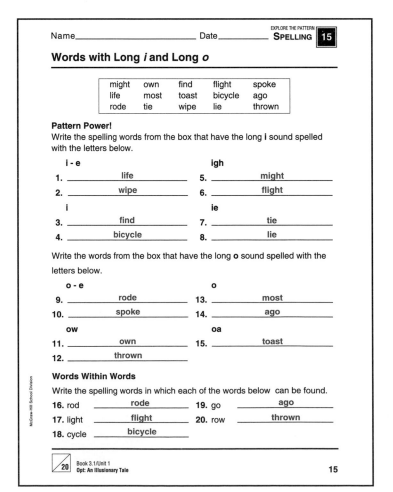

Words with Long *i* and Long *o*

might	own	find	flight	spoke
life	most	toast	bicycle	ago
rode	tie	wipe	lie	thrown

Pattern Power!

Write the spelling words from the box that have the long **i** sound spelled with the letters below.

i - e
1. life
2. wipe

i
3. find
4. bicycle

igh
5. might
6. flight

ie
7. tie
8. lie

Write the words from the box that have the long **o** sound spelled with the letters below.

o - e
9. rode
10. spoke

ow
11. own
12. thrown

o
13. most
14. ago

oa
15. toast

Words Within Words

Write the spelling words in which each of the words below can be found.

16. rod _rode_
17. light _flight_
18. cycle _bicycle_
19. go _ago_
20. row _thrown_

Words with Long *i* and Long *o*

might	own	find	flight	spoke
life	most	toast	bicycle	ago
rode	tie	wipe	lie	thrown

Words in Sentences

Write a spelling word to complete each sentence.

1. A _bicycle_ has two wheels and handlebars.
2. Long _ago_, dinosaurs roamed the Earth.
3. I _might_ go to camp this summer for two weeks.
4. Did Bobby have one or two slices of _toast_ for breakfast?
5. _Wipe_ your muddy shoes on the doormat!
6. The ball was _thrown_ ten feet into the air.
7. Our teacher _spoke_ in a low voice.
8. This building has only one _flight_ of stairs.
9. Stacy _rode_ to school in a bus last year.
10. Many people who live in the city don't _own_ a car.
11. If you don't _tie_ your shoelaces, you'll trip over them.
12. We read a book about the long _life_ of Benjamin Franklin.

Opposites

Write the spelling word from the box that is the antonym, or opposite, of each word below.

lie	find	most	tie

13. fewest _most_
14. lose _find_
15. truth _lie_
16. untie _tie_

Opt: An Illusionary Tale • SPELLING

Proofread and Write — Spelling 17

Name_____ Date_____ SPELLING **17**

Words with Long *i* and Long *o*

Proofreading

There are six spelling mistakes in this paragraph. Circle the misspelled words. Write the words correctly on the lines below.

Many years (agow) the Wright brothers lived in Dayton, Ohio. Orville and Wilbur Wright were inventors. They used their (bysickle) shop to build the first airplane. First they did tests with kites to see if their idea (mite) work. Then they did (flite) tests on gliders in Kitty Hawk, North Carolina. When the brothers couldn't (fynd) anyone to make an engine for their plane, they built one themselves. Finally, in 1903, Orville Wright flew the first plane that had an engine and a propeller. No one else (rowd) with him, not even his brother.

1. _____ago_____   2. _____bicycle_____   3. _____might_____

4. _____flight_____   5. _____find_____   6. _____rode_____

Writing Activity

Imagine that you have your own bicycle shop. Write how you manage the shop. Use at least four spelling words in your explanation.

_____

_____

_____

_____

_____

Posttest — Spelling 18

Name_____ Date_____ SPELLING **18**

Words with Long *i* and Long *o*

Look at the words in each set. One word in each set is spelled correctly. Use a pencil to color in the circle in front of that word. Before you begin, look at the sample sets of words. Sample A has been done for you. Do Sample B by yourself. When you are sure you know what to do, you may go on with the rest of the page.

Sample A
- Ⓐ cind
- ● kind
- Ⓒ kynd
- Ⓓ kinde

Sample B
- ● light
- Ⓕ lyte
- Ⓖ liet
- Ⓗ lygte

1.
- Ⓐ spoak
- Ⓑ spowke
- Ⓒ spok
- ● spoke

2.
- Ⓔ aggo
- Ⓕ agow
- ● ago
- Ⓗ ugo

3.
- ● might
- Ⓑ miht
- Ⓒ mighte
- Ⓓ mitte

4.
- Ⓔ tost
- ● toast
- Ⓖ towst
- Ⓗ toste

5.
- Ⓐ fighnd
- Ⓑ finde
- Ⓒ fynd
- ● find

6.
- Ⓔ bycycle
- Ⓕ bisickal
- ● bicycle
- Ⓗ bysikel

7.
- ● lie
- Ⓑ li
- Ⓒ luy
- Ⓓ ligh

8.
- Ⓔ flite
- ● flight
- Ⓖ flyt
- Ⓗ fligt

9.
- ● own
- Ⓑ oan
- Ⓒ owne
- Ⓓ ohn

10.
- Ⓔ liffe
- Ⓕ lyff
- ● life
- Ⓗ ligh

11.
- Ⓐ tye
- Ⓑ ty
- ● tie
- Ⓓ ti

12.
- Ⓔ rowd
- ● rode
- Ⓖ roade
- Ⓗ rodde

13.
- Ⓐ throun
- ● thrown
- Ⓒ trone
- Ⓓ throan

14.
- Ⓔ whipe
- Ⓕ wype
- Ⓖ wiep
- ● wipe

15.
- Ⓐ mose
- Ⓑ moaste
- ● most
- Ⓓ mowst

Practice 22

Name_____ Date_____ **Practice** 22

Problem and Solution

Characters in stories often face **problems**. The answers to their problems are called **solutions**. Read the problems below. Then complete the chart by writing down two ways to solve each problem. **Answers will vary.**

Problem	Solutions Answers will vary.
Your class is going to write letters to pen pals. Everyone's pencil point is broken and there is no sharpener. What can the class do?	1. **Use pen or crayons to write your letters.** 2. **Buy a new pencil sharpener.**
A vacant lot across the street from your school is covered with rocks. Nobody likes looking at the lot. What can your school do?	3. **Make a rock garden out of the rocks.** 4. **Clear the rocks and plant a garden.**
It is your friend's birthday. You forgot to buy a present. What can you do?	5. **Give your friend one of your favorite things.** 6. **Promise your friend that you'll buy a present tomorrow.**

6 Book 3.1/Unit 1
Max Malone

At Home: Help students to identify problems in their neighborhoods. Brainstorm together to find some solutions.

22

Practice 23

Name_____ Date_____ **Practice** 23

Vocabulary

Supply the correct words from the list.

scene   ceiling   eager   including   section   cents

Juliana was _____**eager**_____ to see the new house. She couldn't wait! There was even a picture of a carnival painted in her new bedroom. "It's on the _____**ceiling**_____," her father had said. "You'll be able to see it as you lie in bed." Juliana thought a carnival was a great _____**scene**_____ to watch before falling asleep.

There was another thing that Juliana liked about her new house. Even _____**including**_____ a ten-minute bus ride, the house was still closer to school.

Juliana's mother bought her a new book bag for the daily trip. It was a present to celebrate their moving. The bag cost seven dollars and eighty _____**cents**_____. They found it in the sports _____**section**_____ of the department store.

"Of all places!" Juliana's mother exclaimed as she picked up the bag. "You never know where you'll find things!"

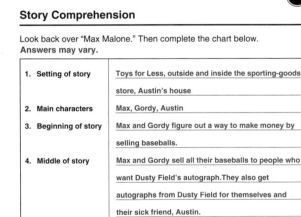

23 **At Home:** Have students use each vocabulary word in a sentence.

Book 3.1/Unit 1
Max Malone 6

Tanya's Books

Tanya's Books

Tanya ran out of books to read. So one day she decided to write her own book. She was *eager* to start. "It will have neat stuff, *including* pictures," she said.

Tanya's mother gave Tanya ninety *cents* to buy a new pen. Then Tanya began to write. Her story was about a house where the *ceiling* became the floor. In one *scene*, the family in the house tried to eat breakfast upside down.

The story was so funny, Tanya decided to write a longer story. This second story had five sections. Each *section* told about a friend of hers.

When Tanya finished her second story she gave each of her friends a copy. Everyone liked it.

1. What did Tanya do when she ran out of books to read?
   She started writing her own stories.
2. What does the floor become in Tanya's first book?
   the ceiling
3. What word tells how Tanya feels about writing her books?
   eager
4. What word describes one setting and event in Tanya's first book?
   scene
5. How much money did Tanya's mother give her?
   ninety cents

5 Book 3.1/Unit 1
Max Malone

At Home: Encourage students to talk about what kind of story they would write if they ran out of books to read.

23A

Practice 24

Name_____ Date_____ **Practice** 24

Story Comprehension

Look back over "Max Malone." Then complete the chart below. **Answers may vary.**

1. Setting of story	Toys for Less, outside and inside the sporting-goods store, Austin's house
2. Main characters	Max, Gordy, Austin
3. Beginning of story	Max and Gordy figure out a way to make money by selling baseballs.
4. Middle of story	Max and Gordy sell all their baseballs to people who want Dusty Field's autograph. They also get autographs from Dusty Field for themselves and their sick friend, Austin.
5. End of Story	Max and Gordy visit Austin and give him a baseball autographed by Dusty Field.

Now match each detail.

6. __c__ sells all the baseballs for $5   a. Dusty Field
7. __e__ had his appendix taken out   b. Max
8. __a__ a baseball player   c. Toys are Less
9. __b__ gets idea to buy baseballs for $5   d. Gordy
10. __d__ helps Max sell the baseballs   e. Austin

24 **At Home:** Have students think of some ways to make money similar to the way Max and Gordy did.

Book 3.1/Unit 1
Max Malone 10

Max Malone... • PRACTICE

Use an Index

An **index** can help you find information in a nonfiction book. The numbers for pages with illustrations are set in italics.

---
622 – Index

M
magazines, financial 33, *34*
merit system, 101, *532*
merchant class, 36, *88*
    rise of in England, *385, 412*
money systems, 65, 89–101
mutual funds, 56, 92
    failure of, 109–120

N
Native American money, 34
newspaper, listings of exchange rates,
    56–58
numbers, 35
    early mathematics 59

numismatics, 67–73
    coin collecting, 122

O
Old World, 45
    gold in, 310
    money used in, 99, 134, 238, 259–261
oversupply, 145, 267

P
Pacific Island coins, 67, 90
    rise of the dollar, 578, 655–678
    shells, 202, 349
    trading, 381, 399, *412, 424*
pound, English, 78–80

---

1. On what page would you find information on Native American money?
   34

2. Where would facts about money systems be found?
   pages 65, 89-101

3. Besides page 202, where else would you read about shells being used as Pacific Island money? _____ **349**

4. If you wanted to know how paper money is printed in the United States, would this page of the index help you to find out? _____ **no**

5. Which page probably has an illustration of a financial magazine? _**34**_

6. On which pages would you find information about the failure of mutual funds? _**109–120**_

Problem and Solution

You can often find **solutions**, or answers, to even the most difficult **problems.** Finish the chart by writing down how Max and Gordy solved each of their problems.

Problem

1. Max and Gordy have $2.50 each and want to buy as many 20¢ baseballs as they can.

2. Max and Gordy feel shy about selling their baseballs to people at the sporting-goods store.

3. Max and Gordy both want their own Dusty Field-autographed baseballs.

4. Max and Gordy forget to save a baseball for Austin.

5. Max and Gordy know that Austin is sad about not seeing Dusty Field.

Solution

They talk to a store manager who sells them all the balls for $5.00.

They force themselves to call out to people to buy their baseballs for Dusty Field's autograph.

They sell 46 baseballs and save 2 for themselves.

They buy a baseball with the money they earned.

They give Austin a new baseball autographed by Dusty Field.

Story Elements

A **plot** is what happens in a story. The **characters** are who the story is about. Read the story before you answer each question.

Tippy was a small brown dog. Fluffy was a black cat with long hair. Both animals lived with their owner, Lisa. One day Lisa let her pets out into the backyard. Both animals wanted to see something new. Right away, Fluffy jumped over the fence. Tippy dug a hole under the fence and crawled through.

Fluffy and Tippy happily ran from yard to yard. Suddenly a big dog appeared. It was the largest, scariest dog Fluffy and Tippy had ever seen. The dog barked and growled. Fluffy and Tippy turned around and ran straight back to their yard.

1. Who are the main characters? _**Tippy, a dog and Fluffy, a cat**_

2. What do the main characters want to do? _**see something new**_

3. How are the characters able to do this? **Fluffy jumps over the fence, and Tippy crawls under the fence to get out of the backyard.**

4. What problem do Tippy and Fluffy run into? **They meet a large dog that growls at them.**

5. What do the animals do next? **They run back to their own backyard.**

6. Do you think the animals learned anything from their experience?
   Answers may vary. Possible answer: Home is the best place to be.

Compound Words

A **compound word** is made by joining two smaller words. The meanings of the two smaller words can help you figure out the meaning of the compound word.

Look at each of the compound words. Write the two words that make up each compound word. Then use the meanings of the two smaller words to write the meaning of the compound word.

popcorn

1. _**pop**_ + _**corn**_

2. meaning = _**corn that can be popped**_

homeland

3. _**home**_ + _**land**_

4. meaning = _**the land in which a person makes his or her home**_

sweatshirt

5. _**sweat**_ + _**shirt**_

6. meaning = _**a shirt that absorbs sweat**_

seacoast

7. _**sea**_ + _**coast**_

8. meaning = _**the place where the sea meets the land**_

sandbox

9. _**sand**_ + _**box**_

10. meaning = _**a box that holds sand**_

Max Malone... • RETEACH

Name_____ Date_____ **Reteach** 22

Problem and Solution

> Charactors in stories often face difficulties or **problems** that they must solve. The answers to their problems are called **solutions**.

Read the story. Then answer each question.

> Amy and her brother, Mark, wanted to buy their mother a purple scarf for her birthday. Their father said the scarf cost $10.00. Amy and Mark had only $7.50 saved.
>
> "I know how we can earn the rest of the money," Mark said. "We can sell lemonade at the corner."
>
> The children bought lemonade mix for $1.50. They spent all day Saturday selling lemonade. They made $2.50. When they subtracted the cost of the mix, they had earned $1.00.
>
> "We still don't have enough money," Amy said. Then she had an idea. She made a poster that read, "Dog Grooming: 50¢ a dog." Soon, Amy and Mark had the $1.50 they needed.

Problems

1. Why couldn't Amy and Mark buy the scarf for their mother right away?

   They didn't have enough money.

2. What problem did Amy and Mark have after they first tried to earn money? They still didn't have enough money to buy the scarf.

Solutions

3. What solution did Amy come up with to solve their problem? They would groom dogs to earn money.

4. Did Mark and Amy solve their problem? Yes; they earned enough money to buy the scarf for their mother's birthday.

4 / Book 3.1/Unit 1
Max Malone
At Home: Have students think of ways to earn money. Then have students make posters advertising their ideas.
22

Name_____ Date_____ **Reteach** 23

Vocabulary

Choose the word that matches the meaning. Then fill in the crossword puzzle.

ceiling   cents   eager   including   scene   section

Across

1. part _____section_____

4. pennies _____cents_____

5. wanting very much _____eager_____

Down

1. a setting _____scene_____

2. top part of a room _____ceiling_____

3. containing _____including_____

(crossword puzzle grid with answers: SECTION across; CENTS across; EAGER across; SCENE, CEILING, INCLUDING down)

Story Comprehension   **Reteach** 24

Circle the answer to each question about "Max Malone."

1. Why doesn't Austin go to see his baseball hero?

   He is too upset.   He is too young.   (He is recovering from surgery.)

2. What do Max and Gordy do at Toys for Less?

   sell baseballs   (buy baseballs)   autograph baseballs

3. What do Max and Gordy do at the sporting-goods store?

   autograph baseballs   buy baseballs   (sell baseballs)

4. What do Max and Gordy give to Austin?

   an appendix   46 baseballs   (an autographed baseball)

23–24
At Home: Have students create their own crossword puzzle using the words from the story.
Book 3.1/Unit 1
Max Malone 4

Name_____ Date_____ **Reteach** 25

Use an Index

> An **index** tells you where different subjects in a book are located. The page numbers of illustrations are listed in italics in an index.

This is a portion of an index for a book called *Your Money*. Use it to answer the questions below.

D
diamonds, 33
dime, 21, 66
dollar, 12, 34–36, *56*

E
Easter Island coins, 92
English nicknames, 45

F
fifty-dollar bill, 101, 121–122
Fort Knox, 66, 78

G
gold, 199, 356–359

Q
quarter, how word was used, 77

P
pound, 39, *88,*
    English, 55
    Irish, 99
penny, 89
    made of copper, 90

R
roll, of coins, 36, 87, 99–100
Royal Treasury, 338, *341*
    keeping track of money, 400

1. On what page would you find information about a quarter? _77_

2. On what page would you find an illustration of a dollar? _56_

3. How many pages contain information about gold? _5_

4. On what page would you find out something about the copper penny? _90_

5. On how many pages is Fort Knox mentioned in this book? _2_

5 / Book 3.1/Unit 1
Max Malone
At Home: Have students write two more questions based on this index.
25

Name_____ Date_____ **Reteach** 26

Problem and Solution

> The **solution** is the way that a character solves his or her **problem**.

Max and Gordy solve a few problems in "Max Malone." Read each problem. Then circle the letter next to the solution that you read about in the story.

1. Max and Gordy want to know how many balls they can buy for $5.00.

   a. Gordy uses math to find out the answer.

   (b.) They talk to the store manager of Toys for Less.

   c. They make a deal with the owner of the sporting-goods store.

2. Max and Gordy want people to buy their baseballs.

   (a.) They call out to people on line at the sporting-goods store.

   b. They make a poster.

   c. They test out their ideas on Austin.

3. Max and Gordy need a baseball for Austin.

   a. The sporting-goods store owner gives them a free baseball.

   b. Dusty Field gives them a baseball of his own.

   (c.) Max and Gordy buy a baseball for Austin.

4. Austin is too sick to meet Dusty Field.

   (a.) Max and Gordy bring Austin an autographed baseball.

   b. Austin's mother gets an autographed baseball for her son.

   c. The sporting-goods store owner mails Austin some baseball cards.

26
At Home: Have students describe a problem that they helped to solve.
Book 3.1/Unit 1
Max Malone 4

Max Malone... • RETEACH

Story Elements

Characters are the people or animals that a story is about. The **plot** is what happens to those characters during the story.

Read the selections. Circle the letter that stands for the correct answer.

Kyle and Tipper spent the day fishing. There was not a cloud in the sky. The lake was calm and still. The two friends saw turtles and frogs swimming through the water. But they didn't see fish!

"Oh well," said Kyle, "we could try again tomorrow."

"Or we could go to the movies," said Tipper.

1. **CHARACTER:** Who are the main characters in the story?
   (a.) Kyle and Tipper   **b.** the fish   **c.** the turtles and frogs

2. **PLOT:** What is the plot of the story?
   a. The movie is playing.
   b. It is not cloudy.
   (c.) Kyle and Tipper didn't catch any fish.

   It was Saturday. Genelle and Jackie were going to the mall by bus. Suddenly they heard a popping sound. The bus had a flat tire.

   "How are we going to get to the store?" asked Genelle.

   "I don't know," answered Jackie. "We'll have to wait until a tow truck comes."

3. **CHARACTER:** Who are the main characters in the story?
   a. the mall   **b.** the tow truck   (c.) Genelle and Jackie

4. **PLOT:** What is the plot of the story?
   a. Genelle and Jackie are bored.
   (b.) The girls' bus has a flat tire on the way to the mall.
   c. There is a sale at the mall.

Compound Words

A **compound word** is made by joining two smaller words. You can usually figure out the meaning of a compound word by looking at the two smaller words and putting their meanings together.

Make a compound word by joining a word in the list to the end of one of the words below. Then write the meaning of the compound word. You may use some words more than once. **Answers may vary.**

selves   boat   yard   balls   board   cloth   noon

1. sail   _____sailboat_____   _____a boat that has a sail_____

2. after   _____afternoon_____   _____the time after 12 P.M., or noon_____

3. table   _____tablecloth_____   _____a cloth that covers a table_____

4. our   _____ourselves_____   _____us, our group_____

5. base   _____baseballs_____   _____balls used for playing baseball_____

6. house   _____houseboat_____   _____a boat that is also a house_____

7. back   _____backyard_____   _____the yard in back_____

8. floor   _____floorboard_____   _____a board in a floor_____

Max Malone... • EXTEND

Name_____ Date_____ **Extend** 22

Problem and Solution

Read the following story about Sarah. Then complete the Problem-Solution Chart to show how Sarah might solve her problem.

Sarah waited in the car for her mother. Sarah had an idea that she wanted to write in her journal before she forgot it. But it was too dark. Then she remembered she had some glow-in-the-dark ink pens in her backpack. Help Sarah solve her problem.

Sarah's Problem-Solution Chart

PROBLEM

What is the problem? **It is too dark for Sarah to write in her journal.**

Who has the problem? _____ **Sarah has the problem.**

SOLUTION BOX

Sarah could use the glow-in-the-dark ink pens to write in her journal. This way she could see what she was writing.

_____

_____

RESULT BOX

Sarah got her idea into her journal before she forgot it. She also

used her time waiting for her mother wisely.

_____

Book 3.1 / Unit 1
Max Malone

At Home: Think of a problem a student might have, such as how to get homework finished on soccer-practice days. Write down possible solutions to the problem, and the result of each solution.

22

Name_____ Date_____ **Extend** 23

Vocabulary

ceiling	cents	eager
including	scene	section

Write each word in the box on a card. Write definitions for each word on other cards. Play a matching game with a partner. Place the word cards face down on one side and the definitions face down on another side. Turn over two cards at a time, one from each side. If the word matches the definition, keep the cards. If not, turn them over and let your partner have a turn.

Extend 24

Story Comprehension

Imagine that you were at the sidewalk sale where Max and Gordy sold baseballs. On another sheet of paper, draw the sidewalk stands you would like to see there and label them. Put all the illustrations together into a booklet and gather them for the library corner. Or, organize your illustrations as a class and make one large book of sidewalk stands.

At Home: Look up entrepreneur together in the dictionary and discuss how Max and Gordy were entrepreneurs. Think of any other young people you know who are like Max.

23–24

Book 3.1/ Unit 1
Max Malone

Name_____ Date_____ **Extend** 25

Use an Index

Many books have an index. An index is at the back of the book. It lists specific information in the book and pages on which the information is located. Look at this part of an index. Then answer the questions below.

D	E
day, length, 21	eagles, 39
deserts, 90–91	ears, 82
dew, 68	parts, 83
digestion, 76	hearing, 85
dinosaurs, 27	Earth, 20
extinction, 28	earthquakes, 22
dogs, 53	earthworms, 25
ducks, 32	ecology, 69
	ecosystems, 70
	water, 71
	land, 73

1. Suppose you wanted to find a picture of an ear. What page would you check? _____ **Page 82 or 83**

2. Some main topics have subtopics. Where would you read about water ecosystems? _____ **Page 71**

3. On what page would you find out about how dinosaurs became extinct? _____ **Page 28**

4. Under what main topic would you find information about hearing?
_____ **Under ears**

5. Under what main topic would you find information about the living and nonliving things in a body of water? _____ **Under ecosystems**

Book 3.1/Unit 1
Max Malone

At Home: Go through indexes of books at home. Point out any differences you find.

25

Name_____ Date_____ **Extend** 26

Problem and Solution

There are solutions for most problems. Max and Gordy showed how to solve some problems. They also showed how to treat a good friend.

Suppose your school needs sports equipment. What ways can you think of to raise the money for your school to buy the equipment it needs?

_____
_____
_____
_____
_____
_____
_____
_____
_____
_____
_____
_____
_____
_____
_____
_____
_____
_____
_____

26

At Home: Talk about daily problem/solution situations that students regularly face and deal with. Help them to see where they are adept at coming up with solutions and where they may need more practice.

Book 3.1 / Unit 1
Max Malone

Max Malone... • EXTEND

Story Elements

Complete the story map below. Tell what event in the story happened as a result of how the character felt. Under the character's name, draw a picture of the character's face showing how he felt.

CHARACTER	Character's Feelings	Story Event
Gordy	He wanted to start selling the baseballs.	**Gordy started calling out, "Get your baseballs autographed by Dusty Field. Just fifty cents. Sure to become a collectable."**
Max	Max had forgotten all about Austin.	**Max and Gordy bought a three dollar real league baseball and asked Dusty to sign it for Austin.**
Austin	Austin felt disappointed because he could not go to the sporting goods store to get Dusty's autograph.	**Max and Gordy surprised Austin with a real league baseball signed by Dusty Field.**

Book 3.1 / Unit 1
Max Malone

At Home: Ask students to draw a character they have read about, but have never seen in an illustration or on TV. Draw some conclusion about how easily readers picture their characters through the words they read.

27

Compound Words

every	mid	base	air	balls
thing	them	selves	one	

Use the words in the box to make compound words you can use in the sentences below.

1. The outfielder caught the fly ball in _____ **midair** _____.
2. Max and Gordy bought forty-six _____ **baseballs** _____.
3. They wanted signatures for _____ **themselves** _____, too.
4. In the end, _____ **everyone** _____ was happy.

Use some of the compound words that you built to write a story.

_____
_____
_____
_____
_____
_____
_____
_____
_____
_____
_____
_____

28

At Home: Ask students to look at a newspaper for more compound words.

Book 3.1 / Unit 1
Max Malone

Panel 1 (Grammar 19)

Name_____ Date_____ LEARN **Grammar** 19

Predicates

- Every sentence has two parts.
- Every sentence has a predicate.
- The **predicate** of a sentence tells what the subject does or is.
  Two boys go to the toy store.
  The predicate is <u>go to the toy store.</u>

Which word or words tell what the subject does or is? Draw a line under the predicate.

1. The boys <u>talk with the store manager.</u>
2. They <u>buy a box of baseballs.</u>
3. The friends <u>count forty-eight balls.</u>
4. Dusty Field <u>is a famous baseball player.</u>
5. People <u>stand in line for Dusty's autograph.</u>
6. The boys <u>sell baseballs to the kids.</u>
7. Dusty <u>signs the baseballs.</u>
8. Austin <u>is a friend of the boys.</u>
9. Austin <u>misses Dusty Field.</u>
10. The boys <u>give Austin a ball signed by Dusty.</u>

10 Book 3.1/Unit 1
Max Malone Makes a Million

Extension: Have students work in pairs. Ask each student to write two sentences that tell what happens in a baseball game. Then tell students to draw a line under the predicates in their partner's sentences. 19

Panel 2 (Grammar 20)

Name_____ Date_____ LEARN AND PRACTICE **Grammar** 20

Finding Predicates

- Every sentence has two parts.
- Every sentence has a predicate.
- The predicate of a sentence tells what the subject does or is.

Match each group of words in the first column with its predicate in the second column. Write the predicate.

1. A toy store **has a sale**.
2. The boys **spend five dollars**.
3. A long line of people **is in front of the store**.
4. At first, Max **is nervous**.
5. Many people **buy balls from the boys**.
6. Dusty Field **is tall and thin**.
7. A real league ball **costs three dollars**.
8. Austin **is happy to see his friends**.
9. Austin's fish **eats shrimp**.
10. From his bag, Gordy **takes out Austin's ball**.

is in front of the store

spend five dollars

is tall and thin

has a sale

takes out Austin's ball

is happy to see his friends

buy balls from the boys

is nervous

costs three dollars

eats shrimp

20 Extension: Have students complete the following sentence by using different predicates: Once a friend _____. Book 3.1/Unit 1 **Max Malone Makes a Million** 10

Panel 3 (Grammar 21)

Name_____ Date_____ PRACTICE AND REVIEW **Grammar** 21

Writing Predicates to Complete Sentences

- Every sentence has two parts.
- Every sentence has a predicate.
- The predicate of a sentence tells what the subject does or is.

Add a predicate to each group of words. Write the sentence.

1. A baseball pitcher _____.
   throws the ball
2. A catcher _____.
   calls the pitches
3. On his face, the catcher _____.
   wears a mask
4. A batter _____.
   swings the bat
5. After three strikes, a batter _____.
   is out
6. After a hit, the batter _____.
   is on base
7. Players on the field _____.
   are all athletes
8. The highest score _____.
   wins the game

Answers will vary. Suggested answers are shown.

8 Book 3.1/Unit 1
Max Malone Makes a Million

Extension: Ask each student to write on a strip of oak tag a sentence about another sport. Have students cut their sentence into two parts so the predicate is one part. Then display the subjects of students' sentences and invite students to find and match the missing predicates. 21

Panel 4 (Grammar 22)

Name_____ Date_____ MECHANICS **Grammar** 22

Using Quotation Marks in Sentences

- Use **quotation marks** before and after a person's exact words.

Put the quotation marks where they should be. Write the correct sentences on the lines.

1. That's it! Max cried out.
   "That's it!" Max cried out.
2. You're a genius, said Gordy.
   "You're a genius," said Gordy.
3. How many can we buy? asked Gordy.
   "How many can we buy?" asked Gordy.
4. Let's ask the manager, said Max.
   "Let's ask the manager," said Max.

Proofread these sentences. Write them correctly on the lines.

5. max said that's a great idea
   Max said, "That's a great idea."
6. the boys sold the baseballs
   The boys sold the baseballs.
7. wow said Gordy
   "Wow!" said Gordy.
8. explain how the boys made a million
   Explain how the boys made a million.

22 Extension: Have students write a conversation using quotation marks. Book 3.1/Unit 1 **Max Malone Makes a Million** 8

Predicates

A. Decide which part of the sentence is the predicate. Mark your answer.

1. A young woman in the store helped the boys.
   - ⓐ helped the boys ●
   - ⓑ A young woman
   - ⓒ in the store

2. The box of baseballs cost five dollars.
   - ⓐ The box
   - ⓑ cost five dollars ●
   - ⓒ The box of baseballs

3. Some of the kids had scraps of paper.
   - ⓐ scraps of paper
   - ⓑ had scraps of paper ●
   - ⓒ Some of the kids

4. Max and Gordy sold all the baseballs.
   - ⓐ Max and Gordy
   - ⓑ sold all the baseballs ●
   - ⓒ all the baseballs

B. Decide which predicate fits the sentence. Mark your answer.

5. The manager of the store _____.
   - ⓐ door opens
   - ⓑ opening the door.
   - ⓒ opened the door. ●

6. The baseball player _____.
   - ⓐ wore jeans ●
   - ⓑ wearing jeans
   - ⓒ worn jeans

7. The ball that Dusty signed _____.
   - ⓐ for Austin
   - ⓑ is for Austin ●
   - ⓒ gave to Austin

8. A real baseball _____.
   - ⓐ be three dollars
   - ⓑ three dollars cost
   - ⓒ costs three dollars ●

Predicates

- The **predicate** of a sentence tells what the subject does or is.

Mechanics:
- Begin every sentence with a capital letter.
- End every sentence with a special mark.
- Use quotation marks before and after a person's exact words.

Work with a partner. One of you reads the sentences aloud. The other proofreads. Listen for the sentences that are missing a predicate. Write the corrected sentences on the lines. The proofreader reads the corrected sentences aloud.

1. the Giant Summer Sale
   _____ **The Giant Summer Sale is happening this weekend.**

2. max read the sign on a box
   _____ **Max read the sign on a box.**

3. the perfect things to buy
   _____ **The perfect things to buy are candlesticks.**

4. do you know what he bought
   _____ **Do you know what he bought?**

5. the baseballs in the box
   _____ **The baseballs in the box are new.**

6. at first, only a few kids
   _____ **At first, only a few kids knew about the game.**

7. they sold all the baseballs
   _____ **They sold all the baseballs.**

8. tell me how the story ends
   _____ **Tell me how the story ends.**

Max Malone... • SPELLING

Page 19

Words with /ū/ and /ü/

Pretest Directions

Fold back the paper along the dotted line. Use the blanks to write each word as it is read aloud. When you finish the test, unfold the paper. Use the list at the right to correct any spelling mistakes. Practice the words you missed for the Posttest.

To Parents

Here are the results of your child's weekly spelling Pretest. You can help your child study for the Posttest by following these simple steps for each word on the word list:

1. Read the word to your child.
2. Have your child write the word, saying each letter as it is written.
3. Say each letter of the word as your child checks the spelling.
4. If a mistake has been made, have your child read each letter of the correctly spelled word aloud, and then repeat steps 1-3.

1. _____	1. music
2. _____	2. broom
3. _____	3. soup
4. _____	4. fruit
5. _____	5. huge
6. _____	6. drew
7. _____	7. truth
8. _____	8. pool
9. _____	9. goose
10. _____	10. excuse
11. _____	11. dew
12. _____	12. juice
13. _____	13. crew
14. _____	14. group
15. _____	15. produce

Challenge Words

_____	ceiling
_____	eager
_____	including
_____	scene
_____	section

Page 20

Words with /ū/ and /ü/

Using the Word Study Steps

1. LOOK at the word.
2. SAY the word aloud.
3. STUDY the letters in the word.
4. WRITE the word.
5. CHECK the word.
   Did you spell the word right?
   If not, go back to step 1.

Spelling Tip

Make up clues to help you remember the spelling.

u and **i** love fr**ui**t

Word Scramble

Unscramble each set of letters to make a spelling word.

1. csium __music__   2. wred __drew__   3. ewd __dew__

4. morbo __broom__   5. tuhtr __truth__   6. cueji __juice__

7. opsu __soup__   8. olop __pool__   9. wcre __crew__

10. fitur __fruit__   11. soeog __goose__   12. pugro __group__

13. gueh __huge__   14. suxcee __excuse__   15. ecrudpo __produce__

To Parents or Helpers:

Using the Word Study Steps above as your child comes across any new words will help him or her spell well. Review the steps as you both go over this week's spelling words.

Go over the Spelling Tip with your child. Ask your child if he or she knows other words that clues can be used to remember spelling. Help him or her write those words.

Help your child unscramble the spelling words.

Page 21

Words with /ū/ and /ü/

music	fruit	truth	excuse	crew
broom	huge	pool	dew	group
soup	drew	goose	juice	produce

Word Sort

Fill in the blanks with the words that have the /ū/ and /ü/ sounds spelled with the letters shown.

u - e
1. __huge__
2. __excuse__
3. __produce__

ew
7. __drew__
8. __dew__
9. __crew__

ou
12. __soup__
13. __group__

oo
4. __pool__
5. __broom__
6. __goose__

ui
10. __fruit__
11. __juice__

u
14. __music__
15. __truth__

Unscramble It

Unscramble each spelling word below and write it correctly on the line.

16. eguh __huge__
17. cumis __music__
18. tuifr __fruit__

Page 22

Words with /ū/ and /ü/

music	fruit	truth	excuse	crew
broom	huge	pool	dew	group
soup	drew	goose	juice	produce

Analogies

An **analogy** is a statement that compares sets of words that are alike in some way: *Night* is to *day* as *black* is to *white*. This analogy points out that *night* and *day* are opposite in the same way that *black* and *white* are opposite.

Use spelling words to complete the analogies below.

1. *On* is to *off* as *tiny* is to __huge__.
2. *Wet* is to *dry* as *lie* is to __truth__.
3. *TV* is to *picture* as *radio* is to __music__.
4. *Carrot* is to *vegetable* as *apple* is to __fruit__.
5. *Peanut* is to *peanut butter* as *orange* is to *orange* __juice__.

In the Dictionary

Many dictionary entries have sample sentences that show how the word can be used. Complete each sample sentence with a spelling word.

6. The artist __drew__ a picture of a garden.
7. Do you like to swim in a __pool__ or in the ocean?
8. Use a __broom__ to sweep the floor.
9. Give a good reason or an __excuse__ for your lateness.
10. Some companies __produce__ parts for cars.

Challenge Extension: Write the Challenge Words on the board in scrambled order and ask students to write them in ABC order.

Worksheet 23

Words with /ū/ and /ü/

Proofreading

There are five spelling mistakes in the fairy tale. Circle the misspelled words. Write the words correctly on the lines below.

When the (mewzik) started, a very strange thing happened. A picture in the fairy tale book came to life. It was amazing. First, a (quce) stepped out from the page. Then a (groop) of chicks from the picture came out and sat around it in a circle.

What do you think happened next?

Well, the chicks began to sing and dance. Suddenly, a parade of (froot) marched across the page. What a silly sight to see bananas, oranges, and pears marching!

Finally, the record stopped playing. Of course, everyone stopped dancing, singing, and marching. And that's the (truthe)!

1. ___music___   2. ___goose___   3. ___group___

4. ___fruit___   5. ___truth___

Writing Activity

Write a list of amazing things that could happen in your own fairy tale. Use at least five spelling words.

_____

_____

_____

_____

_____

Worksheet 24

Words with /ū/ and /ü/

Look at the words in each set. One word in each set is spelled correctly. Use a pencil to color in the circle in front of that word. Before you begin, look at the sample sets of words. Sample A has been done for you. Do Sample B by yourself. When you are sure you know what to do, you may go on with the rest of the page.

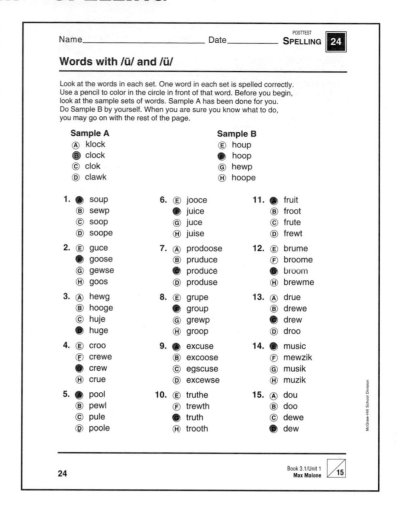

Sample A
- Ⓐ klock
- ⬤Ⓑ clock
- Ⓒ clok
- Ⓓ clawk

Sample B
- Ⓔ houp
- ⬤Ⓕ hoop
- Ⓖ hewp
- Ⓗ hoope

1.
- ⬤Ⓐ soup
- Ⓑ sewp
- Ⓒ soop
- Ⓓ soope

2.
- Ⓔ guce
- ⬤Ⓕ goose
- Ⓖ gewse
- Ⓗ goos

3.
- Ⓐ hewg
- Ⓑ hooge
- Ⓒ huje
- ⬤Ⓓ huge

4.
- Ⓔ croo
- Ⓕ crewe
- ⬤Ⓖ crew
- Ⓗ crue

5.
- ⬤Ⓐ pool
- Ⓑ pewl
- Ⓒ pule
- Ⓓ poole

6.
- Ⓔ jooce
- ⬤Ⓕ juice
- Ⓖ juce
- Ⓗ juise

7.
- Ⓐ prodoose
- Ⓑ pruduce
- ⬤Ⓒ produce
- Ⓓ produse

8.
- Ⓔ grupe
- ⬤Ⓕ group
- Ⓖ grewp
- Ⓗ groop

9.
- ⬤Ⓐ excuse
- Ⓑ excoose
- Ⓒ egscuse
- Ⓓ excewse

10.
- Ⓔ truthe
- Ⓕ trewth
- ⬤Ⓖ truth
- Ⓗ trooth

11.
- ⬤Ⓐ fruit
- Ⓑ froot
- Ⓒ frute
- Ⓓ frewt

12.
- Ⓔ brume
- Ⓕ broome
- ⬤Ⓖ broom
- Ⓗ brewme

13.
- Ⓐ drue
- Ⓑ drewe
- ⬤Ⓒ drew
- Ⓓ droo

14.
- ⬤Ⓔ music
- Ⓕ mewzik
- Ⓖ musik
- Ⓗ muzik

15.
- Ⓐ dou
- Ⓑ doo
- Ⓒ dewe
- ⬤Ⓓ dew

Practice 29

Make Predictions

Read each selection. Then make **predictions** about what might happen based on the titles and stories.

Then answer the questions to predict an outcome.

Things That Snap and Bite

Animal World is a safari park. You can drive through the park and see animals living freely, as they do in the wild. Be careful not to open your window! Some animals can be dangerous.

1. What kinds of animals do you predict live in Animal World?

   Answers would include animals that snap and bite, such as

   crocodiles, lions, and tigers.

2. Which parts of the story helped you make your prediction?

   The animals are wild. They snap and bite.

Rufus to the Rescue

My dog Rufus is so clever. Sometimes I think he actually understands what I am saying. Last week I got stuck climbing a tree. I shouted, "Rufus! Go home and fetch Dad!" Rufus barked at me and ran off.

3. What do you predict will happen? **Rufus will bring Dad back to help**

   the child stuck in the tree.

4. Which parts of the story helped you to predict your outcome?

   The title; also, Rufus is clever and seems to understand.

   He barked and ran off when the child asked him to get help.

Book 3.1/Unit 1 Champions of the World — 29

At Home: Have students look at a book, magazine, or newspaper. Ask them to guess what the stories are about by looking at the titles.

Practice 30

Vocabulary

Choose the correct word from the box to complete each sentence. Then write the word on the line.

| celebrated | cork | fans | pitcher | score | wrap |

1. Kate **celebrated** her birthday by having a party.
2. A baseball's center is made out of **cork**.
3. Our **pitcher** threw the ball for the batter to hit.
4. The **fans** cheered when David stepped onto the stage.
5. I **wrap** the gift with colorful paper.
6. The goal tied the **score** between the two teams.

Write two sentences that use two of the vocabulary words in each sentence. **Answers will vary.**

7. _____

8. _____

At Home: Challenge students to write a short story about a sports event using three of the vocabulary words.

Book 3.1/Unit 1 Champions of the World — 30

Fast Ball

Lou wanted to be a baseball player like his father. Long ago, Lou's father had been a *pitch*er on a winning team.

Pictures of Lou's father hung in Lou's bedroom. In one picture, *fans* cheered and *celebrated* as Lou's father threw the winning pitch. This pitch had made the *score* 3-0.

One afternoon, Lou went outside to practice. He wondered if he could pitch as well as his dad. It was cold, so he had to *wrap* a scarf around his neck. Then he threw the ball against a brick wall. Whack! The ball burst open and its *cork* fell out!

"Looks like I might be able to pitch", he thought. "I guess I'll give baseball a try!"

1. What is the name of the person who throws the ball to the batter?

   pitcher

2. What is inside a baseball?

   cork

3. What did Lou do with the scarf?

   He had to wrap it around his neck.

4. What was 3-0 in one of Lou's father's games?

   the score

5. What do you think Lou will do next in this story?

   He will join a baseball team.

Book 3.1/Unit 1 Champions of the World — 30A

At Home: Have students talk about games and sports they like. Also encourage them to talk about any sports or games any of their family members may play.

Practice 31

Story Comprehension

1. What did the Toms River Little League team do? **The team won the Little League World Championship in 1998.**

2. What was the nickname for the Toms River team? **"the Beast from the East"**

3. What team did the Toms River team play against in the final game? **a baseball team from Japan**

4. How long had it been since a U.S. team had won the Little League World Series? **five years, in 1993**

5. What did the people of Toms River, New Jersey, do when the Little League team came home from the game? **They had a parade to celebrate their team winning the world championship; the team rode on a fire truck.**

6. What is special about Mark McGwire and Sammy Sosa? **They both broke the old home run record the same year.**

7. In your own words, tell about the home run record and how it was set. **Answers will vary.**

8. Is "Champions of the World" a true story? How do you know? **Yes; it gives facts and information, instead of telling a story that a writer made up.**

At Home: Have students look for pictures of people playing baseball. Then have them make a collage of pictures mixed with facts that they learned about baseball from reading "Champions of the World."

Book 3.1/Unit 1 Champions of the World — 31

Champions of the World • PRACTICE

Practice 32

Name_____ Date_____ Practice **32**

Use a Search Engine

Study the make-believe Web site addresses shown below. Use them to answer the questions below.

http://www.majorleaguebaseball.com/	http://www.bigleagueslugger.com/
http://www.baseballcamps.com/	http://www.baseballscholarships.com/
http://www.tomsriver.com/	http://www.halloffame.com/

Fill in the blank with a Web site address. Pick the Web site most likely to help you.

If you wanted information about:

1. a summer camp for baseball players

    http://www.baseballcamps.com/

2. big-league slugger baseball bats

    http://www.bigleagueslugger.com/

3. the Little League World Series champs from Toms River, New Jersey

    http://www.tomsriver.com/

4. a sports scholarship for playing baseball in college

    http://www.baseballscholarship.com/

5. next year's complete major-league baseball schedule

    http://www.majorleaguebaseball.com/

6. how to visit the Hall of Fame in Cooperstown, N.Y.

    http://www.halloffame.com/

Practice 33

Name_____ Date_____ Practice **33**

Steps in a Process

Steps that you follow in order are called **steps in a process**. Writing down the steps in order will help you to remember them.

Think about the following activities. Each of them has several steps that need to be followed. Write down the steps in the process for each activity below. **Answers will vary. Possible examples follow.**

Find a book at the library.

1. Look up the number for the book.

2. Write down the number of the book.

3. Find the floor and bookshelf.

4. Locate the book that has the number.

Make a cup of chocolate milk.

1. Take the milk out of the refrigerator.

2. Take chocolate syrup from the cupboard.

3. Pour chocolate syrup into a glass.

4. Fill the rest of the glass with milk.

5. Stir it until it is mixed.

Make a costume for a costume party.

1. Decide which character you want to be.

2. Draw a picture of your costume.

3. Gather or buy materials and supplies.

4. Cut out the materials to be sewn together.

5. Sew your costume together.

33
At Home: Have students write down five steps that they follow when they do their homework.
Book 3.1/Unit 1
Champions of the World
14

Practice 34

Name_____ Date_____ Practice **34**

Compound Words

You can figure out the meaning of a compound word by looking at the two smaller words within it and putting the two meanings together.

Below are definitions of some compound words. Complete the chart.

Definition	Compound Word	Two Words	
1. the town where a person makes his or her home	hometown	home	town
2. balls that are used to play the game of basketball	basketballs	basket	balls
3. made at home, not at a factory or a store	homemade	home	made
4. the place made for walking at the side of a road	sidewalk	side	walk
5. the days at the end of the school or work week	weekend	week	end
6. case to store books	bookcase	book	case

Book 3.1/Unit 1
Champions of the World
6
At Home: Ask students to name the compound word that means **the work that you do at school.**
34

Practice 35

Name_____ Date_____ Practice **35**

Prefixes

A **prefix** is a word part that can be added to the beginning of a word to change the word's meaning. Knowing what a prefix means can help you figure out what a word means. The prefixes **un-** and **dis-** both mean "not" or "the opposite of."

Prefix + word	Meaning
dis + appears = disappears	the opposite of appears, to pass from sight
un + like = unlike	not alike, different

Write the prefix of each word. Write the word's meaning. Then use the word in a sentence of your own. **Answers will vary.**

1. **disagree**   Prefix: __dis__   Meaning: not agree, opposite of agree

    Sentence: _____

2. **unwrapped** Prefix: __un__   Meaning: not wrapped, opposite of wrapped

    Sentence: _____

3. **disobey**   Prefix: __dis__   Meaning: opposite of obey, not obey

    Sentence: _____

4. **unlucky**   Prefix: __un__   Meaning: not lucky

    Sentence: _____

5. **displease** Prefix: __dis__   Meaning: opposite of please

    Sentence: _____

35
At Home: Ask students to name three other words that begin with the prefix dis- and then tell you their meanings.
Book 3.1/Unit 1
Champions of the World
10

Champions of the World • RETEACH

Reteach 29

Name_____ Date_____ Reteach **29**

Make Predictions

> Reading titles can help you to **predict** what a story will be about.

Read each title. Then read the predictions of what the story will be about. Write an **X** next to the prediction that makes the most sense.

1. "The Beauty of Nature"
   - ____ **a.** a car factory
   - ____ **b.** life in the city
   - _X_ **c.** forests and mountains

2. "Basketball's Greatest Moments"
   - _X_ **a.** famous basketball games
   - ____ **b.** how to make a basketball
   - ____ **c.** a fishing village

3. "Look Left, Look Right, Look Left Again"
   - ____ **a.** making a quilt
   - ____ **b.** a boy and his many pets
   - _X_ **c.** crossing the street safely

4. "Free as a Bird"
   - _X_ **a.** a man who loves to fly airplanes
   - ____ **b.** a woman who owns a rare coin
   - ____ **c.** how to bake bread

Reteach 30

Name_____ Date_____ Reteach **30**

Vocabulary

Use words from the list to finish the story.

celebrated   cork   fans   pitcher   score   wrap

Marlene loves baseball. She is one of the game's biggest ___fans___. When she ___celebrated___ her ninth birthday, her parents took her to see a baseball game. Through most of the game, the ___score___ was tied. One batter hit the ball so hard that the ball popped open and the ___cork___ fell out. Marlene watched as the ___pitcher___ tried to ___wrap___ the leather around the inside of the ball.

6

Story Comprehension — Reteach **31**

Put a ✔ next to every sentence that tells something true from "Champions of the World."

- ____ **1.** The team from Toms River, New Jersey, lost a World Championship Little League game in 1998.
- _✔_ **2.** The Little League team from New Jersey was playing the final game of the season against a baseball team from Japan.
- _✔_ **3.** The Little League team from Toms River rode on a fire truck in a victory parade.
- ____ **4.** Roger Maris has the home-run record of all time.

Reteach 32

Name_____ Date_____ Reteach **32**

Use a Search Engine

> Pretend you've used a **search engine**. This is what you might see on your computer.

Use the information to answer the questions below.

Track Down | home-run champs | SEARCH

Track Down has found **40** web sites for **home-run champs**

1. **Welcome to the World of the Babe**
   complete listing of home runs hit—dates, places, pitchers
   —http://www.baberuth.com/
2. **The Japanese Play Baseball, Too**
   statistics for Japanese leagues
   —http://www.japanesesluggers.com/
3. **The National League Is the Land of Giants**
   complete hitting records for all players ever to appear in league play
   —http://www.nationalleague.com/
4. **McGwire and Sosa Aren't the Only Ones to Hit a Home Run**
   the history and legends of the greatest home runs ever hit
   —http://www.longball.com/
5. **Little League Home Runs**
   features biographies of the best home-run hitters
   —http://www.littleleaguesluggers.com/

1. What sort of information is being sought here? ___home-run champs___
2. What is the name of the search engine chosen? ___Track Down___
3. Which entry found above would be the Web site for Babe Ruth?
   ___http://www.baberuth.com/___
4. What Web address would tell you the most about the players in the National League? ___http://www.nationalleague.com/___
5. If these entries didn't tell you what you needed to know, where else could you look? ___in the other 35 entries not yet shown on the screen___

Reteach 33

Name_____ Date_____ Reteach **33**

Steps in a Process

> A series of steps you follow in order is called **steps in a process**. Writing down steps in the correct order will help you remember them.

In "Champions of the World," you learned how to make a baseball. The steps are written below, but they are out of order. Next to each step, write a number from 1 to 4 to show the order. Use the story if you need help.

Process: Make a Baseball

Step _2_ Put 219 yards of wool around the yarn.

Step _4_ Sew the ball closed with 108 stitches.

Step _3_ Cover the wool with a piece of cowhide.

Step _1_ Put 150 yards of cotton yarn around a piece of cork.

Now write down four steps that you would use to make a sandwich for lunch. **Answers may vary.**

Process: Make a Sandwich

Step 1: ___Take out two pieces of bread.___

Step 2: ___Slice cheese and a tomato.___

Step 3: ___Spread mustard on the bread.___

Step 4: ___Put the cheese and tomato between the slices of bread.___

Champions of the World • RETEACH

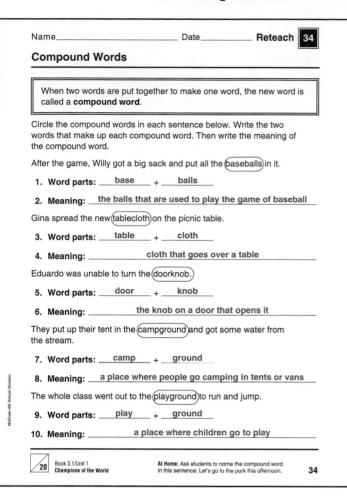

Compound Words

> When two words are put together to make one word, the new word is called a **compound word**.

Circle the compound words in each sentence below. Write the two words that make up each compound word. Then write the meaning of the compound word.

After the game, Willy got a big sack and put all the (baseballs) in it.

1. **Word parts:** ___base___ + ___balls___

2. **Meaning:** __the balls that are used to play the game of baseball__

Gina spread the new (tablecloth) on the picnic table.

3. **Word parts:** ___table___ + ___cloth___

4. **Meaning:** _____cloth that goes over a table_____

Eduardo was unable to turn the (doorknob.)

5. **Word parts:** ___door___ + ___knob___

6. **Meaning:** _____the knob on a door that opens it_____

They put up their tent in the (campground) and got some water from the stream.

7. **Word parts:** ___camp___ + ___ground___

8. **Meaning:** __a place where people go camping in tents or vans__

The whole class went out to the (playground) to run and jump.

9. **Word parts:** ___play___ + ___ground___

10. **Meaning:** _____a place where children go to play_____

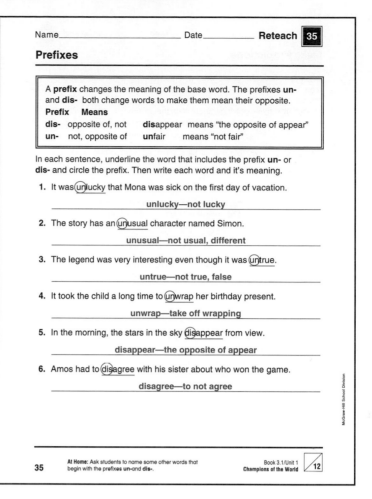

Prefixes

> A **prefix** changes the meaning of the base word. The prefixes **un-** and **dis-** both change words to make them mean their opposite.
> **Prefix**   **Means**
> **dis-**   opposite of, not   **dis**appear   means "the opposite of appear"
> **un-**   not, opposite of   **un**fair   means "not fair"

In each sentence, underline the word that includes the prefix **un-** or **dis-** and circle the prefix. Then write each word and it's meaning.

1. It was (un)lucky that Mona was sick on the first day of vacation.

   _____unlucky—not lucky_____

2. The story has an (un)usual character named Simon.

   _____unusual—not usual, different_____

3. The legend was very interesting even though it was (un)true.

   _____untrue—not true, false_____

4. It took the child a long time to (un)wrap her birthday present.

   _____unwrap—take off wrapping_____

5. In the morning, the stars in the sky (dis)appear from view.

   _____disappear—the opposite of appear_____

6. Amos had to (dis)agree with his sister about who won the game.

   _____disagree—to not agree_____

Champions of the World • EXTEND

Make Predictions

Often you predict, or guess what will happen next, in something you
read. Sometimes your predictions are correct and sometimes they
are not. Read each passage below, then stop and predict what will
happen next by answering the question that follows.

How do you know what's up and what's down?
What is it that keeps you from floating around?

1. Do you predict that this will be a poem, a riddle, a story, or an

   informative article? Explain. **Answers will vary, but most students**

   will predict a poem or riddle because of the rhyming words.

   What do you think the answer might be?
   The answer is simple . . . it's gravity.

2. Did these two lines make you change your prediction? **The rhyming**

   continues, so most students will keep their prediction the same.

*Everything has gravity. An apple and a dog have gravity. You have
gravity. Gravity pulls at everything on Earth, and everything on Earth
pulls back.*

3. Is your prediction still the same? Now what do you believe will come next?

   Most students will change their prediction and will predict

   that more science-related information will follow.

*Everything on Earth is pulled toward the center of the Earth. That is why
Earth's gravity holds apples, dogs, you, and even air, water, and rocks
down. Without gravity we would have no air to breathe or water to drink.
Could we survive?*

4. Does this passage confirm your latest prediction? Can you answer the last

   question in the passage? **Answers will vary, but student's predictions**

   should be confirmed. No, we could not survive without gravity.

Book 3.1 / Unit 1
Champions of the World

At Home: Go back over this exercise with students to see
that the predictions were made through understanding of
the text, not just wild guesses.

29

Vocabulary

Sometimes compound words make up new words. Think about words
such as *downpour, paperback,* or *cattail*. Be creative with the words
in the box to make compound words. Write your compound word in a
sentence. See the examples.

celebrated	cork	fans	pitcher	score	wrap

1. ___**Corkfans**___ like to be near bulletin boards.

2. Halloween is a ___**fanscelebrated**___ holiday.

3. _____

4. _____

Story Comprehension

Work like an inventor. Follow steps to make something.

1. Read the list of materials below. Decide which materials you could use
   to make a tool for sending a message.

electric wire	paper clips	mirror
light bulb	paper	string
battery	pen	paper cups

2. What are you making?

3. Decide your steps in creating your invention.

4. Draw a picture of what you made.

At Home: Talk about what goes into having ideas for inventions. It
requires some wondering about how things work. Walk around, listing
30–31   your home things that could be improved by a new invention.

Book 3.1/Unit 1
Champions of the World

Use a Search Engine

A computer catalog in a library lists all of the books in the library. A
computer search can find books by subject, by title, and by author.

The left column below lists what you know about a book. In the right
column write **author, title,** or **subject** to show which kind of search
you would have the computer catalog perform.

What You Are Looking For

A book about baseball	subject
A book by Allen Say	author
A book titled *Max Malone Makes a Million*	title
A book by Charlotte Herman	author
A book about optical illusions	subject
A book about Sammy Sosa or Mark McGwire	subject
A book titled *Grandfather's Journey*	title

Book 3.1 / Unit 1
Champions of the World

At Home: Discuss with students the different ways of
searching for information in our computer age.

32

Steps in a Process

In "Champions of the World," you read about how to make a baseball.
Think about how you would make your own sports card.
Choose the size of card or paper you want to use.
Decide on the sport you want to be good at.
Draw a picture of yourself playing this sport.
Add color to the picture.
Decide on the information that belongs on the back.
List your name, where you were born, and the year.
List all the other important information.
What other finishing touches do you want to add?
Share the sports cards with classmates.

At Home: Look through a newspaper to find pictures or
statistics on favorite sports figures.

33

Book 3.1/Unit 1
Champions of the World

Champions of the World • EXTEND

Compound Words

In each sentence, there are two words that you can put together to make a compound word listed in the Word Box. Write the compound word on the line.

overhead	basketball	baseball	afternoon
airplane	grandfather	something	sunshine

1. The plane flew over my head.   **overhead**

2. The plane is in the air.   **airplane**

3. Please meet me at noon or after.   **afternoon**

4. The waves seem to shine in the sun.   **sunshine**

5. The ball went in the basket.   **basketball**

6. Some days I can't think of a thing to do.   **something**

7. Juan's father plays a grand piano.   **grandfather**

8. The ball just missed me at first base.   **baseball**

Book 3.1 / Unit 1
Champions of the World

At Home: Make a word box together of items in the room that can be put together to make a compound word.

34

Prefixes

A **prefix** is a word part that can be added to the beginning of a word to change the word's meaning. Knowing what a prefix means can help you figure out what a word means. The prefixes *un-* and *dis-* both mean "not" or "the opposite of."

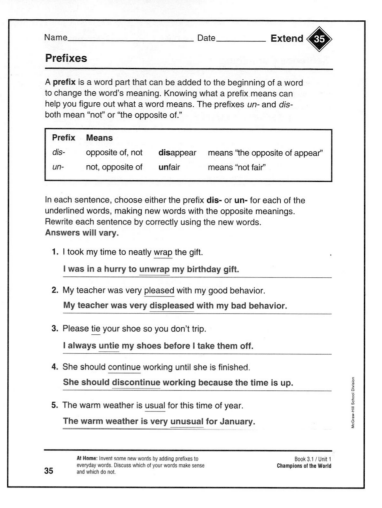

Prefix	Means		
dis-	opposite of, not	**dis**appear	means "the opposite of appear"
un-	not, opposite of	**un**fair	means "not fair"

In each sentence, choose either the prefix **dis-** or **un-** for each of the underlined words, making new words with the opposite meanings. Rewrite each sentence by correctly using the new words. **Answers will vary.**

1. I took my time to neatly <u>wrap</u> the gift.

   I was in a hurry to <u>unwrap</u> my birthday gift.

2. My teacher was very <u>pleased</u> with my good behavior.

   My teacher was very <u>displeased</u> with my bad behavior.

3. Please <u>tie</u> your shoe so you don't trip.

   I always <u>untie</u> my shoes before I take them off.

4. She should <u>continue</u> working until she is finished.

   She should <u>discontinue</u> working because the time is up.

5. The warm weather is <u>usual</u> for this time of year.

   The warm weather is very <u>unusual</u> for January.

35

At Home: Invent some new words by adding prefixes to everyday words. Discuss which of your words make sense and which do not.

Book 3.1 / Unit 1
Champions of the World

T51

Champions of the World • GRAMMAR

Sentence Combining

- Two related sentences can be joined with a comma and the word *and*.
  Separate: A baseball is sewn by hand. It has 108 stitches.
  Joined: A baseball is sewn by hand, and it has 108 stitches.

Combine each pair of sentences. Use a comma and the word *and*.

1. The pitcher throws the ball. Cardone swings.

   The pitcher throws the ball, and Cardone swings.

2. Cardone hits the ball. The ball goes flying.

   Cardone hits the ball, and the ball goes flying.

3. Cardone hits a home run. The team pulls ahead.

   Cardone hits a home run, and the team pulls ahead.

4. The Toms River team wins the World Series. The fans go wild.

   The Toms River team wins the World Series, and the fans go wild.

5. The team rides in a parade. The players wave to their fans.

   The team rides in a parade, and the players wave to their fans.

5 Book 3.1/Unit 1
Champions of the World
Extension: Have students write two related
sentences of their own about the Toms River team
and then use the word *and* to join them.
25

Compound Sentences

- A sentence that contains two sentences joined by *and* is called a **compound sentence**.

Write a compound sentence by joining each pair of sentences. Use a comma and the word *and*.

1. Chris Cardone bats for the first time. He hits a home run.

   Chris Cardone bats for the first time, and he hits a home run.

2. Todd Frazier is the star pitcher. He also hits a home run.

   Todd Frazier is the star pitcher, and he also hits a home run.

3. Brad Frank tags the player. The player is out.

   Brad Frank tags the player, and the player is out.

4. A U.S. team wins the World Series. It's the first time since 1993.

   A U.S. team wins the World Series, and it's the first time since 1993.

5. Toms River has a parade. About 2,000 fans come out to cheer.

   Toms River has a parade, and about 2,000 fans come out to cheer.

26
Extension: Ask students to write a compound sentence
about parades, using the word *and*.
Book 3.1/Unit 1
Champions of the World 5

Writing Compound Sentences

- Two related sentences can be joined with a comma and the word *and*.
- A sentence that contains two sentences joined by *and* is called a **compound sentence**.

Copy the following story, but make it sound better. Use *and* to join each pair of underlined sentences. Place a comma before *and* when you join the sentences to make them into compound sentences.

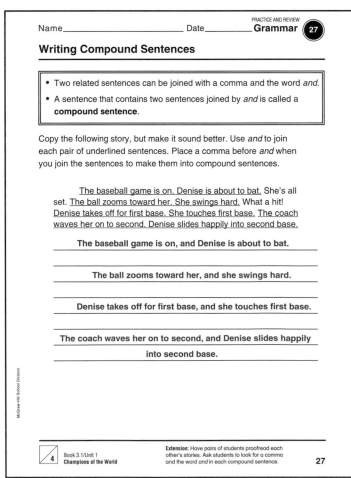

The baseball game is on. Denise is about to bat. She's all set. The ball zooms toward her. She swings hard. What a hit! Denise takes off for first base. She touches first base. The coach waves her on to second. Denise slides happily into second base.

The baseball game is on, and Denise is about to bat.

The ball zooms toward her, and she swings hard.

Denise takes off for first base, and she touches first base.

The coach waves her on to second, and Denise slides happily into second base.

4 Book 3.1/Unit 1
Champions of the World
Extension: Have pairs of students proofread each
other's stories. Ask students to look for a comma
and the word *and* in each compound sentence.
27

Proofreading Compound Sentences

- Use a comma before *and* when you join two sentences to form a compound sentence.
- Begin every sentence with a capital letter.

Combine each pair of short sentences into one longer sentence. Place a comma in the correct place and begin the second part of the sentence with a small letter. Then rewrite the paragraph.

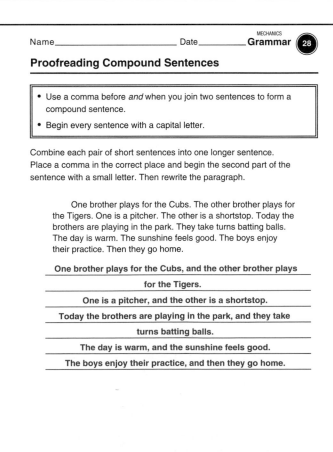

One brother plays for the Cubs. The other brother plays for the Tigers. One is a pitcher. The other is a shortstop. Today the brothers are playing in the park. They take turns batting balls. The day is warm. The sunshine feels good. The boys enjoy their practice. Then they go home.

One brother plays for the Cubs, and the other brother plays for the Tigers.

One is a pitcher, and the other is a shortstop.

Today the brothers are playing in the park, and they take turns batting balls.

The day is warm, and the sunshine feels good.

The boys enjoy their practice, and then they go home.

28
Extension: Invite students to write a short story about
their favorite sport. Tell students to include two
compound sentences in their story.
Book 3.1/Unit 1
Champions of the World 5

Grammar 29 — TEST

Name_____ Date_____ **Grammar** 29

Sentence Combining

A. Write **yes** if two sentences have been combined. Write **no** if two sentences have not been combined.

I. One team scored 12 points, and the other team scored 9 points.

_____ **Yes** _____

2. The Toms River team wins the game and the championship.

_____ **No** _____

3. Cardone hits the ball, and the ball is gone.

_____ **Yes** _____

4. Todd Frazier hits a home run, and he saves the ball.

_____ **Yes** _____

B. If the sentence is a compound sentence, write **compound**. If it is not a compound sentence, write **no**.

5. Sammy Sosa and Mark McGwire set records. _____**No**_____

6. Sosa hit 66 home runs, and McGwire hit 70. _____**compound**_____

C. Use *and* to combine each pair of sentences. Write the new sentence on the line.

7. The batter hit the ball. It sailed over the fence.

The batter hit the ball, and it sailed over the fence.

8. He hit a home run. His team won the game.

He hit a home run, and his team won the game.

Grammar 30 — MORE PRACTICE

Name_____ Date_____ **Grammar** 30

Sentence Combining

- A sentence that contains two sentences joined by *and* is called a compound sentence.
- Use a comma before *and* when you join two sentences to form a compound sentence.
- Every sentence begins with a capital letter.
- Every sentence ends with a special mark.

Read the paragraph about the picture. First write the underlined sentences as a compound sentence. Use a comma and the word *and*. Then write the other three sentences correctly on the lines.

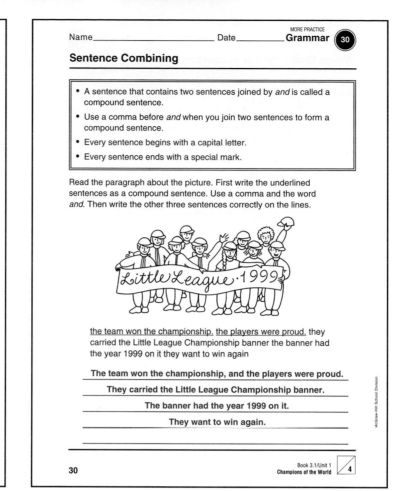

<u>the team won the championship.</u> <u>the players were proud.</u> they carried the Little League Championship banner the banner had the year 1999 on it they want to win again

The team won the championship, and the players were proud.

They carried the Little League Championship banner.

The banner had the year 1999 on it.

They want to win again.

Champions of the World • SPELLING

Words from Physical Education

Pretest Directions

Fold back the paper along the dotted line. Use the blanks to write each word as it is read aloud. When you finish the test, unfold the paper. Use the list at the right to correct any spelling mistakes. Practice the words you missed for the Posttest.

To Parents

Here are the results of your child's weekly spelling Pretest. You can help your child study for the Posttest by following these simple steps for each word on the word list:

1. Read the word to your child.

2. Have your child write the word, saying each letter as it is written.

3. Say each letter of the word as your child checks the spelling.

4. If a mistake has been made, have your child read each letter of the correctly spelled word aloud, and then repeat steps 1-3.

1. _____	1. player
2. _____	2. strike
3. _____	3. parade
4. _____	4. mitt
5. _____	5. batter
6. _____	6. bases
7. _____	7. glove
8. _____	8. action
9. _____	9. crowd
10. _____	10. baseball
11. _____	11. mound
12. _____	12. season
13. _____	13. foul
14. _____	14. outfield
15. _____	15. record

Challenge Words

_____ celebrated
_____ cork
_____ pitcher
_____ score
_____ wrap

Words from Physical Education

Using the Word Study Steps

1. LOOK at the word.

2. SAY the word aloud.

3. STUDY the letters in the word.

4. WRITE the word.

5. CHECK the word.
   Did you spell the word right?
   If not, go back to step 1.

Spelling Tip

Look for word chunks or smaller words that help you remember the spelling of the word.

play + er = player

base + ball = baseball

Find and Circle

Where are the spelling words?

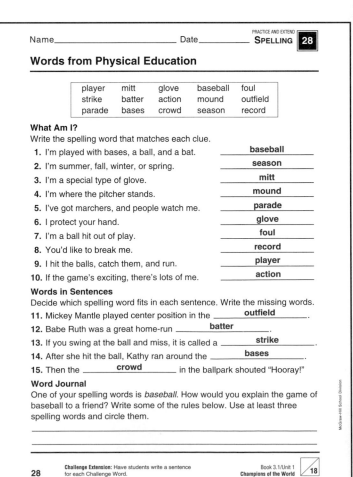

To Parents or Helpers:
Using the Word Study Steps above as your child comes across any new words will help him or her spell well. Review the steps as you both go over this week's spelling words.
Go over the Spelling Tip with your child. Ask him or her to find helpful chunks or smaller words in other new words. Help your child find and circle the spelling words in the puzzle.

Words from Physical Education

player	mitt	glove	baseball	foul
strike	batter	action	mound	outfield
parade	bases	crowd	season	record

Rhyme Time

Write the one-syllable spelling word that rhymes with each of these words.

1. bike **strike**   2. hit **mitt**

3. love **glove**   4. found **mound**

5. howl **foul**   6. loud **crowd**

Write the two-syllable spelling words that rhyme with the words below.

7. mayor **player**   8. vases **bases**

9. charade **parade**   10. traction **action**

11. matter **batter**   12. reason **season**

Find Spelling Words

Find six spelling words in the paragraph. Write each word on the line.

A batter hit the ball during a baseball game. The ball got stuck in the muddy outfield. No one could find it. The player ran around the bases and reached home. The hit broke a record. It was the shortest home run in history.

13. **batter**   14. **baseball**   15. **outfield**

16. **player**   17. **bases**   18. **record**

Words from Physical Education

player	mitt	glove	baseball	foul
strike	batter	action	mound	outfield
parade	bases	crowd	season	record

What Am I?

Write the spelling word that matches each clue.

1. I'm played with bases, a ball, and a bat. **baseball**

2. I'm summer, fall, winter, or spring. **season**

3. I'm a special type of glove. **mitt**

4. I'm where the pitcher stands. **mound**

5. I've got marchers, and people watch me. **parade**

6. I protect your hand. **glove**

7. I'm a ball hit out of play. **foul**

8. You'd like to break me. **record**

9. I hit the balls, catch them, and run. **player**

10. If the game's exciting, there's lots of me. **action**

Words in Sentences

Decide which spelling word fits in each sentence. Write the missing words.

11. Mickey Mantle played center position in the **outfield**.

12. Babe Ruth was a great home-run **batter**.

13. If you swing at the ball and miss, it is called a **strike**.

14. After she hit the ball, Kathy ran around the **bases**.

15. Then the **crowd** in the ballpark shouted "Hooray!"

Word Journal

One of your spelling words is *baseball*. How would you explain the game of baseball to a friend? Write some of the rules below. Use at least three spelling words and circle them.

_____

_____

_____

28
Challenge Extension: Have students write a sentence for each Challenge Word.
Book 3.1/Unit 1
Champions of the World 18

Champions of the World • SPELLING

Words from Physical Education

Proofreading

There are six spelling mistakes in this paragraph. Circle the misspelled words. Write the words correctly on the lines below.

It was too hot to play (basebal) but we did anyway. Joey was the first (battir) The pitcher dug her heels in and threw the ball hard. Joey swung and missed.

"(Stryke) one!" the umpire called.

On the next pitch, Joey hit the ball hard. However, the ball popped up in the air behind him. "(Foule) ball!" cried the umpire. The third time, Joey swung at the ball again. This time he hit the ball over the wall in the (outfeeld.)

"This is one for the (rekerd) books," said our coach.

1. _____baseball_____ 2. _____batter_____ 3. _____strike_____

4. _____foul_____ 5. _____outfield_____ 6. _____record_____

Writing Activity

Write a short story about a baseball game. It can be about a real game or one that you make up. Use at least four spelling words in your story.

_____

_____

_____

_____

Words from Physical Education

Look at the words in each set. One word in each set is spelled correctly. Use a pencil to color in the circle in front of that word. Before you begin, look at the sample sets of words. Sample A has been done for you. Do Sample B by yourself. When you are sure you know what to do, you may go on with the rest of the page.

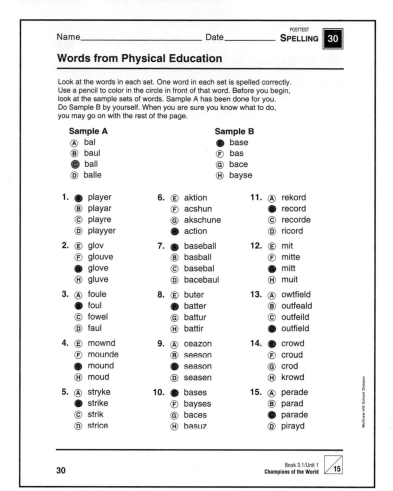

Sample A
- Ⓐ bal
- Ⓑ baul
- ● ball
- Ⓓ balle

Sample B
- ● base
- Ⓕ bas
- Ⓖ bace
- Ⓗ bayse

1.
- ● player
- Ⓑ playar
- Ⓒ playre
- Ⓓ playyer

2.
- Ⓔ glov
- Ⓕ glouve
- ● glove
- Ⓗ gluve

3.
- Ⓐ foule
- ● foul
- Ⓒ fowel
- Ⓓ faul

4.
- Ⓔ mownd
- Ⓕ mounde
- ● mound
- Ⓗ moud

5.
- Ⓐ stryke
- ● strike
- Ⓒ strik
- Ⓓ strice

6.
- Ⓔ aktion
- Ⓕ acshun
- Ⓖ akschune
- ● action

7.
- ● baseball
- Ⓑ basball
- Ⓒ basebal
- Ⓓ bacebaul

8.
- Ⓔ buter
- ● batter
- Ⓖ battur
- Ⓗ battir

9.
- Ⓐ ceazon
- Ⓑ seeson
- ● season
- Ⓓ seasen

10.
- ● bases
- Ⓕ bayses
- Ⓖ baces
- Ⓗ basuz

11.
- Ⓐ rekord
- ● record
- Ⓒ recorde
- Ⓓ ricord

12.
- Ⓔ mit
- Ⓕ mitte
- ● mitt
- Ⓗ muit

13.
- Ⓐ owtfield
- Ⓑ outfeald
- Ⓒ outfeild
- ● outfield

14.
- ● crowd
- Ⓕ croud
- Ⓖ crod
- Ⓗ krowd

15.
- Ⓐ perade
- Ⓑ parad
- ● parade
- Ⓓ pirayd

Practice 36

Name_____ Date_____ **Practice** 36

Unit 1 Vocabulary Review

A. Read each word in Column 1. Then find a word in Column 2 that means the opposite. Write the letter of the word on the line.

_c_ 1. ceiling   **a.** wrong

_d_ 2. enormous   **b.** stop

_a_ 3. correct   **c.** floor

_e_ 4. within   **d.** tiny

_b_ 5. continue   **e.** outside

B. Supply the correct vocabulary word.

| scene | journey | celebrated | gift |
| fans | cents | guard | |

1. The _____**fans**_____ roared when Cora hit the home run.

2. Denny bought a _____**gift**_____ for his grandmother.

3. The _____**journey**_____ across the mountains took three days.

4. The large ball cost 75 _____**cents**_____ more than the small one.

5. The class _____**celebrated**_____ Leo's birthday by giving him a party.

6. When Jane saw the lovely _____**scene**_____, she wanted to paint a picture of it.

7. Harry and Jim stood _____**guard**_____ around the campfire.

12 Book 3.1/Unit 1
Unit 1 Vocabulary Review

At Home: Have students write a sentence for each vocabulary word in Part A.

36

Practice 37

Name_____ Date_____ **Practice** 37

Unit 1 Vocabulary Review

A. Answer each question.

1. **royal** Who might be members of a royal family?
   Sample answer: king, queen, prince, princess

2. **wrap** Why would someone wrap a package?
   Sample answer: to send it in the mail

3. **astonished** What amazing sight astonished you?
   Sample answer: a kitten as small as a mouse

4. **eager** What is something you would be eager to do?
   Sample answer: visit a friend

B. Write the vocabulary word that means almost the same as the underlined word.

| section | scattered | enormous | unusual | straighten | gift |

1. That kind of stone is very rare. _____**unusual**_____

2. Wally finished the first part of the book. _____**section**_____

3. Janet spread the seeds on the soil. _____**scattered**_____

4. Nancy will fix the crooked picture. _____**straighten**_____

5. The Statue of Liberty is huge. _____**enormous**_____

6. My friend gave me a wonderful present. _____**gift**_____

37

At Home: Have students write a question for each vocabulary word in Part B. Then answer the question. Use Part A as a guide.

Book 3.1/Unit 1
Unit 1 Vocabulary Review 10

Reteach 36

Name_____ Date_____ **Reteach** 36

Unit 1 Vocabulary Review

A. Use words from the list to finish the crossword puzzle.

| surrounded | legend | scene | groaning | cork | including |

Across

1. The painting showed a beautiful _____**scene**_____.

3. Mark thought he heard an animal _____**groaning**_____.

4. _____**Cork**_____ is used to make floats and bottle stoppers.

Down

1. The house was _____**surrounded**_____ by bushes.

2. There will be six of us _____**including**_____ the baby.

Crossword:
1 Across: S C E N E
1 Down: S U R R O U N D E D
2 Down: I N C L U D I N G
3 Across: G R O A N I N G
4 Across: C O R K

| fans | pitcher | enormous | score | wrap |

B. Supply the correct word from the list.

The _____**pitcher**_____ took his time. The _____**score**_____ was tied. He couldn't let anyone reach home. Oh, no! It was a home run! The _____**fans**_____ let out an _____**enormous**_____ yell. That will _____**wrap**_____ up the game.

10 Book 3.1/Unit 1
Unit 1 Vocabulary Review

At Home: Have students write a story about a baseball game using at least three vocabulary words.

36

Reteach 37

Name_____ Date_____ **Reteach** 37

Unit 1 Vocabulary Review

A. Read each question. Choose a word from the list to answer the question. Write your answer on the line.

| length | guard | astonished | eager |

1. If you saw a sandwich fall from the sky, how might you feel?
   _____**astonished**_____

2. If you measured a piece of paper from top to bottom, what would you be measuring? _____**length**_____

3. If you couldn't wait to go to the circus, how would you feel?
   _____**eager**_____

4. If you had the job of keeping something safe, what would your job be?
   _____**guard**_____

B. Supply the correct word.

| ceiling | cents | scattered | embarrass |

1. When Jeff dropped the baseball cards, they _____**scattered**_____ all over the floor.

2. We didn't sing "Happy Birthday" to Jack because it would _____**embarrass**_____ him.

3. James wanted to paint stars on the _____**ceiling**_____ of his room.

4. After she bought the hat, Hannah had 50 _____**cents**_____ left.

37

At Home: Have students look for vocabulary words in magazines and copy the sentences in which the words appear.

Book 3.1/Unit 1
Unit 1 Vocabulary Review 8

Unit 1 Review • EXTEND and GRAMMAR

Vocabulary Review

Unscramble each word putting the letters in the order of the numbers.

1. e e c s a t r d t
   8 6 2 1 3 5 7 9 4
   s c a t t e r e d

2. g s n e i t h r a t
   6 1 10 9 5 2 7 3 4 8
   s t r a i g h t e n

3. r c c t r o e
   4 1 6 7 3 2 5
   c o r r e c t

4. s b e a r s a m r
   9 3 1 7 6 8 4 2 5
   e m b a r r a s s

5. g i i c n l n u d
   9 1 7 3 2 4 8 5 6
   i n c l u d i n g

Write a paragraph including all the words you unscrambled.

Answers will vary.

At Home: Have children cut out magazine pictures that illustrate the following words: **journey, surrounded, unusual, towering.** Have them scramble the letters in the word and give clues, along with the picture, to help a friend unscramble the word.

36

Vocabulary Review

Read the sentences. Then circle TRUE or FALSE. Then make the FALSE statements TRUE.

1. When you are hungry, you are **eager** to eat. (TRUE) FALSE

2. We walk on the **ceiling.** TRUE (FALSE)
   False. We walk on the floor.

3. The teams' **scores** were red and blue uniforms. TRUE (FALSE)
   False. The teams' uniforms were red and blue.

4. We felt safe because the dog was keeping **guard** of our house.
   (TRUE) FALSE
   True

5. The car is so **enormous** that only four of us could fit and we had to leave the boxes behind. TRUE (FALSE)
   False. The car is so small that . . .

6. We **celebrated** her birthday with cake and gifts. (TRUE) FALSE
   True

7. I was **astonished** to open a book and find words to read.
   TRUE (FALSE)
   False. I knew that I find and read words in books.

At Home: Write each of the words on a separate card: **length, continue, within, cents, fans,** and **wrap.** Pick a card and use this word in a TRUE or FALSE sentence. Ask someone to guess if it is TRUE or FALSE.

37

Sentences

Read the passage and look at the underlined section. Is there a mistake? What type of mistake is it? Mark your answer.

> My grandfather was born in Japan. he crossed the ocean to come to America. There he saw huge cities. He liked San Francisco best He
> (1)   (2)
> decided to live there.

1. ● Capitalization
   ⓑ Punctuation
   ⓒ Spelling
   ⓓ No Mistake

2. ⓔ Capitalization
   ● Punctuation
   ⓖ Spelling
   ⓗ No Mistake

> I like spelling words about animals. In class, teacher says, "Spell hippopotamus." On no, the word is too long! What do I do now, I
> (3)
> remember Hip, Pop, Tam, and us. I got it rght!
> (4)

3. ⓐ Capitalization
   ● Punctuation
   ⓒ Spelling
   ⓓ No Mistake

4. ⓔ Capitalization
   ⓕ Punctuation
   ● Spelling
   ⓗ No Mistake

> Visit the land of Opt. There you will meet a king who looks taller than
> (5)
> the queen. look again. You will see that the queen seems taller.
> (6)

5. ⓐ Capitalization
   ⓑ Punctuation
   ⓒ Spelling
   ● No Mistake

6. ● Capitalization
   ⓕ Punctuation
   ⓖ Spelling
   ⓗ No Mistake

Read the passage and look at the underlined section. Is there a mistake? If there is, how do you correct it? Mark your answer.

> I saw balloons float in the air. Were many sizes and colors. They had
> (7)
> various shapes. Some balloons. I thought I was dreaming.
> (8)

7. ● Add a subject.
   ⓑ Add a predicate.
   ⓒ Join two sentences with *and*.
   ⓓ No mistake.

8. ⓔ Add a subject.
   ● Add a predicate.
   ⓖ Join two sentences with *and*.
   ⓗ No mistake.

> The beach. Many people go to the beach during summer. I love the
> (9)
> beach. I come here to swim. I come here to build sand castles.
> (10)

9. ⓐ Add a subject.
   ● Add a predicate.
   ⓒ Join two sentences with *and*.
   ⓓ No mistake.

10. ⓔ Add a subject.
    ⓕ Add a predicate.
    ● Join two sentences with *and*.
    ⓗ No mistake.

T57

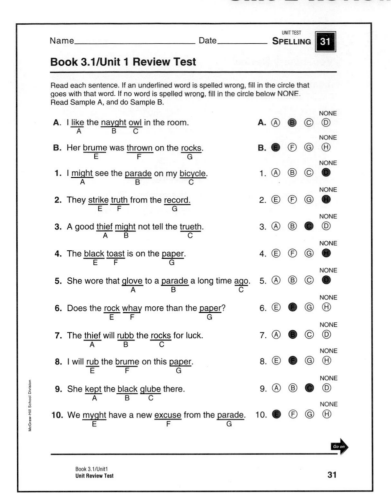

Name_____ Date_____ UNIT TEST
SPELLING **31**

Book 3.1/Unit 1 Review Test

Read each sentence. If an underlined word is spelled wrong, fill in the circle that goes with that word. If no word is spelled wrong, fill in the circle below NONE.
Read Sample A, and do Sample B.

A. I <u>like</u> the <u>nayght</u> <u>owl</u> in the room.
A B C
A. Ⓐ ● Ⓒ Ⓓ NONE

B. Her <u>brume</u> was <u>thrown</u> on the <u>rocks</u>.
E F G
B. ● Ⓕ Ⓖ Ⓗ NONE

1. I <u>might</u> see the <u>parade</u> on my <u>bicycle</u>.
A B C
1. Ⓐ Ⓑ Ⓒ ● NONE

2. They <u>strike</u> <u>truth</u> from the <u>record</u>.
E F G
2. Ⓔ Ⓕ Ⓖ ● NONE

3. A good <u>thief</u> <u>might</u> not tell the <u>trueth</u>.
A B C
3. Ⓐ Ⓑ ● Ⓓ NONE

4. The <u>black</u> <u>toast</u> is on the <u>paper</u>.
E F G
4. Ⓔ Ⓕ Ⓖ ● NONE

5. She wore that <u>glove</u> to a <u>parade</u> a long time <u>ago</u>.
A B C
5. Ⓐ Ⓑ Ⓒ ● NONE

6. Does the <u>rock</u> <u>whay</u> more than the <u>paper</u>?
E F G
6. Ⓔ ● Ⓖ Ⓗ NONE

7. The <u>thief</u> will <u>rubb</u> the <u>rocks</u> for luck.
A B C
7. Ⓐ ● Ⓒ Ⓓ NONE

8. I will <u>rub</u> the <u>brume</u> on this <u>paper</u>.
E F G
8. Ⓔ ● Ⓖ Ⓗ NONE

9. She <u>kept</u> the <u>black</u> <u>glube</u> there.
A B C
9. Ⓐ Ⓑ ● Ⓓ NONE

10. We <u>myght</u> have a new <u>excuse</u> from the <u>parade</u>.
E F G
10. ● Ⓕ Ⓖ Ⓗ NONE

Go on

Book 3.1/Unit1
Unit Review Test
31

Name_____ Date_____ UNIT TEST
SPELLING **32**

11. The <u>theef</u> was <u>thrown</u> from the <u>bicycle</u>.
A B C
11. ● Ⓑ Ⓒ Ⓓ NONE

12. This <u>thinng</u> was <u>kept</u> for the <u>season</u>.
E F G
12. ● Ⓕ Ⓖ Ⓗ NONE

13. Did you have <u>juice</u> with <u>toast</u> and <u>soop</u>?
A B C
13. Ⓐ Ⓑ ● Ⓓ NONE

14. I will <u>record</u> the <u>strike</u> on <u>paper</u>.
E F G
14. Ⓔ Ⓕ Ⓖ ● NONE

15. Dad makes <u>toste</u> and <u>juice</u> after we are <u>awake</u>.
A B C
15. ● Ⓑ Ⓒ Ⓓ NONE

16. She <u>kept</u> a <u>record</u> of the <u>ekscuse</u>.
E F G
16. Ⓔ Ⓕ ● Ⓗ NONE

17. When he is <u>awayk</u> he <u>might</u> have <u>juice</u>.
A B C
17. ● Ⓑ Ⓒ Ⓓ NONE

18. We <u>might</u> have a <u>parade</u> this <u>seezon</u>.
E F G
18. Ⓔ Ⓕ ● Ⓗ NONE

19. The <u>black</u> <u>rocks</u> were <u>throne</u> in the field.
A B C
19. Ⓐ Ⓑ ● Ⓓ NONE

20. We <u>kept</u> <u>joos</u> with <u>soup</u> in the kitchen.
E F G
20. Ⓔ ● Ⓖ Ⓗ NONE

21. The <u>parade</u> made a new <u>reckord</u> <u>strike</u>.
A B C
21. Ⓐ ● Ⓒ Ⓓ NONE

22. The player <u>might</u> <u>strycke</u> out this <u>season</u>.
E F G
22. Ⓔ ● Ⓖ Ⓗ NONE

23. The <u>breeze</u> <u>might</u> help <u>lyfe</u> in the sea.
A B C
23. Ⓐ Ⓑ ● Ⓓ NONE

24. We <u>keptt</u> the <u>broom</u> in the blue <u>cage</u>.
E F G
24. ● Ⓕ Ⓖ Ⓗ NONE

25. That <u>paper</u> was new a <u>season</u> <u>ago</u>.
A B C
25. Ⓐ Ⓑ Ⓒ ● NONE

32
Book 3.1/Unit1
Unit Review Test
25

Notes

Story Elements

 OBJECTIVES Students will create book covers to illustrate story elements. Students will write and solve clues based on story elements and act out scenes from selections.

Visual

COVER IT

 Materials: paper, crayons or colored pencils, index cards

Invite students to create a book cover for a favorite story. Briefly discuss story elements: character, setting, and plot—as they relate to a story the class has recently shared.

* Have students select another story. Encourage them to consider story elements they would like to highlight in their book covers.

* Suggest that students use the story setting as a backdrop for portraying one or more characters and some aspect of the plot.

* Ask students to print the book title and the author's name on an index card.

* Work with students to create an exhibit of book covers, and schedule time for students to present their work to the class. ▶**Spatial**

Auditory

NAME THAT STORY!

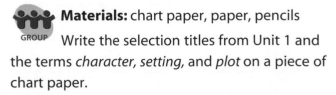 **Materials:** chart paper, paper, pencils

Write the selection titles from Unit 1 and the terms *character, setting,* and *plot* on a piece of chart paper.

* Have students in small groups choose a selection and discuss the characters, setting, and plot.

 Tell students to write clues based on the story elements.

* When students have finished writing, have each group take turns presenting its clues and challenging other groups to identify the story.
▶**Interpersonal, Logical/Mathematical**

Kinesthetic

ACT IT OUT

Materials: classroom props

Use the following activity to illustrate how the actions of characters advance the plot of a story.

* On separate pieces of paper, record key scenes from selections in Unit 1.

* Assign each pair of students a key scene. Tell students to discuss the scene and practice acting it out.

* Give partners the opportunity to dramatize the scene for the class. ▶**Bodily/Kinesthetic**

See Reteach 1, 5, 20, 27

Parts of a Book

OBJECTIVES Students will use a table of contents to prepare and answer questions, act out the meaning of glossary words, and illustrate glossary words.

Alternate Activities

Auditory

PAGES, PLEASE!

Materials: student text, paper and pencil

GROUP Guide students as they practice using a table of contents. Choose a book that all students have as you work with this activity.

- Have students open their books to the table of contents and spend a few minutes discussing its format.

WRITING Tell students to work together in small groups to write questions based on the table of contents. For example, *On what page does* Opt: An Illusionary Tale *begin?*

- Ask each group to present their questions to another group and challenge classmates to find the answers. ▶**Logical/Mathematical**

Kinesthetic

MIME THE MEANING

Materials: student text

PARTNERS Prepare a list of action words from a glossary that students can easily act out.

- Give each pair of students two words from the list, and have them read the definitions in the glossary.

- Tell partners to cooperate as they try a variety of ways to act out the words.

- Have pairs of students take turns acting out their words for the class. Invite class members to guess the words and locate the definitions in the glossary. ▶**Bodily/Kinesthetic**

Visual

WORD PICTURES

 Materials: student text, paper, and crayons ONE or colored pencils

On individual slips of paper, write words from the glossary that lend themselves to illustration.

- Have each student pick a slip of paper and read the definition of the word in the glossary.

- Tell students to draw a picture that illustrates the meaning of the word and to write a caption using the word.

- Have students create a booklet of their illustrated words. Tell them to organize their word pictures in alphabetical order. ▶**Spatial**

See Reteach 4, 11, 18, 25

Make Predictions

OBJECTIVES Students will create story boards, make up story endings, and act out a comic strip.

Visual

STORYBOARD

Materials: paper, crayons or colored pencils

Use the following activity to give students practice with predicting story events and outcomes.

- Write story starters on strips of paper, and give a strip to each pair of students.

- Have partners work together to create a storyboard that continues the story and tells how the story ends.

- Invite students to present their storyboards to the class. Tell student presenters to pause after each frame to give classmates time to make their own predictions. ▶**Spatial**

Auditory

STORY ENDINGS

Materials: paper, pencil

Have students make up possible story endings.

- Read the following incomplete story to students: *Every morning before Brenda leaves for school, she feeds Snowball, her little kitten. One day Brenda called his name, but Snowball was nowhere to be found. Brenda looked everywhere for him. She looked under her bed and in her closet. She searched everywhere, even outside in the garden. It was getting late, and Brenda had to leave for school. She picked up her knapsack, and . . .*

 Ask students to write a good ending for the story.

- When students have finished writing, invite volunteers to share their story endings with the class. Ask each volunteer to explain what was considered in predicting the story ending. ▶**Linguistic**

Kinesthetic

A LIVING COMIC STRIP

Materials: comic strips, overhead projector

Have students in small groups dramatize a comic strip.

- Cut comic strips into frames, leaving out the last frame in each one.

- Give each group a set of frames to put in order, and explain that the last frame is missing. Ask students to discuss what they think the last frame might be.

- Have group members decide what happens in the last frame and then practice acting out the entire comic strip.

- Call on individual groups to present their living comic strips to the class. ▶**Bodily/Kinesthetic**

See Reteach 6, 13, 29

Compound Words

OBJECTIVES Students will write clues for compound words, hunt for two words that together form compound words, and match words to form compound words.

Alternate Activities

Auditory

COMPOUND WORD RIDDLES

Materials: index cards, paper and pencils

Use this activity to review compound words from stories students have read in Unit 1.

- Write the compound words you select on individual index cards.

- Have each student select a card and write clues for each section of the compound word. For example, for *airport,* clues might be "what we breath plus a place where ships dock."

- Tell students to take turns presenting their clues to their group. Have a volunteer write the words on the chalkboard to create a word bank.

Ask students to write sentences that contain words from the word bank.
▶**Linguistic**

Visual

COMPOUND WORD HUNT

Materials: old magazines or newspapers, scissors, tape, and paper

Explain that students will hunt for words that can be used to make compound words.

- Distribute pages from an old magazine or newspaper to each student.

- Ask them to cut out pictures and tape them together on a sheet of paper to create visual examples of compound words. Have students write the compound word on the back of each picture combination.

- Invite students to show their pictures to the class and have the class guess the compound word.
▶**Spatial**

Kinesthetic

COMPOUND WORD MATCH

Materials: index cards, paper bag, tape

Use the following activity to review familiar compound words.

- Display a list of compound words, and give each student two index cards.

- Have students each pick a different compound word and write the two words that make it up, one on each word card.

- Collect the word cards in a paper bag, and have each student draw two cards and tape them to the tops of their shoes.

- Then have students, one at a time, search for a partner to make a compound word.

- Continue the activity until all cards have been matched to form the compound words.
▶**Bodily/Kinesthetic**

See Reteach 7, 28, 34

Problem and Solution

OBJECTIVES Students will illustrate solutions for problems, discuss solutions to realistic problems, and dramatize solutions to story problems.

Alternate Activities

Visual

A PICTURE SOLUTION

Materials: paper, crayons or colored pencils

Use the following activity to guide students as they identify solutions to problems.

- List several realistic "problems" on the chalkboard, such as having a sad friend and feeling bored on a rainy day.

- Have students select a problem and draw a picture that illustrates a solution.

- Ask students to present their picture solutions to the class and explain the reasoning behind their solutions. ▶**Logical/Mathematical**

Auditory

THE BEST SOLUTION

Materials: paper and pencils

Have students form small discussion groups to encourage cooperation in seeking solutions.

- Pose several realistic problems to students, such as losing a pet, losing a borrowed item, or hurting a friend's feelings.

 Have each group select one problem for discussion and appoint a group recorder to write the problem and its proposed solutions.

- Tell students to take turns suggesting solutions to the problem.

- Afterward, the group recorder can read the solutions aloud, and group members can discuss the solutions and determine the most effective one. ▶**Interpersonal**

Kinesthetic

A DRAMATIC SOLUTION

Materials: chart paper, classroom props

Use the following activity to identify alternative solutions to problems in stories students have recently read.

- On chart paper, list several story titles and the problems the characters faced in the stories.

- Divide the class into three teams. Ask each team to select a story and prepare a presentation in which they dramatize the solution to a problem that is found in the story and an alternate solution which the team creates.

- Schedule class time for teams to present their dramatizations to the class. ▶**Bodily/Kinesthetic**

See Reteach 8, 12, 22, 26

Prefixes

✓OBJECTIVES Students will pantomime words that begin with the prefixes *un-* and *dis-*, and use words with the prefixes *un-* and *dis-* in sentences.

Alternate Activities

Kinesthetic

PREFIX PANTOMIME

Materials: index cards; classroom props

ONE Use the following activity to review words that can be made with the prefix *un-*.

- Write the following words on individual index cards: *tie, fed, cover, do, fold, combed, pack, heated, excited, opened,* and *wrap.*

- Place the cards face down, and have students take turns picking a card.

- Ask each student to mime for the class the original word and then the word with the prefix.

- Have classmates identify the base word and the prefix. ▶**Bodily/Kinesthetic**

Visual

ADD A PREFIX

Materials: paper and pencil

ONE Have students practice using words with the prefixes *un-* and *dis-* in context.

- Write the following words on the board: *honest, happy, pleasant,* and *like.*

- Display the following sentences. Have students copy and complete each sentence adding *un-* or *dis-* to one of the words on the chalkboard—and placing the new word with the prefix *un-* or *dis-*.

Maria seems sad and _____.

I enjoy most vegetables, but I _____ turnips.

Someone who cheats is _____.

The smoke made the air _____.

- Have volunteers read the completed sentences aloud. ▶**Linguistic**

Auditory

SENTENCE OPPOSITES

Materials: paper and pencil

PARTNERS Have students use the prefixes *un-* and *dis-* to write sentences opposite in meaning.

- Write the following words on the board: *certain, loyal, able, broken, comfortable, agree, clear, familiar, popular, trust, selfish,* and *obey.*

 Have students write two sentences using **WRITING** words from the list.

- Tell partners to dictate their sentences to each other and rewrite each sentence, using the word with the prefix *un-* or *dis-*. ▶**Linguistic**

See Reteach 14, 21, 35

Steps in a Process

OBJECTIVES Students will unscramble a set of instructions, write a set of directions for doing or making something, and follow a set of instructions.

Alternate Activities

Visual

ORDER STEPS IN A PROCESS

Materials: photocopies of a set of directions
Draw students' attention to the importance of clue words (*first, second, next, last, later, then*) in recognizing steps in a process.

- Prepare directions that explain how to make or do something. Photocopy the directions, and make a separate strip for each step.

- Give each student a set of scrambled direction strips, and have students use visualization and the clue words to order the steps in the proper sequence.

- Ask a volunteer to read the ordered set of directions to the class. ▶**Logical/Mathematical**

Auditory

HOW-TO INSTRUCTIONS

Materials: slips of paper, pencil, scissors
Use the following activity to illustrate the importance of clue words in a set of instructions.

 Have students write a set of simple how-to instructions without using clue words. Explain that each step should be written on a separate slip of paper.

- Ask students to scramble the strips of paper and give them to partners.

- Have partners order the steps in sequence and rewrite the instructions, using clue words.

- Tell partners to discuss how the clue words make the instructions easier to follow.
  ▶**Logical/Mathematical**

Kinesthetic

FOLLOWING DIRECTIONS

Materials: simple sets of directions, classroom props such as containers, measuring cups, and math manipulatives, drawing materials
Have students in small groups demonstrate how to follow steps in a process.

- Prepare several sets of directions for students to follow. Directions may include steps in a recipe or instructions on how to draw a picture or build something.

- Give each group a set of directions, and have group members take turns demonstrating for the class different steps in the process, using a variety of classroom props. ▶**Bodily/Kinesthetic**

See Reteach 15, 19, 33

Notes

A Communication Tool

Although typewriters and computers are readily available, many situations continue to require handwriting. Tasks such as keeping journals, completing forms, taking notes, making shopping or organizational lists, and the ability to read hand-written manuscript or cursive writing are a few examples of practical application of this skill.

BEFORE YOU BEGIN

Before children begin to write, certain fine motor skills need to be developed. Examples of activities that can be used as warm-up activities are:

* **Simon Says** Play a game of Simon Says using just finger positions.
* **Finger Plays and Songs** Sing songs that use Signed English, American Sign Language or finger spelling.
* **Mazes** Mazes are available in a wide range of difficulty. You can also create mazes that allow children to move their writing instruments from left to right.

Determining Handedness

Keys to determining handedness in a child:

* Which hand does the child eat with? This is the hand that is likely to become the dominant hand.
* Does the child start coloring with one hand and then switch to the other? This may be due to fatigue rather than lack of hand preference.
* Does the child cross midline to pick things up or use the closest hand? Place items directly in front of the child to see if one hand is preferred.
* Does the child do better with one hand or the other?

The Mechanics of Writing

DESK AND CHAIR

* Chair height should allow for the feet to rest flat on the floor.
* Desk height should be two inches above the level of the elbows when the child is sitting.
* The chair should be pulled in allowing for an inch of space between the child's abdomen and the desk.
* Children sit erect with the elbows resting on the desk.
* Children should have models of letters on the desk or at eye level, not above their heads.

PAPER POSITION

* **Right-handed children** should turn the paper so that the lower left-hand corner of the paper points to the abdomen.
* **Left-handed children** should turn the paper so that the lower right-hand corner of the paper points to the abdomen.
* The nondominant hand should anchor the paper near the top so that the paper doesn't slide.
* The paper should be moved up as the child nears the bottom of the paper. Many children won't think of this and may let their arms hang off the desk when they reach the bottom of a page.

The Writing Instrument Grasp

For handwriting to be functional, the writing instrument must be held in a way that allows for fluid dynamic movement.

FUNCTIONAL GRASP PATTERNS

* **Tripod Grasp** With open web space, the writing instrument is held with the tip of the thumb and the index finger and rests against the side of the third finger. The thumb and index finger form a circle.
* **Quadrupod Grasp** With open web space, the writing instrument is held with the tip of the thumb and index finger and rests against the fourth finger. The thumb and index finger form a circle.

INCORRECT GRASP PATTERNS

* **Fisted Grasp** The writing instrument is held in a fisted hand.

* **Pronated Grasp** The writing instrument is held diagonally within the hand with the tips of the thumb and index finger on the writing instrument but with no support from other fingers.
* **Five-Finger Grasp** The writing instrument is held with the tips of all five fingers.

TO CORRECT WRITING INSTRUMENT GRASPS

* Have children play counting games with an eye dropper and water.
* Have children pick up small objects with a tweezer.
* Do counting games with children picking up small coins using just the thumb and index finger.

FLEXED OR HOOKED WRIST

* The writing instrument can be held in a variety of grasps with the wrist flexed or bent. This is typically seen with left-handed writers but is also present in some right-handed writers. To correct wrist position, have children check their writing posture and paper placement.

Evaluation Checklist

Functional writing is made up of two elements, legibility and functional speed.

LEGIBILITY

MANUSCRIPT

Formation and Strokes

☑ Does the child begin letters at the top?

☑ Do circles close?

☑ Are the horizontal lines straight?

☑ Do circular shapes and extender and descender lines touch?

☑ Are the heights of all upper-case letters equal?

☑ Are the heights of all lower-case letters equal?

☑ Are the lengths of the extenders and descenders the same for all letters?

Directionality

☑ Are letters and words formed from left to right?

☑ Are letters and words formed from top to bottom?

Spacing

☑ Are the spaces between letters equidistant?

☑ Are the spaces between words equidistant?

☑ Do the letters rest on the line?

☑ Are the top, bottom and side margins even?

CURSIVE

Formation and Strokes

☑ Do circular shapes close?

☑ Are the downstrokes parallel?

☑ Do circular shapes and downstroke lines touch?

☑ Are the heights of all upper-case letters equal?

☑ Are the heights of all lower-case letters equal?

☑ Are the lengths of the extenders and descenders the same for all letters?

☑ Do the letters which finish at the top join the next letter? (*b, o, v, w*)

☑ Do the letters which finish at the bottom join the next letter? (*a, c, d, h, i, k, l, m, n, r, s, t, u, x*)

☑ Do letters with descenders join the next letter? (*f, g, j, p, q, y, z*)

☑ Do all letters touch the line?

☑ Is the vertical slant of all letters consistent?

Directionality

☑ Are letters and words formed from left to right?

☑ Are letters and words formed from top to bottom?

Spacing

☑ Are the spaces between letters equidistant?

☑ Are the spaces between words equidistant?

☑ Do the letters rest on the line?

☑ Are the top, bottom and side margins even?

SPEED

The prettiest handwriting is not functional for classroom work if it takes the child three times longer than the rest of the class to complete work assignments. After the children have been introduced to writing individual letters, begin to add time limitations to the completion of copying or writing assignments. Then check the child's work for legibility.

Handwriting Models—Manuscript

Handwriting Models—Cursive

A B C D E F G H I

J K L M N O P Q R

S T U V W X Y Z

a b c d e f g h i j

k l m n o p q r s

t u v w x y z

Selection Titles

Honors, Prizes, and Awards

CLOSED, I AM A MYSTERY
Book 1, p.10
by *Myra Cohn Livingston*

Poet: *Myra Cohn Livingston,* winner of National Council of Teachers of English Award for Excellence in Poetry for Children (1980); ALA Notable (1984) for *Christmas Poems;* ALA Notable (1987) for *Cat Poems;* ALA Notable (1992) for *Poem-Making: Ways to Learn Writing Poetry*

GRANDFATHER'S JOURNEY
Book 1, p.14
by *Allen Say*

Caldecott Medal, Boston Globe-Horn Book Award, ALA Notable, Booklist Editor's Choice, Blue Ribbon, *New York Times* Best Illustrated, School Library Journal Best Books of the Year (1994)
Author/Illustrator: *Allen Say,* winner of Caldecott Honor, ALA Notable (1989), Boston Globe-Horn Book Award (1988) for *The Boy of the Three-Year Nap;* Christopher Award (1985) for *How My Parents Learned to Eat*

OPT: AN ILLUSIONARY TALE
Book 1, p.80
by *Arline and Joseph Baum*

IRA-CBC Children's Choice (1988), National Science Teachers' Association Outstanding Science Trade Book for Children (1987)

ABUELITA'S LAP
Book 1, p.138
by *Pat Mora*

Author: *Pat Mora,* winner of National Association for Chicano Studies Creative Writing Award (1983); New America: Women Artists and Writers of the Southwest Award (1984)

FOG
Book 1, p.140
by *Carl Sandburg*

Poet: *Carl Sandburg,* winner of Pulitzer Prize for history (1940); ALA Notable (1993) for *More Rootabagas*

CITY GREEN
Book 1, p.144
by *DyAnne DiSalvo*

Author/Illustrator: *DyAnne DiSalvo,* winner ALA Notable (1996) for *You Want to Vote, Lizzie Stanton?*

THE SUN, THE WIND AND THE RAIN
Book 1, p.174
by *Lisa Westberg Peters*
Illustrated by *Ted Rand*

Illustrator: *Ted Rand,* winner of Christopher Award (1991) for *Paul Revere's Ride;* ALA Notable, National Council for Social Studies Notable Children's Book Award (1998) for *Mailing May;* National Council for Social Studies Notable Children's Book Award (1998) for *Storm in the Desert*

Selection Titles	Honors, Prizes, and Awards
DREAM WOLF Book 1, p.206 by *Paul Goble*	**Author/Illustrator:** *Paul Goble,* winner of ALA Notable, Caldecott Medal (1979) for *The Girl Who Loved Wild Horses;* ALA Notable (1985) for *Buffalo Woman;* ALA Notable (1989), Aesop Accolade (1994) for *Iktomi and the Boulder: A Plains Indian Story;* ALA Notable (1993) for *Love Flute*
WHO AM I? Book 1, p.254 by *Felice Holman*	**Poet:** *Felice Holman,* winner of Lewis Carroll Shelf Award, ALA Notable (1978) for *Slake's Limbo;* ALA Best Book for Young Adults (1985) for *The Wild Children;* Flora Steiglitz Straus Award (1990) for *Secret City, USA*
THE LITTLE PAINTER OF SABANA GRANDE Book 1, p.292 by *Patricia Markun Maloney* Illustrated by *Robert Casilla*	**National Council for Social Studies Notable Children's Book Award (1994)**
THE PATCHWORK QUILT Book 1, p.320 by *Valerie Flournoy* Illustrated by *Jerry Pinkney*	**Coretta Scott King Award, ALA Notable, Christopher Award, Reading Rainbow Book (1986)** **Illustrator:** *Jerry Pinkney,* winner of Newbery Medal, Boston Globe-Horn Book Honor (1977) for *Roll of Thunder, Hear My Cry;* Coretta Scott King Award (1987) for *Half a Moon and One Whole Star;* ALA Notable (1988) for *Tales of Uncle Remus;* ALA Notable, Caldecott Honor, Coretta Scott King Award (1989) for *Mirandy and Brother Wind;* ALA Notable, Caldecott Honor, Coretta Scott King Honor (1990) for *Talking Eggs;* Golden Kite Award Book (1990) for *Home Place;* ALA Notable (1991) for *Further Tales of Uncle Remus;* ALA Notable (1993) for *Back Home;* ALA Notable, Boston Globe-Horn Book Award, Caldecott Honor (1995) for *John Henry;* ALA Notable, Blue Ribbon (1997) for *Sam and the Tigers;* ALA Notable, Christopher Award, Coretta Scott King Award, Golden Kite Honor Book (1997) for *Minty;* Aesop Prize (1997) for *The Hired Hand;* NCSS Notable Children's Book Award (1998) for *The Hired Hand,* and *Rikki-Tikki-Tavi;* Rip Van Winkle Award (1998); 1998 Hans Christian Andersen nominee
PECOS BILL Book 1, p.352 by *Angela Shelf Medearis*	**Author:** *Angela Shelf Medearis,* winner of IRA-Teacher's Choice Award Winner Primary Grades (1995) for *Our People*

Selection Titles	Honors, Prizes, and Awards
IN MY FAMILY Book 2, p.40 by *Carmen Lomas Garza*	**Texas Bluebonnet Master List (1998–99), Pura Belpré Illustration Honor Book (1998)** **Author/Illustrator:** *Carmen Lomas Garza,* winner of Pura Belpré Illustrator Honor (1996); ALA Notable, Pura Belpré Honor Book for Illustrations (1996) for *Family Pictures*
CACTUS HOTEL Book 2, p.58 by *Brenda Z. Guiberson* Illustrated by *Megan Lloyd*	**Parents' Choice Award, ALA Notable, NSTA Award for Outstanding Science Trade Book for Children (1991)** **Illustrator:** *Megan Lloyd,* winner of IRA-CBC Children's Choice (1997) for *Too Many Pumpkins;* ALA Notable (1985) for *Surprises*
BIG BLUE WHALE Book 2, p.86 by *Nicola Davies* Illustrated by *Nick Maland*	**IRA-Teacher's Choice (1998), Blue Ribbon (1997)**
DO OYSTERS SNEEZE? Book 2, p.122 by *Jack Prelutsky*	**Poet:** *Jack Prelutsky,* winner of SLJ Best Book (1979) for *Nightmares: Poems to Trouble Your Sleep; New York Times* Notable Book (1980) for *The Headless Horseman Rides Tonight;* ALA Notable (1993) for *Random House Book of Poetry for Young Children;* ALA Notable (1985) for *New Kid on the Block;* ALA Notable (1990) for *Poems of A. Nonny Mouse;* ALA Notable (1991) for *Something Big Has Been Here;* ALA Notable (1993) for *Talking Like the Rain*
LON PO PO Book 2, p.128 by *Ed Young*	**Caldecott Medal, Boston Globe-Horn Book Award, ALA Notable (1990), NCSS Notable Children's Book Award (1989)** **Author/Illustrator:** *Ed Young,* winner of Caldecott Honor (1968) for *The Emperor and the Kite;* Boston Globe-Horn Book Honor (1983) for *Yeh Shen;* ALA Notable, Boston Globe-Horn Book Honor (1984) for *The Double Life of Pocohontas;* ALA Notable (1986) for *Foolish Rabbit's Big Mistake;* ALA Notable (1989) for *Cats Are Cats;* ALA Notable (1989) for *China's Long March;* ALA Notable (1991) for *Mice Are Nice;* ALA Notable (1992) for *All Of You Was Singing;* ALA Notable, Boston Globe-Horn Book Award, Caldecott Honor (1993) for *Seven Blind Mice;* ALA Notable (1994) for *Sadako;* ALA Notable (1995) for *Ibis;* Aesop Accolade (1996) for *The Turkey Girl;* National Council for Social Studies Notable Children's Book Award (1998) for *Genesis* and *Voices of the Heart*

Selection Titles	Honors, Prizes, and Awards
ANIMAL FACT/ANIMAL FABLE Book 2, p.160 by *Seymour Simon* Illustrated by *Diane de Groat*	**A Child Study Association Book of the Year (1979), Texas Blue Bonnet Master List (1982-83)** Author: *Seymour Simon,* winner of Texas Blue Bonnet Master List (1996–7) *Sharks;* NSTA Outstanding Science Tradebook for Children (1997) *The Heart;* ALA Notable (1985) *Moon,* (1986) *Saturn,* (1987) *Sun,* (1988) *Mars,* (1993) *Our Solar System* and *Snakes*
THE MANY LIVES OF BENJAMIN FRANKLIN Book 2, p.180 by *Aliki*	Author: *Aliki (Brandenberg),* winner of NSTA Outstanding Science Tradebook for Children (1990) and Library of Congress Children's Book Award (1972) for *Fossils Tell of Long Ago*
CLOUDY WITH A CHANCE OF MEATBALLS Book 2, p.208 by *Judi Barrett* Illustrated by *Ron Barrett*	*New York Times* **Best Illustrated, IRA-CBC Children's Choice (1978)**
DREAMS Book 2, p.250 by *Langston Hughes*	Poet: *Langston Hughes,* winner of ALA Notable (1995) for *Sweet and Sour Book*
THE BAT BOY AND HIS VIOLIN Book 2, p.254 by *Gavin Curtis* Illustrated by *E. B. Lewis*	**The New York Public Library 100 Best Books for Reading and Sharing (1998); Coretta Scott King Honor for Illustration (1999)**
TWO BAD ANTS Book 2, p.284 by *Chris Van Allsburg*	**NSTA Outstanding Science Trade Book for Children (1988), IRA-CBC Children's Choice (1989)** Author/Illustrator: *Chris Van Allsburg,* winner of ALA Notable, Caldecott Medal (1982), Boston Globe-Horn Book Honor, for *Jumanji;* ALA Notable (1984), for *The Wreck of the Zephyr;* ALA Notable, Boston Globe-Horn Book Honor (1985), for *The Mysteries of Harris Burdick;* ALA Notable, Boston Globe-Horn Book Honor, Caldecott Medal (1986) for *The Polar Express;* ALA Notable (1988) for *The Z Was Zapped,* (1993) for *Widow's Broom,* (1994) for *The Sweetest Fig*
CHARLOTTE'S WEB Book 2, p.332 by *E. B. White* Illustrated by *Garth Williams*	*Newbery Honor (1953)* *Illustrator: Garth Williams*, winner of Newbery Honor (1959) for *The Golden Name Day*; (1959) for *The Family Under the Bridge*; and (1961) for *The Cricket in Times Square*

Trade Books

Additional fiction and nonfiction trade books related to each selection can be shared with children throughout the unit.

GRANDFATHER'S JOURNEY

Going West
Jean Van Leeuwen, illustrated by Thomas B. Allen(Dial Books for Young Readers, 1992)

A family travels west by covered wagon in the 1800s to start a new life.

Alice Ramsey's Grand Adventure
Don Brown (Houghton Mifflin, 1997)

The true story of the first woman to travel across the United States by car.

When Jessie Came Across the Sea
Amy Hest, illustrated by P.J. Lynch (Candlewick Press, 1997)

Jessie leaves her poor village in Eastern Europe to travel to America in search of a better life.

PHOEBE AND THE SPELLING BEE

Nim and the War Effort
Milly Lee, illustrated by Yangsook Choi (Farrar, Straus & Giroux, 1998)

In her effort to collect the most newspapers in her class, Nim has a conflict between her own customs and winning a contest.

Brave as a Mountain Lion
Ann Herbert Scott, illustrated by Glo Coalson (Clarion Books, 1996)

A young Shoshini boy tries to be as brave as his ancestors when he has to perform on stage in a spelling bee.

Wilma Unlimited: How Wilma Rudolph Became the World's Fastest Woman
Kathleen Krull, illustrated by David Diaz (Harcourt Brace Jovanovich, 1997)

The inspiring story of the Olympic gold medalist who overcame seemingly insurmountable odds.

Technology

Multimedia resources can be used to enhance children's understanding of the selections.

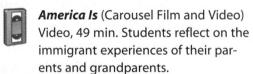 *America Is* (Carousel Film and Video) Video, 49 min. Students reflect on the immigrant experiences of their parents and grandparents.

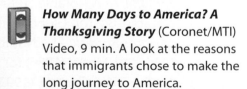 *How Many Days to America? A Thanksgiving Story* (Coronet/MTI) Video, 9 min. A look at the reasons that immigrants chose to make the long journey to America.

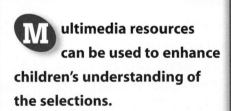 *Just Grandma and Me* (Educational Access/ESI) CD-ROM, Macintosh and Windows. In this animated interactive program, students join Grandma on a trip to the seaside.

 GeoBee Challenge (Educational Access/ESI) CD-ROM, Macintosh and Windows. Players compete in an interactive geography quiz game.

 Playing Fair (Values Series) (BFA Educational Media) Video, 10 min. A discussion on teamwork and fair play.

OPT: AN ILLUSIONARY TALE

Walter Wick's Optical Tricks
Walter Wick (Scholastic Inc., 1998)

Readers will discover that the brain makes assumptions based upon experiences.

Picture Puzzler
Kathleen Westray (Ticknor & Fields, 1994)

Optical illusions based on American folk art motifs are demonstrated in eye-catching illustrations.

Re-Zoom
Istvan Banyai (Viking, 1995)

Readers are in for some surprises as they turn each page and realize that the perspective has changed.

MAX MALONE

Yard Sale
James Stevenson (Greenwillow, 1996)

Read about what happens to the people of Mud Flat when they have a yard sale.

If You Made a Million
David Schwartz, illustrated by Steven Kellogg (Mulberry Books, 1994)

Learn about money, investments, check writing, and earning money; written in an easily understood style.

One Grain of Rice
Demi (Scholastic, 1997)

Discover how a clever girl outsmarts a rajah and saves her village in India from starvation.

CHAMPIONS OF THE WORLD

Our Little League
Chuck Solomon (Crown, 1988)

Follow the Little Mets team from Brooklyn as they prepare for their big game.

The Field Beyond the Outfield
Mark Teague (Scholastic, 1992)

In spite of Ludlow's parents' attempts to redirect his interests from imaginary creatures to the real-life game of baseball, Ludlow's imagination still comes alive on the playing field.

Baseball Saved Us
Ken Mochizuki, illustrated by Dom Lee (Lee & Low, 1993)

A Japanese American boy learns to play baseball in an internment camp, which helps him connect with others when his family is released.

 Opt: An Illusionary Tale (Reading Rainbow/GPN) Video, 30 min. A look at illusions.

 My Shadow (Reading Rainbow/GPN) Video, 30 min. An examination of light and shadow and how shadow puppets are made.

 Draw to Learn (Educational Software) Computer software Macintosh, IBM. An introduction to pencil and paper art, from simple, realistic drawings to 3-D drawings.

 All the Money in the World (AIMS Multimedia) Video, 23 min. A young boy wishes for all the money in the world. When his wish is granted, he learns about the world's economy and things that money can't buy.

 HyperEntrepreneur (HyperTrain/ESI) Computer software, Macintosh and DOS. Players use simulations to learn about starting, owning, and operating a business.

 Mister Gimme (Learning Corp. of America) Video, 29 min. A young boy learns about goals and achievements when he tries a "get-rich-quick" scheme.

 Casey at the Bat (AIMS Multimedia) Video, 7 min. E.L. Thayer's classic work is animated for students.

 Learning to Be a Good Sport (Coronet/MTI) Video, 11 min. This animated program teaches the elements of good sportsmanship.

 The Rag Tag Champs (Pied Piper/AIMS Multimedia) Video, 48 min. Jake fights to get his personal life and his baseball team on track.

Directory of Resources

Abdo & Daughters
4940 Viking Drive, Suite 622
Edina, MN 55435
(800) 458-8399 • www.abdopub.com

Aladdin Paperbacks
(Imprint of Simon & Schuster Children's
Publishing)

Atheneum
(Imprint of Simon & Schuster Children's
Publishing)

**Bantam Doubleday Dell Books for
Young Readers**
(Imprint of Random House)

Blackbirch Press
1 Bradley Road, Suite 205
Woodbridge, CT 06525
(203) 387-7525 • (800) 831-9183

Blue Sky Press
(Imprint of Scholastic)

Boyds Mills Press
815 Church Street
Honesdale, PA 18431
(570) 253-1164 • Fax (570) 251-0179 •
(800) 949-7777

Bradbury Press
(Imprint of Simon & Schuster Children's
Publishing)

BridgeWater Books
(Distributed by Penguin Putnam)

Candlewick Press
2067 Masssachusetts Avenue
Cambridge, MA 02140
(617) 661-3330 • Fax (617) 661-0565

Carolrhoda Books
(Division of Lerner Publications Co.)

Charles Scribners's Sons
(Imprint of Simon & Schuster Children's
Publishing)

Children's Press (Division of Grolier, Inc.)
P.O. Box 1796
Danbury, CT 06813-1333
(800) 621-1115 • www.grolier.com

Child's World
P.O. Box 326
Chanhassen, MN 55317-0326
(612) 906-3939 • (800) 599-READ •
www.childsworld.com

Chronicle Books
85 Second Street, Sixth Floor
San Francisco, CA 94105
(415) 537-3730 • (415) 537-4460 • (800)
722-6657 • www.chroniclebooks.com

Clarion Books
(Imprint of Houghton Mifflin, Inc.)
215 Park Avenue South
New York, NY 10003
(212) 420-5800 • (800) 726-0600 •
www.hmco.com/trade/childrens/
shelves.html

Crowell (Imprint of HarperCollins)

Crown Publishing Group
(Imprint of Random House)

Dial Books
(Imprint of Penguin Putnam Inc.)

Dorling Kindersley (DK Publishing)
95 Madison Avenue
New York, NY 10016
(212) 213-4800 • Fax (800) 774-6733 •
(888) 342-5357 • www.dk.com

Doubleday (Imprint of Random House)

E. P. Dutton Children's Books
(Imprint of Penguin Putnam Inc.)

Farrar Straus & Giroux
19 Union Square West
New York, NY 10003
(212) 741-6900 • Fax (212) 633-2427 •
(888) 330-8477

Four Winds Press
(Imprint of Macmillan, see Simon &
Schuster Children's Publishing)

Greenwillow Books
(Imprint of William Morrow & Co, Inc.)

Grosset & Dunlap
(Imprint of Penguin Putnam, Inc.)

Harcourt Brace & Co.
525 "B" Street
San Diego, CA 92101
(619) 231-6616 • (800) 543-1918 •
www.harcourtbooks.com

Harper & Row (Imprint of HarperCollins)

HarperCollins Children's Books
10 East 53rd Street
New York, NY 10022
(212) 207-7000 • Fax (212) 202-7044 •
(800) 242-7737 •
www.harperchildrens.com

Henry Holt and Company
115 West 18th Street
New York, NY 10011
(212) 886-9200 • (212) 633-0748 • (888)
330-8477 • www.henryholt.com/byr/

Holiday House
425 Madison Avenue
New York, NY 10017
(212) 688-0085 • Fax (212) 421-6134

Houghton Mifflin
222 Berkeley Street
Boston, MA 02116
(617) 351-5000 • Fax (617) 351-1125 •
(800) 225-3362 • www.hmco.com/trade

Hyperion Books
(Imprint of Buena Vista Publishing Co.)
114 Fifth Avenue
New York, NY 10011
(212) 633-4400 • (800) 759-0190 •
www.disney.com

Ideals Children's Books
(Imprint of Hambleton-Hill Publishing, Inc.)
1501 County Hospital Road
Nashville, TN 37218
(615) 254-2480 • (800) 336-6438

Joy Street Books
(Imprint of Little, Brown & Co.)

Just Us Books
356 Glenwood Avenue
E. Orange, NJ 07017
(973) 672-0304 • Fax (973) 677-7570

Alfred A. Knopf
(Imprint of Random House)

Lee & Low Books
95 Madison Avenue
New York, NY 10016
(212) 779-4400 • Fax (212) 683-1894

Lerner Publications Co.
241 First Avenue North
Minneapolis, MN 55401
(612) 332-3344 • Fax (612) 332-7615 •
(800) 328-4929 • www.lernerbooks.com

Little, Brown & Co.
3 Center Plaza
Boston, MA 02108
(617) 227-0730 • Fax (617) 263-2864 •
(800) 343-9204 • www.littlebrown.com

Lothrop Lee & Shepard
(Imprint of William Morrow & Co.)

Macmillan
(Imprint of Simon & Schuster
Children's Publishing)

Marshall Cavendish
99 White Plains Road
Tarrytown, NY 10591
(914) 332-8888 • Fax (914) 332-1082 •
(800) 821-9881 •
www.marshallcavendish.com

William Morrow & Co.
1350 Avenue of the Americas
New York, NY 10019
(212) 261-6500 • Fax (212) 261-6619 •
(800) 843-9389 •
www.williammorrow.com

Morrow Junior Books
(Imprint of William Morrow & Co.)

Mulberry Books
(Imprint of William Morrow & Co.)

National Geographic Society
1145 17th Street, NW
Washington, DC 20036
(202) 828-5667 • (800) 368-2728 •
www.nationalgeographic.com

Northland Publishing
(Division of Justin Industries)
P.O. Box 62
Flagstaff, AZ 86002
(520) 774-5251 • Fax (800) 257-9082 •
(800) 346-3257 • www.northlandpub.com

North-South Books
1123 Broadway, Suite 800
New York, NY 10010
(212) 463-9736 • Fax (212) 633-1004 •
(800) 722-6657 • www.northsouth.com

Orchard Books (A Grolier Company)
95 Madison Avenue
New York, NY 10016
(212) 951-2600 • Fax (212) 213-6435 •
(800) 621-1115 • www.grolier.com

Owlet (Imprint of Henry Holt & Co.)

Willa Perlman Books
(Imprint of Simon & Schuster
Children's Publishing)

Philomel Books
(Imprint of Putnam Penguin, Inc.)

Puffin Books
(Imprint of Penguin Putnam, Inc.)

G.P. Putnam's Sons Publishing
(Imprint of Penguin Putnam, Inc.)

Penguin Putnam, Inc.
345 Hudson Street
New York, NY 10014
(212) 366-2000 • Fax (212) 366-2666 •
(800) 631-8571 •
www.penguinputnam.com

Random House
201 East 50th Street
New York, NY 10022
(212) 751-2600 • Fax (212) 572-2593 •
(800) 726-0600 • www.randomhouse/kids

Rourke Corporation
P.O. Box 3328
Vero Beach, FL 32964
(561) 234-6001 • (800) 394-7055 •
www.rourkepublishing.com

Scholastic
555 Broadway
New York, NY 10012
(212) 343-6100 • Fax (212) 343-6930 •
(800) SCHOLASTIC • www.scholastic.com

Sierra Junior Club
85 Second Street, Second Floor
San Francisco, CA 94105-3441
(415) 977-5500 • Fax (415) 977-5799 •
(800) 935-1056 • www.sierraclub.org

Simon & Schuster Children's Books
1230 Avenue of the Americas
New York, NY 10020
(212) 698-7200 • (800) 223-2336 •
www.simonsays.com/kidzone

Smith & Kraus
4 Lower Mill Road
N. Stratford, NH 03590
(603) 643-6431 • Fax (603) 643-1831 •
(800) 895-4331 • www.smithkraus.com

Teacher Ideas Press
(Division of Libraries Unlimited)
P.O. Box 6633
Englewood, CO 80155-6633
(303) 770-1220 • Fax (303) 220-8843 •
(800) 237-6124 • www.lu.com

Ticknor & Fields
(Imprint of Houghton Mifflin, Inc.)

Usborne (Imprint of EDC Publishing)
10302 E. 55th Place, Suite B
Tulsa, OK 74146-6515
(918) 622-4522 • (800) 475-4522 •
www.edcpub.com

Viking Children's Books
(Imprint of Penguin Putnam Inc.)

Watts Publishing
(Imprint of Grolier Publishing;
see Children's Press)

Walker & Co.
435 Hudson Street
New York, NY 10014
(212) 727-8300 • (212) 727-0984 • (800)
AT-WALKER

Whispering Coyote Press
300 Crescent Court, Suite 860
Dallas, TX 75201
(800) 929-6104 • Fax (214) 319-7298

Albert Whitman
6340 Oakton Street
Morton Grove, IL 60053-2723
(847) 581-0033 • Fax (847) 581-0039 •
(800) 255-7675 • www.awhitmanco.com

Workman Publishing Co., Inc.
708 Broadway
New York, NY 10003
(212) 254-5900 • Fax (800) 521-1832 •
(800) 722-7202 • www.workman.com

Directory of Resources (side tab)

Multimedia Resources

AGC/United Learning
6633 West Howard Street
Niles, IL 60714-3389
(800) 424-0362 • www.unitedlearning.com

AIMS Multimedia
9710 DeSoto Avenue
Chatsworth, CA 91311-4409
(800) 367-2467 •
www.AIMS-multimedia.com

BFA Educational Media
(see Phoenix Learning Group)

Broderbund
(Parsons Technology;
also see The Learning Company)
500 Redwood Blvd
Novato, CA 94997
(800) 521-6263 • Fax (800) 474-8840 •
www.broderbund.com

Carousel Film and Video
260 Fifth Avenue, Suite 705
New York, NY 10001
(212) 683-1660 • e-mail:
carousel@pipeline.com

Cloud 9 Interactive
(888) 662-5683 • www.cloud9int.com

Computer Plus (see ESI)

Coronet/MTI
(see Phoenix Learning Group)

Davidson (see Knowledge Adventure)

Direct Cinema, Ltd.
P.O. Box 10003
Santa Monica, CA 90410-1003
(800) 525-0000

Disney Interactive
(800) 900-9234 •
www.disneyinteractive.com

DK Multimedia (Dorling Kindersley)
95 Madison Avenue
New York, NY 10016
(212) 213-4800 • Fax: (800) 774-6733 •
(888) 342-5357 • www.dk.com

Edmark Corp.
P.O. Box 97021
Redmond, CA 98073-9721
(800) 362-2890 • www.edmark.com

Encyclopaedia Britannica Educational Corp.
310 South Michigan Avenue
Chicago, IL 60604
(800) 554-9862 • www.eb.com

ESI/Educational Software
4213 S. 94th Street
Omaha, NE 68127
(800) 955-5570 • www.edsoft.com

GPN/Reading Rainbow
University of Nebraska-Lincoln
P.O. Box 80669
Lincoln, NE 68501-0669
(800) 228-4630 • www.gpn.unl.edu

Hasbro Interactive
(800) 683-5847 • www.hasbro.com

Humongous
13110 NE 177th Pl., Suite B101, Box 180
Woodenville, WA 98072
(800) 499-8386 • www.humongous.com

IBM Corp.
1133 Westchester Ave.
White Plains, NY 10604
(770) 863-1234 • Fax (770) 863-3030 •
(888) 411-1932 •
www.pc.ibm.com/multimedia/crayola

ICE, Inc.
(Distributed by Arch Publishing)
12B W. Main St.
Elmsford, NY 10523
(914) 347-2464 • (800) 843-9497 •
www.educorp.com

Knowledge Adventure
19840 Pioneer Avenue
Torrence, CA 90503
(800) 542-4240 • (800) 545-7677 •
www.knowledgeadventure.com

The Learning Company
6160 Summit Drive North
Minneapolis, MN 55430
(800) 685-6322 • www.learningco.com

Listening Library
One Park Avenue
Greenwich, CT 06870-1727
(800) 243-4504 • www.listeninglib.com

Macmillan/McGraw-Hill
(see SRA/McGraw-Hill)

Maxis
2121 N. California Blvd
Walnut Creek, CA 94596-3572
(925) 933-5630 • Fax (925) 927-3736 •
(800) 245-4525 • www.maxis.com

MECC
(see the Learning Company)

Microsoft
One Microsoft Way
Redmond, WA 98052-6399
(800) 426-9400 • www.microsoft.com/kids

National Geographic Society Educational Services
P.O. Box 10597
Des Moines, IA 50340-0597
(800) 368-2728 •
www.nationalgeographic.com

National School Products
101 East Broadway
Maryville, TN 37804
(800) 251-9124 • www.ierc.com

PBS Video
1320 Braddock Place
Alexandria, VA 22314
(800) 344-3337 • www.pbs.org

Phoenix Films
(see Phoenix Learning Group)

The Phoenix Learning Group
2348 Chaffee Drive
St. Louis, MO 63146
(800) 221-1274 • e-mail:
phoenixfilms@worldnet.att.net

Pied Piper (see AIMS Multimedia)

Scholastic New Media
555 Broadway
New York, NY 10003
(800) 724-6527 • www.scholastic.com

Simon & Schuster Interactive
(see Knowledge Adventure)

SRA/McGraw-Hill
220 Daniel Dale Road
De Soto, TX 75115
(800) 843-8855 • www.sra4kids.com

SVE/Churchill Media
6677 North Northwest Highway
Chicago, IL 60631
(800) 829-1900 •www.svemedia.com

Tom Snyder Productions (also see ESI)
80 Coolidge Hill Rd.
Watertown, MA 02472
(800) 342-0236 • www.teachtsp.com

Troll Associates
100 Corporate Drive
Mahwah, NJ 07430
(800) 929-8765 • Fax (800) 979-8765 •
www.troll.com

Voyager (see ESI)

Weston Woods
12 Oakwood Avenue
Norwalk, CT 06850
(800) 243-5020 • Fax (203) 845-0498

Zenger Media
10200 Jefferson Blvd., Room 94,
P.O. Box 802
Culver City, CA 90232-0802
(800) 421-4246 • (800) 944-5432 •
www.Zengermedia.com

BOOK 1, UNIT 1

Vocabulary   Spelling

GRANDFATHER'S JOURNEY

Vocabulary
- astonished
- enormous
- journey
- scattered
- surrounded
- towering

Words with short vowels

bag	ever	mix	thing
black	hid	**much**	van
body	**kept**	**rocks**	window
buzz	leg	rub	

PHOEBE AND THE SPELLING BEE

Vocabulary
- continue
- correct
- embarrass
- groaning
- legend
- unusual

Words with long *a* and long *e*

awake	creek	**paper**	team
breeze	grade	plane	thief
carry	marry	**raise**	weigh
cream	neighbor	sail	

OPT

Vocabulary
- gift
- guard
- royal
- within
- length
- straighten

Words with long *i* and long *o*

ago	lie	**own**	**tie**
bicycle	life	**rode**	toast
find	might	spoke	wipe
flight	most	thrown	

MAX MALONE

Vocabulary
- ceiling
- cents
- eager
- including
- scene
- section

/ū/ and /ü/

broom	**excuse**	huge	produce
crew	fruit	juice	soup
dew	**goose**	music	truth
drew	group	pool	

TIME FOR KIDS: CHAMPIONS OF THE WORLD

Vocabulary
- celebrated
- cork
- fans
- pitcher
- score
- wrap

Words from Physical Education

action	crowd	mound	**record**
baseball	foul	outfield	**season**
bases	glove	**parade**	strike
batter	mitt	**player**	

Boldfaced words appear in the selection.

BOOK 1, UNIT 2

Vocabulary   Spelling

CITY GREEN

Vocabulary:
- area
- excitement
- halfway
- heap
- schedule
- stems

Two-syllable words with accented first syllable

battle	even	floppy	maple
bottle	fellow	frozen	**open**
candle	fifty	lazy	silent
carrots	flavor	**lettuce**	

THE SUN, THE WIND AND THE RAIN

Vocabulary:
- canyons
- flowed
- grains
- handful
- peaks
- traded

Words with initial *bl, br, cr, fl, gr, pl*

blind	brisk	flame	grand
blink	**broad**	flash	plate
block	crazy	flood	plenty
brake	**crumble**	grab	

DREAM WOLF

Vocabulary:
- buffalo
- darkness
- echoes
- herds
- ripe
- shelter

Words with initial *sp, str, scr, spr, sk, sl*

scream	skin	spend	**stream**
screen	sleeve	spider	string
scrub	**slept**	spring	strong
skate	slice	sprinkle	

SPIDERS AT WORK

Vocabulary:
- capture
- liquid
- ruin
- serious
- skills
- struggles

Plurals—add *s, es*, and change *y* to *i* add *es*

addresses	companies	inches	pairs
blankets	daisies	**jungles**	pockets
branches	enemies	libraries	**states**
bunches	**flies**	**mountains**	

TIME FOR KIDS: WEB WONDERS

Vocabulary:
- crops
- earthquake
- hatch
- respect
- soldiers
- woven

Words from Science

bait	fang	**silk**	**thread**
beetle	**fiber**	**sticky**	weave
breathe	prey	**strands**	web
cell	science	taste	

Boldfaced words appear in the selection.

BOOK 1, UNIT 3

Vocabulary   ## Spelling

MOSES GOES TO A CONCERT

Vocabulary				
concert				
conductor				
ill				
instrument				
musician				
orchestra				

Words with final *nk, mp, ng, nd, nt*

behind	husband	stamp	**thump**
belong	ink	student	trunk
faint	paint	swing	young
friend	parent	**thank**	

THE LITTLE PAINTER OF SABANA GRANDE

blossoms
dawn
faded
imaginary
miserable
shallow

Words with *tt, ll, bb, dd, pp, ss*

butter	ladder	possible	**small**
grass	lesson	ribbon	supper
happen	**little**	rubber	**unhappy**
hobby	**middle**	silly	

THE PATCHWORK QUILT

anxious
attic
costume
examined
gazed
pattern

/ou/ spelled *ow, ou*; /oi/ spelled *oi, oy*

allow	count	loyal	shout
choice	**enjoy**	noisy	**spoil**
cloudy	foil	poison	voyage
clown	**found**	power	

PECOS BILL

combine
invented
located
prairie
stumbled
wilderness

adding *ed* and *ing*

beginning	escaping	robbed	splitting
blamed	fried	**saving**	stirred
buried	hurried	shaking	supplied
divided	moving	spied	

TIME FOR KIDS: A VERY COOL PLACE TO VISIT

beauty
creeps
furniture
palace
pure
visitors

Words from Science

arctic	**freezes**	igloo	snowflake
chill	frost	matter	solid
degree	heat	**melt**	thaw
dense	**ice**	**northern**	

Boldfaced words appear in the selection.

BOOK 2, UNIT 1

Vocabulary | Spelling

THE TERRIBLE EEK

Vocabulary
- **completely**
- **humans**
- **meal**
- **motion**
- **reply**
- **weight**

Spelling

Words with initial *ch, sh, th, wh*

chain	shadow	thick	whether
cheese	shelf	**thirsty**	whip
cherry	shock	thirty	whisker
chicken	**shone**	thousand	

IN MY FAMILY

Vocabulary
- **comforting**
- **designed**
- **dozens**
- **encouraging**
- **members**
- **relatives**

Spelling

Words with final *ch, sh, tch, th*

approach	finish	sketch	teach
coach	fourth	splash	tooth
crash	itch	**squash**	**underneath**
fetch	peach	stitch	

CACTUS HOTEL

Vocabulary
- **discovered**
- **insects**
- **remains**
- **ribs**
- **tough**
- **treat**

Spelling

/ô/ spelled *a, o, au, ough;* /u̇/ spelled *oo, u, o*

across	cookie	**pulls**	**tall**
always	footprint	saucer	wolf
bought	fought	song	woman
cause	often	sugar	

BIG BLUE WHALE

Vocabulary
- **adult**
- **calm**
- **feast**
- **mammal**
- **swallow**
- **vast**

Spelling

Compound Words

afternoon	cardboard	notebook	someone
anything	everything	outside	**sometimes**
barnyard	**fingernails**	playground	without
basketball	newspaper	sidewalk	

TIME FOR KIDS: J.J.'S BIG DAY

Vocabulary
- **clams**
- **compared**
- **experts**
- **gain**
- **powdered**
- **switched**

Spelling

Words from Math

data	mass	ounce	scale
gallon	measure	pint	second
gram	meter	**pounds**	week
hour	month	**problems**	

Boldfaced words appear in the selection.

BOOK 2, UNIT 2

Vocabulary | Spelling

Lon Po Po

Vocabulary
- claws
- **delighted**
- **disguised**
- **furious**
- **paced**
- **route**

Spelling

Soft *c* /s/ spelled *ss, ce, c, s*
Soft *g* /j/ spelled *j, g, dge, ge*

circle	**jewels**	message	stage
city	jolly	once	**sunset**
giant	judge	rage	twice
gym	ledge	**sisters**	

Animal Fact/ Animal Fable

Vocabulary
- **attack**
- **bother**
- **expects**
- **label**
- **rapidly**
- **temperature**

Spelling

/är/ spelled *ar;*
/ûr/ spelled *ur, or, ir, er, ear*

alarm	market	**sharp**	**words**
curtain	merchant	skirt	world
firm	**person**	startle	worth
learn	search	**turtle**	

The Many Lives of Benjamin Franklin

Vocabulary
- **advice**
- curious
- **discuss**
- **experiment**
- hero
- **scientific**

Spelling

/âr/ spelled *are, air;*
/ôr/ spelled *or, ore;*
/îr/ spelled *ear, eer*

beard	fair	**important**	store
dare	**force**	**near**	storm
deer	glare	sore	**weary**
engineer	hair	stare	

Cloudy with a Chance of Meatballs

Vocabulary
- **avoid**
- **brief**
- frequently
- **gradual**
- periods
- report

Spelling

Contractions

didn't	I'll	shouldn't	won't
doesn't	I'm	they've	you'll
don't	it's	we're	you're
he's	she'll	we've	

Time for Kids: Pure Power

Vocabulary
- energy
- entire
- future
- model
- pollution
- produce

Spelling

Words from Social Studies

climate	**gas**	natural	**solar**
coal	globe	**planet**	**sunlight**
fossil	lumber	recycle	windmills
fuels	**millions**	save	

Boldfaced words appear in the selection.

BOOK 2, UNIT 3

Vocabulary | Spelling

THE BAT BOY AND HIS VIOLIN

Vocabulary
- accept
- equipment
- invisible
- mistake
- perform
- talented

Spelling

/ər/ er, ar, or; /əl/ le, el, al

barrel	**dinner**	**metal**	**stumble**
cellar	favor	motor	**summer**
center	**fiddle**	sailor	travel
collar	**handle**	signal	

TWO BAD ANTS

Vocabulary
- bitter
- crystal
- gripped
- kingdom
- vanished
- whirling

Spelling

Silent letters k, w, l, b, gh

calf	folk	knock	whole
comb	**frightening**	**known**	wrinkle
crumb	**height**	limb	wrong
daylight	knife	palm	

DO ANIMALS THINK?

Vocabulary
- brain
- communicate
- crafty
- social
- solve
- subject

Spelling

Homophones

ant	due	**one**	**too**
ate	eight	sew	two
aunt	meat	**so**	won
do	meet	**to**	

"WILBUR'S BOAST" FROM CHARLOTTE'S WEB

Vocabulary
- boasting
- considering
- conversation
- hesitated
- interrupted
- seized

Spelling

Suffixes -ly, -ful, -able, -tion, -sion

busily	discussion	powerful	useful
collection	expression	**quietly**	valuable
comfort-able	invention	**sadly**	**wonderful**
direction	possession	unbelievable	

TIME FOR KIDS: KOALA CATCHERS

Vocabulary
- crate
- loops
- rescuers
- snug
- starve
- strip

Spelling

Words from Social Studies

bay	**forests**	mainland	**safe**
coast	gulf	**migrate**	valley
continent	**harmed**	outdoors	**wildlife**
country	**island**	port	

Boldfaced words appear in the selection.

Listening, Speaking, Viewing, Representing

☑ Tested Skill

☐ Tinted panels show skills, strategies, and other teaching opportunities

LISTENING	K	1	2	3	4	5	6
Learn the vocabulary of school (numbers, shapes, colors, directions, and categories)							
Identify the musical elements of literary language, such as rhymes, repeated sounds, onomatopoeia							
Determine purposes for listening (get information, solve problems, enjoy and appreciate)							
Listen critically and responsively							
Ask and answer relevant questions							
Listen critically to interpret and evaluate							
Listen responsively to stories and other texts read aloud, including selections from classic and contemporary works							
Connect and compare own experiences, ideas, and traditions with those of others							
Apply comprehension strategies in listening activities							
Understand the major ideas and supporting evidence in spoken messages							
Participate in listening activities related to reading and writing (such as discussions, group activities, conferences)							
Listen to learn by taking notes, organizing, and summarizing spoken ideas							
SPEAKING							
Learn the vocabulary of school (numbers, shapes, colors, directions, and categories)							
Use appropriate language and vocabulary learned to describe ideas, feelings, and experiences							
Ask and answer relevant questions							
Communicate effectively in everyday situations (such as discussions, group activities, conferences)							
Demonstrate speaking skills (audience, purpose, occasion, volume, pitch, tone, rate, fluency)							
Clarify and support spoken messages and ideas with objects, charts, evidence, elaboration, examples							
Use verbal and nonverbal communication in effective ways when, for example, making announcements, giving directions, or making introductions							
Retell a spoken message by summarizing or clarifying							
Connect and compare own experiences, ideas, and traditions with those of others							
Determine purposes for speaking (inform, entertain, give directions, persuade, express personal feelings and opinions)							
Demonstrate skills of reporting and providing information							
Demonstrate skills of interviewing, requesting and providing information							
Apply composition strategies in speaking activities							
Monitor own understanding of spoken message and seek clarification as needed							
VIEWING							
Demonstrate viewing skills (focus attention, organize information)							
Respond to audiovisual media in a variety of ways							
Participate in viewing activities related to reading and writing							
Apply comprehension strategies in viewing activities							
Recognize artists' craft and techniques for conveying meaning							
Interpret information from various formats such as maps, charts, graphics, video segments, technology							
Evaluate purposes of various media (information, appreciation, entertainment, directions, persuasion)							
Use media to compare ideas and points of view							
REPRESENTING							
Select, organize, or produce visuals to complement or extend meanings							
Produce communication using appropriate media to develop a class paper, multimedia or video reports							
Show how language, medium, and presentation contribute to the message							

Reading: Alphabetic Principle, Sounds/Symbols

☑ Tested Skill

☐ Tinted panels show skills, strategies, and other teaching opportunities

PRINT AWARENESS	K	1	2	3	4	5	6
Know the order of the alphabet							
Recognize that print represents spoken language and conveys meaning							
Understand directionality (tracking print from left to right; return sweep)							
Understand that written words are separated by spaces							
Know the difference between individual letters and printed words							
Understand that spoken words are represented in written language by specific sequence of letters							
Recognize that there are correct spellings for words							
Know the difference between capital and lowercase letters							
Recognize how readers use capitalization and punctuation to comprehend							
Recognize the distinguishing features of a paragraph							
Recognize that parts of a book (such as cover/title page and table of contents) offer information							
PHONOLOGICAL AWARENESS							
Identify letters, words, sentences							
Divide spoken sentence into individual words							
Produce rhyming words and distinguish rhyming words from nonrhyming words							
Identify, segment, and combine syllables within spoken words							
Identify and isolate the initial and final sound of a spoken word							
Add, delete, or change sounds to change words (such as cow to how, pan to fan)							
Blend sounds to make spoken words							
Segment one-syllable spoken words into individual phonemes							
PHONICS AND DECODING							
Alphabetic principle: Letter/sound correspondence	☑	☑	☑				
Blending CVC words	☑	☑					
Segmenting CVC words	☑						
Blending CVC, CVCe, CCVC, CVCC, CVVC words	☑	☑	☑				
Segmenting CVC, CVCe, CCVC, CVCC, CVVC words	☑	☑	☑				
Initial and final consonants: /n/n, /d/d, /s/s, /m/m, /t/t, /k/c, /f/f, /r/r, /p/p, /l/l, /k/k, /g/g, /b/b, /h/h, /w/w, /v/v, /ks/x, /kw/qu, /j/j, /y/y, /z/z	☑	☑					
Initial and medial short vowels: a, i, u, o, e	☑	☑	☑				
Long vowels: a-e, i-e, o-e, u-e (vowel-consonant-e)		☑	☑				
Long vowels, including ay, ai; e, ee, ie, ea; o, oa, oe, ow; i, y, igh		☑	☑				
Consonant Digraphs: sh, th, ch, wh		☑					
Consonant Blends: continuant/continuant, including sl, sm, sn, fl, fr, ll, ss, ff		☑					
Consonant Blends: continuant/stop, including st, sk, sp, ng, nt, nd, mp, ft		☑					
Consonant Blends: stop/continuant, including tr, pr, pl, cr, tw		☑					
Variant vowels: including /ü/oo; /ô/a, aw, au; /ü/ue, ew		☑	☑				
Diphthongs, including /ou/ou, ow; /oi/oi, oy		☑	☑				
r-controlled vowels, including /âr/are; /ôr/or, ore; /îr/ear			☑				
Soft c and soft g			☑				
nk		☑	☑				
Consonant Digraphs: ck	☑	☑					
Consonant Digraphs: ph, tch, ch			☑				
Short e: ea			☑				
Long e: y, ey			☑				
/ü/oo		☑	☑				
/är/ar; /ûr/ir, ur, er		☑	☑				
Silent letters: including l, b, k, w, g, h, gh			☑				
Schwa: /ər/er; /ən/en; /əl/le;			☑				
Reading/identifying multisyllabic words		☑	☑				

Reading: Vocabulary/Word Identification

☑ Tested Skill

Tinted panels show skills, strategies, and other teaching opportunities

WORD STRUCTURE	K	1	2	3	4	5	6
Common spelling patterns							
Syllable patterns							
Plurals		☑					
Possessives		☑					
Contractions		☑					
Root, or base, words and inflectional endings (-s, -es, -ed, -ing)		☑	☑	☑		☑	
Compound words			☑	☑	☑	☑	☑
Prefixes and suffixes (such as un-, re-, dis-, non-; -ly, -y, -ful, -able, -tion)				☑	☑	☑	☑
Root words and derivational endings				☑	☑	☑	☑

WORD MEANING	K	1	2	3	4	5	6
Develop vocabulary through concrete experiences							
Develop vocabulary through selections read aloud							
Develop vocabulary through reading							
Cueing systems: syntactic, semantic, phonetic							
Context clues, including semantic clues (word meaning), syntactical clues (word order), and phonetic clues	☑	☑	☑	☑	☑	☑	☑
High-frequency words (such as the, a, an, and, said, was, where, is)							
Identify words that name persons, places, things, and actions							
Automatic reading of regular and irregular words							
Use resources and references (dictionary, glossary, thesaurus, synonym finder, technology and software, and context)							
Synonyms and antonyms			☑	☑	☑	☑	☑
Multiple-meaning words			☑	☑	☑	☑	☑
Figurative language			☑	☑	☑	☑	☑
Decode derivatives (root words, such as like, pay, happy with affixes, such as dis-, pre-, un-)							
Systematic study of words across content areas and in current events							
Locate meanings, pronunciations, and derivations (including dictionaries, glossaries, and other sources)							
Denotation and connotation							☑
Word origins as aid to understanding historical influences on English word meanings							
Homophones, homographs							
Analogies							☑
Idioms							

Reading: Comprehension

PREREADING STRATEGIES	K	1	2	3	4	5	6
Preview and predict							
Use prior knowledge							
Establish and adjust purposes for reading							
Build background							

MONITORING STRATEGIES	K	1	2	3	4	5	6
Adjust reading rate							
Reread, search for clues, ask questions, ask for help							
Visualize							
Read a portion aloud, use reference aids							
Use decoding and vocabulary strategies							
Paraphrase							
Create story maps, diagrams, charts, story props to help comprehend, analyze, synthesize and evaluate texts							

(continued on next page)

✓ Tested Skill

Tinted panels show skills, strategies, and other teaching opportunities

SKILLS AND STRATEGIES	K	1	2	3	4	5	6
Recall story details	✓						
Use illustrations	✓	✓					
Distinguish reality and fantasy	✓	✓	✓				
Classify and categorize	✓						
Make predictions	✓	✓	✓	✓	✓	✓	✓
Recognize sequence of events (tell or act out)	✓	✓	✓	✓	✓	✓	✓
Recognize cause and effect		✓	✓	✓	✓	✓	✓
Compare and contrast	✓	✓	✓	✓	✓	✓	✓
Summarize	✓	✓	✓	✓	✓	✓	✓
Make and explain inferences			✓	✓	✓	✓	✓
Draw conclusions			✓	✓	✓	✓	✓
Distinguish important and unimportant information					✓	✓	✓
Recognize main idea and supporting details	✓	✓	✓	✓	✓	✓	✓
Form conclusions or generalizations and support with evidence from text			✓	✓	✓	✓	✓
Distinguish fact and opinion (including news stories and advertisements)				✓	✓	✓	✓
Recognize problem and solution			✓	✓	✓	✓	✓
Recognize steps in a process		✓	✓	✓	✓	✓	✓
Make judgments and decisions				✓	✓	✓	✓
Distinguish fact and nonfact				✓	✓	✓	✓
Recognize techniques of persuasion and propaganda							✓
Evaluate evidence and sources of information							✓
Identify similarities and differences across texts (including topics, characters, problems, themes, treatment, scope, or organization)							
Practice various questions and tasks (test-like comprehension questions)							
Paraphrase and summarize to recall, inform, and organize							
Answer various types of questions (open-ended, literal, interpretative, test-like such as true-false, multiple choice, short-answer)							
Use study strategies to learn and recall (preview, question, reread, and record)							

LITERARY RESPONSE	K	1	2	3	4	5	6
Listen to stories being read aloud							
React, speculate, join in, read along when predictable and patterned selections are read aloud							
Respond through talk, movement, music, art, drama, and writing to a variety of stories and poems							
Show understanding through writing, illustrating, developing demonstrations, and using technology							
Connect ideas and themes across texts							
Support responses by referring to relevant aspects of text and own experiences							
Offer observations, make connections, speculate, interpret, and raise questions in response to texts							
Interpret text ideas through journal writing, discussion, enactment, and media							

TEXT STRUCTURE/LITERARY CONCEPTS	K	1	2	3	4	5	6
Distinguish forms of texts and the functions they serve (lists, newsletters, signs)							
Understand story structure							
Identify narrative (for entertainment) and expository (for information)							
Distinguish fiction from nonfiction, including fact and fantasy							
Understand literary forms (stories, poems, plays, and informational books)							
Understand literary terms by distinguishing between roles of author and illustrator							
Understand title, author, and illustrator across a variety of texts							
Analyze character, character's point of view, plot, setting, style, tone, mood		✓	✓	✓	✓	✓	✓
Compare communication in different forms							
Understand terms such as *title, author, illustrator, playwright, theater, stage, act, dialogue,* and *scene*							
Recognize stories, poems, myths, folktales, fables, tall tales, limericks, plays, biographies, and autobiographies							
Judge internal logic of story text							
Recognize that authors organize information in specific ways							
Identify texts to inform, influence, express, or entertain							
Describe how author's point of view affects text				✓	✓	✓	✓
Recognize biography, historical fiction, realistic fiction, modern fantasy, informational texts, and poetry							
Analyze ways authors present ideas (cause/effect, compare/contrast, inductively, deductively, chronologically)							
Recognize flashback, foreshadowing, symbolism							

(continued on next page)

☑ Tested Skill

Tinted panels show skills, strategies, and other teaching opportunities

VARIETY OF TEXT	K	1	2	3	4	5	6
Read a variety of genres							
Use informational texts to acquire information							
Read for a variety of purposes							
Select varied sources when reading for information or pleasure							
FLUENCY							
Read regularly in independent-level and instructional-level materials							
Read orally with fluency from familiar texts							
Self-select independent-level reading							
Read silently for increasing periods of time							
Demonstrate characteristics of fluent and effective reading							
Adjust reading rate to purpose							
Read aloud in selected texts, showing understanding of text and engaging the listener							
CULTURES							
Connect own experience with culture of others							
Compare experiences of characters across cultures							
Articulate and discuss themes and connections that cross cultures							
CRITICAL THINKING							
Experiences (comprehend, apply, analyze, synthesize, evaluate)							
Make connections (comprehend, apply, analyze, synthesize, evaluate)							
Expression (comprehend, apply, analyze, synthesize, evaluate)							
Inquiry (comprehend, apply, analyze, synthesize, evaluate)							
Problem solving (comprehend, apply, analyze, synthesize, evaluate)							
Making decisions (comprehend, apply, analyze, synthesize, evaluate)							

Study Skills

INQUIRY/RESEARCH	K	1	2	3	4	5	6
Follow directions							
Use alphabetical order							
Identify/frame questions for research							
Obtain, organize, and summarize information: classify, take notes, outline							
Evaluate research and raise new questions							
Use technology to present information in various formats							
Follow accepted formats for writing research, including documenting sources							
Use test-taking strategies							
Use text organizers (book cover; title page—title, author, illustrator; contents; headings; glossary; index)		☑	☑	☑	☑	☑	☑
Use graphic aids, including maps, diagrams, charts, graphs		☑	☑	☑	☑	☑	☑
Read and interpret varied texts including environmental print, signs, lists, encyclopedia, dictionary, glossary, newspaper, advertisement, magazine, calendar, directions, floor plans		☑	☑	☑	☑	☑	☑
Use reference sources, such as glossary, dictionary, encyclopedia, telephone directory, technology resources		☑	☑	☑	☑	☑	☑
Recognize Library/Media center resources, such as computerized references; catalog search—subject, author, title; encyclopedia index		☑	☑	☑	☑	☑	☑

Writing

Tested Skill

Tinted panels show skills, strategies, and other teaching opportunities

MODES AND FORMS	K	1	2	3	4	5	6
Interactive writing							
Personal narrative (Expressive narrative)			☑	☑	☑	☑	☑
Writing that compares (Informative classificatory)			☑	☑	☑	☑	☑
Explanatory writing (Informative narrative)		☑	☑	☑	☑	☑	☑
Persuasive writing (Persuasive descriptive)			☑	☑	☑	☑	☑
Writing a story	☑	☑	☑	☑	☑	☑	☑
Expository writing	☑	☑	☑	☑	☑	☑	☑
Write using a variety of formats, such as advertisement, autobiography, biography, book report/report, comparison-contrast, critique/review/editorial, description, essay, how-to, interview, invitation, journal/log/notes, message/list, paragraph/multi-paragraph composition, picture book, play (scene), poem/rhyme, story, summary, note, letter							
PURPOSES/AUDIENCES							
Dictate messages such as news and stories for others to write							
Write labels, notes, and captions for illustrations, possessions, charts, and centers							
Write to record, to discover and develop ideas, to inform, to influence, to entertain							
Exhibit an identifiable voice in personal narratives and stories							
Use literary devices (suspense, dialogue, and figurative language)							
Produce written texts by organizing ideas, using effective transitions, and choosing precise wording							
PROCESSES							
Generate ideas for self-selected and assigned topics using prewriting strategies							
Develop drafts							
Revise drafts for varied purposes, elaborate ideas							
Edit for appropriate grammar, spelling, punctuation, and features of polished writings							
Proofread own writing and that of others							
Bring pieces to final form and "publish" them for audiences							
Use technology to compose text							
Select and use reference materials and resources for writing, revising, and editing final drafts							
SPELLING							
Spell own name and write high-frequency words							
Words with short vowels (including CVC and one-syllable words with blends CCVC, CVCC, CCVCC)							
Words with long vowels (including CVCe)							
Words with digraphs, blends, consonant clusters, double consonants							
Words with diphthongs							
Words with variant vowels							
Words with r-controlled vowels							
Words with /ər/, /əl/, and /ən/							
Words with silent letters							
Words with soft c and soft g							
Inflectional endings (including plurals and past tense and words that drop the final e when adding -ing, -ed)							
Compound words							
Contractions							
Homonyms							
Suffixes including -able, -ly, or -less, and prefixes including dis-, re-, pre-, or un-							
Spell words ending in -tion and -sion, such as station and procession							
Accurate spelling of root or base words							
Orthographic patterns and rules such as keep/can; sack/book; out/now; oil/toy; match/speech; ledge/cage; consonant doubling, dropping e, changing y to i							
Multisyllabic words using regularly spelled phonogram patterns							
Syllable patterns (including closed, open, syllable boundary patterns)							
Synonyms and antonyms							
Words from Social Studies, Science, Math, and Physical Education							
Words derived from other languages and cultures							
Use resources to find correct spellings, synonyms, and replacement words							
Use conventional spelling of familiar words in writing assignments							
Spell accurately in final drafts							

(continued on next page)

☑ Tested Skill

Tinted panels show skills, strategies, and other teaching opportunities

GRAMMAR AND USAGE

	K	1	2	3	4	5	6
Understand sentence concepts (word order, statements, questions, exclamations, commands)							
Recognize complete and incomplete sentences							
Nouns (common; proper; singular; plural; irregular plural; possessives)							
Verbs (action; helping; linking; irregular)							
Verb tense (present, past, future, perfect, and progressive)							
Pronouns (possessive, subject and object, pronoun-verb agreement)							
Use objective case pronouns accurately							
Adjectives							
Adverbs that tell how, when, where							
Subjects, predicates							
Subject-verb agreement							
Sentence combining							
Recognize sentence structure (simple, compound, complex)							
Synonyms and antonyms							
Contractions							
Conjunctions							
Prepositions and prepositional phrases							

PENMANSHIP

	K	1	2	3	4	5	6
Write each letter of alphabet (capital and lowercase) using correct formation, appropriate size and spacing							
Write own name and other important words							
Use phonological knowledge to map sounds to letters to write messages							
Write messages that move left to right, top to bottom							
Gain increasing control of penmanship, pencil grip, paper position, beginning stroke							
Use word and letter spacing and margins to make messages readable							
Write legibly by selecting cursive or manuscript as appropriate							

MECHANICS

	K	1	2	3	4	5	6
Use capitalization in sentences, proper nouns, titles, abbreviations and the pronoun I							
Use end marks correctly (period, question mark, exclamation point)							
Use commas (in dates, in addresses, in a series, in letters, in direct address)							
Use apostrophes in contractions and possessives							
Use quotation marks							
Use hyphens, semicolons, colons							

EVALUATION

	K	1	2	3	4	5	6
Identify the most effective features of a piece of writing using class/teacher generated criteria							
Respond constructively to others' writing							
Determine how his/her own writing achieves its purpose							
Use published pieces as models for writing							
Review own written work to monitor growth as writer							

For more detailed scope and sequence including page numbers and additional phonics information, see McGraw-Hill Reading Program scope and sequence (K-6)

Scoring Chart

The Scoring Chart is provided for your convenience in grading your students' work.

- Find the column that shows the total number of items.
- Find the row that matches the number of items answered correctly.
- The intersection of the two rows provides the percentage score.

TOTAL NUMBER OF ITEMS

NUMBER CORRECT	1	2	3	4	5	6	7	8	9	10	11	12	13	14	15	16	17	18	19	20	21	22	23	24	25	26	27	28	29	30
1	100	50	33	25	20	17	14	13	11	10	9	8	8	7	7	6	6	6	5	5	5	5	4	4	4	4	4	4	3	3
2		100	66	50	40	33	29	25	22	20	18	17	15	14	13	13	12	11	11	10	10	9	9	8	8	8	7	7	7	7
3			100	75	60	50	43	38	33	30	27	25	23	21	20	19	18	17	16	15	14	14	13	13	12	12	11	11	10	10
4				100	80	67	57	50	44	40	36	33	31	29	27	25	24	22	21	20	19	18	17	17	16	15	15	14	14	13
5					100	83	71	63	56	50	45	42	38	36	33	31	29	28	26	25	24	23	22	21	20	19	19	18	17	17
6						100	86	75	67	60	55	50	46	43	40	38	35	33	32	30	29	27	26	25	24	23	22	21	21	20
7							100	88	78	70	64	58	54	50	47	44	41	39	37	35	33	32	30	29	28	27	26	25	24	23
8								100	89	80	73	67	62	57	53	50	47	44	42	40	38	36	35	33	32	31	30	29	28	27
9									100	90	82	75	69	64	60	56	53	50	47	45	43	41	39	38	36	35	33	32	31	30
10										100	91	83	77	71	67	63	59	56	53	50	48	45	43	42	40	38	37	36	34	33
11											100	92	85	79	73	69	65	61	58	55	52	50	48	46	44	42	41	39	38	37
12												100	92	86	80	75	71	67	63	60	57	55	52	50	48	46	44	43	41	40
13													100	93	87	81	76	72	68	65	62	59	57	54	52	50	48	46	45	43
14														100	93	88	82	78	74	70	67	64	61	58	56	54	52	50	48	47
15															100	94	88	83	79	75	71	68	65	63	60	58	56	54	52	50
16																100	94	89	84	80	76	73	70	67	64	62	59	57	55	53
17																	100	94	89	85	81	77	74	71	68	65	63	61	59	57
18																		100	95	90	86	82	78	75	72	69	67	64	62	60
19																			100	95	90	86	83	79	76	73	70	68	66	63
20																				100	95	91	87	83	80	77	74	71	69	67
21																					100	95	91	88	84	81	78	75	72	70
22																						100	96	92	88	85	81	79	76	73
23																							100	96	92	88	85	82	79	77
24																								100	96	92	89	86	83	80
25																									100	96	93	89	86	83
26																										100	96	93	90	87
27																											100	96	93	90
28																												100	97	93
29																													100	97
30																														100

Personal Narrative: Writing a Letter

Scoring Rubric: 6-Trait Writing

6. Exceptional	5. Excellent	4. Good	3. Fair	2. Poor	1. Unsatisfactory
Ideas & Content crafts an intriguing, elaborately-detailed personal story of an event.	**Ideas & Content** creates a cohesive, focused picture of an actual event, with an extensive set of features.	**Ideas & Content** crafts a solid, clear description of an event with details that help convey a main idea to the reader.	**Ideas & Content** has some control of the narrative; may not elaborate clearly, or may lose control of the story line.	**Ideas & Content** does not seem to grasp the task to tell a personal story; writer may present images, without a narrative purpose.	**Ideas & Content** does not tell a personal story; writing may go off in several directions, without a sense of purpose; few explicit connections are made between ideas.
Organization unfolds a carefully-organized narrative, in a thoughtfully-crafted sequence that moves a reader smoothly through the events.	**Organization** unfolds a consistent, carefully-organized narrative, in a sequence that moves the reader smoothly through the text.	**Organization** has a well-planned narrative strategy; ideas are connected; has a clear beginning and ending.	**Organization** may not have a clear story structure, or may have trouble tying ideas together; reader may be confused by misplaced or poorly-developed details.	**Organization** shows an extreme lack of organization, so as to interfere with comprehension of the story.	**Organization** shows an extreme lack of organization, so as to interfere with understanding the text; there may be no evident structure at all.
Voice shows unusual originality, depth, and emotions that speak directly to the reader.	**Voice** shows originality, reflectiveness, and a strong personal message that speaks directly to the reader.	**Voice** makes a strong effort to share an authentic personal message directly with the reader.	**Voice** may not connect with the idea of a personal story; may get the basic message across, without a sense of involvement with topic or audience.	**Voice** is not involved in sharing an experience with a reader; does not focus on anything of personal importance or interest.	**Voice** does not address a reader, or has no grasp of sharing understandable feelings and ideas.
Word Choice makes imaginative use of both figurative and everyday language in a natural way; sophisticated choices create a striking picture in the reader's mind.	**Word Choice** makes thoughtful, imaginative use of figurative and everyday language in a natural way; uses words that paint a vivid picture in the reader's mind.	**Word Choice** shows an overall clarity of expression, and an effective control of both new and everyday words.	**Word Choice** may not experiment with words that express a strong feeling; may not choose specific or colorful words that create a picture for the reader.	**Word Choice** does not choose words that express a clear feeling or picture for the reader; some word choices may detract from the meaning of the story.	**Word Choice** uses words that do not fit the task, or are vague and confusing to the reader.
Sentence Fluency crafts varied, capable sentences that flow naturally; dialogue, if used, sounds natural and strengthens the story; may experiment effectively with fragments or other devices.	**Sentence Fluency** crafts creative, effective sentences that flow with a smooth rhythm; dialogue, if used, sounds natural and strengthens the story.	**Sentence Fluency** crafts careful, easy-to-follow sentences; may successfully use fragments and/or dialogue to strengthen the story.	**Sentence Fluency** may have trouble with complex sentences; sentences are understandable, but may be choppy, rambling, or awkward.	**Sentence Fluency** constructs incomplete, rambling, or confusing sentences; may show trouble understanding how words and sentences fit together.	**Sentence Fluency** constructs incomplete, rambling, or confusing sentences; text is hard to follow, and to read aloud.
Conventions is skilled in a wide range of conventions; proper use of the rules of English enhances clarity, meaning, and narrative style; editing is largely unnecessary.	**Conventions** shows strong skills in a wide range of conventions; proper use of the rules of English enhances clarity and narrative style.	**Conventions** may make some errors in spelling, capitalization, punctuation, or usage, but these do not interfere with understanding the text; some editing may be needed.	**Conventions** makes mistakes that are noticeable to the audience, and which may interfere with a smooth reading of the story.	**Conventions** makes repeated errors in spelling, word choice, punctuation, and usage; sentence structures may be confused.	**Conventions** makes severe errors in most or all conventions, so as to consistently interfere with readability; some parts of the text may be impossible to follow or understand.

0: This piece is either blank, or fails to respond to the writing task. The topic is not addressed, or the student simply paraphrases the prompt. The response may be illegible or incoherent.

Personal Narrative: Writing a Letter

8-Point Writing Rubric

8	7	6	5	4	3	2	1
The writer	The writer	The writer	The writer	The writer	The writer	The writer	The writer
• has crafted an outstandingly well-developed and highly-organized personal narrative that communicates a definite sense of purpose and audience.	• presents a well-developed and consistently organized personal narrative with a strong overall sense of purpose and audience.	• presents an organized, cohesive personal narrative with a consistent sense of purpose and audience.	• has crafted a personal narrative of satisfactory organization with a general sense of audience and purpose.	• has made an adequate attempt at organizing a personal narrative, though sense of audience and purpose are not always consistent.	• chooses a good topic to share in a personal narrative, but does not adequately organize events or fully develop ideas.	• makes a largely unsuccessful attempt to construct a personal narrative out of personal experience.	• has not successfully developed a personal narrative.
• conveys a full-bodied picture of an event through the use of transitions and detailed descriptions.	• conveys an authentic, clear picture of an event through the use of transitions and descriptions.	• details a good overall picture of the event through the use of some transitions and the development of satisfactory descriptions.	• sometimes uses transitions to connect events.	• demonstrates limited use of transitions, and misses opportunities to elaborate on important descriptions.	• does not adequately use transitions, and provides limited descriptions of important observations and experiences.	• has not explained events in logical sequence; writing is often unfocused.	• has not articulated a main idea, or overall focus, for the piece.
			• sometimes uses elaboration to enhance descriptions.			• does not use transitions or descriptions to communicate important events.	• does not use transitions, imagery, or descriptions in the writing.
• adeptly uses innovative figurative language, vivid imagery, and authentic expression of feelings to recreate the event.	• often uses figurative language, thoughtful imagery, and expression of feelings.	• uses some thoughtful figurative language, imagery, and expression of feelings, though elaboration is not always consistent.	• occasionally uses figurative language and imagery, but may not fully explain thoughts and feelings related to the event.	• articulates a good opening statement or paragraph, but may lose focus soon thereafter.	• may not develop an opening sentence or paragraph.	• fails to use figurative language; vocabulary is simplistic.	• uses limited, below-grade-level vocabulary to explain events.
• frequently uses sophisticated vocabulary and complex sentence structure to enhance meaning.	• often uses advanced vocabulary and a variety of sentence structures to maintain high interest.	• chooses meaningful vocabulary and varies sentence structure to add interest to the narrative.	• uses familiar grade-appropriate vocabulary, but does not consistently vary sentence structure.	• uses some solid imagery, but omits descriptions of important thoughts and feelings.	• frequently misses the opportunity to provide images, thoughts, and feelings.	• exhibits serious lack of language control.	• demonstrates lack of language control severe enough to impair reader understanding of the main idea.
				• may make mistakes in grammar, usage, and mechanics that somewhat detract from readability.	• displays problems with organization.		
					• makes mistakes in grammar, usage, and mechanics that distract the reader from fully understanding the narrative.		

0: This piece is either blank, or fails to respond to the writing task. The topic is not addressed, or the student simply paraphrases the prompt. The response may be illegible or incoherent.